Marketing
Identities

D1738718

Marketing Identities

The Invention of Jewish Ethnicity in *Ost und West*

David A. Brenner

WAYNE STATE UNIVERSITY PRESS
DETROIT

Library of Congress Cataloging-in-Publication Data

Brenner, David A., 1964–
Marketing identities : the invention of Jewish ethnicity in Ost
und West / David A. Brenner.
p. cm.
Includes bibliographical references and index.
ISBN 0-8143-2684-6 (pbk. : alk. paper)
1. Jews—Germany—Intellectual life. 2. Jews, East European—
Germany—Intellectual life. 3. Jews, East European—Germany—
Public opinion. 4. Public opinion—Jews. 5. Ost und West (Berlin,
Germany : 1901) 6. Germany—Ethnic relations. I. Title.
DS135.G33B736   1998
943'.155004924—dc21   97-50452

Cover:
Leo Winz (lower right) and others on
the *Kaiser Wilhelm II* steamer
of Norddeutscher Lloyd
(*Ost und West* [October 1908]: 605–6);
cover of *Ost und West* between
1901 and 1906.

For

MY

GRANDPARENTS

Contents

Acknowledgments   9
Introduction: Multiple Identities   15

1. Promoting an Ethnic, Pan-Jewish Identity   21
2. *Ost und West* and the History of European Jewish Identity   54
3. "Intellectuals" Reading "Parvenus": The Intellectual
   Nationalist as *Ostjude* and the Assimilating Parvenu as
   Westjude in *Ost und West*   77
4. The Philanthropic Parvenue and the Uplifted *Ostjude:*
   German-Jewish Women and *Ost und West*   98
5. Antisemitism and the German-Jewish Male: *Ost und*
   West's Promotion of Ethnic Jewish Identity to
   German-Jewish Men   139
Conclusion: The Meaning of *Ost und West*—Jews and
   Germans, Identity and Self-Hatred   159

Notes   171
Primary, Secondary, and Archival Sources Cited   219
Index   235

Acknowledgments

This book originated in 1989–90 as Eastern Europe was disintegrating and with it the German Democratic Republic. To reflect on East-West issues and the imagining of communities and nations—even in turn-of-the-century Jewish contexts—appeared utterly unavoidable. Later, in 1990–91, the Federal Republic of Germany served as my base. As I began "dissertating" there, the inhabitants—characterized as *Ossis/Wessis*—were confronting and crossing boundaries that seemed prefigured in the discursive universe that was *Ost und West*. The predicament of "the Wall within the head" not only was reminiscent of the two (pre-Holocaust) European Jewries, but it also raised the question, more urgently than ever, of the "Germanies," of their "inventions," "ethnicities," and "self-stereotyping." This study also came to fruition during the election campaigns of 1991–92 in the United States and the ensuing analysis of sound bites, political rhetoric, and the mass media that they provoked. What follows, then, is itself history and a commentary—through a glass darkly, as it were—on those years. In that sense (and others), all responsibility for its contents is my own.

It would be difficult to thank everyone who made *Marketing Identities* possible. My doctoral committee, for starters, deserves special mention. Under the tutelage of my advisers, John M. Hoberman and Janet K. Swaffar, the dissertation achieved its completion in August 1993. It was John who

9

first inspired me to come to the University of Texas and who has helped me overcome lapses into a cumbersome, jargony style. Janet showed an interest in my development at an early stage of my Austin sojourn, encouraging me at every step in the writing process and never letting me forget my obligations to pedagogy and the profession. Katherine Arens critiqued (too) many drafts of the dissertation and returned them all with superhuman alacrity. By a twist of fate, Kirsten Belgum was also researching journals and nationalism; this study reflects her insights into methodology. Seth Wolitz first brought my attention to the extensive holdings of *Ost und West* at the Harry Ransom Center, and he graciously permitted me to mine his inexhaustible knowledge of Jewish cultures and their history.

Other teachers also proved helpful. Hans Otto Horch in Aachen generously hosted my initial year of Ph.D. research there and warrants credit for being the pioneer in the field of German-Jewish periodical studies. Walter Wetzels, Robert King, Peter Hess, David Price, and Mark Louden all offered advice in Austin. At the postdoctoral stage, I am grateful for the insights of Sander Gilman, David Sorkin, and Michael Brenner—all of whom commented on earlier drafts of the manuscript—not to speak of the two anonymous readers of Wayne State University Press. Thanks also go to Marion Kaplan, who critiqued an early version of chapter 4. Arthur Evans, director of the press, has always been obliging and accommodating. His editorial and production staff—Jennifer Backer, Meg Humes, and Alice Nigoghosian, and copy editor Wendy Warren Keebler—made an attractive spectacle out of a word-processed manuscript and a skeletal list of illustrations.

At the University of Colorado, William Safran and many others critiqued my work and offered support. I have left until last one colleague who offered invaluable help as he struggled with similar issues of German and Jewish cultural history. Michael Berkowitz, despite his busy schedule, was a "gentle" reader and source of constant support, always taking time for seemingly endless E-mail inquiries.

It is my pleasure finally to thank those institutions that provided generous grants at crucial stages of this project: the German Academic Exchange Service (DAAD) and the Alexander von Humboldt Foundation. I also received assistance and hospitality at the following libraries and archives: the Leo Baeck Institute (New York), the Humanities Research Center (Austin), the YIVO Institute for Jewish Research (New York), the Central Zionist Archives (Jerusalem), the Germania Judaica (Cologne), the Alliance Israélite Universelle (Paris), and the Archiv Bibliographia Judaica (Frankfurt a.M). Thanks go especially to Diane Spielman and Michael Heymann. I am also grateful to the staffs of Interlibrary Loan at the University of Texas, the Technische Hochschule Aachen, and the University of Colorado.

Portions of this book have been previously published in earlier forms. Part of chapter 3 originally appeared as "Out of the Ghetto and into the

Tiergarten: Redefining the Jewish Parvenu in *Ost und West*, 1901–1906," *German Quarterly* 66.2 (spring 1993): 176–94. Parts of the introduction and of chapter 5 appeared as "Promoting East European Jewry: *Ost und West*, Ethnic Identity, and the German-Jewish Audience," *Prooftexts* 15.1 (January 1995): 63–88. A portion of chapter 4 appeared as "Neglected 'Women's' Texts and Contexts: Vicki Baum's Jewish Ghetto Stories," *Women in German Yearbook* 13 (1997): 101–22. I thank the editors and journals for permission to revise and reprint my work.

Without the friendship of several individuals, this work may never have achieved completion. Words are not sufficient to thank my sister Lynn and brother-in-law Jeff, Robert Boone, Jeff Grossman, Achim Jaeger, Itzik Gottesman, the Oppenheims, Stan Taylor and Katie Kelfer, Carol Harvel, Glenn and Ursula Levine, Stephan March, Michael Gumbert, and many, many others. Jeff, Itzik, Achim, and Glenn merit distinction for many stimulating conversations related to questions dealt with in the book.

I wish also to thank my parents and stepparents, Larry and Gloria, Gladys and Jules, for their personal and financial support—and not just their patient understanding. Along with them, my enduring love goes out to my wife, Rachel. She not only took an interest in the project from day one, sharing her expertise as a member of Germany's post-Holocaust Jewish community, but she also put up with my most unpoetic, ultra-*wissenschaftlich* moments.

Ithaca, NY

December 25. What I discern of contemporary Jewish literature in Warsaw through Löwy, and of contemporary Czech literature partly through my own insight, points to the fact that many of the benefits of literature—the stimulating of minds, the integrated cohesion of national consciousness, often unrealized in public life and always on the verge of disintegration, the pride and support that a nation derives from a literature of its own in the face of the hostile surrounding world, this keeping of a diary by a nation that is something entirely different from historiography and results in a more rapid (and yet always closely scrutinized) development, the elaborate spiritualization of civic life in its full range, the combining of dissatisfied elements that are immediately put to use precisely in this sphere where stagnation can only do harm, *the constant organization of a people with respect to its whole that is created by the hustle and bustle of magazines,* the restricting of the nation's attention to its own affairs and the admission of what is foreign only by way of reflection, the birth of a respect for those active in literature, the awakening in the younger generation of higher aspirations, which though transient leaves its permanent mark, the acknowledgment of literary events as objects of political concern, the refinement of the antithesis between fathers and sons and the possibility of discussing this, the presentation of national faults in a manner that can be very painful but also liberating and deserving of forgiveness, the beginning of a lively and therefore self-confident book trade and the craving for books—all these effects can be produced by a literature whose development is not unusually broad in scope, but seems to be because it lacks notable talents.

Franz Kafka, *Diaries,* 1911 (emphasis added).

INTRODUCTION

Multiple Identities

Between 1901 and 1923, the Berlin-based magazine *Ost und West* promoted European Jewish culture to Jewish audiences in Germany. The common goal of the editors of the journal was to reverse Jewish "assimilation"[1] in Western and Central Europe by constructing an ethnic-national identity that included East European or "Eastern" forms of Jewishness.[2] This study of *Ost und West* is thus concerned with the question of whether German Jews were interested in adopting elements of East European Jewish identity at this time. And, if this was the case, was it possible to have both a German and a pan-Jewish[3] identity in Wilhelminian Germany (or the *Kaiserreich*), where Jews were already suspected of nonconformity, if not disloyalty?[4]

Ost und West reveals the possibilities and limitations of such multiple identities for turn-of-the-century German Jews. Even though the editors of the journal succeeded in creating a public sphere for pan-Jewishness (*Gesamtjudentum*), they were confronted with serious obstacles. East European Jews—referred to as "Eastern Jews" or *Ostjuden*[5] in this book—had been perceived negatively by many Western Jews (*Westjuden*) and non-Jews since the Enlightenment. Since the late eighteenth century, an elite of intellectuals and policymakers had called on the *Ostjuden* to become less Jewish and to "regenerate" themselves into a group more like "the Germans." The *Ostjuden* were increasingly caricatured in literature, the

15

arts, and the sciences, a development that had reached a high point as *Ost und West* began publication.

As a means of correcting these negative images of Eastern Jews, *Ost und West* attempted to legitimize public expressions of Jewishness in the West. In this sense, the journal sought to "reeducate" Jews in Germany. Despite its emphasis on reeducation, however, *Ost und West* did not simply advance the interests of a Jewish nationalist avant-garde. Instead, its founders knew that they would have to reflect the presuppositions of the broader Jewish audience if they were to attract more readers. To influence Jewish readers in Germany who knew little about Eastern Jewry, *Ost und West* appealed specifically to the three main audiences in the *Kaiserreich:* Jewish intellectuals, middle-class Jewish women, and middle-class Jewish men. Leo Winz (1876–1952), the transplanted Ukrainian Jew and public relations adept who published the magazine, was well suited to this task. And judging by its wide circulation—*Ost und West* reached at least 10 percent of the 625,000 Jews in Germany at its height[6]—the journal was a success. At least in the public sphere, it brought *Westjuden* closer to *Ostjuden.*[7]

Winz, in fact, was a veteran "image maker" who had served between 1905 and 1908 as the head of public relations (*Chef der Propaganda*) at the oldest major German advertising firm, Haasenstein and Vogler. Besides owning and investing in a range of businesses, he was also the publisher of the largest, most widely circulated Jewish newspaper in Germany (the *Gemeindeblatt der jüdischen Gemeinde zu Berlin*) from 1927 to 1934, as well as the founder of *Der Schlemiel. Ein illustriertes jüdisches Witzblatt* [The Schlemiel: An Illustrated Jewish Humor Magazine] (1904–23). Keenly aware of the need to conduct audience research and always aiming for higher advertising revenues, Winz was something of a Robert Maxwell of the German-Jewish press—a savvy entrepreneur and sponsor of the arts, music, boxing, and film. To date, there exists no biography of Winz or of his main associates at *Ost und West*, Binjamin Segel (1867–1931), Theodor Zlocisti (1874–1943), and Arno Nadel (1878–1943). Yet he and his colleagues were responsible for publishing the first rich trove of materials that promoted an ethnic, pan-Jewish identity.

In its first three years, *Ost und West* was best known for images that glorified Eastern Jewry. The magazine thus differed visibly from competing German-Jewish publications in boldly asserting its Jewishness. As soon as the reader picked up an issue, he or she knew that the stories, essays, and illustrations were provided by Jews, about Jews, and for Jews.[8] The very first issue (January 1901), for example, featured an essay titled "Jüdische Renaissance" by Martin Buber (1878–1965), a review of Robert Jaffé's *Ahasver* (1900) by Samuel Lublinski (1868–1910), a story by Isaac Leib Peretz (1851–1915) in German translation, drawings by Ephraim Moses Lilien (1874–1925), and an article on the Hebrew language by Simon Bernfeld (1860–1940). In this and later issues, European (in particular,

16

Ashkenazic) Jewry was presented as having a proud ethnic heritage and a diverse cultural tradition. Many of the early contributors to *Ost und West*—Buber, Lilien, Davis Trietsch[9] (1870–1935), to name a few—were also active in the Zionist organization. There they were involved in creating new Jewish images through "agitation and propaganda," terms that did not carry a negative connotation at the time.

Although the first three years of *Ost und West* signaled a "Jewish Renaissance," the magazine soon became formulaic, especially in its attempts to create a new Jewish aesthetic. After Buber and Lilien distanced themselves from Winz in 1903, positive images of the *Ostjude* in the journal were gradually superseded by negative criticisms of the *Westjude*. Having seen how difficult it would be to change the attitudes of German Jews, Winz and his associates reasoned that the best defense was a good offense. It was not enough to "repackage" the Eastern Jew, who remained dirty, poor, and superstitious in the minds of Westerners. Rather, a new approach was needed that subtly attacked the *Westjuden* themselves. The *Westjude* thus became the butt of a concerted campaign based on anticapitalism and anti-Western thought, and the magazine came to rely on this critique after its first three years.

Ost und West's "negative" approach suggests that pinpointing a common enemy fostered a greater sense of belonging than new ideals and myths. What is remarkable about the magazine, however, is that negative images of Jews were able to coexist alongside positive ones. On the one hand, this inconsistency revealed both the possibilities and the limitations of ethnic identity in the journal; on the other hand, it was an inevitable function of stereotyping. In this study, *stereotyping* is defined as a mental shorthand central to all thinking and to the formation of human identities. Looking at stereotypes in this manner reveals that positive stereotyping was the flip side of negative stereotyping. In other words, the two existed on a continuum. Many contributors to *Ost und West* did not depict the *Ostjuden* in negative terms. Instead, they reversed the categories, rendering Eastern Jews as "noble" or "traditional" instead of culturally backward. At the same time—using a similar strategy—the magazine tried to reach out to German Jews by adapting negative stereotypes of *Ostjuden:* elements of these stereotypes were transferred onto representations of *Westjuden*. For the purposes of this study, these "recycled" stereotypes have a cognitive-psychological function: they represent necessary stages in the process of Jewish self-definition. As we shall see, Winz and his associates came to understand this process of self-definition and were able to exploit it as a promotional technique.

Images of Jews in *Ost und West* were not always transparent and often resist a single interpretation. The magazine's Jewish nationalist editors were, for instance, not willing to part entirely with Western enlightened thinking, and they rarely glorified Eastern Jews such as the Hasidim, whom they thought of as unenlightened. One major subthesis of this investigation

17

is that stereotypes in *Ost und West* based on Western Jewish criteria were as prevalent as stereotypes based on Eastern Jewish criteria.

By interpreting both positive and negative Jewish self-images in *Ost und West* as they appear in literary texts, essays, editorials, and works of art, we shall see how the journal helped to redefine European Jewish identity. As an early example of the promotion of ethnic identity, *Ost und West* may shed light on later attempts by Jews and other minority groups to promote multiple identities. At the same time, this study goes beyond the analysis of cultural politics to reveal how Jews living in Germany perceived themselves in the decades leading up to National Socialism and the *Shoah* (or *khurbn*). It suggests that they perceived themselves as different from other Germans. It also suggests that, for all their prejudice toward Eastern Jews, German Jews were capable of tolerating Jewish diversity. In appealing to the Jews of Germany, *Ost und West* urged a healthy respect for differences rather than an elitist glorification of one Jewish identity over another. As a result, it brought Eastern and Western Jewry closer than many assumed was possible, at least in the limited public sphere of Jewish journalism. In this public realm, then, there existed an East-West Jewish symbiosis, if not a German-Jewish one.

Historians have long used biological metaphors such as *symbiosis* to discuss the status of Jewish identity in the German lands. They have stressed, particularly after the Holocaust, the negative dimensions of symbiosis. As a result, they tend to devalue the idea of the "German Jew," the idea that an individual could be, at one and the same time, both German and Jewish. As a result, much of post-Holocaust historiography denounces those Jews living in Germany before 1933 as delusional, assimilationist, or self-hating.[10]

A symptom of this bias against multiple Jewish identities has been to censure German-Jewish attitudes, behavior, and actions toward the Eastern Jews. Recent scholarship on East-West Jewish relations has focused on the mutual alienation of these groups. This reaction is in part a response to decades of denial concerning Western Jewish prejudice toward Eastern Jews. Researchers understandably have wanted to compensate for the neglect of Yiddish-speaking Jewry, a neglect that can be traced back to the Enlightenment. Steven E. Aschheim's *Brothers and Strangers* (1982) represents one in a chorus of voices seeking to rescue the *Ostjude* from German-Jewish domination. Aschheim demonstrates that German Jews, like their non-Jewish compatriots, harbored negative attitudes toward Eastern Jewry. He documents the wide-scale production of negative stereotypes of *Ostjuden* by Jews and non-Jews. Yet, while duly noting that the idealization of *Ostjuden* in World War I took on cultic proportions, his conclusions and those of more strident critics of Western Jewry suggest that all attempts to reconcile Eastern and Western Jewish cultures were doomed from the start.[11]

While acknowledging that German Jews thought and behaved negatively toward their fellow Jews, this study does not favor Eastern Jews. In

18

fact, its primary insight is that *both* Jewish groups—the Eastern Jewish producers of *Ost und West* and the Western Jewish recipients of the magazine—employed tried-and-true techniques of stereotyping. By the same token, stereotyping cannot be written off as deceptive or divorced from historical reality just because it is carried out by cultural and political institutions.[12] Such a position plays into the dualism that this investigation—like *Ost und West* before it—has tried to avoid.

In scholarship since the mid-1980s, a more balanced viewpoint about East-West Jewish differences has been emerging. Jack Wertheimer's *Unwelcome Strangers* (1987) complements Aschheim's research by investigating the political and socioeconomic realities that shaped the responses of Jewish Easterners and Westerners to each other. Wertheimer asks how German Jews behaved when they encountered Eastern Jews, and he concludes that they showed "empathy" for their Eastern *coreligionists* even if they occasionally showed little "sympathy" for Eastern Jewish *customs*. In arguing that *Westjuden* despised *Ostjuden* less than non-Jews did, he implies that a measure of Jewish communal solidarity prevailed.

Is it therefore justified to label the contempt of Western Jews for Eastern Jews as "Jewish antisemitism"? Antisemitic attacks on Eastern Jews certainly made German Jews look—and feel—bad. According to Sander Gilman's thesis of Jewish self-hatred, Western Jews hated not only their Eastern brethren but also, as a result of psychological projection, the Eastern Jew within *themselves*.[13] This theory assumes that German Jews felt threatened by the prospect of "hordes" of Jewish aliens pouring across the Eastern border. Even though Jewish migration to Germany never exceeded a few hundred per year until 1918 and even though the new Jewish immigrants were statistically insignificant in comparison to the host populations—the total number of *Ostjuden* who settled in Germany never exceeded 100,000—their presence was immediately noticed by government officials and political opportunists. On this basis, Aschheim, Trude Maurer,[14] and others have argued that worried Jewish communities feared an antisemitic backlash and tried to keep the numbers of immigrants down or at least less visible.

Wertheimer, by contrast, presents compelling evidence that the Jews in Germany responded positively to the challenge posed by antisemitic attacks on Jews from the East. To be sure, some German Jews blamed Eastern Jews for antisemitism, pinpointing them as a source of shame or embarrassment.[15] And the established Jews of the West may have avoided contact with immigrant "Russians" and "Galicians," even treating them with condescension.[16] But, writes Wertheimer, the Jewish middle classes in Germany

> also displayed compassion for the suffering of their coreligionists. . . . [T]hey provided various types of support—legal aid, political support, and care for the needy. While we have no way of knowing what the "average" German Jew

19

said in the privacy of his home, we have numerous ways of documenting what German Jews said and did publicly. And from the evidence at our disposal, it appears that their actions on behalf of the immigrants were incompatible with hatred.[17]

What was taking place here will not surprise researchers of migration in the twentieth century. People from the same place who have immigrated at different times classify themselves as "greenhorn" or "assimilated"—a phenomenon typified by, but not specific to, European Jews.

Wertheimer's point is not that Jews were incapable of mutual animosity. Rather, he claims that Western and Eastern Jews may have benefited from each other. And the extent of their interactions and their cultural similarities suggest that a relationship existed upon which *Ost und West* might build. The idea of a pan-Jewish public sphere was no pipe dream: there was a ready-made market in Germany for the magazine and its version of Eastern Jewish culture.[18] If we understand *Ost und West* as a public relations enterprise that brought specific images of Jewishness to specific audiences, we must draw upon both Aschheim's cultural history and Wertheimer's social history so that a clearer picture of the media's influence on fin-de-siècle European Jews may emerge.[19] For this study is not a history of Jewish self-representation or of its subcategories, such as Jewish nationalism. Instead, this study explores the discourse[20] of Jewish identity in an institutional framework: a German-Jewish periodical. It is thus more concerned with the promotion of Jewish identity in *Ost und West* than with its theoretical formulation or semiotics.

Such an approach to Jewish identity and identity politics is long over-due. By looking at minority self-stereotyping as both a discursive and a socio-psychological phenomenon, models of Jews in Germany as self-hating or assimilating are revealed for what they are: ideological dogma. At the same time, the study of *Ost und West*—a twenty-three-year, 10,000-page discursive universe—is "local history" of a particularly rich microcosm. My anthropological approach to this institution complements and gives a more complete picture to other general histories of the period.

1

Promoting an Ethnic, Pan-Jewish Identity

More than any other factor, the westward migration of hundreds of thousands of East European Jews between 1880 and 1914 led to the creation of *Ost und West*. That migration was the result of anti-Jewish policies and the idea that the Jews formed a separate nation or ethnicity. The sheer size of the migration was unparalleled in modern European history. Even if the new Jewish immigrants were statistically insignificant in comparison to their host populations in the West, their presence was always noted—and rarely with enthusiasm.

Jews in Poland, Russia, and the Ukraine had been relocating westward since the seventeenth century. The Chmielnicki massacres of 1648 and the Russo-Swedish War of 1655 drove thousands of Eastern Jews into Germany. Those who remained itinerant were known as "beggar Jews" (*Betteljuden*) or, more pejoratively, *Schnorrer* and *Polacken*. Only after the pogroms of 1880, however, did a truly mass exodus take place which altered the course of modern Jewish history. These pogroms gave a boost to the cause of Jewish nationalism which in the next twenty years received additional impetus from events across Europe. Among these events were the blood libel at Tisza Eszlár in Hungary (1882–83), the Dreyfus trials in France (1895, 1899), and the formation of the *Bund* (the General Jewish Workers' Union in Lithuania, Poland, and Russia) in 1897.[1]

The post-1880 wave of East European Jewish migration came as a surprise to Jews in the West. For as late as the 1860s, contacts between

Eastern and Western Jews were scarce, with the occasional exception of the boarder or Sabbath guest who was a *Betteljude*.[2] In 1868–69, cholera and famine overtook Jews in the western part of the Tsarist empire. When the victims came to Prussia seeking economic and medical aid, German Jews quickly formed ad hoc committees and raised funds to help their coreligionists. To what extent their response was dictated by altruism and to what extent by fear of anti-Jewish reprisals is not clear. Whatever the case, their philanthropy brought a speedy end to the crisis. While some of the Russian-Jewish refugees stayed on in Prussia, most trekked to points farther West. The ad hoc committees were dissolved, and the problem appeared forgotten.

What had appeared impossible in 1868–69, however, came true over the next half century: Jewish emigration from Russia rose dramatically. While only 40,000 to 50,000 Jews migrated westward during the 1870s, tens of thousands more abandoned their homes in the 1880s. The prospect of a new future in the West led Jews to flee political and economic oppression under Tsar Nicholas II, especially after the restrictive May Laws of 1881. Even more Jews emigrated when Moscow and St. Petersburg were declared off-limits to them in 1891; after the Russo-Japanese War and the Revolution of 1905, more than 100,000 Jews left the Tsarist empire each year. The most popular destination was the United States, but large numbers also went to Argentina, Canada, England, and France. By 1914, at least 2.5 million Russian Jews had settled in Western countries.

Jews living in Russian territories were not the only ones uprooted at the end of the nineteenth century. Their immediate neighbors, Jews from the Austro-Hungarian empire and the Kingdom of Rumania, were also part of the new Diaspora. Victimized by boycotts and professional restrictions, Jews from Galicia increasingly left the Habsburg Empire after the 1870s. Many Rumanian Jews also moved westward after their country failed to abide by the Berlin Treaty of 1878, refusing to grant them citizenship and other basic rights. Approximately 400,000 Jews left their homes in the Galician, Bohemian, Moravian, Hungarian, and Rumanian lands between 1870 and the outbreak of World War I. Although many sought new opportunities in the industrialized nations of the West, an even larger number migrated within the Austro-Hungarian empire. Among them were the fathers of Sigmund Freud (1856–1939) and Franz Kafka (1883–1921).

Not unexpectedly, this mass flight placed a large burden on Western governments. For the most part, they had left Jewish immigration from the East unregulated. Yet what had previously been little more than a nuisance now assumed large proportions. Politicians and special interests called for legislation that would protect "natives" against the threat of undesirable aliens, and such calls grew more frequent when a Europe-wide economic crisis began in 1873. In this unstable climate, antisemites tried to find ways to make visible the "Jewish characteristics" of unwanted immigrants.

The consensus of historians is that "[w]herever they settled in appreciable numbers, newly arrived Jews from the East sparked far-reaching and disruptive public controversies over attitudes and policies toward aliens."[3] The debate over Eastern Jewish aliens was no less controversial in the *Jewish* communities of the West which, until the end of the nineteenth century, had been relatively unencumbered by their Eastern brethren.[4]

Whether real or perceived, the challenge posed by Jewish immigration was most pronounced in the *Kaiserreich*. Although Jewish migration to Germany never exceeded a few hundred per year until 1918, some Jews and non-Jews were obsessed with the idea that droves of Jewish aliens were streaming across the eastern border that Germany shared with both Austro-Hungary and Russia. And this fear was not entirely unfounded, since most *Ostjuden* had to cross German borders to proceed westward.

But three factors made the *Kaiserreich* look more susceptible to Jewish mass migration than it actually was: (1) the impossibility of policing the borders, (2) the need to stimulate foreign investment, and (3) the granting of civil rights to Jews.

First, it was impractical to regulate, much less bar, immigration by Jews. Neither imperial decree nor tighter supervision was able to reduce the flow of human traffic. Although the borders were successfully sealed between 1885 and 1890, the decision to import seasonal workers from Poland made it difficult to separate desirable from undesirable immigrants. Indeed, those Jews simply passing through—the "transmigrants"—were a motley group. Some were penniless refugees on foot; others were rail travelers holding ship's passage to the New World. Stationing 10 percent of all Prussian gendarmes on the border, requiring identification cards, threatening fines and imprisonment—none of these measures could dam the flow of Jewish (and non-Jewish) refugees, especially after the Russian revolution of 1905. In addition to political considerations, the expensive cost of travel documents and the availability of many human smugglers also encouraged Jews to cross the border illegally.

Second, Germany signed trade agreements with Austro-Hungary and Russia in the early 1890s, granting most-favored-nation trading status to those states. As a result, subjects of both nations could move about freely in Germany and conduct their business free of harassment. Galician, Bohemian, Moravian, Hungarian, and Russian Jews could now travel to Germany on business. The new treaties shielded them from group discrimination; only individuals could be prevented from entering the country. Allowing Jewish refugees into the *Reich* was also in Germany's self-interest, since the German shipping industry profited greatly from transporting Eastern Jews to England and America via the ports of Hamburg and Bremen. In fact, Jewish transmigration exceeded 700,000 during the peak years between 1905 and 1914. Jews made up 50 percent of passengers on Germany's growing commercial fleet according to some accounts.[5]

Third, the German parliament found its hands tied in trying to cope with the new influx. Since the *Reich* had become unified in law, old barriers to Jewish emancipation had fallen away, making it difficult to single Jews out for special treatment. On November 1, 1867, the Constitution of the North German Confederation (article 3, paragraph 3) had eliminated all laws that restricted the settlement of *Betteljuden*, and all religious discrimination was outlawed on July 3, 1869.[6] When the newly unified empire granted Jews complete legal equality in 1871, Jewish aliens seeking German citizenship were no longer at a disadvantage vis-à-vis other aliens. In theory, then, it was harder than ever to discriminate against Jews who came under the jurisdiction of the *Kaiserreich*.

If government officials in the Wilhelminian Empire truly wanted to curtail unwanted immigration after 1880, why did they not simply pass a law forbidding all foreign Jews to enter Germany? The reason is simple: administrative measures were already in place to bar such immigration. The power to confer and to take away citizenship had traditionally rested with the individual German states (*Länder*), and this was no different under the *Kaiserreich*. Each state, from its minister of the interior down to the lowest policeman, had an extensive bureaucracy for regulating resident aliens. The requirements for citizenship—permission from the country of origin, home ownership in Germany, an unblemished civic record, the ability to support all dependents—were in practice *minimal* requirements. People who had lived for decades in Germany were routinely denied citizenship. Except for women who married German citizens and except for men who held public office or served a school or community, naturalization was a long and often arbitrary process.

Since administrators (*Beamte*), rather than legislators, set the conditions under which aliens could become residents, the potential for abuse was always present. In Bavaria, Prussia, or Hesse, state officials could decide autocratically what papers were necessary for entry into their territories. If an immigrant was fortunate enough to be issued a residency permit, the permit might entitle him or her to stay for only a few days at a time. Certain states limited the economic activities of foreigners; others put a freeze on the hiring of foreign workers. Aliens were also forbidden to participate in the political process or to hold meetings in languages other than German. Failure to meet any of these requirements was grounds for deportation. Moreover, anyone deemed "troublesome" (*lästig*) or a danger to "public interests" or "security" was subject to immediate expulsion. Often thousands of aliens were exiled on such pretexts.

Since the German states were permitted to regulate immigration as they saw fit, they could—and often did—discriminate more against Jews than against other foreigners.[7] Although East European Jews made up only 10 percent of all foreigners in the *Kaiserreich*, the *Länder* took steps to treat them differently. Polish Catholics were no doubt caught in the middle between the nationalism and the economic self-interest of their German hosts, who imported them as seasonal workers and permitted them to settle temporarily in German lands between April and November. Yet East European Jews suffered even greater harassment. Regarded as "troublesome" and unfit for heavy labor in agriculture or industry because of "laziness," many were kept out of Germany. Eastern Jews earned their living "through haggling and begging" and had "an aversion to every sort of respectable work," in the words of the Berlin police commissioner.[8] As a result of such attitudes, those Jews who made it into Germany had an unusually heterogeneous profile. Whereas Poles and other Slavs were almost invariably seasonal workers, the East European Jews in Germany formed at least four very different subgroups:

> (1) [T]he largest by far consisted of transmigrants who moved through Germany in ever-increasing numbers on their way from Russia, Rumania, and Austro-Hungary to other Western lands; (2) a second group was made up of transients who sought to remain in the country temporarily, either to find work, to absorb German culture, or to raise funds by begging for help from German Jews; (3) still another distinct group was formed by young Jews from the East who studied in Germany's renowned institutions of higher learning; (4) and, finally, immigrant Jews attempted to establish themselves as permanent residents, and even citizens, of the Reich.[9]

Even though anti-Jewish policies drove many Jews out of Eastern Europe in the final decades of the nineteenth century, few of these émigrés were what we today would term asylum seekers. Like migrant workers, they were drawn to the more industrialized West by the promise of new economic opportunities. In addition, they knew that their fellow Jews in England, France, Germany, and the New World enjoyed comparatively greater freedom and prosperity. Those who were adventurous enough felt compelled to seek their fortunes in the unfamiliar surroundings of the West.

One Jew who took part in the turn-of-the-century mass migration of East European Jewry was Leo Winz, the publisher and chief editor of *Ost und West*. Winz founded the journal in 1901 while still a student in Berlin. Because this study focuses on the promotion of ethnic identity, one of its aims is to understand how a young Eastern Jew, with only an insignificant amount of startup capital, could build up a Jewish publishing business that had a net worth of one quarter of a million marks (approximately two million present-day U.S. dollars) and whose customers went beyond the sphere of émigré intellectuals such as himself.

Winz moved to Berlin in 1892, at the age of sixteen, and his early career was typical of many young Eastern Jews in search of education and advancement. By coming to Berlin, these young émigrés were repeating Jewish history, reenacting the journey of Salomon Maimon (1753–1800) from *shtetl* "backwardness" to German "enlightenment."[10] While they could still attend Russian universities, there was little need for such pilgrimages, and between 1881 and 1886, fewer than 100 Russian Jews were registered as students in all of Germany. But the situation in Russia changed radically in July 1887, when Tsar Nicholas II imposed an anti-Jewish *numerus clausus*, forcing Winz and growing numbers of Jews to seek higher education abroad.[11] At first, the young Russians flocked to Switzerland, which offered a high level of political freedom, yet by 1900, Germany had become just as popular.[12]

To resist these new arrivals and appease antisemites, the authorities in the various German states began restricting the numbers of East European Jews admitted to study. Worse, German officials and politicians manufactured an *Ausländerfrage* as a pretext to spy upon and deport Russian Jews, claiming that "bomb-throwing subversives" were destabilizing institutions of higher learning in Germany.[13] This defamatory campaign, which drew on traditional stereotypes of the *Ostjude*, was quite successful: after 1905, " 'Russian,' 'radical,' and 'eastern Jew' became linked together . . . as a single type of undesirable in the eyes of many a German."[14] Such were the obstacles that Winz and others faced if they wished to maintain their Eastern Jewish identity in such an environment; neither he nor most of his Eastern colleagues were ever permitted to become citizens of the *Reich*.

Though Russian Jews studying in Germany always had been confronted with xenophobia, prejudice toward them seemed to worsen in direct relation to their growing (if numerically insignificant) presence. Statistics confirm how conspicuous they were becoming: more than 25 percent of all foreign students who matriculated in the *Kaiserreich* were Russian Jews.[15] In Berlin, Eastern Jews made up 25 percent of the Jewish student body in 1905–6, having made up less than 10 percent of all Jewish students in 1887–88.[16] In fact, the number of émigrés multiplied tenfold during the 1890s and quadrupled further in the decade prior to 1914. By 1912–13, more than 2,500 Russian Jews attended Prussian universities and technical schools, and 500 of them studied in Berlin.[17] Such an expanding audience was ripe for a publication like *Ost und West* which promoted a visible Jewish ethnicity. Winz and contributors to the journal were no doubt aware that the percentage of Eastern Jews among all Wilhelminian Jews had nearly doubled from 7 percent to 12.8 percent in the first decade of the twentieth century, partly as a result of the influx of Russian-Jewish students.[18]

Study in Germany, a necessity for Russian-Jewish youth in the 1880s, became immensely popular after 1900.[19] Although nurtured on Eastern Jewish values, many of these Jews were impressed by the promise of a German education. The attraction was the same as it had been for the Jewish Enlighteners (*maskilim*) of the previous generation: Germany, Russia's closest Western neighbor, was viewed as combining political stability with scientific advancement. The technological achievements of the Wilhelminian age inspired Russian Jews to become doctors, chemists, and engineers. Whereas Winz and some of his associates had studied literature, art, and philosophy in the 1890s, nearly 85 percent of foreign Jews were enrolled in medical studies by 1912.[20] Careers in the sciences also were less affected by antisemitism than law or academia, which were notorious dead ends for Jews in both Tsarist Russia and Imperial Germany.

In the wake of the Holocaust, it is difficult today to remember how young *Ostjuden* internalized, indeed relished, things German.[21] But Wilhelminian Germany was on the rise, economically and culturally, a fact that even its opponents conceded. To the generation of Russian Jews unable to study in Russia, Germany symbolized freedom and upward mobility, and it was a mere border crossing away. One person who shared this attitude and who illegally spirited himself over the frontier was Chaim Weizmann (1874–1952). A chemist who went on to become the leader of the World Zionist Movement and the first president of the state of Israel, Weizmann wrote in 1949 (just four years after the *Shoah*):

> For the Jews and the intellectuals generally of Russia, the West ended at the Rhine, and beyond that boundary there was only an unknown world. They knew Germany, they spoke German, and they were vastly impressed by German achievement, German discipline and German power. They knew, as I did, that Russia was rotten through and through, eaten up by graft, incompetence and indolence. . . . Germany, it is true, was also anti-Semitic, but German anti-Semitism did not show as much on the surface. It bore a milder aspect.[22]

For similar reasons, Russian Jews of all political and ideological leanings settled in Germany prior to World War I. They included Jewish nationalists and socialists, Hebraists and Yiddishists, liberals as well as anarchists. Their luminaries were Aḥad Haᶜam (1858–1927), Micha Josef Berdichevsky (1865–1921), Saul Tchernichowsky (1875–1943), Alexander "Parvus" Helphand (1867–1924), and many others.

Since both Jewish and non-Jewish Germans harbored negative images of *Ostjuden*, the Russian Jews' fondness for the *Kaiserreich* went unreciprocated. These Jews, seldom accepted in the new communities, were compelled to create their own.[23] Their impromptu colonies (*Kolonien*) became a new frame of reference in their exile from the Pale. The concentration of Russian Jews of similar ages and backgrounds eased their transition and relieved their isolation. These support networks also bypassed the German-Jewish establishment. Its institutions were based in Berlin, but its members often seemed indifferent to the large community of émigrés.

Many a Russian Jew came to identify more with his adopted group of expatriates (*lantslayt*) than with the "old country." New bonds replaced older ones. Ethnic Jewishness was substituted for a more traditional identity, a process that further undermined the old loyalties of the students. Like certain Third World intellectuals today, these Eastern Jews felt stifled upon returning home from the West. Weizmann, for instance, found his hometown culturally and economically bereft.[24] Intellectually a Westerner, he felt that he had been cast into "foreign hands" (*goyishe hent*) whenever he visited there.[25] Some Russian Jews thus internalized a number of Western attitudes toward the East, including an elitist attitude toward the *shtetl*. Weizmann's disdain for the ghettoized Pale of Settlement, the Russian territory where most Jews were forced to reside, was a logical result of living abroad and developing bicultural sensibilities.[26] In their tolerance for multiple sensibilities, indeed *identities*, Weizmann, Winz, and their contemporaries resembled the early *maskilim*.

But while Russian-Jewish intellectuals may have been enlightened, they were not yet Westerners. Outside their narrow community, they were labeled *Polacken* or even *Bolschewisten*. What really sustained them in the face of such nonacceptance was political opposition to the Tsarist regime, regardless of whether such opposition was ethnic Jewish, liberal, socialist, or anarchist. Often these Jewish students looked westward for new ideologies to challenge Russian domination. Perhaps the most idiosyncratic thing about them was the forum in which they interacted: the Western-style debate.[27] Otherwise aloof from German university life, these young Russian-Jewish émigrés socialized in political meetings. Large, private disputations became their alternative to the duels and drinking evenings (*Kommers*) of the established German-Jewish fraternities.

The most famous of these disputing organizations was the Russian Jewish Scientific Society (*Russischer jüdischer wissenschaftlicher Verein*), founded in Berlin in 1889. Along with the proto-Zionist fraternity *Kadimah* (Vienna, founded in 1883), it was the forerunner of *Jung Israel* (Berlin, founded in 1892), *Hasmonäa* (Berlin, founded in 1892), and related groups which also balanced Western Jewish with Eastern Jewish concerns.[28] The members of the *Verein*, at first moderate devotees of Jewish nationalism, had become Zionists by 1898. Besides Weizmann, other famous Zionists emerged from their ranks: Leo Motzkin (1867–1933), Nachman Syrkin (1868–1924), Shmarya Levin (1867–1935), and Victor Jacobson (1869–1934).[29] Winz was involved in the *Verein*, *Jung Israel*, and other groups whose members strove to unify their Eastern Jewish identity with a broader, ethnic Jewish identity.[30] Typical for their activities was the formation of a nationalist society called *Bildung: Verein zur Förderung der Literatur in jüdisch-deutscher Mundart* (founded in 1896) which distributed Yiddish literature among Jews under the aegis of the *Verein*.[31]

The major activities of the *Verein*, however, remained lectures and debates. These Saturday night disputations, involving as many as 150 students, took on the air of a sporting event. These almost martial encounters had a distinctive masculine style (not least of all because their audience was exclusively male). Here Jewish intellectuals honed their rhetorical skills so that they might better stereotype their opponents. Although these forums had a seditious air, they were largely ignored by the Berlin police, who were more interested in breaking up socialist meetings than those of Jewish nationalists.[32] And more foreign Jewish students probably

joined the nationalist clubs than the socialist ones.[33] On occasion, however, the Jewish socialists would come to debate the *Nationaljuden*. They
often brought with them notables, such as Helphand or Leon Trotsky
(1879–1940), in the hope of forcing Jewish nationalists to succumb by dint
of authority, if not argument.[34] For the already convinced, these public
contests served to reinforce their commitment to one or another Jewish
ideology.

Despite their largely Russian clientele, the *Verein* and related societies
were open to all Eastern Jews regardless of their origin. Among their
members were Galician Jews, who were greatly outnumbered in Berlin by
their coreligionists from the Pale. If the Russian Jews were more politicized,
the Galicians were more scholarly, perhaps the result of having been raised
in the somewhat more stable circumstances of the Habsburg empire. This
holds true for Binjamin Segel (1867–1931). Although overshadowed by
his fellow Galicians Martin Buber (1878–1965) and Markus Ehrenpreis
(1869–1951), Segel was a talented scholar, folklorist, and ethnographer.
He attended universities in Lemberg, Vienna, and Berlin. At *Ost und West*,
he quickly became the main editorialist, producing more articles, essays,
and stories for the magazine than anyone else in its twenty-three years of
publication.

Like Winz, who studied with professors such as Georg Simmel (1858–
1918), Hermann Strack (1848–1922), Chaim Steinthal (1823–1899; see
chapter 5 below), and even the antisemite Heinrich von Treitschke (1834–
1896), Segel, too, concentrated in the humanities at the Berlin university.[35]
But here is where all comparisons end. Not only did Winz and Segel
represent a rare alliance—Russian Jew and Austrian Jew—but their status
under German law was also different. Winz had to leave Germany during
World War I, whereas Segel was permitted to stay. While Winz signed
his letters *"Mit Zionsgruß"* and claimed to be a Zionist his entire life,
Segel wrote propaganda for the liberal, anti-Zionist camp after the war.
Winz's opinions were largely unpublished; Segel's were as numerous as his
pseudonyms and were not limited to *Ost und West*.

Having been raised in the multiethnic Habsburg Empire, Segel had
witnessed the large-scale migrations of Jews within that empire in the last
decades of the nineteenth century. As a result, he favored Jewish cultural
autonomy on a nonterritorial basis. To call for state-sanctioned Jewish
particularism may have been possible in Austro-Hungary, but it was virtually
unheard of in the *Kaiserreich*. For while the Jewish middle-class elite of
the Habsburg Empire may have identified with the enlightened values
of German culture, most Austro-Hungarian Jews did not see themselves
as "Germans": "The very different nature of the Austrian state structure,
the reality of a multinational state, and the demographic configuration of
Habsburg Jewry allowed Jews to be culturally German, Czech, Magyar, or
Polish, politically Austrian, and ethnically Jewish all at the same time. A

nation-state like Germany could never tolerate such a tripartite identity."[36] For this reason, this study focuses on role of Jewish ethnicity in Germany. Jews in Austro-Hungary were, to be sure, readers of *Ost und West* and were often discussed in its pages. Yet in Vienna, Eastern Jews never became the issue in communal affairs that they were in Berlin.[37] Perhaps this is why there never was a Habsburg equivalent of *Ost und West*.[38] For the need to promote the *Ostjuden* in the Habsburg Empire was not nearly as compelling; above all, it was home to nearly twice as many Eastern Jews as Germany.

Ignoring such distinctions, Germans and German Jews alike lumped Russian Jews together with other *Ostjuden* from Austria, Hungary, Galicia, the Bukovina, Poland, and Rumania. Few cared to notice that the émigré Jews of Berlin were often as detached from one another as they were from German Jewry. (The foreign student community seemed so differentiated, in fact, that one commentator quipped that there were as many cliques as there were émigré Jews in Berlin.)[39] The potential for uniting these various individuals, and the remainder of Jews in Germany, lay in a peculiar institution: the emerging Jewish public sphere in Germany. As we shall see, *Ost und West* was to play a special, integrative role at the center of this public sphere. Moreover, the most important tool for consolidating ethnic identity in the Jewish journalism of the time was stereotyping. Not surprisingly, then, the most conspicuous bonding between Russians and Galicians took place in the world of stereotypes, the means by which *Ost und West* and others defended themselves against so-called assimilationists in the West.

In stigmatizing Western Jews as assimilationists, Eastern Jewish students ran the risk of widening the already considerable gap between themselves and their Western Jewish peers. Even in the twentieth century, contacts between the two student worlds were rare. Undeterred, however, some young *Westjuden* took up cudgels for the *Ostjuden* and became members of organizations such as the *Verein*. The most notable case was Heinrich Loewe (1867–1950). As a citizen of the *Kaiserreich*, Loewe was able to use his privileged status to protect Eastern Jewry, and he was one of the earliest Western Jews to espouse an ethnic Jewish identity.[40] In addition, the *Verein* also frequently invited German scholars such as Moritz Steinschneider to deliver lectures, foreshadowing the primacy given to history and literature in *Ost und West*.

One of Loewe's greatest contributions was to found in 1894 a reading room for Eastern Jews, the *Berlin Jüdische Leseballe*.[41] The role of this and other lending libraries and reading societies (*Lesegesellschaften*) in German-Jewish society has been only recently the object of study, but their impact seems undeniable.[42] These institutions not only edified and entertained their members, they also served the cause of ethnic (and class) integration by giving their members a sense of belonging. In addition, the preexisting network of Jewish libraries gave a necessary boost to *Ost und West* and related Jewish periodicals.[43] Winz knew how crucial they were in the circulation of his magazine. Not only can his name can be found on the donors' lists of the libraries, but Winz was, in fact, the head librarian at the *Lesehalle* in the late 1890s (see fig. 1).

The growth of institutions dedicated to the reading of "Jewish" texts shows that ethnic Jewishness was rapidly becoming a meaningful identity, a way of uniting Jews in Germany in an imaginary textual realm. As a European Jewish journalist writing in German, Russian, Hebrew, and Yiddish, Winz was a prime mover in the ethnic Jewish public sphere from its earliest days onward. While living in Berlin in the 1890s, he had served as the German correspondent for the Hebrew weekly *Ha-Tsefirah* (Warsaw, 1862–1928, edited by Nahum Sokolow). He also wrote for the Russian-Jewish monthly *Voskhod* (St. Petersburg, 1881–1906, various editors), a cultural journal similar to *Ost und West*. As a young publicist, Winz cultivated a wide range of contacts among Jewish journalists so that, at the mere age of twenty-five, he was selected to lead the press corps at the 1901 Zionist Congress in Basel.

Winz found the German-language Jewish public sphere of his time wanting. While the Jewish Liberal weekly *Allgemeine Zeitung des Judentums* (Berlin, 1837–1922, edited in succession by Ludwig Phillipson, Gustav Karpeles, Ludwig Geiger, and Albert Katz), the neo-Orthodox weekly *Der Israelit* (Frankfurt, 1860–1938, edited by S. Schachnowitz), and the anti-Zionist, pro-German monthly *Im deutschen Reich* (Berlin, 1895–1921, edited by Alfred Levy) were, to some extent, models for *Ost und West*, Winz was eager to avoid the partisan policies of these establishment newspapers.[44] His idea was to appeal to a much broader Jewish audience with a message of pan-Jewish ethnicity. There was the recently founded *Israelitisches Familienblatt*, a weekly "family journal" published by Max Lessman in Hamburg, Frankfurt, and Berlin (1898–1938), which would become the most widely circulated Jewish periodical of Imperial and Weimar Germany. But the *Familienblatt* was too close to the assimilationist *Centralverein deutscher Staatsbürger jüdischen Glaubens* (Central Association of German Citizens of the Jewish Faith) despite the pretense of being apolitical.[45] There was no immediate German-language predecessor that fulfilled Winz's agenda, not even the Zionist party organ *Die Welt* (Vienna, 1897–1914) or the German Zionist weekly *Jüdische Rundschau* (Berlin, 1899–1938; until 1902 *Israelitische Rundschau*). The only direct Jewish nationalist models were lesser known and short-lived. The best known of these was the monthly *Zion. Monatsschrift für die nationalen Interessen des jüdischen Volkes* (Berlin, 1895–1900), which was edited until 1897 by Heinrich Loewe. In 1898, Loewe outlined plans for a monthly to be called *Der Orient. Monatsschrift für Kultur und Leben der jüdischen Nation*.[46] Not unlike *Ost und West*, its program stressed the "cultural dimensions" of the new Jewish nationalist

Figure 1. Circulation desk at the Berlin Jewish Lesehalle. *Leo Winz in background, left.* Ost und West *(November 1908): 687–88.*

orientation and called for a synthesis of European humanism and Jewish particularity. Another feature of *Der Orient* that reappeared in *Ost und West* was Loewe's rhetoric of nonpartisanship. *Der Orient* insisted that all parties should have a voice, "since every orientation represented another expression of the people's soul [*Volksseele*] and the life of the nation." Only then could the Jewish press become democratized and transcend "the quarrels of the day and narrow-minded partisanship."[47]

In hindsight, the activities of the *Russischer jüdischer wissenschaftlicher Verein* and similar societies provided the training grounds for future journalists such as Winz and Loewe. Loewe, in 1902, became the editor of *Ost und West*'s major competitor, the *Jüdische Rundschau*. The polemics in which the members of the *Verein* participated as students thus found their way into the journals and newspapers they later published. Debates held by the *Verein* were the first examples of a Jewish nationalist public sphere in Germany. Finally, the *Verein* and related groups were the first to recognize the importance of propaganda techniques in attracting Western Jews to their cause.[48] The *Verein*'s role as a liaison between Eastern Jews and German Jews was thus influential. In the end, however, it proved less decisive for Loewe's—and party Zionist—journalism than for Winz's.

How did *Ost und West* stress the commonalities of Jews, East and West? What were the foundations of an ethnic—and visible—Jewish identity that could apply equally to *Ostjuden* and *Westjuden?* Each group defined itself, at certain times and in certain contexts, according to religious criteria. Moreover, Jews from both cultures shared one basic attitude toward Jewish religion: being Jewish had, past and present, implied some degree of observance of biblical commandments and injunctions. And even if they shunned religious affiliation, most agreed with the tradition that a Jew was someone who descended from a Jewish mother.

Yet the widespread acceptance of the idea of matrilineal descent points to a second dimension of Jewish self-definition: ethnicity. In the parlance of the nineteenth century, Jewish ethnic cohesiveness was conceived of in terms of nationhood. Self-labeled Jews felt that they formed a unique nation, even if they did not possess a state of their own. The myth of tribal allegiance was extremely powerful, and by the turn of the century, the ethnic-national definition increasingly began to prevail over older versions of Jewish identity. Jews shared not only a religious culture but in addition a host of other mindsets and practices that extended beyond the shared experience of antisemitism.[49] We shall follow Benedict Anderson's lead in defining the nation as an imagined social grouping which finds its binding commonalities in language, culture, religion, or politics.[50] As *Ost und West* appeared on the scene, some Jews already had developed an awareness that they belonged to a nation, most notably in the Zionist movement which was formally established in 1897 by Theodor Herzl (1860–1904). This awareness was promoted in *Ost und West* (and elsewhere) under the banner of "Jewish nationalism" (*Nationaljudentum*) or "Jewish ethnicity" (*Stammesjudentum*).[51]

Even in their most intellectual formulations, Jewish nationalism and Jewish ethnicity were rarely defined lucidly.[52] Nevertheless, the idea of common nationhood was a powerful source of identification for most Jews. For many, it became a matter of utmost concern at the fin de siècle that Jews were a nation without political sovereignty. If Jews were an independent people, how could they ever achieve autonomy within the boundaries of a non-Jewish state? This was the dilemma that Zionism attempted to resolve by promoting Jewish settlement in Palestine. While generally supportive of the ideas of Zionism, *Ost und West* remained steadfastly nonpartisan for all of its twenty-three years. What Winz and his colleagues ended up advocating was a vague idea of European Jewish consciousness. This strategy was more likely to appeal to German Jews than the more definitive goal of a Jewish state in Palestine or the more taboo option of Jewish cultural autonomy in Germany. Within German and Western culture, *Ost und West* came to specialize in the "touch of Jewishness," the so-called *jüdische Note*.[53] This was the key to the journal's understated ideal of nationalist Jewry, an ideal at times better captured by the term *ethnic Jewishness* than by *Jewish nationalism.*

Ost und West repeatedly spoke of a "harmonious" Jewish identity, an identity poised between tradition and modernity and between East and West. But beginning in the last half of the nineteenth century, nativist organizations in Germany and Austria made it more difficult to maintain such a harmonious Jewishness. The most persistent challenges to the idea of Jewish ethnicity came from the antisemitic camp. In response, some Jews internalized antisemitism; others recast it as a Jewish-based form of racialism (Jewry as a race). The charge of Jewish "parasitism" in the German economy or in German culture was capable of moving even nationalist Jews to elaborate apologetics. *Ost und West*, too, called on Jews to dissimilate from German culture and to modernize their occupational structure. Agriculture and artisanry came to be preferred to the historical Jewish concentration in trade and commerce. Whether this demand for professional restructuring was solely a reaction to anti-Jewish sentiment is a question for further discussion below, where I shall describe this set of Jewish self-representations as "Western-enlightened."

The Jewish nationalist renaissance heralded by *Ost und West* was not simply a reaction to antisemitism, however. Political and social discrimination certainly had an impact on the self-image of *Ost und West*'s readers, but this threat was countered by deeply held Jewish values and messianic longings that were centuries older than Jew hatred. Antisemitism "only deepened resolve and forced public statements [from Jews], but did not create Jewish ethnic consciousness," writes the historian Marsha Rozenblit.[54] In *Ost und West*, antisemitism bolstered Jewish identity, encouraging those who already wanted to affiliate more demonstratively with the Jewish people.

The persistence of Jewish consciousness in Europe cannot be explained by Jew hatred alone. At the same time, what many people took for Jewish cohesion—or even conspiracy—was actually an illusion. For Jewish nationalism, the one ideology capable of uniting (Ashkenazic) Jewry, was understood very differently in Eastern and Western Europe. In the East, an ethnic-national identity was still a lived reality for many Jews into the twentieth century. In the West, this form of Jewish identity always had been at risk, a risk that increased after Jews were urged to assimilate to the dominant culture in the spirit of "enlightenment."

It is one of the goals of this book to problematize this typology of East and West. For now, though, it should suffice to note that Jewish nationalism did not achieve concrete form in Germany until Jewish student organizations and Zionism arose in the 1890s. Even as many German Jews began to feel that loyalty to the German state might coexist with Jewish national consciousness, loyalty to the *Kaiserreich* almost always took precedence. Indeed, Western Jewish nationalism—and to a lesser extent, Eastern—drew on a century-old history of *German* nationalism. For the early German nationalists, language, symbols, songs, and myths expressed a people's peculiar "national essence."[55] Although Jewish leaders knew how closely linked Western Jewish nationalism was to its German godparent, they were concerned that patriotic Germans would take offense at visible displays of Jewishness. Most German Zionists insisted upon international negotiations as the sole means of acquiring a legally recognized Jewish homeland. The ethnic Jewish movement in the West is thus referred to by historians as "Jewish state nationalism" or "political Zionism."[56]

Since Zionism was only one form of Jewish nationalism—indeed, of Western Jewish nationalism—one must differentiate carefully among Jewish nationalisms in turn-of-the-century Europe.[57] Traditional Jewish consciousness provided the building blocks for Eastern Jewish nationalism, whose theorists, such as Aḥad Haʿam, felt that a spiritual renewal had to precede any restoration of a Jewish state. Aḥad Haʿam's Jewish nationalism, in its historical setting, was also known as "cultural Zionism" (or "spiritual Zionism"). It is mainly in its Palestinocentrism that it varied from the "Diaspora nationalism" of Simon Dubnow (1860–1941) and related forms of Jewish cultural autonomy. Yet history generally has been less kind to these Jewish nationalists of Eastern Europe than to their Western brethren. Though at times highly organized in self-defense and anti-Tsarist cells, they were ultimately as powerless as their constituencies. The only significant Jewish party besides the Zionists that evolved in Russia was the *Bund*, and its demands for Jewish national autonomy were realized only partially after the 1917 revolution.

The distinction between Western and Eastern Jewish nationalism is also related to the distinction between the nation-state (the goal of étatist or civic nationalisms) and the cultural nation (the goal of cultural or ethnic nationalisms). This distinction was regarded as well established in nineteenth-century German thought and was codified, for instance, in the writings of historian Friedrich Meinecke.[58] Western Jewish nationalists were more concerned with developing étatist than ethnic nationalism, despite the fact that they tried to integrate the latter whenever possible. Herzl's model was Jewish life in Western Europe, founded on the idea of "civility" and republican notions of statehood. Western Jewish nationalists—be they Zionists or Territorialists[59]—rejected the idea that the Jews could ever be fully integrated into a state where they formed a political minority. The survival of the Jews in a modern world required more than limited self-rule or minority rights; it required nothing less than a homeland. The Western Jewish nationalists called for a Jewish national renaissance, assuming that the momentum of a cultural renewal would help them realize the goal of statehood. They differed from the Eastern Jewish nationalists, however, in assuming that the new homeland, rather than the cultural renewal, would give purpose and direction to the course of Jewish history. Advocating a strong break with the past of Jewish oppression, they sought to "normalize" the Jews by urging a high degree of acculturation to modern ways. Only then might Jews also reap the fruits of Western civilization, fruits such as étatist nationalism.

While Herzl and his sympathizers were committed to realizing Jewish national hopes, their plans were thoroughly characterized by "enlightened" Western thinking, a fact repeatedly pointed out by Jewish Easterners. Even in its most separatist manifestations, Western Jewish nationalism took the progressive optimism of emancipation and transferred it from the individual to the ethnic collective. Herzl, for all his apparent elitism, accurately mirrored the cultural concerns of most Western Jews, and his sense of Zionism often took on the contours of a Western Jewish "ethnocentrism."[60] At the time that his Jewish consciousness was being forged through covering the first Dreyfus trials for the Viennese *Neue Freie Presse*, he was still unfamiliar with the Eastern proto-Zionists of the Hovevei Zion movement, Leon Pinsker (1821–1891) and Moses Leib Lilienblum (1843–1910). Nor had Herzl read the works of German-Jewish forerunners, such as Moses Hess (1812–1875). In fact, the preponderance of Russian-Jewish nationalists at the First Zionist Congress (Basel, 1897) astounded him. Although these Eastern Zionists, led by Menachem Ussishkin (1863–1941), profoundly affected Herzl's later policies, the cultural gap was too large to brook. The first Zionist congresses, for all their ostensible unity, laid down the battle lines between the two orientations toward Jewish nationalism.

Foreign students such as Winz played a major role in this schism. Although they had received Western university educations, they were nevertheless loyal to Eastern Jewish culture and values. All of them had encountered Western-style political Zionism in the course of their intellectual odyssey in Germany. Their mounting objections to it led them to ally themselves with Western Jewish intellectuals receptive to Eastern Jewish ideas. Eventually, they formed the "Democratic Faction" (*Demokratische Fraktion*), a splinter group inspired in large part by Aḥad Haᶜam and cultural Zionism.[61] This circle, established in 1900, included Buber, Weizmann, Berthold Feiwel (1875–1937), and Leo Motzkin (1867–1933). The Faction and its supporters sought to democratize the Zionist movement while also actively promoting Jewish culture and social reform in the Diaspora. Not surprisingly, many of *Ost und West*'s earliest contributors were associated with the Faction.[62]

To make matters worse for Herzl, Western Jewish nationalism was not received warmly by non-Jews in Germany. In the *Kaiserreich*, more than in Herzl's native Austro-Hungary, Jewish nationalist aspirations ran counter to the prevailing sentiment that Jews should be either "denationalized" or deported. Jewish nationalism entailed a "renationalization" of Jewish life, and it was bound to elicit images of separatism for Germans who thought of themselves as part of a homogeneous nation. The controversy surrounding the so-called Jewish Problem (*Judenfrage*) in the nineteenth century crystallized around the question of Jewish integration: would the Jews become full-fledged Germans or not? Even though the World Zionist Organization had its headquarters in Germany between 1904 and 1914, the charge of dual loyalty thwarted the success of Jewish nationalism in the *Kaiserreich*. In German-Jewish communal politics, Zionism never did achieve dominance, accounting for fewer than 10 percent of votes cast in every *Gemeinde* election prior to 1920.

How did Jewish nationalism come to be regarded as less legitimate than other nationalisms in a *Reich* unified in the name of Germanhood (*Deutschtum*)? Here one must distinguish between "liberal" (or "civic") and "conservative" (or "ethnic") nationalism.[63] Liberal German nationalists, in the immediate aftermath of 1871, were prepared to admit the legitimacy of other nationalist movements within Germany. But this rhetorical legitimacy was soon suppressed under the impact of new events. The economic crisis of 1873 became the pretext for a coalition of conservatives and antisemites to challenge liberal versions of German nationalism. Between 1872 and 1886, the German state conducted a *Kulturkampf* to restrict Catholics—who made up one third of the German population—from competing loyalties.[64] More and more, the idea of Germany as a nation-state came to compete with the idea of Germany as an ethnic, monocultural nation.

As if in imitation of German conservatism, the Western Jewish precedent of "unification" nationalism frowned upon nationalisms formulated by Eastern Jews. The Zionist leadership, in turn, was perceived as too utopian by those in favor of more Jewish autonomy in Poland, Russia, and Austria, where the majority of Jews still lived. The call for a speedy solution to the Jewish predicament in Eastern Europe went out from Russian and Galician Jewish intellectuals. As activists, they sought to redress Jewish problems immediately (*Gegenwartsarbeit*) and to correct the deliberate approach of the political Zionists.[65] They advocated both practical work in Palestine ("practical Zionism") and immediate relief in the Diaspora as solutions to the problem of Jewish mass migration.

Although they were outraged by the poverty and political repression of their Eastern coreligionists, the Jews of Western Europe only recently had achieved legal equality themselves. They were thus eager to protect their newly acquired status, which seemed incompatible with Jewish nationalism of any kind. In particular, they worried that more *Ostjuden* on German soil could jeopardize their own precarious footing before the law.[66] Germany had never allowed significant numbers of Jewish immigrants to settle within its borders, and it was therefore easy for antisemites such as Wilhelm Marr (1818–1904) and court preacher Adolf Stoecker (1835–1909) to play on the fears of Jews and non-Jews.[67] German "citizens of the Jewish faith" (as some German Jews fashioned themselves) feared that they would be accused of harboring dual loyalties, and antidefamation became the centerpiece of their Jewish identities. In short, they assumed that the condition for their emancipation was the surrender of all claims to a separate nationality.

The more the *Kaiserreich* was guided by a myth of its own homogeneity, the more impossible it appeared to make Jewish nationalism an acceptable form of identity there.[68] For this reason, Zionist extremists opted for a similar myth of cultural homogeneity as a solution to the dilemma of dual loyalty. Whereas the new German antisemitism was antedated by an indigenous tradition of Eastern Jewish nationalism,[69] Western Jewish nationalists had no such tradition. Instead, they flirted with conservative Western views of ethnic identity. Clothing their ideology in the discourse of racialism, some Zionists accepted the idea that Jews formed a scientifically verifiable, if not superior, race.[70]

Yet these Western Jewish nationalists, by imitating conservative European nationalism, threatened to become as Western as the enlightened Jews they stereotyped in their literature.[71] The most extreme also resisted the nationalism of Eastern Jewry, a move that precipitated the three most controversial events in the Zionist movement at the turn of the century: the formation of the Democratic Faction, the debate surrounding the publication of Herzl's *Altneuland*[72] in October 1902, and the "Uganda Controversy" of 1904. As a result of these crises, more Eastern Jews distanced themselves from party Zionism, and cultural Zionism became a force to be reckoned with.

Ost und West played a central role in the *Altneuland* controversy surrounding Aḥad Haᶜam, Herzl, and Max Nordau (1849–1923). The controversy came at a critical juncture in the journal's history and was a revealing prelude to the Uganda affair which subsequently divided the Zionist movement. In *Ha-Shiloah* in the fall of 1902, Aḥad Haᶜam wrote a scathing review of *Altneuland*, Herzl's utopian novel. *Ost und West* decided to print a translation of his critique. Before publishing, Winz, as a matter of courtesy, sent Herzl advance proofs of the article, asking if he wanted to publish a response in the same issue. Herzl, in a rage, hoarded the proofs and refused to respond to Winz. Instead, he commissioned his loyal deputy, Nordau,[73] to write a reply for the Zionist party organ *Die Welt*—a reply that reached every important German-language Jewish publication before the *Ost und West* issue in question ever appeared. As a result of this scandal, Winz privately charged that Herzl had been condescending toward him and toward Eastern Jewish journalists in general.[74] *Ost und West*'s response, "Die Juden von Gestern," drew attention to Nordau's paternalistic West European biases and his limited understanding of Eastern Jewish traditions. The relatively mild editorial, probably written by Binjamin Segel, was sufficiently critical to inflame the ire of Nordau and other Zionists. Their overreaction is but one illustration of how many Jewish nationalists regarded Herzl as a near monarchical figure.[75] As a consequence of this scandal, Segel and Winz were unwelcome among Zionists for years,[76] a status that was repaired neither by *Ost und West*'s special issue on Herzl at the time of his death nor by letters of apology to Nordau, who originally had been a hero of the cultural Zionists.

This dispute worked to *Ost und West*'s advantage in one sense. The journal received new publicity, and Winz was encouraged to campaign all the more stridently for Eastern Jewry, particularly in the wake of the Kishinev pogroms of April 6 and 7, 1903, which occurred just before "Die Juden von Gestern" went to press. Furthermore, the rapid ascent of *Ost und West* as a leading German-Jewish periodical did not pass unnoticed. Within the field of Jewish publishing, Winz appears to have been envied and scorned by the likes of Heinrich Loewe and Martin Buber. Loewe, an old rival of Winz's, generated a number of attacks in the *Jüdische Rundschau*.[77] Buber was for a brief time the editor of the Herzl-backed party organ *Die Welt*.[78] In his letters to Herzl, Buber made clear his dislike for Winz, whom he knew well, having contributed regularly to *Ost und West* until 1905.[79] Just how envious Buber was of Winz's success as a publicist is evidenced in his 1903 sketch for a journal entitled *Der Jude*.[80] This ambitious project, which he conceived along with Weizmann, Lilien, and Alfred Nossig (1864–1943), was intended to result in a literary and cultural monthly similar to Winz's journal. Because of lack of funds and *Ost und West*'s greater appeal, *Der Jude* was shelved until 1916, when interest in Eastern Jewry was sufficient to warrant another major pan-Jewish journal.[81]

The *Altneuland* affair was but one more example of how urgent the message of pan-Jewishness was. Somehow, despite the controversies, a bridge had to be built between Jewish nationalists from both Europes. *Ost und West* was well suited to this project, as we shall see, for ideology and public relations came to assume equal importance in it.

How did *Ost und West* deal with the widening rupture in the Jewish nationalist camp? To be sure, Winz and Segel were fully aware of the Western nature of political Zionism. When challenged, as they were in the *Altneuland* affair, they responded with Eastern-style Jewish ethnicity. Yet they were also aware that *Ost und West* would have to make certain concessions to Western Jewish readers in order to be a truly pan-Jewish magazine. Fine-tuning *Ost und West* to German-Jewish culture(s) was absolutely essential if the journal was to attract new readers.

It was a subtle game to market Jewish ethnicity to *Westjuden*. Jewishness was a difficult "product" to promote to Jews in Germany who were, by and large, fairly well integrated despite only having received full civil rights in 1871. As a result, many Wilhelminian Jews were not receptive to reminders of a "ghetto"[82] heritage that they were actively involved in forgetting. The idea that they should profess or declare their Jewish identity seemed foolish, about as absurd as Zionism seemed to most prior to 1897.[83] What is more, the journal was attempting to market East European Jewry at a time when

Ostjuden were largely viewed negatively in German and German-Jewish culture. However, because they lived in and "between" two cultures, the editors of *Ost und West* understood how to balance the journal's advocacy of East European Jewish culture with the demands of its Western Jewish audiences.

To Winz and his associates, the decision to publish *Ost und West* in German rather than in Yiddish or Hebrew did not imply that the magazine would conform to German cultural mores. Individual and group identities in the journal were constructed less by German politics than by internal Jewish politics. While a resolution granting Yiddish and Hebrew equal status as the Jewish national languages was passed at the Czernowitz conference of 1908, German had been a lingua franca of East-Central European Jewry since the nineteenth century. People who thought of themselves as "ethnic Jews" might therefore use all three—Yiddish, Hebrew, and German (or another national vernacular)—for Jewish ethnicity was not defined uniquely by language.

Ost und West claimed to have subscribers the world over, from Gluchow to Galveston and from Copenhagen to Capetown. If we believe its inside front cover promotions, *Ost und West* was read in more than four hundred cities across the globe, a third of them in Germany, a third in Austro-Hungary, and a sixth in Russia. Yet, despite these pretensions to an international readership, the magazine was first and foremost directed at Jews living in the German *Reich*. Indeed, archival evidence reveals that Winz had difficulties marketing it in Eastern Europe.[84] Jews living there likely saw *Ost und West* as "too German." At the same time, the journal differed significantly from other German-Jewish cultural reviews. Unlike the *Allgemeine Zeitung des Judentums* (1837–1922) and the *Jüdische Rundschau* (1898–1938), both of which were hardly nonpartisan, *Ost und West* was the first journal in Germany with a genuinely pan-Jewish nationalist perspective, seeking to unite Jews of all nations, sects, and political ideologies. It represents a large-scale solution to the so-called Jewish Question (*Judenfrage*), comparable to the so-called Greater German (*großdeutsch*) solution sought by German cultural reviews such as the *Deutsche Rundschau* (founded in 1864).[85]

Ost und West was the first significant publication to bring together Western and Eastern Jewish artists and intellectuals. Its accomplishments thus lie more in the realm of cultural transmission than in intellectual or artistic originality. As a showcase for both Eastern and Western Jewish culture, *Ost und West* was customarily the first place in the West where thinkers such as Aḥad Haᶜam, Nathan Birnbaum (1864–1937), and Martin Buber were published. The journal also featured Jewish artists. Those born in the East included Lilien, Lesser Ury (1861–1931), Leopold Pilichowski (1869–1933), Mark Antokolski (1843–1902), Samuel Hirshenberg [Hirszenberg] (1863–1908), Enrico [Henryk] Glicenstein (1870–1942), and Boris Schatz

(1867–1932). Those born in the West included Max Liebermann (1847–1935), Jozef Israëls (1847–1935), and Hermann Struck (1876–1944). A transitional figure between East and West was Ury, who arrived in Berlin from Poland at the age of twelve; his works were featured regularly in *Ost und West*.[86]

But *Ost und West* was produced primarily neither for the Jewish avant-garde nor for loyal Jewish readers in Eastern Europe. To enlarge its readership in Germany and the West, *Ost und West* sought to reach beyond Jewish writers and educators and thereby to enlist the interest of Western Jews who did not belong to the cultural elite. In becoming sensitive to the values and norms of a broader cross-section of German Jewry, *Ost und West* negotiated a fragile rapprochement between Eastern Jewish cultural nationalism and Western Jewish étatist nationalism.[87] In promoting Eastern Jewish culture to a Jewish readership in the West, *Ost und West* had to make *Ostjudentum* palatable to them. Many Jews in Germany, after all, felt threatened by conspicuous displays of Jewishness, and the Jewish nationalist outlook of *Ost und West* was potentially offensive to them. Therefore, to make the cultural autonomy of Eastern Jewry acceptable to a Western audience, *Ost und West* tempered its Jewish particularism with a more universalist outlook.

Prudent appeals to ethnicity and to a carefully delimited "uniquely Jewish cultural nuance" (*spezifisch-jüdische Kulturnuance*) show the pains taken in *Ost und West*'s official 1901 program to balance the Jewish East with the Jewish West: "We thus want to extol Jewish life, not as it exists today, but as it should be and is on its way to becoming. What we mean is a Jewish life that is self-aware, inwardly secure and sanctified, faithful and thriving, where the good particularity of our race unfolds within the framework of a beautiful humanity and a serene labor for the cultural progress of all."[88] The rhetoric here of a newly self-aware Jewish "race" was thoroughly compatible with Western notions of cultural progress and aesthetic humanism. Jewish cultural nationalism thus appeared side by side with a bourgeois-liberal ideology in this magazine. *Ost und West* was willing to match its audience's "horizon of expectations"[89] by making occasional concessions to "enlightened" manners and morals. Nevertheless, even while urging German Jews to become integrated, *Ost und West* was sprinkled with hardy doses of Eastern Jewish particularity.

This programmatic note of Jewishness (*jüdische Note*) was enshrined visually in the journal's brown-yellow front cover (see fig. 2). Designed by the Jewish *Jugendstil* artist Lilien in collaboration with Winz, the drawing depicts an impressive female figure who fills the entire left side of the tableau (physically West). Though she wears a Renaissance-style blouse, her bottom half is draped in a garment patterned with Stars of David—the dominant motif of the graphic.[90] A Star of David also adorns her hair; the bejeweled head covering in the back evokes Jewish tradition. In a state of inspiration, she gazes into a small, treelike root. Whereas the root blossoms on the upper right side of the tableau (physically East), it expands to encircle the lower left side of the page (physically West) in thorns.

While the growth of this plant appears to recapitulate Jewish history, rendering Western Jewish life as a bitter Diaspora, one might interpret the entire image differently. If the robust Jewish female on the left signifies Eastern Jewishness, as suggested by "Ost" in the title directly above her, the small plant against the dark background on the right may symbolize the embryonic state of Jewish nationalism in the West. In this, as in other cases, Winz and his colleagues showed a preference for multivalence over lucidity when attempting to market the idea of pan-Jewishness. Indeed, *Ost und West*'s cover was far more complex than similar images produced by Lilien around the same time.[91]

Female figures such as the one here would become a staple of Zionist iconography in the early days of the movement, a Jewish counterpart to Germania, Marianne, and Britannia.[92] Most images of her disappeared after a few years, however, as did this particular one in 1906. By contrast, the magazine's masthead never changed in twenty-three years of publication (see fig. 3). Like the cover, it was also drawn by Lilien and also outlines the historical transition from traditional to enlightened Jewish identity. "West" begins at the exact center of "Ost und West," indicating who the journal's target audience was. Whereas the "O" in "Ost" is covered with a flourish that resembles a yarmulke, the head covering of observant Jews, the "W" in "West" is crowned by a mustache shape, symbolizing the westernization of the traditional Jewish beard. In addition, the "W" looks imprisoned, even though the bars enclosing it are part of a Star of David.

This and other distinctions between Western and Eastern Jewish identity in *Ost und West*'s iconography recall Aḥad Haᶜam's dictum regarding European Jews: they were free but enslaved.[93] In the West, one could only be a "Jew" at home; on the street, one had to behave like a "man" or a *Bürger*. Religion had come to be a private matter, a denomination meant to be inconspicuous. Jews in the East, however, were "Jews" in public and "men" in private. *Ost und West*'s visual imagery, though it expressed similar contradictions, supported more overt forms of Jewishness.

Ost und West was accordingly the first European Jewish journal to feature works of art and photography. Photography, in particular, virtually ensured the magazine's success. Nine years prior to *Ost und West*, Georg Meisenbach had invented autotypy, the first technique that allowed photographs to be reproduced directly. Meisenbach worked in Berlin, and his cheap, fast procedures spread to competitor firms. One such firm was Zander and Labisch, which supplied these reproductions (or "clichés") to Winz and whose owner, Richard Labisch, was a backer of *Ost und West*. A significant number of Eastern Jews, in fact, were employed in the photo-reproduction industry in Berlin. The first and most influential periodical in Germany to draw on the possibilities of these new technologies was the

Figure 2. E. M. Lilien, cover of Ost und West *between 1901 and 1906.*

Figure 3. E. M. Lilien, masthead of Ost und West, *1901–23.*

Ullstein Verlag's weekly magazine, the *Berliner Illustrirte Zeitung* (1895–1933). The astounding success of the *BIZ* was at least partly a result of its photographs, and it set the trend for *Ost und West* and other illustrated magazines.[94]

Making one's ethnicity visible was understood as central to a pan-Jewish identity that incorporated both Eastern-traditional and Western-enlightened models.[95] As suggested already, pan-Jewishness was easier to realize in the print media than in the mentality (or behavior) of actual European Jews.[96] Journalism, in the nineteenth century, had become the most powerful means of propagating images of the nation, and this applied to the Jewish nation as well.[97] Imagining the nation achieved its acme in the context of magazines and newspapers. By developing a new Jewish iconography, *Ost und West* was on its way to becoming an ethnic Jewish journal.

Another way that *Ost und West* reinforced the broad nature of pan-Jewishness was to inundate its readers with a diversity of genres. The resulting heterogeneity made the journal's ideal of Jewish ethnicity look more plausible—and more desirable. At the same time, the multiplicity of genres, and hence contributions, concealed a weakness: *Ost und West's* cultural significance far outweighed its political power. Furthermore, it soon became clear that quantity was more important than quality for Winz and his associates. Their elitist pretensions proved to be largely hype. By integrating essays with fiction, folklore, art, and photographs, *Ost und West* became something that *Ha-Shiloah* (Berlin and Warsaw, 1896–1914), *Voskhod*, and its other Jewish predecessors were not: it became *middle-brow*. This meant two things: first, that the journal was directed at a German-Jewish public that was by and large middle-class; and, second, that it tried to present content of a challenging but not highly intellectual nature to this audience.

By making *Ost und West* a middle-brow magazine, Winz and his associates showed how skillful they were at marketing Jewish ethnicity. The journal's mix of "high" and "low" culture appealed to all of German Jewry, male and female, intellectual and nonintellectual, upper- and lower-middle-class.[98] Women, as suggested by the cover art and a multitude of other evidence, formed a significant target audience for the journal; for a full discussion of this, see chapter 4 below.

A typical issue began with a few pages of advertisements. Then came an editorial or review essay, followed almost without fail by an illustrated arts feature. The middle section included articles and essays on Jewish literature, culture, history, current events, and religion; these, too, were sprinkled with illustrations. The final pages were the most varied: a given issue could include poetry, literature, folklore, music, a summary of the press, short literary reviews, aphorisms, quotes, and chess. To close, there were more advertisements. Indeed, Winz once claimed that *Ost und West* had more advertising than any other general publication in Germany (see fig. 4).[99]

In line with this appeal, the typical ordering of genres in *Ost und West* favored Western rather than Eastern Jewish readers.[100] Rhetoric and context also suggest that most contributions to *Ost und West* had the Western Jewish reader in mind. The plastic arts, for instance, were a genre notoriously absent from the traditional Eastern Jewish world before the nineteenth century. In addition, even if many of the artists featured in the journal hailed from the East, they were packaged for the Western Jewish reader. The only truly Eastern Jewish products in *Ost und West* were fiction, folklore, and the press review—all of which appeared in German translation. The writers published most regularly—Peretz, Sholem Asch (1880–1957), Sholem Aleichem (1859–1916), and David Pinski (1872–1959)—were well known for their sensitivity to West European trends. In fact, most of the Eastern Jewish belles-lettres that appeared in *Ost und West* were humoristic and thus readily accessible to German-Jewish audiences.

Like Winz, the most frequent contributors to the journal had both Eastern and Western Jewish allegiances. Most hailed from Poland, the Ukraine, Lithuania, and Galicia, including Aḥad Haᶜam, Buber, Birnbaum, Segel, Felix Perles (1874–1933), Arno Nadel (1878–1943), and Theodor Zlocisti (1874–1943). But each of these men knew the difference between Eastern and Western Jewish life and applied it when involved in editorial decisions. What was originally Eastern Jewish had to be promoted to German Jews. The ensuing canonization of Western Jewish contents and genres merely proved that Winz and his associates could play the game of German-Jewish culture at least as well as the German Jews themselves.

Despite all the pro-West gestures in *Ost und West*, the few surviving testimonies from *Westjuden* document their distaste for Winz's unstinting promotion of the *Ostjude*.[101] What few people have acknowledged, however, is that prior to Buber's translations (or, better, rewritings) of Hasidic tales, *Ost und West* was the largest transmitter of Eastern Jewish literature, art, folklore, and folk song to the Western Jewish public. Besides acting as an editor and publisher, Winz was also a collector of Eastern Jewish art and music and a patron to those who produced it.[102] Besides earning money for Winz (and its contributors), *Ost und West*'s practical functions included spotlighting these *Ostjuden* and publicizing relief efforts for Russian, Rumanian, and other "needy" non-German Jews. *Ost und West* was in this respect a leading publicity organ for Jewish philanthropy in Eastern Europe and elsewhere. *Ost und West* saw no contradiction in championing Eastern Jewish grass-roots initiatives while at the same time endorsing Western-based relief efforts, as long as they were not overly paternalistic.

Winz's ultimate coup as a publisher and proof of his skill as a consummate politico was to secure an agreement in 1906 from the Alliance Israélite

Figure 4. Example of a page of advertisements, including Berlin department stores.
Ost und West *(June 1911).*

Universelle, whereby this quintessentially Western Jewish organization agreed to finance part of *Ost und West*'s production in exchange for space in the journal and discounted subscriptions for its 10,000 German members.[103] But no one has yet explained why an essentially philanthropic organization such as the Alliance sponsored a journal devoted to introspection about and the revitalization of Jewish culture.[104] *Ost und West*'s liaison with the Alliance from 1906 to 1914 was a marriage of convenience. The Central Committee of the Alliance was looking for a cheap, expedient way to woo the German-Jewish public and prevent it from absconding to other organizations since it feared German influence in Turkey and its other spheres of influence.[105] The Alliance was thus at best a halfhearted backer of *Ost und West* between 1906 and 1914. Concerned mainly with Jews in the Arab world, the Paris-based organization had little in common with the East European Jewish nationalism of *Ost und West*. Western and liberal in outlook, it tended to view East European and Oriental Jews as "uncivilized" and in need of regeneration.[106]

Even though the magazine's association with the Alliance resulted in a new subtitle ("Illustrierte Monatsschrift für das gesamte Judentum. Organ der Alliance Israélite Universelle"), the Eastern Jewish nationalism of *Ost und West* was still as pronounced as ever. Notwithstanding areas of partial agreement, the magazine was often at odds with the ideology of the Alliance. In editorials, Segel and Winz explicitly advocated more decentralization from Paris, more indigenous teachers for the Alliance's schools, and more practically geared school curricula. Coming full circle, *Ost und West*'s assessment of the Alliance resembled its earliest criticisms of the political Zionists: both groups emphasized diplomacy at the expense of true cultural work. Because of the special nature of their partnership, the Alliance repeatedly felt a need to dissociate itself from opinions stated in *Ost und West*. Time and again, the Alliance published disclaimers in its section of the magazine urging the Zionists to direct their attacks not at the organization but rather at *Ost und West*'s editors.[107]

Like the Alliance, *Ost und West* on occasion did misrepresent features of Eastern Jewish culture. Some of the translations into German that appeared reveal a selective reinvention of "native" traditions.[108] Nonetheless, *Ost und West*'s contributors were among the foremost scholars of their day. Even when they made mistakes, their example inspired others, such as Fritz Mordechai Kaufmann (1888–1921), the founder of *Die Freistatt* (Eschweiler, 1912–14), to try to do a better job. Along with *Neue jüdische Monatshefte* (Berlin, 1916–1924) and Buber's *Der Jude* (Berlin, 1916–1924), *Die Freistatt* was indebted to *Ost und West* for its early attempts to publicize Eastern Jewish culture.[109]

What most observers have failed to note is that Winz's magazine pioneered the advocacy of East European Jewry in the West long before the emergence during World War I of what Gershom Scholem has dubbed the "cult of the *Ostjuden.*"[110] Two decades before the Jewish renaissance of the 1920s, *Ost und West* had helped create an alternative space for a minority culture within German culture and European culture at large.[111] The Eastern Jewish immigrant culture of the Weimar Republic was the beneficiary of such efforts, as well as the nationalist *Jüdische Volkspartei*, which emerged victorious in a number of *Gemeinde* elections after 1920.[112]

Winz, though habitually asked to serve on the executive board of the *Volkspartei*, preferred to direct his efforts at the larger (Jewish) public. Like all successful efforts in magazine publishing and advertising, *Ost und West* sought to make its readers desire something they had not previously felt they needed.[113] It attempted to make the notion of Jewish particularism acceptable to integrated Jews living the West. Through a complicated system of cultural signs, Jewish readers were made to perceive themselves as desiring separatism, no longer feeling the need to act upon earlier assimilationist urges. Under Winz's management, *Ost und West* delivered a consistent message: cultural nationalism was in the best interest of the Jewish middle classes in Germany and throughout Europe.

To make Eastern Jewry acceptable to Western Jews and to persuade German Jews to view their Eastern cousins as equals, the East European Jewish editors of *Ost und West* set out to redefine German-Jewish identity by purveying new, positive images of Jews. Idealization, however, proved less effective than denigration. *Ost und West* specialized in taking negative stereotypes of *Ostjuden* (and Jews in general) and grafting them onto Western Jews. This technique, which remains part of the repertoire of image making today, borrows from the insights of group psychology. *Ost und West* thus belittled *Westjuden* as products of an "enlightened" Western milieu, a variation on older antisemitic stereotypes of the Jew as a product of Eastern ghettos.[114] Chapters 3 through 5 of this study examine the repackaging of such stereotypes and how these stereotypes (appearing within different genres and contexts) were adapted to the specific audiences of *Ost und West*.

The stress throughout this study will be on the conscious use of stereotypes, even though it is the unconscious element that gives stereotypical images their remarkable power. Most scholars in the field agree that stereotyping plays a decisive role in shaping personal and group identity, since stereotypes regulate how humans beings perceive themselves and their world. But any adequate definition of stereotyping must recognize that stereotypes are contingent and therefore manipulable. For the purposes of this study, I shall designate stereotypes as the products of normal cognitive processes by which individuals attempt to make sense of the world. Since stereotypes function as a type of mental shorthand, the issue is not whether they are true but to what extent they guide and determine how human beings define themselves.[115] At the same time, however, stereotypes can be strongly influenced by the individual's psychology as well as the self-image of the groups with which he or she identifies.

How do we account, then, for the fact that some stereotypes appear to make better sense of the world than others? Psychoanalytic approaches to stereotyping distinguish between pathological and nonpathological stereotyping. Stereotypes ultimately derive from the child's opposition of "good" self and "bad" other.[116] In adults, a perceived threat to the integrity of the "good" self may cause a person to react defensively by imagining a "bad" other. Pathological stereotyping involves a regression to the infant's antithesis of "good" self and "bad" other, whereby the individual psyche repeatedly transfers "bad" feelings about the self (inadequacy, fear, powerlessness, etc.) onto other groups or persons. This mechanism of projecting "bad" feelings is operative in Western Jewish stereotyping of Eastern Jews as unclean, indecent, and culturally inferior. Eastern Jews, however, were not immune to this mechanism; they also rejected negative Jewish self-images by projecting them onto a perceived other, at times engaging in stereotyping of *Westjuden*.

The distinction between pathological and nonpathological stereotyping is perhaps more usefully rendered in the cognitive distinction between stereotypes and types.[117] According to one critic,

> [o]ne difference between stereotype and type may lie in narrative rhetoric. With stereotyped characters, the narrator suggests that we have sufficient evidence for a final judgement and conveys clearly what our judgement should be. Types, on the other hand, are used heuristically, as the starting-points for constructing deeper and more complex characters, and here the narrator will refrain from foisting judgements on the readers. Thus types and stereotypes are not two opposed categories but distant bands on the same spectrum.[118]

In its treatment of Jews, *Ost und West* fluctuates between these categories, otherwise known as good and bad, or positive and negative, stereotyping. Whereas Eastern Jews are rendered as idealized *types*, the Western Jews described in *Ost und West* usually qualify as *stereotypes* in the scheme above. Stereotypes were particularly prominent in literature, the main object of this study. The journal's fiction, because it was short fiction, precluded complex character development.[119]

Despite the large body of research on stereotyping, the promotion of positive and negative images has received less attention. Instead of employing value-laden categories such as "pathological" and "nonpathological," we will use a value-neutral analysis which outlines how "well" or "poorly" stereotypes are marketed to specific social and cultural groups. Such an analysis acknowledges that stereotypes are protean. That is, the categories into which each stereotype can be divided are bipolar (good self and bad other), but the categories themselves are "mutable and constantly shifting."[120] This inherent instability of stereotypes enabled the image makers at *Ost und West* to appeal to different markets. This study thus affirms that stereotypes of the Jew differ from culture to culture, from era to era, from institution to institution, and from market to market.[121] The manipulation of stereotypes was the successful strategy behind *Ost und West*'s promotion of ethnic Jewishness to its German-Jewish audiences.

Seeing stereotypes as a marketing stratagem available to the stereotyped group qua agents or "subjects" contributes to our understanding of Jewish audiences in Germany.[122] *Ost und West*'s positive stereotyping of *Ostjuden* and negative stereotyping of *Westjuden* suggest how German Jews understood the issues of their day. Stereotyping also reveals how openly Jewish they were willing to be, and thus the limits of their self-definition as Jews. *Ost und West*'s definitions of Jewishness were marketed carefully to three Jewish readerships in Germany: intellectuals, middle-class women, and middle-class men. Despite its focus on one journal, then, this study concentrates primarily on Wilhelminian Jewry. The events of World War I persuaded Winz to modify the magazine's focus after 1918. For the war not only brought forth renewed antisemitism in Germany and the East, but it also reminded Winz and his associates that antisemites were not as interested in differentiating among Jews as they were.

Finally, one caveat is in order with regard to *Ost und West*'s public. Even though this study makes claims regarding the nature of the magazine's audience, it is not really a reception study.[123] Detailed reactions to *Ost und West* from Jews in the *Kaiserreich* have not survived. Despite that, we know that many German Jews were aware of the journal; the controversies it unleashed suggest as much.[124] Most important, *Ost und West*'s high level of circulation also makes it valid to draw conclusions about its audience based on its texts.[125]

Ost und West's promotional strategies provide the chief evidence for conclusions about its readers. Stereotypes, in particular, influenced the audience's interpretation of what it meant to be a Jew; they offered up both attractive and repulsive images of Jews. As we shall see, *Ost und West* appealed to each of its audiences by using different stereotypes. Each group of readers was defined against a specific foil: Jewish male intellectuals were defined against the negative representation of a Western Jewish social climber; German-Jewish women were defined against a stereotyped Western Jewish female parvenu (*parvenue*); German-Jewish men, particularly in wartime, were defined against the image of cowardly and self-hating enemies. Using such clues, we can see how *Ost und West* perceived its audiences, and we can construct a fuller portrait of Jewish audiences in Germany and their perceptions of Jewish identity. Because these perceptions were affected by political and social changes between 1901 and 1923, the magazine regularly had to adapt its stereotyping techniques. Thus, in its twenty-three-year existence, *Ost und West* moved from the stereotyping of Jewish undesirables to the stereotyping of antisemites. The product—ethnic identity—did not change, only its promotion did.

Ost und West is also useful as a barometer of German-Jewish identity because it sought to change its readers rather than merely to reflect their wishes. Yet relying on stereotypes to influence readers did not guarantee success. What made *Ost und West* so effective in promoting Jewish consciousness, perhaps even more than other texts? The answer may lie in its status as a journal, a more suitable genre for this enterprise than a novel.[126] Because it appeared in serial fashion, *Ost und West* could constantly revise its stereotypes in order to keep in touch with its audiences. The fact that it appeared every month also enabled *Ost und West* to adapt to political and social changes. By varying its written and visual contributions, the journal ultimately was able to reach three different Jewish audiences in Germany. European Jews shared a broadly conceived set of allegiances, and periodicals, like perhaps no other historical artifact, indicate the range of meanings that were acceptable to an ethnic group. By imagining themselves to be part of this group, the readers of *Ost und West* were seeking community. What they found was a ready-made public sphere. In this sense, the journal provided them with an already constructed fellowship, an artificial national identity, a textual homeland. Appearing as they did in the second most widely circulated Jewish periodical in Germany and one of the most widely circulated in Eastern Europe, the collected narratives in *Ost und West* affirmed the maxim "You are what you read," which especially applied to Jews, whose identity had been traditionally reinforced through reading and rereading the Hebrew Bible, Talmud, Midrash, and other sources.

Ost und West did not affect all readers in the same way. Differences in background and viewpoint affect how readers experience texts. These "outside" factors affect what reading theorists refer to as "schemata," the organizing structures built up from prior experiences that the individual reader brings to bear on a text.[127] Yet, for all their diversity, Jewish audiences in Germany had many similar backgrounds and viewpoints and, by extension, similar schemata. It does not matter that recorded responses to *Ost und West* are few and far between or that we know very little about the reading habits of Wilhelminian Jews. What matters is how Winz and the journal's editors chose to market Eastern Jewish culture in the *Kaiserreich*. Promoting a newer Jewish identity simply meant addressing *Ost und West*'s three major readerships of German-Jewish intellectuals, German-Jewish middle-class women, and German-Jewish middle-class men. As a propaganda effort, the magazine specialized in approaching each readership on its own terms. It had to cast its net wide, but it did so with nuance. This strategy for cultivating submarkets was compatible with *Ost und West*'s gimmick of bringing a "Jewish nuance" (*jüdische Nuance*) to European culture, and the magazine presented a broad, nonpartisan consensus that was based in Jewish ethnicity. A comparison with the contemporaneous Hebrew press, where similar debates raged more polemically, shows that *Ost und West* was at least as interested in marketing a cultural identity as in promoting specific political ideologies to its various Jewish clienteles.[128]

Over its twenty-three years of publication, *Ost und West*'s message did not vary, despite its innovative Western-style approach to promoting Jewish identity. The journal attempted to awaken the Jewish minority's "desire" to retain its ethnic distinctiveness, hoping that this minority might overcome its "need" to integrate into German culture.

The following chapter illuminates the sources for European Jewish identity in the nineteenth century, showing how *Ost und West* exploited both Eastern and Western Jewish identities to promote its vision of pan-Jewishness. At the same time, however, *Ost und West* both influenced and mirrored its readers, thus raising the question of what were the absolute limits of Jewish self-definition in turn-of-the-century Germany. What did *Ost und West*'s audiences perceive as "un-Jewish"? Its stereotypes of Jews also reveal what the journal considered insufficiently Jewish. These stereotypes are best expressed as prohibitions: you shall not convert; you shall not be ignorant of Jewish culture; and you shall not be a social-climbing capitalist. If a Jew could escape these negative images, then there was a range of acceptable ways in which he or she might define himself or herself. These prohibitions correspond to three definitions of the Jew that express varying degrees of westernization: from traditional Eastern definitions to modern ethnic definitions and finally to Western Jewish definitions. The editors of *Ost und West* preferred national-ethnic definitions and tried to move its readers away from acculturation, defined here as the adoption of non-Jewish cultural traits.[129]

How *Ost und West* used these three types of Jewish identity in appealing to Jewish male intellectuals is the subject of this study's third chapter. It was not difficult to market *Ostjudentum* effectively to an intellectual public already sympathetic to its cause. Early on, the journal pinpointed the Western Jewish parvenu as the source of acculturation, not the ghetto Jews of the East, as was thought previously. The Berlin-based social climber was a revision of earlier stereotypes of Jewish apostates. Owning up to one's geocultural background was held to be the essence of Jewishness in *Ost und West*'s fiction.

The fourth chapter examines appeals to the German-Jewish female audience in *Ost und West*. Even though these Western Jewish bourgeoises formed the core of the magazine's readership, *Ost und West* remained true to its Eastern Jewish origins. It counted on German-Jewish women to react negatively to parvenu *Westjuden*. It even created a female social climber and discouraged her insincere type of philanthropy. The novellas in the journal, while not always directly concerned with Jewish immigrants from the East, range from sentimental paternalism to critical engagement in their representations of *Ostjuden.* All of these novellas were meant to attract women along with Jewish male intellectuals.

Middle-class Jewish males in Germany were less central to *Ost und West*'s project. While they certainly read the journal, their concerns were seldom addressed directly until World War I. The fifth chapter investigates the promotion of Jewishness during wartime, a period that required open displays of Germanness. Until the 1916 census of Jews in the Prussian military (the *Judenzählung*), the German-Jewish male audience of *Ost und West* saw itself as well integrated. It thus favored Western-enlightened definitions of Jewish identity. In keeping with this orientation, *Ost und West*'s war editorials likened anti-German sentiment to antisemitism. At times, the magazine projected upon the Entente powers the images of cowardice, Germanophobia and self-hatred that antisemites often associated with Jewish men. As we shall see, morally bankrupt antisemites served as foils for "tough" Jewish males in the journal's essays and serialized fiction.

The conclusion explores *Ost und West*'s responses to Western-style acculturation and its antithesis, dissimilation. The notion is reexamined that Jews eagerly assimilated to German society and that they were self-hating. After World War I ended, Winz paid more attention to his other enterprises, and in 1923, inflation brought on *Ost und West*'s decline. Nevertheless, the journal already had influenced other periodicals to focus on *Ostjuden,* and its ethnic definitions were increasingly adopted as a model for German-Jewish identity. *Ost und West* ultimately augments our knowledge of how minority groups understand themselves. It may thus illuminate contemporary discussions in Europe and the Americas regarding ethnic identity.

2

Ost und West and the History of European Jewish Identity

The creators of *Ost und West* had to know what made their readers Jewish in order to promote Jewish ethnicity to them. By familiarizing themselves with German-Jewish identity, they hoped to influence how *Westjuden* perceived their Jewishness. Winz and his associates thus conducted what we today would call market research to determine the ways in which German Jews identified themselves as Jews.[1] By partaking of two Jewish cultures, the editors of *Ost und West* already had completed enough informal market research to develop effective methods of publicity. They saw that they could more ably promote ethnic Jewishness—also referred to as "ethnic Judaism" in the following—by being sensitive to the fears and desires of their audience. This chapter, then, will derive the strategies with which *Ost und West* appealed to Jewish groups in the *Kaiserreich* by specifying the Jewish identities they shared.[2]

At the same time, *Ost und West* had to draw on the few similarities of Eastern Jews and Western Jews to promote its ideology of pan-European Jewish identity. Although the differences between the two groups were better known and were the source of much stereotyping, the magazine focused on *anything* that unified them. If Jewish ethnicity was to become an acceptable form of German-Jewish identity, *Ost und West* had to define its *"modernes Judentum"* broadly, extending the limits of Jewish self-definition. *Judentum* was already a broad term by 1901, encompassing both "Judaism" and "Jewishness." In the interest of historical accuracy, the two will be used interchangeably in the following.

Ethnic Judaism in turn-of-the-century Germany was thus an attempt to synthesize the Judaisms of Eastern and Western Europe. Yet *Ost und West's* synthesis was not impartial, for it had the distinctly Eastern flavor of the Pale. But while the journal favored Eastern Jewish ethnicity, it consistently dressed it up in Western clothes. Making a pan-European ethnic Judaism acceptable to Jews in Germany eventually took priority over conjoining Eastern and Western Judaisms.

As already noted, stereotyping proved the best way to prop up ethnic Jewish consciousness in *Ost und West*. Stereotypes were based, however, on the components of popular Jewish identity, and it is these components that will be examined here. Surprisingly few efforts have been made to write a social history of Jewish identity in the modern age.[3] Most historians of European Jewry have relied instead on accounts of ideologues, community leaders, or fellow historians. As a result, their intellectual histories of European Jews all but ignore middle-brow magazines such as *Ost und West* and their specific appeals to Jewish self-understanding. This chapter is an attempt to reconstruct what it meant to be Jewish in Germany around 1900. Its aim is to show how the readers of *Ost und West* viewed their Jewish identities before their first encounter with the journal.

The targeted audiences of *Ost und West* did not construct their Jewishness out of whole cloth. Rather, their Judaism was a patchwork woven together from three types of Jewish identity: "Eastern" or "traditional" Judaism, "Western" or "enlightened" Judaism, and "ethnic" or "national"[4] Judaism. Though somewhat simplified, these three forms of Jewish identity represent the main options available to Jews in the *Kaiserreich*, and each was a variation on a geocultural orientation—East European versus West European.

Eastern/traditional Judaism. In the parlance of European Jews, becoming modern meant leaving Eastern Europe, where the oldest type of Judaism, traditional Orthodoxy, was practiced. This Jewish identity was based, first and foremost, on religion. Its forms of ritual and belief were not unlike those in the remainder of medieval, premodern Europe. Jews leaving this ghettolike environment might not always be strictly observant. Nonetheless, their Orthodox Judaism was to be distinguished from Jewish neo-Orthodoxy in Germany, a Judaism that creatively borrowed from enlightened Western lifestyles. *Ost und West's* essays and fiction drew heavily on Eastern, ancestral modes of seeing the world, and in its early years, the magazine relied especially upon negative religious stereotypes of Jews who intermarried and/or converted.[5] As we will see, this strategy aimed to appeal to recently transplanted *Ostjuden* in Germany. For the East European *shtetl* ("small town") whence many of these Jews came was still characterized by Jewish tradition: little acculturation to the surrounding

Slavic cultures, the preservation of Yiddish speech, a lower-middle-class and proletarian socioeconomic structure, a high birth rate, and a low rate of intermarriage.[6]

Western/enlightened Judaism. From a historical point of view, enlightened Judaism represented the first stage of European Jewish modernization. It does not conform, however, in all particulars with the European Enlightenment, and it certainly goes beyond the scope of the Jewish Enlightenment or *Haskalah*. Jews who left the ghetto, the prototype being Moses Mendelssohn (1729–1786), were accepted into a "semi-neutral" society in the West.[7] As they came into closer contact with the majority culture in Germany after 1800, Jews increasingly adopted middle-class mores. As a result, Western Judaism became a "confession" like Lutheranism. But Jews in Germany never became fully Germanized, and the majority of them certainly were not as upwardly mobile as the fictional Jewish parvenu. Still, the allure of Western secularism was such that *Ost und West* always presented itself as eminently respectable. It conformed, on the surface at least, as much to enlightened, West European norms as to traditional, Eastern Jewish models. The journal required, for instance, that male Jews project an image of patriotism and overt masculinity. In addition, Jewish men were encouraged to imitate non-Jews in their occupations, becoming farmers or craftsmen instead of merchants and moneylenders. The call to open all professions to Jews also was taken up by Jewish nationalists.

Pan-European or ethnic Judaism. This mixture of Eastern and Western Judaism, the creation of multicultural Jews, was grounded in the belief that it was wrong to neglect any aspect of Jewish culture. Although linked to the premodern religion of Jews, it did not dismiss their secular loyalties. While those who did not support Jewish cultural renewal were, by implication, "inauthentic" Jews, those who were willing to avow their Jewish ethnicity publicly might interpret it as they wished. Ethnic Jews (*Stammesjuden*) might be activists, or they might be nonpartisan on issues such as Zionism. In addition, they might derive their definitions of *Judentum* from Eastern religious *and* Western secular models, both of which could be found in *Ost und West*.[8]

Religion and ritual observance lie at the core of Jewish history. The oldest form of Jewish identity available in turn-of-the century Europe was Rabbinic Judaism, a religious-cultural system that had been in existence for more than a thousand years. This form of Jewish identity originally was designed to preserve Jewish consciousness in the post-Exilic age (after 70 c.e.). Traditional Judaism was built not on correct beliefs (orthodoxy) but on correct practices (orthopraxy). As a result, Rabbinic Judaism put forth extensive guidelines for ethical behavior. Although these guidelines were reinforced by the *kehillah,* or autonomous, nonvoluntary Jewish community, traditional Jews obeyed the Torah because God ordained it, not necessarily because of moral or worldly authority. Indeed, following the law was the precondition for all moral action.

This legalistic-sounding orientation only changed with the advent of modernity and exposure to Western ways. The creation of "moral individuals" was a concern of newfangled Enlightenment thinkers in the eighteenth century and foreign to Eastern-traditional Judaism.[9] These largely Christian thinkers, for all their misrepresentation of Jews, correctly understood the centrality of Talmud in premodern Jewish practice. Soon Jews were attracted to the rationality and universalism of the Enlightenment, and moral arguments were used to justify the observance of 613 commandments. The notion of a Jewish ethical mission first emerged in the late 1700s and found its classical formulation in Reform (or "Liberal") Judaism.[10] In fact, the rejection of traditional Jewish identity was important in uniting both Reform and neo-Orthodox German Jews, and it pointed to a basic East-West Jewish difference.[11]

The Eastern Jewish editors of *Ost und West* were highly aware of the Eastern sources for traditional Jewish identity. By defending Eastern Jewish culture, the magazine was defending pre-Enlightenment religious values and implicitly attacking German forms of Judaism that had their social and intellectual foundations in Western secularism. Discussion of religious issues, while not central, became an offshoot of the journal's agenda, and despite its ethnic orientation, *Ost und West* assumed that children of Jewish mothers—matrilineal descent was the traditional benchmark for determining who was a Jew—should have some basic understanding of Judaism qua religion.[12] Being a traditional Jew implied that one had some knowledge of biblical commandments and injunctions. However, *Ost und West* shrewdly avoided denominational controversy by permitting a range of Jewish religious affiliations, from strict observance to unbaptized disinterest.[13] This openness was a potential affront to pious Orthodox readers in the East. Still, the journal excoriated those who had converted out of Judaism. It also took pains to avoid offending Jews who were devout (*gesetzestreu*), allying itself at times with the westernized neo-Orthodox of Germany.[14] Although the journal favored readers who were proud, professing (*selbstbewußt*) Jews, its Jewish nationalist bias actually targeted all readers of Jewish ancestry. In this respect, *Ost und West* could make concessions to enlightened Judaism without having to exclude traditional Jews. Religion was thus inextricably linked with ethnicity in Eastern Jewish self-definition, and no *Nationaljude* could have overlooked this type of Judaism in forging his or her ethnic Jewish identity.[15]

Eastern Jews who were similar in background to the journal's editors and recently transplanted in Germany became the target readers of *Ost und West*, particularly in its early years. But for all their participation in greater European culture, the social and cultural profile of Winz and his colleagues reflected their moorings in Eastern Jewish life. By virtue of geocultural circumstance, they had been shaped by the traditional religiosity and lifestyle. According to most accounts, the world they came from was fairly unproblematic: "it does seem fair to generalize that vast numbers of Jews in Russia to 1917 or in Poland to 1939 were living with one foot in their tradition and the other outside of it, striving—at times tentatively, at times stridently, more often than not unselfconsciously—to reconcile the way of life of their parents with the attractions and challenges of modern existence."[16] Therefore, religious identity remained an influential force in the lives of Jewish Easterners, even after 1900, when Eastern Jewish life was characterized by a certain degree of acculturation and secularization that typically led not to assimilation but to modern Jewish nationalism of one form or another. In this community, there were two legitimate forms of identity, ritual and ethnic, and both often dwelled within the same soul.

The most famous example of this compatibility was the Russian-based Mizrachi Zionist faction.[17] The Orthodox supporters of Mizrachi were prepared to make compromises that more traditional *Ostjuden* were not. As Zionists, they were prepared to accepted Jewish cultural activities (within limitations) as well as diplomatic efforts to colonize Palestine. In contrast, the strictly Orthodox declared it blasphemy to do anything that might bring on the promised messianic age of redemption.

If religious practice was a potential source of conflict among Eastern Jews, their basic understanding of themselves was fairly uniform. In contrast to West and Central European Jewry (ca. 2 million), the Jewish masses of the Pale (ca. 7 million) had, in many respects, shared a common culture until the Tsarist-inspired May Laws of 1881 unleashed migration to the West. With the exception of the two million who eventually emigrated, a large part of Eastern Jewry tended to accept poverty and pogroms as a way of life that would endure until the onset of the messianic age. Nor was the *shtetl* of Eastern Europe, contrary to late-twentieth-century depictions, a utopia. Jews were in the minority in most of these oppressive towns, and in the Pale of Settlement, Jews were severely curtailed in their freedom of movement and other basic rights. But while they harbored no illusions about life in Eastern Europe, the majority wished neither to emigrate nor to assimilate; the force of tradition was too strong. The majority of Russian, Galician, and Rumanian Jews thus convinced themselves to stay put—physically, culturally, and theologically—even after the pogroms of 1903–1906, when emigration reached its zenith.

That Eastern Jewish identity had a long prehistory is often discounted. A legitimate sense of division between East and West preceded the enlightenment and emancipation of European Jewry. Jewish settlements in medieval Eastern Europe may have been even more populous than those in the West.[18] European Jews, in fact, may never have shared a unified identity or set of practices.[19] East European Jewish customs, such as early age of marriage, were losing currency among German Jews in the sixteenth and seventeenth centuries. At this time, German-Jewish *yeshivot* (institutes of traditional learning) were also on the decline; German students had to travel to Poland and other Eastern destinations, and teachers had to be recruited from the same places to work in the West. Indeed, these teachers were the bulwark against a decline of traditional Judaism in the West. Eastern and Western Jews thus regarded themselves as "foreign" even before the negative stereotypes of them achieved their classical formulation in the late eighteenth century. The trope of the westernized Jew (*daytsher*) already had begun to take form in the 1600s.[20]

The cultural gap between Eastern and Western Jews, then, was nothing new by the nineteenth century. That century, however, was marked by an unparalleled antipathy toward Eastern Jews on the part of Western Jews, surpassing prejudice toward *Betteljuden* in previous centuries.[21] The emancipation and enlightenment of the *Westjuden* compounded this new alienation. Political equality required a new Jewish outlook based in patriotism, if not yet in military service. European Jews went from being "Ashkenazic" to being "French," German," or "English." Under the terms of this new social contract, Jewish culture was to become interwoven with that of non-Jews. Political enfranchisement meant that Western Jewry began to affiliate socially and culturally with the emerging nation-states, ending centuries of treatment as a separate corporative entity.[22] The leader of German neo-Orthodoxy, for example, Samson Raphael Hirsch, was a staunch advocate of emancipation. Like Hirsch, Orthodox as well as liberal Jews distanced themselves from *Ostjudentum*.[23]

As a result of enlightenment and emancipation, Jews in Central Europe developed new forms of identity even more different from those of East European Jewry. True, the cultural ideals of both groups remained vaguely similar. Forms of distinction in the *shtetl*, such as education, resembled those in the metropolis (*Großstadt*), rendering Jews at both ends of Europe discernible from their neighbors. But the differences between the two Jewries outweighed their similarities by 1900. Even where the dominance of traditional Judaism in the Pale of Settlement was challenged, these challenges, such as *Haskalah*, took on forms peculiar to the East. The popular movement of Hasidism is one branch of Jewish traditionalism that, for all its differences with Rabbinic Judaism, teamed up with its opponents (the *Mitnagdim*) to fight the *Haskalah*.

In the mid-eighteenth century, the religious and cultural fissure of Eastern and Western Jewry became a full-fledged rift. What scholars refer to as "Western Jewish identity" crystallized and became understood as distinct at this time. This identity, as we shall see, derived from Enlightenment models. In addition, it became linked to the supporters of Enlightenment in France, England, and Germany: the rising middle classes. In most respects—socially, economically, demographically, and linguistically—the

typology of the Western Jews contrasted markedly with that of their Orthodox cousins in the East. Above all, West European Jews tended to be more
acculturated to their host cultures. They thus tended to abandon both Yiddish and Orthodoxy, and they converted and intermarried more than their
Eastern counterparts. By no means impoverished, most were middle-class.
While usually settled in urban areas, they rarely constituted a remarkably
high percentage within the general urban population. In addition, their
birth rate, a source of great concern, was comparatively low. Because of the
confluence of these factors, this Jewry's sense of Jewish identification was
usually confessional rather than traditional or even ethnic.[24]

Even though the Western type of Jewish community corresponds most
readily to the Jewries of Germany, France, and England, the contrast of
Ostjudentum and *Westjudentum* was not purely geographical. Around 1900,
one could find both types represented in East Central Europe. Jews living
in Bohemia and Moravia, the Rumanian Walach region, and parts of Latvia
identified more with the Western type.[25] When seen in historical perspective, however, the discontinuities between East and West are fairly uniform
and predictable. By the advent of *Ost und West*, *westjüdisch* and *ostjüdisch*
designated not only geographical distance but also two diverging stages of
cultural identity.

The Jewish confrontation with Western modernity took on an urgency in Germany that it did not assume elsewhere. Although the outward
manifestations of this East-West transformation inevitably differed from
country to country, Germany played a special role because of its common
border with Russian Poland.[26] The allure of Western Judaism led many a
Polish Jew to migrate to Germany. The Jews of Posen, for example, became
westernized within a hundred years after coming to Berlin in the eighteenth
century, eventually forming the core of the Berlin Jewish *Gemeinde*. While
the shift to enlightened Judaism, or even Jewish secularism,[27] rarely took
place in the lifetime of one individual, it usually required only two or more
generations to complete its development (see fig. 5).[28]

One paradigmatic case of Jewish "Germanification" was Moses Mendelssohn. Commonly hailed as the first acculturated Jew in Germany,
he was only the most visible instance of an already expanding trend.[29]
Mendelssohn was born in Dessau but perfected his German and his command of German philosophy only after following his rabbi to Berlin at
age fourteen. A devotee of the Enlightenment and friend to Lessing and
other Christian intellectuals, Mendelssohn maintained that if Jews worked
to eliminate their Yiddish dialect (*Mauschel*), they might cultivate German,
European, and Hebraic learning. Mendelssohn, besides various philosophical treatises, is most famous for translating the Hebrew Bible (*Tanakh*)
into a German written in Hebrew characters. Despite his public persona
as a German Enlightener, or *Aufklärer*, he remained a strictly observant
Jew who refused to entertain the possibility of converting.[30] Yet most of

DIE TRANSFORMATION DER RUSSISCHEN JUDEN.

Vier Generationen.

Talmud-Gelehrter Ahron G . . . . .
geboren 1795 zu Minsk
gestorben 1881.

Rechtsanwalt Saul G . . . . .
geboren 1866 zu Minsk.

Kaufmann Moses G . . . . .
geboren 1814 zu Minsk
gestorben 1882.

Michael G . . . . .
geboren 1895 zu St. Petersburg.

Unsere Bilder geben eine gute Illustration für die Wandlung im Habitus der russischen Juden ab. Sie stellen vier Glieder e i n e r und derselben Familie dar und dürften manchen unserer westeuropäischen Leser in Erstaunen versetzen, die erfahrungsgemäss häufig eine recht karikierte Vorstellung vom Aeusseren unserer Brüder im Osten haben.

Es ist eine der wesentlichsten Aufgaben unserer Zeitschrift, zwischen dem jüdischen Osten und dem westlichen Judentum Brücken zu schlagen und dem einen das Verständnis für das Wesen der anderen zu erleichtern. Selten ist es uns möglich, wie im gegenwärtigen Fall, durch die Liebenswürdigkeit eines Petersburger Freundes, die Wandlungen in der äusseren Erscheinung einer bestimmten Kategorie von Juden auch im Bilde vorzuführen, und wir benutzen die Gelegenheit mit Freuden. Welche prächtigen Typen sind diese beiden alter Juden, und wie unterscheiden sie sich von der gewohnten Vorstellung.

Es ist zu bedauern, dass nur wenige Bilder von Juden früherer Generationen existieren, besonders von solchen der Urgrossväter und Grossväter der jetzigen Generation. Ihre Existenz würde uns eine würdigere Vorstellung auch von unseren direkteren Vorfahren geben, als die, welche nur zu viele von uns aus volkstümlichen Vorstellungen unserer „Wirtsvölker" geschöpft haben.

Wir haben mit Unrecht unseren Ahnenstolz auf die Judengeschlechter unserer historischen Zeiten beschränkt und der Auffassung unserer Feinde — die zwar bei jedem anderen Volke zutreffen würde — Recht gegeben, wonach eine Unterdrückung, wie die Juden durch viele Jahrhunderte sie erduldet haben, achtunggebietende Gestalten unmöglich macht.

B . . . . . d

Figure 5. B . . . . . d, *"Transformation der russischen Juden."*
Ost und West *(September 1901): 673–74.*

his children, not satisfied with being Jews by denomination, opted for Christianity.

Mendelssohn's visibility beyond Berlin circles influenced both Jewish identity and state policy toward the Jews and other minorities.[31] Among those who consulted Mendelssohn were statesmen and policymakers such as Wilhelm von Humboldt (1767–1835) and Christian Wilhelm von Dohm (1751–1820), author of "Über die bürgerliche Verbesserung der Juden" (On the Civic Improvement of the Jews, 1781). In Prussia in the late eighteenth century, bureaucrats such as Dohm proposed a quid pro quo whereby Jews might acquire civil rights in exchange for "regenerating" themselves, that is, acquiring the manners and morals of Western bourgeois society. Jews could become German *Bürger* in both senses of the term ("citizen" and "bourgeois"), but only if they remade themselves into enlightened Europeans first. In effect, Jews were asked to eliminate nearly all Jewish components of their self-understanding and to revamp their appearance, behavior, and type of education.

Even though he understood the hardships Jews had faced historically, Dohm saw European Jewish life as deficient. What suited the respectable, middle-class (Christian) German should suit the Jew, and Dohm's quid pro quo soon became a model for Jewish emancipation in the German-speaking lands.[32] Presumably, Jews who regenerated themselves according to this enlightenment-emancipation pact might transcend the defects of their condition. Acculturation was held to be a small sacrifice for their greater good. In the nineteenth century, some German Jews acculturated themselves as far as was socially and legally possible, though most drew the line at baptism.[33]

Although the promise of complete integration turned out to be illusory even for those who possessed a baptismal certificate (*Taufschein*), acculturation was central to becoming westernized. It is precisely this westernization that *Ost und West* attempted to reverse by promoting Eastern forms of Jewish identity. What many historians fail to underscore is that the Jews most directly affected by Dohm's program were *Ostjuden*. The growing numbers of *Ostjuden* moving to the West in the 1700s contrasted starkly with the largely Sephardic Jewish population in Western Europe at the time. After being exiled from the Iberian Peninsula at the end of the fifteenth century, Sephardic Jewry had settled in Holland, England, France, and even parts of Germany.[34] Its legacy of cultural achievement functioned as a positive model for Jewish identity throughout Europe. Only a decade after Dohm's essay, the French parliament granted Sephardic Jews complete rights yet hesitated to do the same for the Ashkenazic Jews of Alsace-Lorraine. This prejudice was also inherent in Prussian policymaking: Dohm and his contemporaries sought to eradicate those physical, behavioral, and moral characteristics of Jews most commonly associated with Eastern Jewry.[35] What these bureaucrats recognized was that the recent past of many Jewish newcomers to Germany was an East European past. They saw that the majority of Jews who had migrated to Germany since the seventeenth century came from Poland, Russia, Rumania, Galicia, and Hungary, their customs and traditions nurtured by a premodern Eastern Jewish culture.

Enlightened Judaism further entrenched itself in the German lands in the generations following Mendelssohn. Dohm and Mendelssohn helped codify a new identity for Jews wanting to live in Germany. The key to this social and cultural identity was a Europe-wide system of behavior called *Sittlichkeit*, best translated as "respectability." Respectability was *the* major trend in Western Jewish culture as it developed since the Enlightenment, and it was closely allied with cultural trends described variously as "civilization," "modernity," and "embourgeoisement" (*Verbürgerlichung*).[36] Respectability was a product of the Enlightenment, and thus a set of values that interested Western Jews and other bourgeois groups. As we shall see, it came to figure prominently in *Ost und West* as a public relations strategy.

Historian George Mosse has portrayed respectability as an interlocked set of cultural constructs akin to an ideology, yet its social foundations made respectability a material, lived set of perceptions and practices:

> Respectability was not confined to the refinement of manners as part of the civilizing process that had begun with the change from feudal to court society, but set norms for all aspects of human life. These proved congenial to the upward mobility of the middle classes with their emphasis upon self-control, moderation, and quiet strength. Human passions and fantasies that might escape control were regarded as enemies of respectability, endangering social norms.[37]

Respectability was a proscriptive guide for middle-class success in the modern age. In the perceptions of men and women, the social distinction that it conferred was as important as their economic or political interests. Respectability also came to provide Western Jewish society with an essential glue that could withstand times of crisis. In addition to serving as "everyone's morality," it was attractive to acculturated Jews establishing new forms of Judaism. As a behavioral code for the private as well as for the public sphere, respectability was most visible in the Jewish bourgeois household. A moral (*gesittete*) family came to be the epitome not only of Germanness but also of Jewishness—which is why *Ost und West*, at the start of the twentieth century, advertised itself as a middle-brow publication that was a must in every Jewish home.[38] The identities available to the Jewish subculture in Wilhelminian Germany, although independent of the dominant culture in many respects, evolved from the value system of respectability.

As a Europe-wide ideology, respectability long remained undetected by historians because of its uncanny ability to influence people while simultaneously remaining invisible to them. Jews and other nineteenth-century

Europeans readily succumbed to its dictates. Because it assigned its subjects a definitive place in society, respectability was valued as helping to fight social anarchy and cognitive disarray. Like other sources for European identity, it also made ample use of stereotyping through binary categories such as *masculine* and *feminine*, *normal* and *abnormal*, *native* and *foreigner*, *sick* and *healthy*.[39] The ideology of respectability was thus intended to exclude, even repress, alternative visions of culture. The positive self-image of *Westjudentum* was frequently sustained through the stereotyping of Eastern Jews. Respectability thus became the basis for a new, Western type of Jewish consciousness.

No discussion of the impact of respectability on Jewish identity is complete without mention of *Bildung* ("education" or "culture") that peculiarly German model for character formation.[40] Like respectability, *Bildung* became one of the central ideals of the German Enlightenment in the late eighteenth century.[41] Promising a "cure of the inward man," *Bildung* came to be associated by German Jews with those attitudes of tolerance and liberal ideas that had enabled them to enter bourgeois society.[42] The Jewish affinity for *Bildung* can be traced back to the value placed on learning and ethical idealism in Eastern Jewish culture. Even until World War II, *Bildung* and respectability were the guiding ideals adhered to by German Jews.[43] Non-Jewish Germans in the state bureaucracy and nationalist organizations adapted these ideals to their own ends. Intellectuals as historically diverse as Wilhelm von Humboldt (1767–1835) and Thomas Mann (1875–1955) sought to define the inward process of *Bildung* as a cultural ideal specifically suited to Germany.[44]

Yiddish and East European Jewish culture had, at best, a tenuous place in the scheme of respectability. Throughout the nineteenth century and most of the twentieth, Eastern Jews were thought to be resistant to both *Bildung* and proper sexual mores. Western Jews were encouraged to repudiate the "ghetto Jew" of the past whose appearance and behavior seemed to deny the Gentile ideal of manly respectability.[45] Not unlike their Victorian counterparts in England, the German ideologues of respectability extolled the naked bodies of Greek sculpture for their purity and chastity while in the same breath condemning homosexuals and *Ostjuden* as criminal threats to society. One main exemplar of this "conservative" respectability was Friedrich Ludwig "Turnvater" Jahn (1778–1852), the founder of the gymnastic and fraternity movements, who combined a cult of physical health with nationalist aspirations.[46] Jahn's successors helped make masculine strength the sine qua non of respectable European nationalisms, both Jewish and non-Jewish, by World War I. Zionists, especially Nordau, sought to prove that the discourse of Jewish nationalism was more masculine than that of its antipode, Jewish liberalism.[47] The same strategies earlier used to exclude Eastern Jews were at times taken up by their advocates. As a Jewish nationalist journal, *Ost und West* used the masculine rhetoric of the surrounding culture, extolling such values as strength of will (*Willensstärke*) and steadfastness (*Festigkeit*).[48]

Once they decisively rejected Eastern Jewish culture for Enlightenment ideals such as respectability and *Bildung*, many German Jews parted ways with traditional Judaism. But what had emerged as a new paradigm in the first half of the nineteenth century took on a conformist mien after 1848. This conservative turn was the result of successful Jewish embourgeoisement, a process marked, above all, by the Germanization of Eastern/traditional Jewish culture. For many Jews, Judaism became a denomination whose adherents were—culturally and economically—bourgeois Germans. Thus, the actual readers of *Ost und West* were most likely Jews of middle-class occupation and/or income.[49] Of the approximately 85 percent of Jews in the *Kaiserreich* considered middle-class, about 25 percent could be classified as belonging to the lower middle class.[50] Even the small Jewish working class ascribed to notions of respectability associated with the German middle class.[51]

Enlightenment Judaism was also internalized as a class orientation by many German Jews. For some, respectability and *Bildung* had become Jewishness itself, a "secular religion" that aimed to replace premodern Judaism.[52] Secular Judaism also incorporated other functions that, before the nineteenth century, had been exercised by religion, such as replacing cultic allegiances with family allegiances. Not unlike its Eastern Jewish counterpart, the German-Jewish family passed on cultural values and norms to its children,[53] but the centrality of the domestic sphere, of the *Hausfrau*, of presentation and display, of "leisured" behavior and German-style education—all these indicated that German Jews adhered to bourgeois norms of respectability.[54] After 1848, the ideology of respectability began to lose its emancipatory appeal, establishing itself as a conservative source of bourgeois identity. Yet its legacy was so powerful that Jews carried on its ideals until new ethnic forms of identity arose alongside the racialist antisemitism of the 1870s and 1880s.[55]

This conclusion is borne out by the politics of German Jews, many of whom had fought for liberalism alongside German Christians. As German-Jewish secularism achieved heightened popularity in the years between 1848 and 1871, liberalism was still dominant as a bourgeois credo.[56] Evidence indicates that German Jews supported liberal political parties which were more likely to accept Jewish civil rights. Prior to 1878, Jews in Germany voted a liberal ticket: 70 percent National-Liberal and 20 percent Left-Liberal. But after that year and the upsurge in antisemitism, the balance shifted to the left. After 1878, 65 percent of German Jews voted Left-Liberal and 15 percent National-Liberal, the remaining Jewish ballots going to centrist parties and to the Social Democrats.[57]

Cultivating a respectable profile also gave middle-class Wilhelminian Jews a firm sense of distinction vis-à-vis Jews living in the East. The pervasiveness of respectability and *Bildung* in German-Jewish middle-class life is attested to by Eastern Jewish perceptions of German Jewry from the end of the nineteenth century. For many *Ostjuden*, their German brethren were too *"daytsh"* in their language, dress, etiquette, worship, work ethic, drive to achieve, and loyalty to the *Vaterland*.[58] German Jews affirmed these values in the context of various associations (*Vereine*). Such institutions imitated those of the non-Jewish middle classes and served to distance *Westjuden* further from traditional Eastern Judaism.[59]

The histories of the German-Jewish and the German middle classes therefore run parallel. But while the success of German Jewry, in all its hope and frustration, must be seen against the background of the em-bourgeoisement of German society as a whole, Jacob Katz and others maintain that Jews integrated not into the German middle classes but into a peculiarly Jewish middle class, or *Bürgertum*.[60] Jews actually created their own subgroup of the German middle class, a distinctive community which conformed to the German middle class in some, but not all, features. A major factor in this development was the limited nature of respectability. Respectability promised Jews an upward mobility that might integrate them into class and nation but provided no guarantee of civil status. After 1871, Jews were fully protected under the laws of Germany, but barriers to equal opportunity continued to exist in the civil service, officers' corps, judiciary, and professorate. Significant threats to Jewish emancipation included the Anti-Semitic Petition of 1881–82, the mass expulsion of 10,000 Eastern immigrants from Prussia in the 1880s, the adoption of the Tivoli Program by the Conservative party in 1892, and the repeated introduction of restrictionist legislation in the *Reichstag* between 1893 and 1902.

Just as the German *Bürgertum* had earlier asserted its identity by distinguishing itself from the aristocracy and the lower classes, so, too, did German Jewry assert its identity by diverging from mainstream middle-class beliefs and practices.[61] For one, most Jews in Germany chose to socialize with and marry other Jews. Moreover, they had different occupations from other Germans, were more educated, lived in larger communities, had fewer children, and were distinguishable in other ways.[62] But these behaviors did not necessarily result from a desire to be separatist. On the contrary, "Jews were more 'Jewish' and less integrated than many have argued, but they were not separate either. Group solidarity need not be confused with segregation."[63] Owing to its high degree of integration, the German-Jewish subculture that developed after Mendelssohn was invisible to itself. Acculturating German Jews in the first half of the nineteenth century were not aware that they had reinterpreted bourgeois mores and rewritten German traditions.[64]

Even if German Jews were not conscious of forming a new type of Jewish identity, their enemies knew better, repeatedly subjecting them to criticism and negative stereotyping. The most commonly denigrated aspect of their subculture was its professional structure. Having achieved success in trade, commerce, and credit prior to the Industrial Revolution, most German Jews were earning a bourgeois-level income by 1848. In this period of German history, they were on average wealthier than their neighbors owing to their head start in the race of industrialization. This advantage, ironically, was the result of being restricted to certain occupations and certain forms of property.[65] Few Jews, as a result, could be found in legal, governmental, military, or academic positions after 1871. A switch to less traditional work, however, could not take place in one generation (especially inasmuch as Jews were having fewer children than ever, and their numbers in the *Kaiserreich* were declining relative to the non-Jewish population). Well into the Weimar period, Jews remained concentrated in the commercial and professional fields; they were underrepresented as artisans, farmers, and industrial laborers. Anticapitalism and antisemitism made Jews even more self-conscious about their lopsided occupational structure. German Jews came to see the "ghetto Jew" as unproductive, earning his living through usury and by his wits. The historical presence of wandering *Betteljuden* encouraged the cliché of the *Schnorrer* incapable of "honest work."[66]

German antisemitism challenged the legitimacy of enlightened Judaism on many fronts. Whether the criterion was respectability or race, the Jews were labeled inferior. Repeatedly, antisemites accused Jews of economic and cultural parasitism, and stereotypes of Jewish parvenus appeared with greater regularity after the stock market crash (*Börsenkrach*) of 1873. For all its furor, antisemitism was not completely internalized by German Jews. Jewish identity preceded antisemitism, just as it had preceded Christian anti-Judaism. Jew hatred, in other words, did not require original responses from the Jews. At the turn of the century, the educated German-Jewish bourgeoisie started to discover Jewish ethnicity for itself. To solidify a nascent Jewish identity that was traditional but modern, Eastern but Western, institutions such as *Ost und West* would now exploit the national allegiances of Jews. The rediscovery of Eastern Jewish culture called for a synthesis of liberal respectability and *shtetl* sensibilities. This encounter of the Western Jewish Enlightenment and traditional Jewish culture had precursors, as we shall now see, which decisively influenced *Ost und West*'s brand of Jewish ethnic identity.

Politically, socially, and culturally, it appeared impossible to unite Eastern and Western Jewish identities at the time *Ost und West* was established. But Winz's grand design was not at all so new: Jewish biculturalism had been around at least since the end of the eighteenth century, starting with Mendelssohn's modifications to traditional Judaism. As the first European Jews who tried to make Western Jewish identity compatible with Eastern

Jewish identity, Mendelssohn and other German-Jewish intellectuals were dubbed the *maskilim* (singular *maskil;* adherents of the *Haskalah*).

The *Haskalah* quickly spread to Poland and Russia, not least of all because its major texts were composed in Hebrew. The early *maskilim* in the East can be considered indirect forebears of *Ost und West*, but their goal was quite different: they attempted to make features of *Western* Jewish identity appealing to *Eastern* Jews. Western Judaism was, however, alien to traditional Judaism, and Jews in Eastern Europe did not embrace respectability and *Bildung* as enthusiastically as Jews in Germany. The *maskilim* explored alternatives such as the biblical and medieval rationalist traditions in their desire to break with a Talmud-based Jewish culture that seemed insular to them. Like their forerunner, Mendelssohn, they strove to liberalize Jewish communities by exposing them to European languages, literature, and science. They also hoped to eliminate Jewish particularism by advocating political and legal equality in Germany, Austria, and Russia.

After the middle of the nineteenth century, the *Haskalah* took on more Eastern features as the center of the European *Haskalah* gravitated toward Russia. In their prenationalist phase before 1881, the *maskilim* attempted to legitimize a westernized Jewish identity to the Jewish masses of the Pale. They were more successful in this undertaking than many historians have indicated. True, the leading *maskilim* belonged both to the cultural elite and to the upper middle class. Nathan Krochmal (1785–1840), Max Lilienthal (1815–1882), Mendele Moykher-Sforim (1835–1917), Sholem Aleichem, and Aḥad Haʿam all were sons of landowners, merchants, bureaucrats, or rabbis.[67] Yet, because they were willing to publish in Yiddish, their ideas came to saturate the educated Jewish elite by the mid-nineteenth century.[68] Despite considerable opposition from a coalition of Hasidic and rival Mitnagdim, the social and cultural reforms of *Haskalah* found some resonance in Russia and parts of Galicia.[69]

The most striking development in the *Haskalah* was the strong ethnic consciousness that emerged in Russia in the wake of the restrictive May Laws of 1881 and the (continued) strangulation of the Pale. As a consequence of these events, many *maskilim* revised their attitudes toward the Enlightenment agenda and began to doubt the possibility of achieving civil equality in the Tsarist empire. Under the repressive regime of Nicholas II, it became clear that the *Haskalah* would be viable in the East only if it integrated the concerns of the *Ostjuden* as a national-ethnic unit. The ethnic element inherent in traditional Eastern Judaism was thus a ready-made source for a new Jewish self-understanding. It was eagerly exploited by a new generation of Jewish intellectuals who were largely educated in yeshivas and rabbinical seminaries.[70] (Before coming to Berlin, Leo Winz was also a *yeshive bokher*). These individuals helped transform the secular identity purveyed by the early *maskilim* into an ethnic-national identity more commensurate with the realities of life in Eastern Europe.

The Enlighteners' updated views were reflected in *Ost und West*, which was indefatigable in recording the emergence of ethnic Judaism. Like the generation of *maskilim* born after mid-century, Winz and his associates (again, mainly Eastern Jews) understood themselves in terms of Jewish ethnicity. In appealing to its public, *Ost und West* drew on both the religious heritage and the secular identity of European Jewry, promoting a type of nationalist *Haskalah*. But just as the *maskilim* had had to develop techniques to promote Western Judaism in the Pale of Settlement, so, too, would *Ost und West* have to be persuasive to interest German Jews in Eastern Jewish identity and thus become a true magazine, as its subtitle promised, "for all Jews" (*das gesamte Judentum*).

How was *Ost und West* to deal with the ever-widening split between Eastern and Western Jewish identity? Winz and his colleagues were clearly worried by the Western nature of political Zionism. Therefore, in their promotion of Eastern-style Jewish ethnicity, respectability was a means but never an end unto itself. Adjusting the norms of Western civility became the key to attracting the different segments of the German-Jewish audience to the traditional values of *Ostjudentum* that, alongside Jewish secularism, fueled the journal's broad interpretation of ethnic Judaism.

The Jewish biculturalism of *Ost und West*, though it originated in the East, needed friends in the West if it was to become truly viable. Few individuals at the fin de siècle understood the possibilities—and pitfalls—of transmitting Jewish culture better than Nathan Birnbaum, one of *Ost und West*'s leading editorialists. Raised in Vienna by acculturating Galician parents, Birnbaum (nom de plume "Mathias Acher") was educated at a humanistic gymnasium, where he became a socialist for a short time. Soon thereafter, he taught himself Yiddish and Hebrew, the beginning of a multifaceted, lifelong project of "re-ethnification."[71] Birnbaum not only adopted most of the forms of ethnic Jewish identity, he also helped create them. He coined the term *Zionism*, molded Diaspora nationalism, created Yiddishism, and toward the end of his life, re-founded *Agudat Yisrael* (*Agudes Yisroel* in Yiddish), a world organization of Orthodox Jewry based on Eastern Judaism, limited cultural autonomism, and opposition to secular Zionism.

Birnbaum was not just a theoretician, however. He was highly aware of the techniques of promoting Jewish ethnicity, having been an outstanding publicist for the Jewish nationalist cause since the mid-1880s. His journal *Selbstemanzipation* (1885–93) was one of the first attempts to reconcile Zionism with other ethnic Judaisms, and in "Das westjüdische Kulturproblem" (published in *Ost und West* in February 1904), he recognized that a broad conception of Jewish ethnicity was crucial to the success of Jewish nationalism in the West:

> And how is nationality actually different from culture? Do you really believe that political "nationalism" can bring western Jewry back to Judaism? What a

mistake! I think what the Jewish national idea needs at present in the West are not "national Jews" who don't make the Jewish cultural nuance a hue stronger, but rather Jews per se—even if they are "assimilators" [*Assimilanten*]—whose portion of Jewish essence has the propensity to increase in size and strength.

Here Birnbaum practices *Ost und West*'s principle of inclusive marketing by granting assimilated Jews latitude in how they define themselves. At the same time, he concludes that the Jews have not become full-fledged Germans, French, or English, for they can never be truly "nationalized" into their respective host states. What people have mistaken for assimilation is the adoption of a modern European general culture (*modern-europäische Allgemein-Kultur*).[72]

Birnbaum thus defended the existence of distinctive Jewish subcultures (*die jüdische Kulturnuance*) and supplied arguments for *Ost und West*'s publicity campaign on behalf of Eastern Jewry. Always the good European, however, he also proposed a synthesis of Western and Eastern Jewish ethnicity using the categories of German intellectual discourse. For Birnbaum, the divisions between political and cultural Zionism corresponded to the current of German thought that distinguished between *Zivilisation* and *Kultur*.[73] Like Meinecke's dichotomy of *Staatsnation/Kulturnation*, the associations evoked by the dichotomy *Zivilisation/Kultur* were an accepted part of intellectual discourse in the *Kaiserreich*. This antithesis, best known today from Thomas Mann's *Bekenntnisse eines Unpolitischen* [Confessions of a Nonpolitical Man] (1918), operated on an East-West continuum. For Mann, Germany embodied *Kultur* and was therefore superior to French and British *Zivilisation* in the West and Russian barbarism in the East. Such an idea of culture centered on an inward feeling and preferred mysticism to rationalism and science: "A culture possesses a soul, while civilization is . . . external and artificial."[74] Whereas *Kultur* put the accent on romanticism and the authentic self, *Zivilisation* was enlightened and industrialized. Whereas a monarchy might be the ideal polity under *Kultur*, *Zivilisation* favored secularism and mass participation in the political process. *Kultur* was usually linked to the "soul of the people" (*Volksseele*) and was epitomized in the rural peasantry. *Zivilisation*, in contrast, was identified with the superficiality and relativism of the city.

This German bias toward culture was reflected in turn-of-the-century discourse on the Jew. Antisemites associated Jews with the mercantilist, urban nature of *Zivilisation*. Jewish nationalists such as Birnbaum drew on the same German paradigm, directing their critiques at a culturally deficient Western Jewry. In this framework, Jews in the West became the true *Ghettojuden*, the products of Diaspora who lacked a genuine *Volksseele*. Birnbaum was also sensitive to Jews who embraced European modernity, however, and his inclusive approach to Jewish nationalism is reflected in his revision of Dohm's quid pro quo. In Birnbaum's version, Eastern Jews would gain entrée into European civilization, and, in exchange, Western

Jews would get a Jewish soul and an ethnic culture. At the same time, Birnbaum was concerned that Western Jews might not hold up their end of the bargain, choosing to balk at such a program. In the following passage from "Etwas über Ost- und Westjudentum" (1904), he describes, *sotto voce*, the differences between Eastern and Western Jews and their respective styles of nationalism in the rhetoric of *Kultur* and *Zivilisation*:

> Yet this much can be crystallized out of the preceding discussion and this is what we wish to suggest at this point: even though culture [*Kultur*] and civilization [*Zivilisation*] have some kind of relationship to each other, they represent in themselves differing qualities of the spiritual life of man. Culture is narrower and deeper, and civilization is more general and broad. Culture is the particularity of a people; civilization, the particularity of a stage in human development. Culture predominates in the innermost recesses of the mind; civilization, in technical, economic, and political life. Finally, not every culture presupposes a particular civilization, nor every civilization a particular culture. Thus, within certain limits conditioned by certain outcomes, a highly developed, or better a profound culture is compatible with a low level of civilization, and a high level of civilization is compatible with a culture that is uncultivated, merely hinted at or already withering.[75]

In this intricate argument, Birnbaum ultimately grants parity to Eastern Jewish tradition and Western Jewish modernity. Then he extends the argument to include Jewish nationalism: "[E]very Eastern Jew, even the 'assimilator' [*Assimilant*], [is] in his expressions a child of the active Eastern Jewish cultural community [*Kulturgemeinschaft*] and every Western Jew, even the 'Zionist,' [is] a piece of the passive Western Jewish peculiarity [*Besonderheit*]."[76] Here, however, Birnbaum slightly favors Eastern Jewish nationalism in maintaining that *Ostjuden* are more easily distinguished in their cultural particularity. To combat the presuppositions of his Western audience, he uses adjectives such as "colorless" and "boring" to describe Western Jews who are alienated from Jewish national customs (*Volkstum*). Having accepted the premises of universalism, these Jews are stuck between two cultures; they do not possess one or the other. Yet, while Western Jews are far too prone to despise their brethren to the East, Eastern Jews also must address their arrogance vis-à-vis the Jewish West. The *Ostjuden* should not scoff at the gifts of civilization, particularly those specifically associated with the Germans: "the order of ideas, method, system."[77]

In this final point, Birnbaum aligned himself with the early *maskilim*. But among his small following in the West, Birnbaum was pegged as a reverse *maskil*, a position he took to its logical conclusion by living his final years as an Eastern-style strictly Orthodox Jew. Certainly few Western Jews were engaged in "reverse assimilation" or the importation of Eastern Jewish nationalism, and Birnbaum must have seemed just another curious utopian in fin-de-siècle Vienna. Yet his life and the lives he influenced testify to the viability of Eastern Jewish ethnic identity in the West. Because he was unabashed in his advocacy and scholarly pursuit of *Ostjudentum* and because he was a keen observer of European Jewish trends, his prescriptions for European Jewish harmony were taken seriously.[78]

Like Birnbaum, *Ost und West* encouraged a synthetic perspective on Eastern and Western Jewish identity. The Eastern Jewish editors of the journal were familiar with both Eastern and Western Jewish culture. This knowledge enabled them to purvey Eastern ethnic Judaism with the hope of appealing to Jews in the West whose self-definition—be it Zionist or liberal—was primarily secular. This bicultural approach originated with the *maskil*-turned-Jewish-nationalist Aḥad Haᶜam, the primary ideologue of *Ost und West*.[79] Owing to his moderate Jewish nationalism, Aḥad Haᶜam represented a cultural Zionism that did not break with Enlightenment ideals but was distinctively Eastern. Not surprisingly, he was a formative influence on Birnbaum, Segel, and the other editorialists of *Ost und West*, showing that the transition between *maskilim* and nationalists was quite fluid. This fluidity suggested that an "ethnic *Haskalah*" was possible.[80] (In contrast, the political Zionists in Herzl's circle often were backed in Russia by middle-class supporters of a conventional *Haskalah*.)[81] Aḥad Haᶜam thus embodied both East and West, Jewish nationalism and Jewish liberalism. This contrasts with the accounts of historians who prefer to relegate him to one camp or the other. Although a critic of Herzl's *Altneuland*, he had been a liberalizer and modernizer as a young man and had studied in Germany and Switzerland. Even later in his life, Aḥad Haᶜam and his allies openly opposed religious Orthodoxy's efforts to garner political control in the Holy Land, demanding that Jewish Palestine diverge from the Diaspora experience in which rabbinical authority had dominated. (Hence he and his followers were more exasperated with the Orthodox leaders in Russia for their hypocritical accommodation to the Tsarist authorities than they ever were with the political Zionists.) Like many a former *maskil*, he revealed his admiration for the West and disdain for life in the Pale of Settlement.[82]

On the basis of their Europe-wide experiences, Aḥad Haᶜam and his disciples grasped the shortcomings of both Eastern and Western Jewish identity. The increasingly frequent linkage of East and West in the lives of many turn-of-the-century Jews is confirmed by reading *Ost und West*. The next generation of young *Westjuden*—including Fritz Mordechai Kaufmann, Georg (Jírí) Langer (1894–1943), Max Meyer (1886–?), and Gerhard (Gershom) Scholem (1897–1982)—became adherents of ethnic Judaism. Unlike most of their contemporaries, they drew the conclusion that Eastern Jewry was more authentic than Western Jewry and worth emulating. Consequently, they broke with the Western respectability of their parents and developed a veritable cult of the *Ostjuden*, frequently based on firsthand knowledge of Eastern Jewish life. Franz Kafka, perhaps the most renowned Western Jewish writer of this period, also deserves mention in this context.

In a 1912 speech to an acculturated Prague Jewish audience in which he introduced a troupe of Eastern Jewish actors he had befriended, Kafka suggested that his Prague Jewish listeners knew more Yiddish than they thought. He also argued in his letters to Felice Bauer (1887–1960) that cultural exchange and mutual tolerance would benefit Jews raised on both sides of the imaginary line separating Europe from Asia.[83]

With the exception of the young Jews cited, Western Jews did not commonly cultivate an interest in the *Ostjuden*. *Ost und West* sought to correct this deficiency by promoting Eastern Jewish identity. Far from a one-sided plan, however, the journal's Eastern Jewishness was balanced out by the pan-Jewish outlook of its creators. Unfortunately, the vogue in historiography has been to designate bicultural Jews as subalterns, estranged from the cultural mainstream.[84] While this notion is correct to a point, the idea that European Jews formed esoteric communities rent by factionalism not only perpetuates the cliché of Jewish secrecy but also marginalizes all those who express multiple identities. In *Ost und West*, one finds contributors who understood both the Jewish East and the Jewish West. Finally, judging by the magazine's large readership, its creators were far from being on the fringe. They shared in a significant community built on the written word.

By drawing on their commonalities, *Ost und West* brought the Jews of Europe together in a symbolic world of words and images where diverse Jewish identities might be narrated. In rendering seemingly conflicting models for identity compatible, the journal made Jewish nationalism palatable to more assimilated Jewish audiences.[85] As a magazine of ethnic culture, *Ost und West* participated in a Europe-wide phenomenon: the rise of print journalism, which was integral in the construction of all nationalisms in the nineteenth century.[86] Journals that featured a nation's culture—referred to here as "national-cultural reviews"—were the ultimate realization of a quest to imagine the nation, and, like other late-nineteenth-century European journals, *Ost und West* was involved in the nation-building enterprise.

What exactly was a national-cultural review (*Kulturrundschau*)? It was a journal that purported to address all members of a single ethnicity or national group. It proceeded from the assumption that these individuals felt united by common bonds, regardless of where they (the "nationals") might reside. Both the *Deutsche Rundschau* (1874–1964) and *Ost und West*, for instance, prided themselves on having subscribers as far away as America. Wilmont Haacke establishes the origin of German national-cultural reviews in the late-eighteenth-century *Nationaljournal*, a spinoff of the *moralische Wochenschriften* ("moral weeklies") in the German territories.[87] Karl Ulrich Syndram characterizes the *Kulturrundschau* of the late nineteenth century as a hybrid of a specialized journal (*Fachzeitschrift*) and a news-oriented daily newspaper with a cultural section (*politisch-aktuelle Tageszeitung mit Feuilleton*).[88] The *Kulturrundschau* thus had elements both of sophisticated art journals, which featured essays, and of family entertainment magazines, which specialized in fiction and poetry. The genres that commonly filled these cultural reviews were the political and cultural-political essay, the literary- and art-historical essay, belles-lettres, popular scholarship, and the review of the press. The target group addressed by the *Kulturrundschau* was the educated middle class or *Bildungsbürgertum*, the leading intellectual class of the nation.[89] To impress this audience, the *Kulturrundschau* displayed its competence and authority by attracting well-known contributors.[90]

One drawback of Syndram's definition is its failure to explain the dynamics of the national-cultural reviews. For example, how did these journals encourage their readers to affiliate ethnically? Late in his book, Syndram provides an answer: stereotyping was required in order to bring together the perceived members of a nation or culture.[91] The stereotyping of rival nations was a time-honored tradition, as is evident in the earliest national-cultural reviews, the *Edinburgh Review* (1802–1929) and the *Revue des deux mondes* (1829–). Like other national-cultural reviews, *Ost und West* addressed readers of many persuasions, making careful use of both positive and negative imagery to construct a new ideal of Jewish ethnicity. Moreover, the journal had Jewish as well as non-Jewish precursors. *Ost und West's* Jewish predecessors presented some of the earliest stereotypes of Eastern Jews. Earlier variants of national-cultural reviews for Jews were Gabriel Rießer's *Der Jude. Periodische Blätter für Religion und Gewissensfreiheit* (1831–33) and Aḥad Haᶜam's *Ha-Shiloah*.

The main German-Jewish prototype of *Ost und West*, the *Allgemeine Zeitung des Judentums*, also was involved in imagining the Jewish nation. Though not strictly speaking a national-cultural review, this weekly newspaper spanned several epochs in German-Jewish history. By stereotyping traditional Jews and Jews from Eastern Europe, the *Allgemeine Zeitung des Judentums* attempted to consolidate its primary audience of liberal Jews. Although it held paternalistic attitudes toward the *Ostjuden*, the *Allgemeine Zeitung des Judentums* did support their emancipation; in fact, it was the first newspaper to translate Peretz and other Eastern Jewish writers into German. It also selectively appropriated ethnic Jewish identity, if only to bolster its Enlightenment definitions of Jewishness. Although generally a vehicle of acculturation that advanced Judaism as a respectable confession, this grandfather of German-Jewish journalism affirmed that Germany's Jews had developed a rich, diverse subculture through their own devices.

Just as the *Allgemeine Zeitung des Judentums* became a true national review in appropriating all forms of Jewish identity, so, too, did *Ost und West* embrace Jewish allegiances that went beyond its ethnic program. Styling itself as *the* alternative to the *Allgemeine Zeitung des Judentums*, *Ost und West* nevertheless drew on all three forms of Judaism in modern Europe: Eastern-traditional, Western-enlightened, and pan-European. At the same time, *Ost und West* had a truly pan-Jewish audience, one that spanned Europe and outnumbered that of the *Allgemeine Zeitung des Judentums* by a factor of ten. Thus, Winz's journal was not only a national-culture review but also a widely read one. More a diverse assemblage than a monolithic synthesis, *Ost und West* played up the religious roots of Jewish ethnicity at the same time as it advocated a modified form of Western respectability. It is this flexible approach to its audience that distinguished it from its predecessors and is the subject of the following chapters.

To Winz and the editors of *Ost und West*, there were two main types of Jewish identity, and each corresponded to a geocultural source: traditional Jewish identity emerged in Eastern Jewish culture, and enlightened Jewish identity emerged in Western Jewish culture. While the pan-Jewish identity *Ost und West* espoused was an attempt to combine Eastern-traditional with Western-enlightened Judaism, the notion of pan-Jewishness had Eastern and Western varieties unto itself. As a result, *Ost und West*'s attempt to unite Jews under the banner of ethnicity was fraught with contradictions—made worse by its own preference for Eastern ethnic Jewishness. Precisely because it was so difficult to overcome the distinctions between Eastern and Western Jewish culture, even for those who wished to unite them, *Ost und West* had to rely on negative stereotyping to bridge the gap. What is more, this negative stereotyping, if it was to be compelling, had to draw on images of both Eastern and Western Jewry.

The following chapters focus in particular on the negative tactics *Ost und West* employed. Negative stereotyping, even of other Jews, was almost always more effective than selling an ideal. Presenting unfavorable images did not have to be brash, however. It could actually be quite subtle, as in the case of *Ost und West*, whose practices of denigration varied for each of its Jewish audience in Germany—male intellectuals, middle-class women, and middle-class men. But each group of readers had one thing in common: it feared losing its Jewish identity through assimilation. By promoting negative images, *Ost und West* capitalized on this fear, hoping that its Jewish audiences would support the idea of ethnic distinctiveness. Winz and his circle thought that the idea of a Jewish essence (*Urjudentum*) would be more attractive to Western Jews if it were juxtaposed with unfavorable images of Jewish apostates, parvenus, and self-haters.

The remainder of this study analyzes how effective *Ost und West* was in promoting ethnic Judaism to its specific Jewish audiences in Germany. Each chapter begins with a general overview of the Jewish audience in question, outlining which versions of *Judentum* were most powerful in its self-understanding. In each case, Winz and his colleagues pinpointed the traditional and modern loyalties of each group of Jews. They then appealed to each audience with an individualized set of stereotypes. Since positive images of Jewish ethnicity failed to find the desired resonance after 1903, *Ost und West*'s negative stereotypes proved more compelling, showing that

75

ethnic Jewish identity had greater drawing power when it was negatively promoted. This negative "marketing," in turn, played upon the Eastern/ traditional and Western/enlightened identities of Jews in Germany. By playing upon both identities in their choice of stereotypes, the editors of *Ost und West* hoped to give the idea of ethnic pan-Jewishness the focus and definition it otherwise lacked.

3

"Intellectuals" Reading "Parvenus": The Intellectual Nationalist as *Ostjude* and the Assimilating Parvenu as *Westjude* in *Ost und West*

This chapter explores how the creators of *Ost und West* used their knowledge of Jewish identities to appeal to a specific Jewish subgroup in Germany: the intelligentsia sympathetic to Eastern Jewry. This almost exclusively male audience was made up of students, journalists, literati, rabbis, and educators. They were the avant-garde of ethnic Jewry in the West, and from its earliest days, the journal drew its editors and main contributors from their ranks.

Assuming the loyalty of Eastern Jewish readers, *Ost und West* set out to attract their Western counterparts. To appeal to German-Jewish intellectuals was no easy matter, however, particularly since Winz and his colleagues eschewed the romanticized images of the *Ostjude* (and the Oriental Jew) that had begun to emerge in Western literature of the nineteenth century. To begin with, they felt that those who idealized the *Ostjude* might overlook the dire social and political conditions under which Eastern Jews lived. They also knew that positive imagery could not by itself spark an ethnic Jewish renaissance. They thus sought negative stereotypes of a specific group of Jews—Jews who were neither Eastern nor Jewish nationalist. On the one hand, this meant criticizing a number of Western Jews, a move that might offend some German-Jewish readers. On the other hand, it meant caricaturing Jews without somehow slipping into the all-too-pervasive clichés of the *Ostjude* as dirty, loud, unmannered, and culturally retrograde.[1] For antisemites in Germany were only too happy to come across such images and take them out of context.

Ost und West needed a different type of Jew to stereotype, one that its elite readers could really disdain—and in good conscience. The most persistent stereotype of all, a stock figure of German letters since the early nineteenth century, was the Jewish social climber, alternatively known as the "parvenu," "arriviste," or "nouveau riche."[2] This character was a distant relative of the court Jews (or *Hofjuden*) granted special privileges by German royals since the sixteenth century. Perhaps because many such "exception" Jews came from Poland, this figure came to be more strongly associated with East European Jews.[3] Designated as a *Geldprotz* after 1873, the parvenu was presumed to have a tendency to "show off" (*protzen*), a behavior attributed to his Eastern Jewish descent.[4] Since he threatened to become indistinguishable from non-Jews, the parvenu's Christian colleagues branded him as different. This did not go unnoticed by the editors of *Ost und West*, who were looking to redefine Jewish identity and community. They turned to this more interesting stereotype in an effort to transcend older simplifications which their avant-garde readers mistrusted.

The negative image of the parvenu thus became the main stereotype in *Ost und West*. Yet, as we shall see, the *Protz* of the journal was not simply new; he was, in fact, diametrically opposed to the Eastern Jewish parvenu encountered in belles-lettres prior to the twentieth century. In *Ost und West*, the Eastern origins of previous Jewish arrivistes were now either effaced or specified as "Western." As a result, the *Western* Jewish parvenu was suddenly held up as a cautionary figure. When publishing literary and historical narratives about Jewish origins, then, *Ost und West* pinpointed the Western Jewish parvenu as the source of acculturation, not the *Ghettojuden* of the East. As this stereotype gained momentum, owning up to one's ethnic background became the essence of authentic Jewishness in *Ost und West*. In the meantime, the ultimate term of opprobrium remained *Assimilant* ("assimilator") or *Abtrünniger* ("apostate"). In league against "bad" Jews, "good" Eastern and "good" Western Jews might find some common ground. The Jewish fold was defined anew so as to exclude those Jews who, like the social climbers, were taken to be wealthy and less educated.

To clarify how Winz and his circle promoted this specific stereotype, this chapter first will describe the intellectual, pro-*Ostjude* audience of *Ost und West*, the readers who were socially and culturally inclined to recoil at the sight of nouveau riche *Westjuden*. The character of the arriviste, as we shall see, became the special target of the journal's short satires set in Berlin. These short satires were calculated to play on both the religious and enlightened loyalties of Jewish intellectuals. Just which loyalties were brought to bear—Eastern or Western, traditional or modern—was not always apparent, however. Even as the journal rejected an assimilated lifestyle in favor of historical Judaism, it accepted modern, Western criticisms of the lopsided professional structure of Jewish Germans, "enlightened" arguments that promoted artisanry and farming over commerce and banking.

This analysis of the Jewish parvenu image rests on the assumption that German-Jewish students, intellectuals, and artists were a major audience of *Ost und West*. But how do we actually know that this was true? And how did *Ost und West*'s editorial team approach them as a unique market?

We can answer these questions by reconstructing *Ost und West*'s audience of Western Jewish cultural elites. It is true that such an undertaking is risky in the absence of precise distribution statistics, detailed letters to the editor, and reader protocols.[5] Yet the stereotypes used by *Ost und West* provide the information needed to fill these gaps. Indeed, the image of the Western Jewish parvenu that pervades the first years of *Ost und West* suggests that Jewish intellectuals—antipodes to the parvenu—were the pioneer subscribers to the magazine.

German-Jewish students and intellectuals, unlike other *Westjuden*, were also more likely to have contact with bona fide *Ostjuden*. As we have seen, the rapprochement of Eastern and Western Jews first began around the turn of the century under the auspices of groups such as the *Russischer jüdischer wissenschaftlicher Verein*. In the 1890s, Birnbaum, Loewe, and others laid the groundwork for pan-Jewish nationalism. These leading lights of the Young Jewish Movement (*die jungjüdische Bewegung*) worked to bring about a synthesis of the German youth movement with the incipient Jewish "Renaissance."[6] The Democratic Faction of the Zionist party was only the most famous offspring of this new alliance of Jewish writers, artists, and journalists. Although small and more Eastern than Western Jewish in composition, this group made up the new ethnic Jewish vanguard in Europe. In selecting its editorials, literature, and art, *Ost and West* shared the Faction's agenda, promoting Jewish nationalist thinkers and thus achieving notoriety for itself. Despite hailing from Russia and Galicia, the editors of the magazine were determined to galvanize the support of Jewish intellectuals in the West—both the Western and Eastern Jewish nationalists.

As in Eastern Europe, pointing the young elites in Central Europe toward ethnic Judaism was a new response to growing economic and racial antisemitism. In an epoch of mounting prejudice in the universities and academic professions, the anti-parvenu narratives of *Ost und West* could be aimed at the German-Jewish *Bildungsproletariat*. This new "proletariat of the educated" consisted of Jewish men (and a handful of women) in their twenties who saw their career prospects turning more and more dismal.[7] Almost all Jews seeking or holding elite positions in Germany were affected by discrimination. After the stock market crash of 1873, rivalries among students in the *Kaiserreich* grew fiercer and were influenced by racialist thinking. Eastern Jews, as the most conspicuous group of foreigners at the university, soon became easy targets for their conservative peers.[8] Denying

Jewish access to higher education became a major thrust of organized antisemitism and climaxed in the Anti-Semitic Petition of 1881–82.[9] What is more, protests against Russian-Jewish students in Germany implicated their more acculturated German-Jewish cousins.[10] A new East-West Jewish ethnic alliance, it was thought, could combat such threats.

Restrictions on Jewish immigrants helped strengthen this new alliance. In the *Kaiserreich*, foreign Jews were rarely offered citizenship and were subject to deportation if they were deemed burdensome (*lästig*) or of no tangible benefit to the German economy. These laws reflected the centuries-old practice of limiting Jews to the commercial and banking sectors. In fact, Jews from the Habsburg Empire were preferred by the German authorities over other foreign Jews, precisely because it was believed that they would stimulate trade and investment.[11] And one major reason Winz and his colleagues chose journalism was to preclude being expelled from the *Kaiserreich*.

The culture industry thus became a main outlet for university-educated Jews from both Europes. Owing to job discrimination, many native-born Jews in Germany (and Austria) who had trained as lawyers or humanists were forced into journalism. (A comparison reveals that Jews in England and France enjoyed more career mobility in the nineteenth century than their coreligionists in Germany.)[12] In an irony of history, the limits placed on Jewish occupations actually led to a preponderance of Jews in the press, that most visible of fields. The best-known publishers in all of Germany, the Ullsteins and the Mosses, were Jews. Out of these circumstances arose the myth that the Jewish press was all-powerful and conspiratorial. But in discussions among Eastern and Western Jews, the crisis of the *Bildungsproletariat* received the most attention—not the realities of prejudice, as one might expect.[13] Jews, like other ill-treated groups, looked upon antisemitism as a hazard of the marketplace, even though many were aware of its deleterious potential as an ideology. Without diverging into self-hatred, leading Jews agreed that the newest wave of antisemitism was a *plausible* consequence of the depressed professional job market of the 1870s which had made the competition for most "academic" metiers keener than ever.

But competition between Jewish and non-Jewish students (together less than 1 percent of the population) and the general retrenchment of German conservatism after the 1880s also can be read as a sign of progress. The social gains German Jews made as the result of emancipation became more elusive as they moved closer to political parity. In practice (though not in law), they were excluded from the bureaucracy, the judiciary, the professoriate, and the officer class. To advance socially demanded one basic sacrifice: getting baptized. The high number of Jewish conversions after 1871— higher than at any other time in German history—shows the relative ease with which this step was taken.[14] Even though baptism (like intermarriage) did not translate into full acceptance, its popularity suggests that acceptance was no longer impossible, at least for those Jews more loyal to Western-enlightened Judaism. Not surprisingly, Jewish university students were highly susceptible to conversion.[15]

As part of a wide-scale outreach program, *Ost und West* and other purveyors of ethnic Judaism tried to limit such damage and frequently appealed to the loyalties of unaffiliated Jews who refused to convert, the so-called *Trotzjuden* ("defiant Jews"). Unlike parvenus and other renegades, *Trotzjuden* or "dissidents" were regarded by many Jews as exhibiting integrity (*Charakter*), and their numbers increased in the *Kaiserreich*.[16] In fact, statistics suggest that conversions were on the decline by 1901, when *Ost und West* began publication.[17] Some Western Jews were thus prepared to reject an assimilated German identity for the Jewish ethnic identity being fashioned by Eastern Jewish students in Germany.

As argued above, the delayed entry of Jews into academic professions pushed many intellectual *Westjuden* in the direction of Jewish nationalism. While the *Trotzjuden* did not fully embrace Jewish nationalism of either variety, others went several steps further, attempting to "re-judaize" or "re-ethnify" themselves through contact with Eastern Jewish life. These young German Jews, whose chances to succeed as *Bildungsbürger* were waning, reacted to the threat of becoming déclassé by portraying their fathers (and the rest of the German-Jewish propertied bourgeoisie) as assimilationists. The Jewish nationalist challenge to the leadership of the established Jewish communities (*Gemeinden*) is but one manifestation of a widening generation gap after 1900, which, as we shall see in *Ost und West*, became a frequent literary motif of the epoch.[18]

Western Jews responded to the lure of ethnic redefinition for a mixture of professional and familial reasons. Having come of age in the 1890s and 1900s, young Jews in Germany had had a very different experience from the previous generation. Their fathers, who subscribed to an ideology of emancipation, had been raised in the hopeful *Nachmärz* period (1848–1871) and had not been subjected to the same degree of academic or professional antisemitism.[19] On account of the demise of liberalism, the new generation was also willing to avow its Jewishness publicly. Starting around 1900, a small group of "returners" (*ba'alei teshuvah*; Hebrew for "penitents") tried to reverse the acculturation patterns of their elders, some of whom were first-generation immigrants from the East. As Aschheim observes:

> There was a delicious irony in this: whereas before, German Jews had been shamed by the presence of their cousins from the East, their own children were now profoundly embarrassed by the affluence and philistinism of their parents and looked East for a source of renewed pride. The great problem of Jewish life, bemoaned one Zionist, was the fact that all Jews were judged by the behavior of a small bourgeoisie. The cult of the *Ostjuden* was one way of attempting to escape this damning judgment by association.[20]

81

Overcoming the stereotype of the parvenu or "capitalist" Jew, whom they felt their fathers embodied, became a major agenda for these younger Jews, and a number of them after 1900 renewed their ties to Judaism. Some, like Nathan Birnbaum, made full-scale returns to Eastern-style Jewish Orthodoxy. Later prominent examples of Western Jewish elites who "dissimilated" in this way include Fritz Mordechai Kaufmann, a Jew from the Rheinland who became a Yiddishist and married a Polish-Jewish woman, and Kafka's friend Georg (Jírí) Langer, who became a disciple of the Belzer *rebbe*, to the chagrin of his liberal Prague Jewish family. In his biography of Birnbaum, sociolinguist Joshua Fishman documents how the "re-ethnification and accompanying re-linguification [of elites] is a common process in the early stages of very many modern ethnicity movements" and how this process shows a "proto-elitist return to (or selection of) roots—often after failure to transethnify 'upwardly' in accord with earlier aspirations."[21]

At its worst, this kind of re-ethnification could decline into elitism. But the elitism that marred fin-de-siècle Jewish nationalism was not confined to Western Jewish groups. The members of the Democratic Faction, for instance, were parodied for their avant-garde intellectualism. Not only Buber, the standard-bearer of the group, but also Weizmann, Motzkin, and Aḥad Haʿam were singled out.[22] Other Eastern Jewish nationalists looked upon as elite were the leaders of the Jewish socialist *Bund*, who were at best partially re-ethnified.[23] Indeed, the *Bund*'s program to mobilize the Jewish lower classes was indebted to a Western model of progressive socialism. But the dual focus of all these groups on Western-style civilization and Eastern-style Jewish culture cannot be called schizophrenic. Rather, it expressed a typical need of Jewish nationalism to exploit the past while responding to current developments. As Fishman points out, "modern ethnicity movements are essentially attempts to achieve modernization, utilizing 'primordial' identificational metaphors and emotional attachments for this purpose. Thus, they are not really 'return' movements (i.e., not really nativization or past-oriented efforts). They exploit or mine the past rather than cleave to it. Partially transethnified elites can uniquely serve such movements because of their own double exposure."[24] Winz and his team were also "doubly exposed." *Ost und West* mined the past with an eye toward the present and thereby showed the value of promoting both traditional and modern components of ethnic Jewishness. Winz, then, found himself attracting to his project Jews who bridged East and West.

Because the audience of Jews who lived both Eastern and Western forms of Judaism eclipsed the tiny elite of dissimilators, the Western audience of *Ost und West* soon grew beyond activists and elites. "Metaphorical returners" to the fold, of course, far outnumbered "genuine returners."[25] Even the Zionist movement could not encompass them all, and, according to Winz, the readership of *Ost und West* was largely non-Zionist by 1903.[26]

Few young German Jews circa 1900 were adherents of Jewish nation-alism, much less *ba'alei teshuvah*. Moreover, the "metaphorical" returners among them were more willing to subscribe to Western Jewish nation-alism than to its Eastern counterpart. As "anti-bourgeois" bourgeoisie, they also had more in common with the larger German youth movement (*Jugendbewegung*) than with traditional Judaism. These young Germans, like their German-Jewish peers, felt trapped between the "Mammonism" of capitalism and the "materialism" of organized labor. They also feared they were losing ground socially, a mood shared by their leading youth organization, the *Wandervögel*.[27]

Despite their image of uniformity, the *Wandervögel* and other such groups were split down the middle into *Besitz-* and *Bildungsbürger* (prop-ertied and educated bourgeois) an internal class division echoed in the Jewish youth movement.[28] The Jewish *Besitz-* and *Bildungsbürger* were also prepared to stereotype each other if necessary. Just as German Jews had traditionally stigmatized *Ostjuden*, so, too, did young Jewish *Bürger* try to create distance between themselves. Many were aware that the Jewish middle class, which included three quarters of all Jews in the *Kaiserreich*, was divided into subclasses: the upper segment included well-to-do en-trepreneurs, doctors, and lawyers; the middle segment included retailers and independent tradesmen; and the lower segment included less-monied artisans and businesspeople, white-collar and communal officials, teachers, and bookkeepers.[29] Short of inventing some new common cause, it was difficult to build consensus within this sizable middle class. The only shared ideals were the norms of respectability observed by more affluent and established Jews. Lower-class Jews in Germany (even some first-generation Easterners) recognized that these ideals were their ticket to status, whereas most middle-class Jews used the idea of respectability to bracket them-selves off from the Jewish lower classes and Eastern Jewish immigrants, on the one hand, and from the Jewish upper classes and parvenus, on the other.

Ost und West sought to make ethnic Judaism part of broader middle-class Jewish identity by tapping into the scruples of the Wilhelminian Jews. These Jews, like middle-class Germans, were subjected to the dictates of en-lightened morality: respectability, hard work, cleanliness, and so on. These dictates, in fact, encouraged *Ost und West* to use stereotypes of parvenu *Westjuden* who had (conventionally) Eastern Jewish defects.[30] Such a strategy ultimately accommodated the journal's intellectual audience, enabling Jews between twenty and forty to break with their parents' *Westjudentum* while also distancing themselves from the negative side of *Ostjudentum*.[31]

Young German-Jewish intellectuals were thus unwilling to abandon the upper-middle-class status they had inherited. And they were the only ones likely to have the leisure (or the finances) to support Jewish nationalism. In the end, the decision to identify ethnically was often a luxury for the

Jewish middle class, helping elites maintain their political leverage over *Ostjuden* and lower-class Jews. The alliance that Winz and his circle tried to forge between Eastern and Western Jewish elites was shaky. It could not be realized on one or the other's terms. Only one avenue remained: to craft a synthesis of traditional and enlightened Judaism under the banner of Jewish ethnicity. But this, as we shall see, meant creating new stereotypes.

This section will explore one type of Jewish self-representation in *Ost und West*, namely the discourse of the Jewish parvenu as a deficient *Westjude*. Whereas much research has focused on the portrayal of Jews—Eastern and Western—in the modern age, little has been written about parvenus.[32] *Ost und West*'s stereotypes of the Jewish parvenu, as suggested earlier, promoted ethnic Judaism to Western and Eastern Jews active in the cultural sphere. At the height of *Ost und West*'s "corrective" stereotyping between 1901 and 1906, the Western Jewish *Protz* was promoted as the embodiment of all Jewish parvenus throughout history. But the magazine did not invent this stereotype; it only marks a transition in the diverse and colorful history of this character in German (and Western) culture. *Ost und West* drew on a long history of attitudes toward socially mobile Jews, attitudes stemming from both Jews and non-Jews. Again, the innovation of Winz and his colleagues was to redefine the origins of the parvenu characters as Western, not Eastern.

Attitudes toward lapsed Jews almost always have demarcated the perceived boundaries between "Jew" and "non-Jew." Yet prior to their emergence from ghetto life in the 1700s, European Jews could disaffiliate from their community in only two ways: through conversion and through heresy. In the wake of the *Haskalah*, Jews were compelled to redefine their identities, a process that entailed disguising their common origins, be they linguistic, territorial, ethnic, or historical. Most Jews preferred the deliberate pace of acculturation over assimilation, since it was a less radical adaptation to non-Jewish society, but some still chose to repress their recent past.[33] Indeed, the raison d'être of Jewish parvenus was the concealment of their social and/or cultural origins.

In Germany, where Jews did not attain many rights and legal freedoms until 1869, many Jews camouflaged their Jewish ancestry. After this time, antisemites—even the Jewish ones—reveled in opportunities to humiliate Jews who masked their origins, which led both Jews and Christians to form antidefamation organizations (*Abwehrorganisationen*) in 1890s Germany. Yet an open profession of Jewish belief or ethnicity was unusual until the emergence of political Zionism, which itself never strayed from Western liberal universalism. But since it was created by Eastern Jewish nationalists, *Ost und West* was alone among German-Jewish journals in openly acknowledging its Jewish roots (indeed, its Eastern Jewish patronage) by featuring the history, literature, art, and folklore of *Ostjuden*. In summary, the magazine's conspicuous displays of Jewishness touted ethnic pride as an antidote to antisemitism.

In urging European Jews to overcome their self-censorship and to "come out of the closet," the myth makers at *Ost und West* used a conspicuous foil: the German-Jewish parvenu. Shame or embarrassment about this figure, defined in Webster's as "a usually crude or pushing person who has recently reached a position of prominence, power or wealth," was meant to make Jewish readers identify with their ethnic roots. When presented in *Ost und West*, representations of Jewish social climbers had a didactic function: they were intended to educate German Jews. Above all, they served as negative exempla in the journal's cautionary tales.

Ost und West's anti-parvenu narratives evolved in response to specific historical developments. The rate of apostasy in Germany was staggering (if belated) when compared to other Western nations. In Berlin, the center of gravity of German Jewry, at least 100 adult conversions to Protestantism (or one for every 600 to 650 Jews) were registered per year in the period from 1882 to 1908. In England, the figures were significantly lower. "Jews were ceasing to be Jewish in England because resistance to their incorporation into society was weak; in Germany, their ties to Judaism were being sundered because the resistance was strong," notes one historian.[34] Narratives of Jewish parvenus—who themselves may or may not have been baptized— were thus attempts to come to terms with the high degree of acculturation that German society required of the Jews.[35]

What, then, did the standard German-Jewish parvenu character look like? Arguably the most powerful and widespread representation of the Jew to be found in post-Enlightenment Germany, the image of the Jewish parvenu derived its archetypal impact from medieval stereotyping of Jews as greedy and usurious.[36] As a social upstart, the Jewish arriviste was depicted as prideful (thus committing the Christian sin of *hubris*). He became, at the same time, the object of envy and projected guilt; he had no right to be in the position he held. In addition, he was frequently portrayed as a lapsed Jew or a convert to Christianity.

The upstart Jew was also marked by wealth and ostentation; not coincidentally, the Jewish parvenu of the *Kaiserreich* was most typically designated as a monied show-off. Western secularism also shaped the typical Jewish arriviste character, even if the religious overtones of the image never faded. The parvenu Jew of prose fiction was thus highly acculturated and typically resided in a large city, such as Berlin. In addition, he was pretentious, though not always cultured or even intelligent. Repeatedly caricatured as pot-bellied, bow-legged, diamond-wearing, gesticulating, large-nosed, and curly haired, he was at core rootless and degenerate, a legacy of nineteenth-century antisemitism and anticapitalism.

Yet the most pervasive nineteenth-century versions of the stereotype had one additional feature: the parvenu was firmly linked to East European

Jewish types.[37] As already indicated, such a reading of the parvenu was common among German Jews who believed themselves more civilized than their Eastern coreligionists. To resist this interpretation of the German-Jewish parvenu, *Ost und West* turned the tables. The journal's literature and essays uncovered the origins of the arriviste and revealed them to be . . . Western![38] Contributors to *Ost und West*, however, were prone to recycle the elements of the older easternized image, giving the new Western Jewish *Protz* the negative traits previously associated with the stereotype of the Eastern Jewish parvenu. Although the contributors to *Ost und West* rarely caricatured the physical appearance or manners of this Western Jewish *Protz*, his hunger for status was familiar to the cultural elites who read the journal.[39] The Western Jewish intellectuals I have described were not at all offended by critical portraits of literary parvenus who were *Westjuden*. On the contrary, they welcomed these images, thus encouraging *Ost und West* to continue its negative promotion campaign to make Eastern Jews and ethnic Jewishness respectable in the eyes of the larger Western Jewish audience.[40]

By now, it should be clear that negative stereotyping of arriviste Jews was central to the mission of *Ost und West*. Exposing the modest origins of many a nouveau riche Jew actually became something of a sport in the journal's appeals to ethnically inclined literati. Cultural origins were at the core of this type of criticism. As a proponent of Eastern Jewish nationalism, *Ost und West* consistently portrayed Eastern Jews as more "rooted" than their Western brethren. In addition, the journal called upon all Jews to acknowledge their parents' (or grandparents') place of origin, be it Germany, Austria, Hungary, Galicia, the Bukovina, Poland, or Russia.[41] Requiring that those Western Jews with family in the East embrace their roots was one way to parry attacks on *Ostjuden*. Since the Enlightenment, most parvenus in the German-Jewish cultural milieu were thought to be recent immigrants from Eastern Europe, and in the historians' controversy of 1878–79, Heinrich von Treitschke identified Eastern Europe as the breeding ground of Jewish parvenuism.[42] *Ost und West*, in turn, defended Eastern Jewry by directing its barbs against Western Jewish parvenus, those whose families had resided in the West for more than one generation.[43]

Even while redefining the Jewish social climber, *Ost und West*'s essays and stories show that it was acutely aware of his literary predecessors. The origin of the magazine's parvenu stereotype is found in four nineteenth-century traditions: (1) the Eastern Jewish tradition critical of the enlightened Jew or *daytsher*;[44] (2) the anticonversion and anti-intermarriage fiction published in Orthodox and Liberal Jewish periodicals in the second half of the nineteenth century;[45] (3) the genre of so-called *Dorf- und Ghetto-geschichten* by Jewish and non-Jewish writers such as Berthold Auerbach (1812–1882), Leopold Kompert (1822–1886), Karl Emil Franzos (1848–

1904), and Leopold Sacher-Masoch (1835–1895); and (4) the non-Jewish literary and historical tradition of the Jewish speculator-cum-*Geldprotz*, exemplified in contributions to the Treitschke dispute as well as in the fictions of Gustav Freytag (1816–1895), Wilhelm Raabe (1831–1910), and a host of others prior to the fin de siècle.[46]

A complete examination of these tropes of the Jewish parvenu would take us far afield. It is also not necessary, for the fourth tradition—the most influential—predominated. Works such as Gustav Freytag's *Soll und Haben* (1855) engaged the interest of a broad audience extending beyond German Jewry and constituted the most immediate and most likely source of parvenus in *Ost und West*. Most of this late-nineteenth-century litera-ture, whether labeled "historical scholarship" or "historical fiction," was written in a "Realist" mode.[47] As we shall see, the imagery and governing aesthetic of this Realism were challenged by *Ost und West*'s contemporary fiction (*Zeitprosa*) of German-Jewish life. This Naturalist fiction became the primary vehicle for challenging the ideological linkage of Jewish parvenus and Eastern Jewish immigrants.

In contrast to other Jewish mass media, *Ost und West* specialized in stereotypes of the Jewish parvenu that placed this character solidly in Western society. Since the majority of the magazine's readers had grown up in Western and Central Europe, this created a potential quandary. Having decided to publish anti-Western parvenu narratives, *Ost und West* was compelled to feature examples of this genre written by Western Jewish writers. In fact, the journal often used Western Jewish authors to denounce Western Jewish parvenus, although many narratives created by Eastern Jews were also used, such as Peretz's "Vier Testamente" (September 1901). Some of the German-Jewish authors, such as Lothar Brieger-Wasservogel (1879–1949),[48] were hard-line Western Zionists even though the editorial staff of the journal was critical of political Zionism, leaning toward the cultural Zionism of Aḥad Haᶜam. Even if they were not part of *Ost und West*'s original constituency of non-arriviste Eastern Jews, Western Jewish writers knew the Western milieu better and thus could produce stereotypes that were more appealing to readers in the West (but were no less acceptable to Eastern Jewish intellectuals).

Winz and his colleagues had discovered that it was not enough to locate "genuine" Jewish national culture in Eastern Europe in order to attract Western Jews to ethnic Jewishness.[49] They saw instead that the view of Eastern Jewish life as more honest and more harmonious was little more than a mythical inversion of the negative stereotyping that was so rampant. Instead of repeating this utopian vision, the contemporary fiction published in *Ost und West* divorced the Jewish parvenu from his Eastern roots to a greater extent than ever before. In turn, he was linked through a system of signs with Western culture. Prior to *Ost und West*, the Jews of the West had portrayed the Jewish arriviste as a direct descendant of the negatively marked *Ostjude* (for example, in the fiction of Karl Emil Franzos).[50] Despite all pretenses, the parvenu of Eastern lineage could never be enlightened or cultured enough. The Jewish social climber had been typified as craving the property of non-Jews in the manner of *Schacher- und Wucherjudentum* ("haggling and usurious Jewry"). The theory of Jewish history behind these stereotypes located spiritual and/or moral renewal in the modern Western Diaspora. It was hoped that the forces of progressivism would defeat the Jewish parvenu and his Eastern cousins.

In contrast to the "unassimilable" nouveaux riches from the East, the new Jewish parvenu of *Ost und West* was defined differently. *He*—the parvenu was inevitably a man—was held to be too modernized and, above all, too westernized. In the journal's contemporary fiction (*Zeitprosa*), this Western parvenu was also blind to the antisemitism that surrounded him. (It was rarely explained that historical limitations on Jewish professions in German territories were to blame for parvenuism.) Non-Jews in these stories were the avaricious ones; they rapaciously stole money and possessions from the Jews. In addition, spiritual renewal was no longer to be found in the West European Diaspora. From this standpoint, Eastern Jewish culture, no longer ideologically tainted, was elevated to the more progressive position.

How did this transition in the history of the parvenu stereotype take place in *Ost und West?* In the first five years of its German-language prose fiction, the "newer" Jewish parvenu became increasingly predominant. In 1901, three of the twelve prose contributions featured this character; in 1902, two of fifteen; in 1903, two of sixteen; in 1904, five of nineteen; and, in 1905, four of eighteen. In other words, the percentage of parvenu stories vis-à-vis other fiction shows a fall and then a slow but steady rise in the first five years of *Ost und West:* in 1901, 25 percent; in 1902, 13 percent; in 1903, 11 percent; in 1904, 26 percent; in 1905, 22 percent. This trend toward stereotyping of Western Jewish parvenus—part of the general trend toward negative stereotyping in *Ost und West*—culminated in four satirical sketches of Berlin Jewish parvenus that appeared in 1904 and 1905.[51] Set in Berlin, *Ost und West's* publication site and largest market, these Naturalist sketches were intended to shock. Instead, they most likely bore out the presuppositions of the journal's more intellectual readers. Since narratives of Western parvenus never ceased to be popular in *Ost und West*, I will close discussion of this genre in 1906, at which time the journal became somewhat less strident, emphasizing scholarship and education over manifestos and myth making. By that time, *Ost und West* had also stabilized financially and had taken on new readers beyond the intellectual audience delineated here.

In targeting its intellectual readers in the German-Jewish community, *Ost und West* appealed to the two types of Jewish identity at the root of their ethnic sensibilities: the Eastern-religious and the Western-enlightened. *Ost und West* published stereotypes of parvenu Jews that played on the ethnic loyalties of these readers, regardless of whether they were more traditional or more modern in orientation.

To begin with, *Ost und West*'s parvenu was a revision of earlier stereotypes of Jewish religious apostates. Lothar Brieger-Wasservogel's "Das alte Testament" (November 1901) is one of many such examples. A satire of German Jews as irreligious arrivistes, this narrative is typical of *Ost und West*'s earliest literary contributions, appearing as it does in the framework of a Naturalist sketch narrated in the present tense.[52] In "Das alte Testament," Baron von Goldstein, a wealthy ennobled businessman, holds an improbable discussion of conscience with an old talking Bible. This Old Testament is the last remaining evidence of his Jewish heritage, a family heirloom originally acquired by his great-grandfather, a Jewish peddler (*Hausierer*).[53]

Goldstein represents *Ost und West*'s new breed of Western-based Jewish parvenus. He is characterized as a successfully assimilated parvenu, proud of what he has achieved through years of hard work. Since being baptized, Goldstein has become a major financier of the Conservative party. He intimates that he will vote for an antisemite in the next *Reichstag* elections just to prove that he is truly a devout Christian. The acquisition of money and power has preoccupied him to such an extent that he is only now, in middle age, on the verge of marrying. At the threshold of complete assimilation, however, his origins become an obstacle. Although a respected and honored citizen and engaged to the precious daughter of General von Hohenheim, Goldstein is still a Jew and a "Finanzaristokrat" (849). For all this Jew's achievements, he is still despised by the *real*—that is, non-Jewish—aristocrats.[54] Integration is a chimera.

Still not acknowledging the antisemitism surrounding him, Goldstein—the apostate-*Protz* par excellence—spitefully glances at the dusty, web-covered Bible every night, "as if he wanted to boast that he had gone beyond that" (850). One evening, the Bible actually begins to talk to him, launching into a critique of the German-Jewish symbiosis. It declares that Jews and Christians "inflict evil upon each another. . . . And all who have dreamed of an inward friendship between Aryans and Semites were starry-eyed idealists" (851). At this point, the talking Old Testament accuses Goldstein of self-deception, reminding him of the tears that he cries when he slips away secretly to the Jewish cemetery. The Bible warns him, on the eve of his marriage to the daughter of von Hohenheim, that intermarriage will be of no benefit and that the children of such a union will only be "unhappy hybrids" (*unglückselige Zwitter*) (854).

How was Goldstein a new but old version of the Jewish parvenu stereotype? In contrast to his nineteenth-century predecessors in *Der Israelit* and elsewhere, he is estranged from his Eastern roots. Whereas it might appear that Goldstein's conversion is a mere confessional matter, Brieger-Wasservogel, in typical *Ost und West* fashion, situated it in a West European context. The conventional Eastern Jewish lineage of the German-Jewish parvenu was thus strikingly absent. Goldstein's earliest possible Eastern Jewish ancestor would have been his great-grandfather, and there is never a suggestion that this man, a Bible-reading peddler, was from Eastern Europe.

Even if there is no reference to any ancient Western Jewish lineage, Goldstein is entirely of the West. Although marked physically as a Jew—he is described as short, overweight, and large-nosed—his behavior is thoroughly "civilized." He is so secularized, in fact, that he is ignorant of the texts that make up the Jewish religious tradition. Although antisemites in the story mock Goldstein behind his back, the Jewish reader of *Ost und West* was encouraged to conceive of Goldstein as the epitome of Western capitalist culture. And although the Bible and the era it represents became the basis for Jewish renewal in "Das alte Testament," the Diaspora, the site of Goldstein's degeneracy, loomed even larger. *Ost und West's* readers had been warned.

In "Das alte Testament," as in many other texts from *Ost und West*, the stereotype of the Jewish parvenu played on the religious Eastern outlook of certain Jewish readers. But the strength of traditional anti-apostate sentiments also made new ideals of Jewish ethnicity difficult to realize in the journal's fiction. As noted previously, *Ost und West* could not reach Western Jewish intellectuals or a larger audience solely by invoking a positive image of Eastern Jewish folk culture. In "Das alte Testament" and elsewhere, the drawing power of the caricature of the Jewish *Geldprotz* was its negative overtones and its focus on present evils instead of a utopian past. Accordingly, satirical German-Jewish *Zeitprosa* such as "Das alte Testament" became the preferred genre in *Ost und West* and was programmatically enshrined as a model in the journal's literary contest of 1902:

> The work must be written in the German language and taken if possible from the life of West European Jews. It cannot of course be one of the popular milieu descriptions that only capture the externalities of Jewish life. Instead it should be a literary contribution to the psychology of modern Jewry. One of the deeper problems that moves the Jews of today should be addressed and an excerpt provided from the individual, social, cultural, or political relations of modern Jews. (February 1902: 129)

This literary model tacitly redefined stereotypes such as the Jewish parvenu as Western. Through this and an accompanying art contest, Winz and company aimed to attract young Jewish nationalists, as readers and contributors, to his new publishing venture.[55] But the magazine never issued a first-place award, though promising to publish other meritorious stories submitted to the competition. From the second-prize honoree, however, we can derive the preferences of the editorial staff and special panel of judges. The story, Ernst Guggenheim's "Der Rabbi" (November 1902), is a mysterious, avant-garde treatment of a young rabbi falling away from Judaism. On account of his doubt, he is banished from the fold by his rabbi father and cantor brother.[56] But the novella was so multivalent as to defy interpretation. Was the villain the father, the brother, or the protagonist? What Guggenheim's novella presumably lacked, for the first prize, was a less concealed treatment of its characters' origins and a more clearly delineated attack on Western Jewish mores.[57]

The failure of *Ost und West*'s literary contest to attract more sophisticated and less clichéd treatments of the Western Jewish predicament shows how difficult it was to construct a believable and truly new Jewish hero. Unlike the vivid Western arriviste, the positive Jewish hero was hackneyed and artificial, a lifeless distillation of a partisan-political standpoint (Zionist, Liberal Jewish, etc.). *Ost und West*'s literary contest thus failed to attract new, plausible models for the elusive "true-to-life Jew."[58] The fictional idealizations of Eastern Jewish cultural traditions that were generated by a cultural critique of the West did not yet work as an attractive theme for a literary contest in *Ost und West.*

The failure of *Ost und West*'s literary contest was predictable, given the more general type of social-critical narratives available to Jewish nationalists. Consider "Mauschel" (1897), Theodor Herzl's better-known but no less poisonous polemic.[59] This essay, published originally under a pseudonym in *Die Welt*, depicted a Jewish Uncle Tom figure who was stunted, degenerate, and shabby. Herzl's attack, in this case, did not befit his great skill as a feuilletonist. Nouveau riche and gaudy, this degenerate Jew, whose traits were borrowed from the repertoire of antisemitism, was a foil for the Zionist agenda. That Herzl's target was generally understood to be the Western Jewish parvenu is evidenced in Winz's decision to republish the essay.

Herzl's successful foray into stereotyping still failed to supplant negative imagery with a positive model for Western Jewish identity formation. Moreover, there was no shortage of negative images of Jews in the surrounding culture, and caricatures were common in *Simplicissimus* (Munich, 1896–1940 and 1954–1967) and *Fliegende Blätter* (Munich, 1844–1944), the leading satire magazines in Germany. As expected, the negative stereotype of the Western Jewish parvenu à la Brieger-Wasservogel was destined to be more attractive to readers than dry models of ethnicity. But, as we have seen, *Ost und West*'s literary contest of 1902 did not pretend to foster positive image making. Instead, Winz and his team urged the creation of a new Jewish parvenu as a foil. Having identified a new evil, *Ost und West* could now save pan-Jewish culture from it.

Predictably, *Ost und West* did not publish stories whose appeal was based on the most modern form of Judaism, Western "confessional" Judaism. Generally, *Ost und West* repudiated secular Jews and strove to redefine their origins in light of an ethnic Judaism that included religious tradition.

91

But as the new parvenu stereotype developed, *Ost und West*'s ethnic bias drew on both religious argument and modern social thought, especially in its criticism of the lopsided professional structure of German Jewry. In addition, the medium for denouncing the Western parvenu was almost exclusively secular: satirical *Zeitprosa*.

As this agenda crystallized in the wake of the literary contest of 1902, *Ost und West* published satirical sketches of so-called Berlin *Tiergartenjudentum* with increasing frequency.[60] The Jews parodied here resided in the fashionable Tiergarten neighborhood on the west side of the city. The Tiergarten was populated by Jews beyond their proportion of the German population, and along with the rest of "Berlin W.," it became the location of choice for parvenus of all faiths. For the Jewish geography of Berlin was as polarized as that of Europe generally. The more westernized Jews lived in the suburbs of Wilmersdorf, Charlottenburg, Schöneberg, and Tiergarten; the more recently immigrated Eastern Jewish population—which grew more rapidly than ever before between 1900 and 1905—traditionally settled on the east side, in the *Scheunenviertel*, the center of Berlin, and Prenzlauer Berg.[61]

Ost und West's literary programmatics were best realized in two outstanding fictions of *Tiergartenjuden* from 1905 that address the social composition of Berlin Jewry: Siegbert Salter's "Szene aus Berlin W. Die Tempelfahrt" (September 1905) and "Das Glück des Hauses Löbenthal. Skizze aus Berlin W." (December 1905).[62] In each work, a sketch of western Berlin life becomes the vehicle for a social-psychological critique of German Jewry as assimilationist (see fig. 6). Both are biting critiques of *Tiergartenjudentum* in the style of Thomas Mann's *Wälsungenblut* (1905).[63] Mann's novella also featured parvenu Jews and may have even influenced Salter's anti-assimilationist tales.[64]

"Szene aus Berlin W. Die Tempelfahrt" was very timely, appearing as it did in the September issue at the Jewish High Holy Day season. In this narrative, Salter portrays a wealthy Jewish *Kommerzienratsfamilie* dining on Yom Kippur eve. Suddenly cognizant that they are eating ham, the family is moved to repent and decides to attend the service at the Reform temple. Having made postservice reservations at Kempinsky's, a first-class restaurant, they hurry out, only to encounter traffic en route to the synagogue. While waiting in line near the temple, the daughter discovers that the mother has accidentally left her pearl-embroidered brocade and expensive earrings at home: "The ladies were inconsolable. Going to temple like that? Not wearing any symbol of status [*Abzeichen*]? Like the wife of just any old businessman?—Impossible" (596). Since they view services as nothing more than an opportunity for conspicuous display, the wife and daughter want to return home to retrieve the jewelry. Taking advantage of the situation, the father dispenses with services altogether, whispering to the coachman (so that the other templegoers will not overhear him): "To Kempinsky's!"

While Salter seems to excoriate Jewish parvenuism on religious grounds alone, his presuppositions concerning Jewish identity and its boundaries are also based on secular criteria. For why has the wife forgotten her costly jewels in the first place? The mishap results from a distraction prior to leaving for temple. Wealthy Gentile philanthropists pay a visit, seeking a contribution for the conversion of black children in German Southwest Africa to Christianity. The Kommerzienrat's wife does not quite comprehend the matter in its entirety, but when a young "poet-philosopher" asks her if she thinks that the little "Neger" should be converted to Judaism, she replies: "'What an idea, Herr Doktor. To Christianity, of course.' But whether to Christianity of a Catholic or Protestant persuasion—this she wasn't sure about" (594). This discussion, though ostensibly about conversion, tacitly raises the question of which "races" can be assimilated. The parvenu's wife reveals the extent of her acculturation in agreeing to respond to this test of national loyalty. In the course of the visit of these "Delegates of the Association for the Conversion of Black Negro Children (*schwarze Negerkinder*) in Southwest Africa," the Jewish parvenus are subtly associated with these African blacks. The implication is that the visitors perceive all Jews, regardless of status, as "white Negroes."[65]

Three months later, in the December 1905 issue of *Ost und West*, another Salter parody of Berlin Tiergarten Jews appeared, entitled "Das Glück des

Figure 6. John Höxter, drawing for Siegbert Salter's "Das Glück des Hauses Löbenthal. Skizze aus Berlin W." Ost und West *(December 1905): 797.*

Hauses Löbenthal. Skizze aus Berlin W." Like the Aarenholds in Thomas Mann's *Wälsungenblut*, the Löbenthals seek to marry their daughter off to a nobleman, a marriage of convenience that weds money to status. The difference between the two novellas lies in the source of the betrayal perpetrated in each. In Salter's story, the Gentile, Baron Reck, turns out to be an impostor who steals money and jewelry from the Jews; in Mann's novella, it is the Jew, Sigmund, who deflowers his sister and leaves her Gentile fiancé with "damaged goods." Despite these differences, both Salter and Mann portray the Jews as ruthless social climbers whose parvenuism knows no bounds. The Löbenthals have repeatedly tried and failed to enter "good society." As classic assimilationists, they delude themselves that prestige will be theirs once their daughter, with her "deep black Oriental eyes and aquiline nose" (799), has married the young baron. The narrator's aperçu that the Löbenthals are received everywhere with open arms—"all the more, since they always came with open hands" (798)—presages Reck's chicanery at the end of the story.

In contrast to the Gentile fiancé in Mann's novella, Baron Reck is portrayed as a decadent, much closer in type to the Jewish *Protz* Sigmund. He pretends to fear his parents' reaction to the marriage and that they might even withhold his inheritance. In the story's dénouement, Reck is absent from the engagement dinner. The duped Löbenthal finds a letter from Reck at his hotel, from which he has checked out earlier that afternoon. Reck maintains in the note that his family has forced him to desist from his plans, and he apologizes for this "indiscretion" that is making his heart "bleed" (800). The jewelry Löbenthal had provided for Reck to choose a gift for his bride is also missing. In the end, Löbenthal never seems to grasp that the impostor baron has robbed him, a narrative irony sustained by Löbenthal's guileless ponderings, such as "Curiously enough," "Strangely," "Quite incomprehensibly" (800). Particularly incomprehensible to him is the circumstance that the "illustrious" Reck family—a cruel hoax—has been able to conceal its existence so effectively, "despite the most thorough-going investigations" (802). In short, the non-Jew is able to double-cross Löbenthal because of the latter's pathological desire to assimilate.

In Salter's "Das Glück des Hauses Löbenthal," the Western Jew becomes a degenerate assimilator and not just another religious apostate. Löbenthal has become completely dissociated from Eastern Jewish customs. Yet details of Salter's portrayal are similar to antisemitic renderings of Eastern Jewish parvenus; in fact, Löbenthal possesses negative characteristics usually reserved for *Ostjuden*, such as greed, exploitation, and marriage brokering. His investments in South Africa and political support for the importation of "coolie" labor render him all the more suspicious. Professionally, then, he is also sullied, a product of the wrong social milieu.

Salter's sketches of *Tiergartenjudentum* contained the basic elements of many other stories in the journal. But neither these nor other early stories in *Ost und West* feature a Jewish character with positive features. Here again, *Ost und West* made negative stereotyping of Western Jewish parvenus its primary vehicle for imagining a new "ethnic" Jew. This new Jew was defined negatively and with an eye toward both Western and Eastern Jewish intellectuals; he was thus neither a parvenu with a conventional Jewish profession (the Kommerzienrat, Löbenthal) nor a religious apostate (Goldstein) nor a boor ignorant of Jewish culture (Goldstein, the Kommerzienrat, and Löbenthal).

The popularity of these sketches in *Ost und West* suggests that Jewish elites had begun to internalize the *jüdischer Protz* as an "anti-Jew" who was Western through and through. If this is the case, the reigning historiographical view that the Eastern Jews were the sole targets of Jewish antisemitism (or "self-hatred") is in need of revision.[66] Escaping from the stereotype of parvenu Jew went hand in hand with the heightened Jewish nationalism of many young Eastern Jews and the antibourgeois sentiments of many young Western Jews. For German-Jewish returners, Eastern Jewry became a symbolic surrogate family, a way to reject their Western Jewish homes.[67] This negative path to Eastern Jewish identity had become hackneyed by 1919, when Kafka penned his "Letter to His Father" (*Brief an den Vater*). Though set in Prague, this document became the most famous literary rejection of the parvenu thought to lurk within every Western Jewish home.[68]

Ost und West's redefinition of Jewish parvenuism for its intellectual audience was influenced by current events. Indeed, the rise of Jewish arriviste characters in the journal after 1903 is inseparable from the political developments of that year. The *Altneuland* controversy, for one, actually may have inspired the satirical sketches of Berlin *Tiergartenjudentum* in *Ost und West*. Although Herzl continued to be beloved within Jewish nationalist circles, these fictions evoked his parvenu-like past as well as his status as a new arrival (*Neuankömmling*) in Jewish circles. The publication of parvenu narratives in *Ost und West* was also bolstered by the Kishinev pogroms of April 6–7, 1903. Along with the pogroms following the Russian revolution of 1905, Kishinev provoked an international outcry comparable only to that accompanying the Shoah (despite the fact that those murdered, wounded, or displaced in 1903 numbered in the thousands rather than the millions).[69] This latest antisemitic violence and mounting attacks on Jews in the decade prior to World War I seemed to justify the literary condemnation of the Jewish *Protz* in *Ost und West.*[70]

One additional factor may have focused *Ost und West's* attack on the Western parvenu: the magazine's debt burden. Insolvency always loomed over *Ost und West* despite evidence of a boom in print media since the 1880s. The move to incorporate in 1904 was as much an attempt to manage debt as a sign of success. In fact, Winz renegotiated contracts with business partners nearly once a year until 1914 (another reason many contemporaries speak of him as an adroit businessman). The fact that most new publishing houses at this time folded within five years testifies to his perseverance.[71]

By 1906, *Ost und West*'s output reached 9,000, qualifying it as the second most widely sold Jewish periodical in Germany and suggesting that its version of a new ethnic Judaism had begun to resonate beyond the intellectual community. Its stereotyping of the Western Jewish arriviste had proved to be successful—and even profitable. Despite renewed antisemitism in Russia, Rumania, and Germany, 1906 was a decisive transition year for *Ost und West*, particularly on account of the deal with the Alliance.[72] That Winz himself may have been something of a parvenu after 1905, at least in the publishing world, is indicated by his relocation in 1907 to Berlin-Charlottenburg. While he never quite made it into the Tiergarten neighborhood, his magazine was appraised in 1914 at 250,000 marks, and for the next decade, he was regarded as a wealthy man.

After 1906, Winz's magazine became something of a trendsetter in the world of German-Jewish journalism. Seeking to profit from the success of *Ost und West*, three other major Jewish literary-cultural monthlies began publication during the Imperial period: *Die Freistatt*, *Der Jude*, and *Neue jüdische Monatshefte*. To varying degrees, each of these journals juxtaposed Eastern Jewish art and literature with negative images of the rich Jewish show-off (*Geldprotz*). Like *Ost und West*, they made their ethnic particularism acceptable to Jews and other would-be *Bildungsbürger* by presenting themselves as an alternative to the existing Jewish publications in Germany and by placing a revival of Jewish ethnicity at the top of their agenda. As in *Ost und West*, these objectives were largely accomplished by means of the conceptual shorthand of stereotyping, in particular the stereotyping of parvenu *Westjuden*.

Each of these ethnic Jewish journals derided its competitors as partisan or as low-brow "family" journalism. Yet they also borrowed generously from their "inferior" colleagues' tactics. As *Ost und West* became more established and its lean years came to a close, Eastern Jews and other intellectuals rapidly lost their status as the journal's main addressees. For despite *Ost und West*'s sophisticated layout and presentation, its editors were never content with appealing to the Jewish avant-garde of both Europes. As outlined in chapters 1 and 2 above, the journal always sought to be middle-brow, reaching out to a broad audience of Central European Jews by using the latest public relations techniques. The next chapters investigate how *Ost und West* reached out to German Jewry as a whole after its first years, in particular to middle-class women and men.

Even though its program was more Eastern than Western Jewish, *Ost und West* came to be read by a less elite Jewry in Germany. The broad Jewish audience valued the magazine for combining ethnic separatism with integrationist elements; the Western Jewish intelligentsia continued to be drawn to its respectable Jewish nationalism.[73] As a pan-Jewish cultural institution, then, *Ost und West* did not just mirror the values and practices of Wilhelminian Jewish culture; it also shaped Jewish self-representations in a constant dialogue with social and political trends. By advancing negative stereotypes of Western-based Jewish arrivistes, *Ost und West* became a major force in redefining Western Jewish identity. As we shall now see, *Ost und West* became even more proficient after 1906 at the revising and dissemination of stereotypes. The Western parvenu character, as expected, never lost its negative appeal. The Eastern-religious and Western-enlightened elements of the parvenu stereotype were both used to appeal to *Ost und West*'s next major subaudience, middle-class German-Jewish women.

4

The Philanthropic Parvenue and the Uplifted *Ostjude:* German-Jewish Women and *Ost und West*

In the last chapter, we showed how the stereotype of the Jewish parvenu became the centerpiece of *Ost und West*'s campaign to promote ethnic Jewish identity among a group of German Jews with a specific social and political profile: male intellectuals. For this group, the Jewish arriviste had become the ultimate affront to Judaism, regardless of whether that Judaism was Eastern, Western, or some combination of the two. The Jewish parvenu character, as depicted in *Ost und West*'s cautionary tales, provided the Jewish cultural elite with a negative role model.

But Jewish male intellectuals in Germany were not the only ones outraged by parvenu Jews. Jewish women also reacted negatively to carica-tures of themselves. In fact, the 1913 creation of a Jewish female parvenu (or *parvenue*) by Binjamin Segel is only one indication of how important women were to become as readers of *Ost und West*. Many factors point to a significant female readership at the peak of the journal's success between 1906 and 1914. Thus, even though most of the parvenus stereotyped in *Ost und West* were men and most of their creators were men, the audience meant to consume these images may have been at least 25 percent female. And while most Eastern Jewish students in Germany and most native German-Jewish literati were men, a significant portion of the magazine's audience were women. Female readers were even addressed directly at times.[1] The authors of "show-off" novellas (*Protznovellen*), then, may have been Jewish males, but their implied readers were just as often Jewish women.[2]

Few of the women reading *Ost und West* were from Eastern Europe, however. The only significant group of Eastern Jewish women living in the West were Russian women students, and they numbered only in the dozens.[3] *Ost und West* was directed at the Jewish woman who was German or Austrian and lived in an urban setting such as Berlin or Vienna. Though she may have been intellectually inclined, she was less likely to be a university student, writer, or artist than to be confined to an upper-middle-class household. Like her sisters of previous generations, the Jewish bourgeoise was quite contemporary in her tastes, as the advertising in *Ost und West* confirms. But unlike her early-nineteenth-century predecessors, who converted out of Judaism, the women who read *Ost und West* were generally opposed to assimilation.[4] In fact, women of all ranks within German-Jewish society were less likely to leave the fold than were men during the Wilhelminian era.[5] There was, as a result, less of a need for Jewish parvenue characters. Besides, when *Ost und West* used negative stereotyping of male parvenus, it already had a receptive audience in middle-class Jewish women.

A comparison with intellectual male readers reveals how it was possible for *Ost und West* to promote the *Ostjuden* to a middle-class audience of Western Jewish women. While the journal had a distinctive Eastern Jewish bias that seemed unlikely to appeal to the Western Judaism of German-Jewish women, Winz and his associates were steadfast in their effort to build a Jewish female audience. First, they assumed that the average Wilhelminian Jewish woman, like her male intellectual counterparts, would detest the Jewish nouveau riche character. To this end, *Ost und West* played on both the enlightened and religious aspects of German-Jewish female identity. Second, the journal's editors experimented with positive stereotypes meant to attract German-Jewish women, who were less likely than Jewish male intellectuals to have engaged in debate about Jewish ethnicity and who may even have been sensitive to *Ost und West*'s negative stereotyping and masculine rhetoric. For a period in the magazine's history, then, it was thought that romanticized images of male Eastern Jews would make ethnic Judaism acceptable to philanthropically inclined Jewish women in the West. This group was more susceptible to such an approach since it was bound to the domestic sphere and was thus not as familiar with real *Ostjuden* as the male intellectual clientele of *Ost und West*.

Yet *Ost und West* could not produce convincing positive stereotypes of *Ostjuden*, as seen above in chapter 3. In their dubious attempts to help Western Jewish women identify with such Jews, the journal's writers came up with Eastern Jewish characters that were as unthreatening as possible. Dependent and childlike, these characters were palimpsests derived from older negative stereotypes of Eastern Jews. This "philanthropic" approach to the *Ostjuden*, often referred to as *Ghettojuden*,[6] was rife for misinterpretation and threatened to subvert *Ost und West*'s mission. Soon it was discarded in favor of more reliable practices: negative stereotyping and satire. In reorienting their approach to Jewish female readers, *Ost und West*'s editors decided to publish stereotypes of the Western Jewish parvenue. Women reading the magazine were urged to detest such social climbers, who, it was suggested, could never become caring mothers and wives.

One caveat: this chapter is not a materialist history of women and reading, something that remains to be undertaken for Wilhelminian Jewish women (and for women in other cultures). Instead, this chapter focuses on the discourse of reading and gender encountered in *Ost und West*. In particular, it looks at how the magazine encouraged a sympathetic, identificatory response from German-Jewish female consumers, though any number of them may have remained cool to the idea of an ethnic, pan-Jewish identity.

In redefining the identity of German-Jewish women through stereotypes, the editors of *Ost und West* also showed a deep understanding of the historical place of women in Judaism. While limited by tradition to the home, where it was their duty to preserve Judaism against challenges from without, Jewish women were permitted extensive contact with the profane world, even the non-Jewish culture surrounding them. This involved no contradiction under Jewish law (*halakha*); women were not required to observe the commandments and prohibitions that obtained for men. In theory they enjoyed more freedom to interact with their Gentile neighbors and their cultures. Men were ideally to spend their days studying Talmud in small groups, while women were supposed to manage the household, if not the family business.[7]

In the eighteenth century, Jewish women in Germany came into ever greater contact with non-Jewish culture. German-Jewish women borrowed from enlightened, non-Jewish institutions such as the bourgeois family and its culture of domesticity. Borrowing was not the same as imitating, however.[8] For example, German-Jewish women were the moral educators in their homes. But unlike their middle-class Christian sisters, they instilled in their families both religious and enlightened values that were uniquely Jewish. *Ost und West* recognized this crucial role played by German-Jewish women, often debunking arguments that the Talmud was antiwoman.[9]

Women living in *Ost und West*'s home base, Berlin, embodied the extremes of tradition and modernity, of Eastern and Western Judaism. For more than a century, these women—even more than their husbands—had belonged to the cultural elite of Germany. (Actually, many of their ancestors had been privileged "exception Jews," who belonged to the economic elite of Prussia.) Names such as Rahel Varnhagen (1771–1833), Henriette Herz (1764–1847), and Dorothea Schlegel (1763–1839) are inseparable from

100

German literary and artistic history around 1800. Yet, unlike these famous assimilating salon hostesses (*Salondamen*),[10] their more numerous Berlin Jewish counterparts of a century later became important agents of *dissimilation* in their homes. Two factors made this possible. First, Wilhelminian Jewish women were less likely than men to cut ties to Judaism. Second, they were highly educated. The majority of German-Jewish women had been literate since the Middle Ages, and one third of all female *Gymnasium* students in Berlin after 1900 were Jewish women—even though Jews made up only 5 percent of the Berlin population.

Precisely such women spearheaded philanthropic and educational activities in the Jewish community and were a major force behind relief efforts to Eastern Jewry. One such Berlin Jewish woman was Felice Bauer, the fiancée of Franz Kafka. Even though Kafka knew of *Ost und West* (but may not have subscribed), Bauer appears to have been a regular reader who brought his attention to important reviews in the journal.[11] While Bauer did not engage herself with Eastern Jewry as thoroughly as Kafka might have wished, she did act upon his suggestion to attend lectures at Siegfried Lehmann's *Jüdisches Volksheim*.[12]

Like many other women, Bauer's Jewish awareness was reinforced in the religious and social spheres. As a result, re-ethnification was not as pressing an agenda for her as it was for her fiancé and other Jewish intellectual men. Yet, at the same time, their traditional and modern loyalties made German-Jewish women receptive to *Ost und West*'s ethnic Judaism. This fact, along with the general participation of women in Eastern and Western Jewish culture since the *Haskalah*, has been the subject of little scholarship. Conventionally, it has been assumed that women were passive recipients rather than active producers of Jewish culture.[13] But, in fact, much of ethnic Jewish culture in Germany was shaped by women. While their contributions to Jewish nationalism may have been less conspicuous than those of men, they were no less significant. Women played an important role in sustaining all types of Jewish culture—Eastern, Western, and ethnic. Often stereotyped as the "inferior" readers of devotional works translated from Hebrew, Eastern Jewish women were the first readers of modern Yiddish literature.[14] Often stereotyped as seductive salon hostesses, Western Jewish women in the age of Enlightenment were champions of German arts and letters.

Studying *Ost und West* helps us grasp how central middle-class women were in the dissemination of ethnic Jewish identity. Nineteenth-century Jewish women acted in myriad ways as cultural intermediaries, especially as agents of class formation and representation.[15] Within the domestic sphere, Jewish women, like their non-Jewish sisters, became avid consumers of culture. In contrast to men, who worked outside the home, middle-class women and children had more time available to read books and journals. As household technology improved and the middle class prospered in

Germany, Jewish women were reading more than ever. Seeing women as active journal readers is thus a counterweight to standard historiography that sees Jewish women as passive recipients.

Outside the home, women of the Jewish middle classes also played a major role in building an urban-oriented Wilhelminian Jewish culture.[16] They subscribed, for example, to the new circulating libraries for Jews.[17] Beyond the realm of books and periodicals, more and more urban bourgeois women were also participating in extrafamilial activities by the 1890s, attending meetings, small salons, and lecture series for women. Having the requisite leisure time and money, German-Jewish women also went to theaters, cafés, and concerts, where they at times outnumbered Gentile women.[18] The *Ost und West Verlag* produced occasional evening performances of music and recitation, the so-called young Jewish *Liederabende*, in an attempt to attract the female audience. The 1912 *Liederabende* in Berlin, Leipzig, Breslau, Munich, Nuremberg, Hamburg, and Hanover were by all accounts an exemplary success.[19] Reviewed in both the Jewish and the non-Jewish press, such concerts were again sponsored by Winz in 1919, filling one Berlin venue with seating for 2,000.[20]

To attract an audience of Western Jewish women to ethnic Jewishness, *Ost und West* instituted up-to-date marketing practices. As a self-proclaimed innovator in the field of print advertising, Winz sought to make his magazine desirable to audiences who may not have felt a direct need for it. *Ost und West* was presented as the perfect consumer item for the German-Jewish family. Its acknowledged goal was to reach as many Jewish households as possible.[21] The magazine's first editorial thus ended with the hope that *Ost und West* might "secure a place in every Jewish home."[22]

This obvious appeal to women showed that Winz was looking to expand the readership of *Ost und West.* In Germany alone, there was a market of 200,000 potential Jewish women readers, approximately 50,000 of whom resided in Berlin. (The potential market in the Habsburg empire was even larger.) In the prewar years, *Ost und West* could afford to charge what the market would bear for advertising space. In fact, its advertising fees were the highest for all Jewish periodicals in Germany.[23] Advertisements could be found at the front and back of each issue; on occasion, they took up a sixth of the space. This led Winz to claim—or, better, to exaggerate—that *Ost und West* carried "*more* advertisements" in its twenty-three-year history "than any other general-interest periodical in Germany."[24] The key to its success, then, was advertisers, not subscribers.

That *Ost und West* was in part geared toward women is in no small measure because of its female director of advertising, Elsa Jacoby. Jacoby, who later married Winz, was not only his personal secretary but also his deputy after 1914. Women were targeted by promotions ranging from books and journals to household and luxury items. (One department store, Berlin's Kaufhaus des Westens, advertised both women's garments and its lending

102

library in *Ost und West*.)[25] Just because images of women permeated such advertisements does not mean, of course, that most readers were women. Nevertheless, the magazine's elegant appearance was pivotal in attracting both advertisers and female consumers. The Winzes, who published the *Gemeindeblatt der jüdischen Gemeinde zu Berlin* after 1927, repeatedly chided the earlier editors of that magazine for their lack of aesthetic refinement.[26]

The purchase of a stylish journal also conferred status, and *Ost und West* cultivated its image as a family journal (*Familienblatt*) of a higher niveau, seeking to become an upper middle class Jewish version of *Die Gartenlaube*.[27] Unlike its popular contemporary, however, *Ost und West* did not suggest that the upper strata of its audience divorce themselves from the "masses"—in this case, the Eastern Jews and the Jewish lower classes in Germany. Nor was *Ost und West* beyond the reach of working-class Jews: a subscription to the magazine was possible at the price of seven marks per year (less than a week's wages for a common laborer).[28] The low price of *Ost und West*, subsidized in effect by advertising revenues, was a key factor in the magazine's success among middle-class Jews. This was especially true for women, who actually may have subscribed on behalf of their families.

While it did not pose as a practical adviser as many German popular magazines did, *Ost und West* complemented etiquette books and other such "professional" texts on advancing in Jewish circles.[29] Contact with the journal decisively enhanced a woman's ability to converse at social gatherings on Jewish issues as well as art and music. This function was crucial since many German upper-middle-class women were brought up to entertain others by discussing literature and art.[30] Women's interest in literature and art, however, did not preclude their being interested in the politics and theology published in *Ost und West*. The journal also helped women educate their children, for Jewish ethnicity was a topic rarely addressed in the theologically oriented religion class (*Religionsunterricht*) offered at school.

Ost und West, like other middle-brow cultural products, ultimately owed much of its success to women. German-Jewish women took advantage of their leisure time to promote Judaism and Jewish ethnicity to their children (and, in some cases, to their husbands).[31] Jewish women at the turn of the century were thus quite different from other middle-class women in Germany. While Goethe, Schiller, and Wagner stand out in the few surviving testimonies about the reading, listening, and viewing habits of German-Jewish women, these women were more and more drawn to the emerging variety of ethnic Jewish culture in places such as *Ost und West*. Indeed, some had never strayed from more traditional Western (or Eastern) forms of Judaism.[32]

German-Jewish women in the *Kaiserreich* were very influential in the areas of philanthropy and social welfare. Although urged to limit themselves to household affairs, they found new public outlets for fulfillment at the outset of the twentieth century in humanitarian and relief work. These primary expressions of Jewish female identity were not without precedent, however. Jewish women had practiced *tsedakah* (Hebrew for "justice," usually translated as "charity") for centuries. Traditional religious identity had led Jewish women to acts of benevolence (*mitzvot*) inside and outside the home.

With the spread of enlightened Judaism in the nineteenth century, education and paid employment became attractive options for Jewish women in the German lands. But religion, in addition to class pretension, was so strong a motivating factor in their public activities that the idea of the career woman was not fully accepted in the Jewish community until after World War I.[33] The identity of German-Jewish women at the end of the nineteenth century, then, was marked by a split between Eastern religiosity and Western secularism.[34] Throughout Central Europe at this time, new spheres of activity opened up for Jewish women having altruistic and social aspirations. The same women often participated in several different Jewish organizations—from traditional to modern, from religious charities to professional social work.[35] In Berlin, for example, a 1909 survey found that, whereas approximately 10,000 Jews belonged to one Jewish charitable organization, more than 7,000 belonged to two, and 1,100 belonged to three.[36] Also, the names of women involved in Jewish communal affairs often appeared in the membership lists of secular organizations, such as Ethical Culture.[37] With 5,000 clubs to choose from in Germany in 1906, Jewish women affiliated rapidly.[38]

Ost und West was one of several institutions that interested German-Jewish women, not least because of its rare combination of religious and enlightened Judaism. In addition to its other features that attracted women readers, the journal served as an update on Jewish philanthropy in Germany. The rise of *Ost und West* after its first years went hand in hand with the rise in Jewish women's associations. By the turn of the century, every sizable town in Germany had such an association, a development that led to the establishment of the Jewish Women's League (*Jüdischer Frauenbund*) in 1904.[39] In addition, women who were Jewish or of Jewish origin also played a leading role in the fin-de-siècle women's movement.[40]

Winz and his associates recognized that philanthropy was central to German-Jewish female identity in this epoch, and they sought to direct this philanthropy toward ethnic Judaism. (In fact, one of the first works of art reproduced in *Ost und West* showed women yearning for Zion; see fig. 7.) This agenda decisively influenced *Ost und West* after 1908, when the German law banning women's political activities (the *Vereinsgesetz*) was abolished.[41] Female Jewish ethnicity became a viable possibility in the *Kaiserreich*, as German-Jewish women's voluntarism moved away from old-fashioned religious *tsedakah* to a more secular approach to social welfare.

Helping the needy, sick, and hungry was the goal of the "social motherhood" ideology of the German women's movement, where some Jews played leading roles.[42] But the philanthropy of these women never lost its distinctive Jewish character. For the new "social housekeeping" approach to philanthropy called for individualized relief and the careful monitoring of clients' needs. And many of these clients were *Ostjuden*.

Eastern Jewish beggars, transients, and travelers often received charity from Jewish women in Germany. Those Jewish women who identified with Eastern Jews were, by *Ost und West*'s standards, making the right gesture. Their motives, even if self-serving, could be redirected into an Eastern Jewish nationalism. Yet they still shared the bourgeois civility of their non-Jewish sisters in Germany. At times, it appeared that their charitable activities were meant to protect or even promote their middle-class (or, in some cases, upper-class) status. This criticism of German-Jewish women is most relevant to their attitudes toward Eastern and other needy Jews. At worst, these women were disapproving of working-class Jews and *Ostjuden;* at best, their behavior was patronizing or paternalistic.[43] Precisely because it is difficult to draw the line between condescension and benevolence, this study will use the neutral term *philanthropic* to describe German-Jewish women's charity toward Jews perceived as their social inferiors.

Before analyzing how *Ost und West*'s writings about *Ostjuden* encouraged this form of altruism, we must first describe the social and cultural context of women's philanthropy toward Eastern Jewry. While the organizations German-Jewish women founded were among the most advanced in the field of social welfare, they also could be dauntingly professional in addressing the so-called plight of the *Ostjude*. *Ost und West* felt it necessary to attack this new philanthropy and its ideological derivatives. In A. Benesra's (Binjamin Segel's) "Philosophie der Zerstreuung" (January 1905), what appeared to be a modified plan for self-help was actually a veiled critique of Jewish welfare practices aimed at the Alliance Israélite Universelle and the Jewish Colonial Association.[44] (This critique, however, also may have been motivated by sexism, for the Alliance was popular with Jewish women, having been one of the first large Jewish organizations to admit women as members. Jewish women were repeatedly addressed in Alliance-sanctioned statements in *Ost und West*.)[45] These institutions, along with the Zionist movement, were regarded as having assumed the character of large fund-raising enterprises.[46] Political Zionism seemed to be expanding the Diaspora by accelerating the pace of Jewish migration. Instead of urging Jews to emigrate whenever possible, Segel advocated on-site efforts to change the political, economic, and social conditions where Jews already lived. He thus maintained that Jewish altruism was synonymous with self-help. By implementing new theories of social welfare and replacing the

Figure 7. Eduard Bendemann, "An den Wassern Babels" [By the Waters of Babylon]. Ost und West (January 1901): 15–16. (Courtesy of the Harry Ransom Research Center, University of Texas.)

old donor-oriented practices, a more equitable relationship might develop between Eastern Jews and Western Jews, one that emphasized the more neutral role of helper over that of custodian. The two were to be brought together under the banner of Jewish ethnicity.

But East-West Jewish relations were, in truth, not as patronizing as Segel described them. Even though many Jewish *Gemeinden* were condescending in their philanthropy, others (with Berlin at the forefront) spent a great deal of money to sensitize their members to the needs of impoverished Jews from the East (see introduction above). *Ost und West*'s altruism was for the most part ideologically neutral. To avoid offending other groups, it was not unusual for Winz and his colleagues to support both autonomous endeavors by Eastern Jews and Western-based relief efforts.[47]

The philanthropy of German-Jewish women at the turn of the century was also in a double bind. At certain times, these women betrayed a "certain distance and feeling of superiority" over Eastern Jews; at other times, their encounters with Eastern Jews were untroubled.[48] In short, there is little evidence that German-Jewish women despised their Eastern coreligionists.[49] Instead, they viewed it as their duty to help immigrant Jews adjust to German society.[50] Not bent on making foreign Jews assimilate,

106

they felt could inculcate them with Western middle-class values without maligning their Eastern Jewish religiosity, style of dress, or manner of speech. When in doubt, then, German Jewry interceded on behalf of Jews from the East, sensing that attacks on foreign Jews called into question their own security as citizens of the *Kaiserreich*.[51] Jewish women also volunteered to aid refugees through sponsoring adult education, girls' clubs, reading rooms, kindergartens, and vocational schools.

An example of this combined mission to educate and to uplift the Jewish lower classes through liberal philanthropy was the Toynbee Halls in London and Vienna. Reported on in *Ost und West* (April 1901) by its founder, Leon Kellner, the Viennese Toynbee Hall fostered Jewish-only education in a context hospitable to both wealthy and indigent Jews. This mission was accomplished by sponsoring free courses, tea evenings, and especially lectures and music. The hall, like similar institutions, was careful to include working-class Jews in these activities. Kellner boasted that Western Jews eventually stopped smirking when the Eastern Jews spoke up in Yiddish or Yiddish-accented German. By at least one account, contacts between women from East and West were cordial.[52] Apparently, the Toynbee Hall in Vienna was a minor success, drawing large audiences and competing successfully with other sensationalist amusements in Vienna, such as the "self-hating Jewish comedy" of the theater and "popular, non-Wagnerian music" of other venues.[53]

One other Viennese "amusement" discussed by Kellner was prostitution. Like Kellner, Jewish women perceived it as their duty to save Eastern Jewish women from the scourge of prostitution and the white slave trade. In this arena, Jewish philanthropy came to the fore again, hoping to uplift the "tainted" Jews of the East. Bertha Pappenheim (1859–1936), leader of the *Jüdischer Frauenbund*, wrote in *Ost und West* that Eastern Jewish prostitution was a shameful and "embarrassing" problem.[54] One of the more policy-oriented attempts to rectify the "debasement" of Eastern Jewish women was Fabius Schach's 1903 proposal in *Ost und West*. Schach, one of the journal's main contributors and himself an *Ostjude* from Riga (Latvia), favored employing the endangered women in domestic service. This was one of a number of proposals to train Russian and Galician Jewish girls to be maids.[55] Schach's plan had the advantage of seeing the moral (*sittlich*) issue as a "bleeding social question." At the same time, he claimed that his plan would rectify the lack of "good help" available.

The need of German-Jewish women to uplift the *Ostjuden* (and *Ostjüdinnen*) was incorporated in a new strategy that aimed to equate their philanthropic outlook with the "Eastern Jewish question." Schach and the other leading writers of *Ost und West* hoped to persuade middle-class women to identify positively with downtrodden Eastern Jews—and especially with young male artists. This strategy was among the journal's earliest efforts to promote Jewish ethnic identity to its female readers using a positive approach that eschewed negative stereotyping. Before describing this approach, we must briefly outline how it developed.

Few negative stereotypes of Western or Eastern Jewish women appear in the early years of *Ost und West*. While negative images of the Jewish male predominate in European history, more specific explanations are likely for the dearth of female caricatures in *Ost und West*. For one, Winz and his associates needed the Jewish female audience. Precisely because this audience was well organized and decidedly middle-class, the men behind *Ost und West* would have to reduce any overt misogyny. If they could not flatter Jewish female readers, then they could at least avoid offending them by adding to the negative images of the Jewish woman then appearing in humor magazines such as *Simplicissimus*. In addition, Winz and the contributors to the journal were undoubtedly aware of the relatively low rate of female apostasy in the *Kaiserreich*. Why criticize Jewish women, when they were one of the forces stemming the tide of assimilation?

Against this backdrop, *Ost und West* made an effort to promote a positive Jewish ethnic identity for women in its early years. In featuring strong role models, *Ost und West's* earliest essays and stories targeted women reared on Western Jewish religiosity and philanthropy. In fact, apostasy and intermarriage among women were thematized in the very first issue of the journal. One short article, "Beethoven's erste Liebe" (January 1901), reveals that Beethoven's first love was a German-Jewish woman who broke off the romance with the composer on her own initiative. What is interpreted as brave resistance to intermarriage set the tone for other discussions of female apostasy in *Ost und West*.[56] Since the journal constantly singled out Vienna's epidemic of baptisms (*Taufseuche*),[57] Winz published a satire featuring a positive *belle juive*.[58] Possibly written by Segel (under the pseudonym of "Ysaye"), "Die Jüdin. Eine Wiener Skizze" (April 1904)[59] directly confronts the issues of conversion and intermarriage. The central figure of this sketch is Renée Rothstein, a Jewish singer making her social debut at a Viennese ball.[60] An excellent artist, a true beauty, and of untarnished reputation,[61] Rothstein embodies the innocent, beautiful Jewess of lore. But as she enters the ball, she is snubbed by the other guests as well as the host. Since the host is also her escort, a minor scandal erupts. Rothstein responds with strength, decrying antisemitism and thus proving to *Ost und West's* (female) readers that apostasy of all kinds can be resisted.

Not all images in *Ost und West* of Jewish women challenged by apostasy were this sympathetic. The earliest and most negative image of the female apostate to appear was an undated painting by Nicolai Pimonenko (1862–1912) titled "Baptized Jewess in Her [Home] Village" (July 1901) (see fig. 8). In a dramatic scene set in Russia, Jews surround a young woman who has converted. This image was sold in reproduction by Winz's Phönix Verlag and was repeatedly advertised in *Ost und West*.[62]

Figure 8. Nicolai Pimonenko, "Getaufte Jüdin im Heimatsdorf." Ost und West *(July 1901): 489–90.*

The negative impact of conversion was also commonly hinted at in prose fiction about Jewish women. In stories such as Salter's "Die Tempelfahrt" (discussed above in chapter 3), the wives and daughters of parvenus were singled out for special treatment. Yet they were also relieved of responsibility: the male parvenu was invariably the butt of satire. Similarly, "Sünde: Aus dem Leben eines kleinen Mädchens" by Josefa Metz (May 1904) depicts Jewish women as more susceptible to minor lapses in observance than to the full-blown parvenuism of Jewish men. Eva Neuberg, the little girl of the satire's subtitle, behaves like a miniature version of her *Tiergartenjudentum* parents. This vain preadolescent is tortured by pangs of conscience while attending a Yom Kippur service at synagogue. The narrator takes the reader into Eva's stream of consciousness as she comes to terms with the sin of having recently eaten ham for the first time. The trivialization of this and other peccadilloes drives her superficial Judaism home to the reader. In the climactic scene, Eva falls asleep during the sermon and dreams of God sitting in judgment over her family. The God of her imagination resembles her assimilationist grandfather, who always kept a bust of Goethe on his desk. To her ultimate relief, Eva dreams that she is written into the Book of Life—not the Book of Death—on this Day of Atonement.

Even though Eva was just a little girl, she represented something new in *Ost und West*: a negative stereotype of a female apostate. While Jewish women reading "Sünde" might laugh at Eva's sins, they were encouraged to ask themselves how well they were educating their own children in things Jewish. What appeared innocuous was to become part of a new agenda intended to raise the ethnic consciousness of Jewish women reading *Ost und West*. The new program, delineated by Fabius Schach, intended to do away altogether with stereotypes that played on women's religious identity. In fact, Schach's "Zur Psychologie des Renegatentums" (July 1903) directly addresses German-Jewish women. In an effort to make them into good Jewish nationalists, he proposes replacing their fears of assimilation with idealized images of Eastern Jewry. At the outset, Schach issues an apologia for apostates, parvenus, and other Jewish renegades. Yet, halfway through his proscriptive essay, Schach turns anti-assimilationist and anti-apostate, calling directly on Jewish women readers to rescue Judaism by giving it an East European orientation.[63]

Schach takes a circuitous route to that conclusion. He begins by making reading his link between Western and Eastern Jewry. In the first paragraphs of "Zur Psychologie des Renegatentums," he offers a rare glimpse into how *Ost und West*'s main writers looked at reading, in particular the reading of Jewish texts. Having studied at the Volozhin *yeshiva*, the largest and best known in Eastern Europe, Schach makes a melodrama out of his own experiences of reading as a teenager: "At night I sit in my little room by candlelight and furtively read German books, trembling in awe, *like a delicate virgin who is reading her chosen one's declarations of love*" (452–53; emphasis added).[64] Here Schach compares an Eastern Jewish teenage boy to a Jewish woman, a connection that would become a preoccupation in *Ost und West* as the journal used positive stereotypes of *Ostjuden* to appeal to Jewish female readers.

To strengthen this connection of Eastern Jewish male to Western Jewish female, Schach's autobiographical narrative of westernization becomes more and more sentimental:

> And it comes over me like a heavenly torrent, as if a new, airy, free soul were entering me. And every German poem is a revelation, every new thought a fount of pure knowledge. And a wild, consuming yearning seizes me: Away from this stifling atmosphere, this world of rigid formulae and dead letters! Into the world of beauty and freedom! The first blossoms of love can never flower more delicately, more divinely than this fervor for culture [*Bildungsbrunst*]. (453)[65]

Reading is more than enlightening here; it becomes transgressive, unorthodox, even erotic. *Ost und West*, along with Schach, clearly hoped that German-Jewish women would be similarly affected by reading—with one crucial distinction: Winz and his associates wanted women to experience enthusiasm when reading about *Eastern Jewish* topics by *Eastern Jewish* authors. Schach offers Jewish women guidelines for reading the Eastern Jewish culture found in *Ost und West* in the following passage, where, in contrast to his earlier worship for Western culture, he begins to take critical stock of his youthful love:

> But then I look back on everything that has been dear to me until now, and I fear I have destroyed something. Two worlds struggle in my young breast;

I separate myself from much of the old with tears in my eyes, and vow that I
will become a messenger of light, a bearer of culture, devoting my life to the
enlightenment of my people. It happened to every one of us this way, just as
it had happened to our ancestors in western Europe a hundred years earlier.
(453)

In this passage, Schach shows empathy for male and female Jews who
acculturated in the Mendelssohnian era. He even appears—contrary to *Ost
und West*'s stereotyping of Jewish parvenus—to comprehend why some Jews
never returned to their traditional roots and never understood the culture
of the old (Eastern) world.[66]

But Schach does not believe that *tout comprendre c'est tout pardonner.*
He thus writes off his euphoria over German literature as a youthful
transgression. What is more, he serves up a new periodization of Jewish
history, indeed, of the history of Jewish assimilation. Drawing a strict line
after 1871, Schach condemns all forms of Jewish apostasy in the Second
Reich and reinterprets the epoch of Mendelssohn, the *maskilim*, and Gabriel
Riesser as the golden age of German Jewry. He is shocked that more Jews
than ever before are being baptized in the *Kaiserreich.* For him, conversion
is tantamount to violating the laws of 1869 and 1871 that granted Jews full
rights before the law (at least on paper). Schach now switches the thrust
of his previous stereotyping and attacks German-Jewish apostates as cold-
hearted opportunists completely lacking in character. In effect, he blames
the victims, arguing that the behavior of apostate Jews fuels antisemitism.
Jewish converts to Christianity—even if they are presumably citizens of the
German empire—are ultimately seen through the eyes of racialist science:
they are "sick" and "degenerate."

Having revised the history of Jewish renegades in such terms, Schach
finally strikes a compromise. His ideal Jew, the type catered to by *Ost
und West*, is a "Jewish modern" (*jüdischer Moderner*).[67] Engaging reader
interest by using the first-person plural, Schach lays out his agenda for
an ethnic Judaism: "We need to educate our Jewish youth better, in a
manner more geared toward the soul (*Seele*). We need good Jewish stories
and good Jewish poems that we can give to young people; we need a
revival of Jewish literature (*Poesie*), an awakening of the Jewish soul, in a
word: a kind of Jewish renaissance" (460). Characteristically, Schach places
culture at the center of his program against apostasy, thus departing little
from earlier pronouncements in *Ost und West* such as the unsuccessful
literary contest.[68] In addition, he contends that what is good for Jewish
youth is good for Jewish adults. Besides Jewish literature, all age groups
need Jewish art, popular Jewish scholarship, Jewish publishing houses,
inexpensive publications, enlightening lectures, and poetry readings. But
how is Schach's ethnic agenda to be realized? "Those are all things that we
need very much, but what we need even more is the Jewish house, i.e., the
Jewish home adorned in beauty and harmony, where Jewish life can feel

111

at home and can evolve freely. And we need Jewish mothers, even more than Jewish fathers, i.e., women whose Judaism is a part of their emotional life (*Gemütsleben*). For only such women are competent and qualified to raise (*erziehen*) our young people to the highest levels" (462). Knowing that Jewish women have the power to keep their men and children within the fold, Schach imagines them creating homes filled with Jewish tradition and Western aesthetics. While not further defining the proper Jewish family environment, Schach clearly sees Jewish mothers as all-important figures. The "us" describing Schach and his audience embraces both the Eastern *yeshive bokher* and his Western middle-class patronesses.

In this peculiar synthesis of young Eastern men and philanthropic Western women, Schach subtly plays off acculturation and its opposite: re-ethnification. In the process, he presents his female readers with positive stereotypes of *Ostjuden* that are reinforced by illustrations accompanying the text. "Im Tempel zu Tripolis" (453–54) derives, interestingly enough, from the Orientalist oeuvre of Ismael Gentz (1862–1914), a non-Jewish artist who lived in the Middle East. In the painting, a small and effeminate East European (or Oriental Jewish) male is studying a sacred text in faint candlelight (fig. 9). The maternal and mostly married (see the head-covered female figure in the magazine's cover art) readers of *Ost und West* were encouraged to sympathize with the stunted man-child of the painting, one of numerous images in the journal of Jewish men studying Talmud.[69]

A second visual image reiterates the theme that Jewish mothers must guard against assimilation. "Weib mit Ziegen" (457–58) by the Western Jewish artist Max Liebermann underlines the message of the second half of Schach's essay. This reproduction depicts a woman leading two goats, but whereas one goat obediently accompanies the woman, the other goat, trying to walk in the opposite direction, must be restrained by a leash (fig. 10). The placement of the painting in this context suggests that children and other dependents are supposed to obey their parents. The trope of the philanthropic Western woman is illustrated in the image of an older women taking care of two smaller creatures.

This sort of interplay between text and image was common in *Ost und West*. It served to conjoin Western and Eastern Jewry by associating Western Jewish mothers with Eastern Jewish boys. In fact, this trope reappeared with increasing frequency in the discourse of West-to-East Jewish philanthropy. For in addition to Schach's autobiographical narrative, which presents an Eastern Jewish teenager as the object of identification, *Ost und West* published other philanthropic narratives of Eastern Jewish artists whom Jewish patronesses had taken under their wing.

Representative of this genre is "Heinrich Redlich. Erinnerungen" (January 1906) by Lina Morgenstern (1830–1910). Morgenstern's memoir describes how she liberated Heinrich Redlich (1840–1889), a young Polish-Jewish artist, from his East European "ghetto." The memoir is typical of

Figure 9. Ismael Gentz, "Im Tempel zu Tripolis."
Ost und West *(July 1903): 453–54. (Courtesy of the*
Harry Ransom Research Center, University of Texas.)

113

other rags-to-riches stories in *Ost und West*, stories in which Jewish artists emerge from lowly origins in the East to become (minor) stars in the West. When recounted by Western Jewish narrators, these accounts made their protagonists more legitimate.

Whereas Redlich was not well known, even by *Ost und West*'s standards, Morgenstern was the leading German-Jewish woman of her generation. Featured in one article and an obituary in *Ost und West*, Morgenstern was actually discussed more than any other woman in the journal. Born in Breslau, an East-West border city (and Freytag's setting for *Soll und Haben*), she was renowned for her philanthropy at an early age. A popular writer, translated into many languages, she was also the founder of the Berlin food pantry and the Berlin Housewives' Association (*Hausfrauenverein*), a leading advocate of Friedrich Fröbel's *Kindergarten* pedagogy, and a distinguished national servant in the Franco-Prussian war.

Figure 10. Max Liebermann, "Weib mit Ziegen." Ost und West (1903): 457–58. (Courtesy of the Harry Ransom Research Center, University of Texas.)

Redlich was the featured artist of the January 1906 issue of *Ost und West*. This was no small feat. Since subscriptions to *Ost und West* were customarily renewed in December, the January issues of *Ost und West* were always especially important. Yet Morgenstern's comments on Redlich are preceded by one other narrative: a biographical introduction to Morgenstern's accomplishments by the scholar Adolf Kohut (1848–1917), titled "Lina Morgenstern." Kohut depicts Morgenstern as the grande dame of German women. But in resolving a perceived tension between Morgenstern's activism and her "virtue," Kohut clearly prefers the latter. For him, Morgenstern's womanhood is bound up with her role as caregiver and as nurturer. In addition, her honor consists in her firm "Israelite" belief in progress and humanitarianism. A housewife with a family, Morgenstern is never a "feminist" in the negative sense; she is always restrained and respectable. She becomes a paragon of Western Jewish motherhood, an inoffensive activist whose love for husband and children comes first (38).

In these and other narratives from *Ost und West*'s middle period, German-Jewish women's philanthropy toward Eastern Jewish men was venerated. Specifically, *Ost und West*'s idolizing of the Eastern Jewish artist and Kohut's favorable view of Western female activism came together in Morgenstern's account of the young Redlich. In this memoir, Redlich is introduced as a veritable Polish-Jewish Horatio Alger, who, by moving to Berlin, has retraced the footsteps of numerous Eastern Jews eager for enlightenment. But even here, enlightenment has its limits: Redlich is stigmatized by his Yiddish accent despite his modest success as an artist in Breslau and elsewhere. Morgenstern confronts the reader with Redlich's tragic death resulting from a severe mental illness that she describes in the final third of the biography. While her view of Redlich as mentally ill almost certainly draws on negative stereotypes of Eastern Jews, it also provides a befitting closure to her hagiographical narrative.

Morgenstern's memoir was not the first account of a German-Jewish woman identifying with an Eastern Jewish artist. In the 1903 volume of *Ost und West*, writer and critic Rosalie Perles illustrates a similar partnership. Perles, the wife of rabbinical scholar Joseph Perles and mother of rabbinical scholar Felix Perles, was a lay leader of the Königsberg Jewish community which was being constantly replenished by Jewish immigrants from the east and south. Her philanthropic outlook is most apparent in an essay entitled "Henryk Glicenstein" (March 1903).[70] For Perles, four traits sum up the sculptor Glicenstein: he is from Russian Poland, he is Jewish, he is indigent, and he is an artistic genius. Once again, a Jewish female sponsor deems a young, poor Eastern Jewish artist worthy of success. Perles goes so far as to claim that Glicenstein is better disposed toward females because his father, a *melamed* (or elementary school teaching assistant), likely beat him. For her, this is why most of Glicenstein's patrons are Jewish women. Despite the goodwill of these guardian angels, Glicenstein's "Eastern Jewishness" has handicapped him in his efforts to ingratiate himself. His external appearance and self-presentation resemble that of a "Polish *yeshiva bokher*" (180) (see fig. 11). And in Munich, where he resided before moving to Italy, Glicenstein is apparently impeded by his deficient manner of speech.[71] By parenthetically adding that "speaking is Glicenstein's weakest side" (182), Perles indicates that the source of corruption here is Yiddish, making Glicenstein one of many Eastern Jews burdened with an inherent difficulty in handling the German language (and, by implication, Western discourse).[72]

At the close of Perles's lengthy biography, we find the same ambivalence that Morgenstern earlier expressed about Redlich. Even though Glicenstein was still living when Perles penned her article, his life is stamped as tragic; his demise, like that of other Eastern Jewish artists depicted in *Ost und West*, appears imminent. In addition, much is made of the gap between his outstanding reputation and his financial poverty. The continual return of old clichés about *Ostjuden* in this and other narratives as tragic charity cases reveals how distant patroness and client actually were. Not surprisingly, Perles's empathy for Glicenstein's "predicament" renders him a messiah figure and a Jewish nationalist. Glicenstein's art is said to have a positive "jüdische Note" despite the fact that most of it was portraiture. Like other reviewers of Eastern Jewish artists in *Ost und West*, Perles believed that her artist's future works would be saturated with Jewish content (192).

Ost und West's strategy was to bring the German-Jewish female audience to Eastern Jewish culture by idolizing the artistic, "authentic" *Ostjude*. This linkage often was underscored by juxtaposing narratives of the Eastern Jewish artist with texts that idealized Jewish women. Perles's narrative of Glicenstein, for example, was foregrounded by Binjamin Segel's expurgated selection of proverbs, "Die Frau im jüdischen Sprichwort" (March 1903). By making such connections, Winz and his colleagues hoped to raise the ethnic consciousness of German-Jewish women.

Yet, while the stereotype of the Eastern Jewish artist in need of uplifting was created for the German-Jewish woman, the stereotype was weighed down by two factors: the burden of the artist's origins and the patronizing of his spiritual benefactors. Thus, Morgenstern's, Perles's, and even Schach's narratives of youthful Eastern artists were not enough to make German-Jewish women identify with Eastern Jewish men in the manner proposed by *Ost und West*. Old attitudes about the backwardness of *Ostjuden* were simply too tenacious. In addition, Jewish women felt compelled to affirm their bourgeois status and Western identity. For it was only by differentiating themselves from Eastern Jewish or working-class inferiors that the bourgeoises of *Ost und West* could themselves become part of the German-Jewish elite.

As we have seen, the traditional philanthropy of German-Jewish women was bound up with older negative images of the *Ostjuden*, a link

Figure 11. Henryk Glicenstein. Ost und West *(March 1903): 177–78. (Courtesy of the Harry Ransom Research Center, University of Texas.)*

that constantly threatened to undermine *Ost und West*'s promotion of ethnic Judaism to the female Jewish audience. What was needed were new criticisms of Western Jewry that went beyond the traditional impetus for charity motivating such figures as Morgenstern and Perles. While the fiction of Vicki Baum (1888–1960), the best known of *Ost und West*'s women writers, seemed to criticize Western Jewry by focusing on weak, dependent Jews in an Eastern ghetto milieu, her philanthropic narratives went one step further. They were ultimately shaped by enlightened Judaism, mixed together with the older trope of the Western Jewish patroness and the dependent Eastern Jewish male artist. Yet these fictions were so open to interpretation that Winz and Segel would feel compelled to counteract their ambiguity, especially their unpleasant images of *Ostjuden*.[73]

Baum, best known today for her *Grand Hotel* (*Menschen im Hotel*, 1929), was already a talent in the making when Winz decided to publish her "Im alten Haus" (January 1910). Although she was a mere twenty-two years old at the time, her skillful command of popular narrative and her understanding of social systems of distinction point to her later success in the Weimar Republic as a creator and editor of middle-brow fiction for the blockbuster Ullstein Verlag, where she was offered a lucrative exclusive contract to become a staff writer and edit a glossy women's magazine.[74] Baum's "Rafael Gutmann" (January and February 1911) showed glimpses of her style of the 1920s in which she developed a narrative economy marked by suspense, tension, foreshadowing, and the interplay of desire and fear.[75]

Winz, ever astute, correctly anticipated that Baum would be a hit. Prior to Baum, women writers rarely appeared in *Ost und West*, not even under male pseudonyms. Many female-sounding names disguised the identities of male authors. In the early years, the non-Jewish poet Dolorosa was the exception, along with several painters. Rachel Mundlak (1887–?), a Polish Jew and the in-house artist after Lilien moved on, was the most visible artist in the magazine, of equal profile with Pilichowsky and Hirshenberg. Other female artists featured were Marie Dillon (1858–?), in May 1904; Helene von Mises, in December 1905; Marie Cohen, in March 1905; Helene Darmesteter, in February 1907; Käthe Münzer, in January 1908; Sophie Blum-Lazarus, in June 1908; Julie Wolfthorn, in December 1911; and Margot Lipmann, in November 1912.

Until Baum's "Im alten Haus," then, there had been very little activity by women in *Ost und West*—all the more reason why regular readers would have taken note of her stories.[76] To point out the journal's new commitment to contributions by women, Baum's second work in *Ost und West*, "Rafael Gutmann," was preceded by a feature on the "interesting" textile designs of a Berlin Jewish woman (fig. 12), "Eine interessante Handarbeit" (January 1911).[77] This gesture also may have been a nod in the direction of the Jewish women's movement, which had evolved rapidly after the 1908 legalization of women's associations in Germany.

A fine preview of Baum's later works, "Im alten Haus" equivocates on Jewish issues as well as women's issues. As a critique of a prototypical Jewish ghetto and its inhabitants, its point of view is neither discernibly Western nor Eastern Jewish; in addition, it reveals nothing to identify its locale as Baum's native Vienna. The main character is a decrepit, elderly Jewish woman who owns a ritual bath (*mikve*).[78] As a metaphor for the assimilation process, she eventually goes blind after allowing herself to be operated on by a doctor. When her children decide to sell the house and leave the Jewish quarter, she drowns herself in the basement *mikve*. On the one hand, the spectacle of sick Jews living and working underground anticipated Nazi

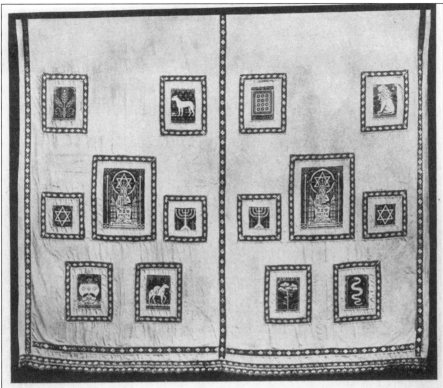

FENSTER-VORHANG.   FILET-ARBEIT.

Entworfen und ausgeführt von Frau Hedwig Wollsteiner.

Eine interessante Handarbeit

führen wir hier den Lesern vor: es ist ein Vorhang, den eine Berliner Dame (Frau Hedwig
Wollsteiner) in vierjähriger unermüdlicher Arbeit
angefertigt hat. Jüdische Symbole sind hier in
freier Uebertragung alter Formen in moderner
Anschauung stilisiert in den viereckigen Feldern
dargestellt. Es ist ein Werk bewundernswerten
Fleisses, dessen Verfertiger ein feines Formgefühl
an den Tag legt. Das Kunstgewerbe wird bei uns
Juden noch immer stark vernachlässigt, mit Aus-
nahme einiger weniger Künstler und der Versuche
in der Kunstgewerbeschule Bezalel wird hierin sehr
wenig geleistet. Ein Stück, wie diesen Vorhang hier,
sollten sich unsere Frauen zum Vorbild nehmen
und die edle Kunst der Handarbeit, eine Kunst,
die ganz und gar in das Gebiet der Frau gehört,
mehr in den Dienst unserer Sache stellen. K. S.

ERKER-VORHANG.   ERKER-VORHANG

Figure 12. Hedwig Wollsteiner, "Eine interessante Handarbeit."
Ost und West *(January 1911): 35–36.*

calumnies directed against Jews; on the other hand, the story's critique of the ghetto, though harsh, was directed at all European Jewish locales in the Diaspora (*galut* in Hebrew or *goles* in Yiddish).

Yet from the Eastern Jewish nationalist standpoint of *Ost und West*, the Diaspora of Western—not of Eastern—Europe was in need of renewal. To underscore its anti-Western, non-Zionist bias, *Ost und West* framed "Im alten Haus" with several photographs of proud-looking Oriental Jews (fig. 13).[79] In addition, the editors juxtaposed the story with an obituary of Lina Morgenstern (fig. 14).[80] While praising Morgenstern's work on behalf of all Jews, the author concurs with Kohut's earlier account (discussed above) by ascribing to her the following roles: mother and wife first, philanthropist second, activist third. This negative understanding of Western Jewish women's roles tacitly belittled Baum's protagonist in "Im alten Haus," not to speak of Baum's own accomplishments as a Western Jewish female writer.

Baum's second story in *Ost und West*, "Rafael Gutmann," avoids women characters for the most part. Yet it has an Eastern Jewish male protagonist, Rafael Gutmann, who is depicted as effeminate or even homosexual ("queer").[81] This type of characterization, as was so often the case in *Ost und West*, enabled female readers to identify with an Eastern Jewish artist. As a typical narrative of philanthropy, the story excoriates the Jewish ghetto, parodying the Yiddish language as *Mauscheln*. Rafael is a traditional (or "Orthodox") Eastern Jew who longs to be westernized.[82] Although the son of a secondhand clothes dealer, he discovers his love of song, becoming a choir boy and soloist at an elegant Liberal Jewish synagogue. He also sings magnificently and speaks flawless German, in stark contrast to his Yiddish-speaking family. Yet his father, Lazar, bent on making a retailer out of him, compels him to leave music and Liberal Judaism behind.

Weak-willed, Rafael accedes to his father's wishes in the second half of the novella.[83] He becomes a caftan-wearing clerk in a dingy store in the Jewish quarter. To make matters worse, his blind ex-mentor, Menkis, betrays him by marrying the non-Jewish soprano Corinna. Yet Rafael is fatally infatuated with Corinna, even composing a folk song for her. (This so-called Russian folk song functions as a cipher for many Yiddish folk songs collected by Winz and published in *Ost und West*. In order to lend these "low" cultural products a degree of legitimacy, one segment of the story is juxtaposed with a *Lied* based on Heine's poem "Das gold'ne Kalb"; see fig. 15.) Ultimately, the young man's desire to make it in the West remains unfulfilled. Typecast as a degenerate, he can resist neither the familiar ghetto milieu nor the allure of Wagner's music; indeed, he knows *Die Meistersinger von Nürnberg* and *Tristan und Isolde* by heart. After escaping the ghetto to attend the opera one final time, Rafael commits suicide, literally divided between the two worlds of East and West, tradition and modernity.

Baum's own childhood was not unlike Rafael's. A musical prodigy,

120

Figure 13. Photos of Oriental Jews.
Ost und West *(January 1910): 25, 39.*

Figure 14. Photo of Lina Morgenstern.
Ost und West *(January 1906): 37–38.*

she studied harp at the Vienna *Konservatorium* and appeared with various orchestras in her teens and twenties. Her family life was also troubled, despite comfortable middle-class surroundings: she depicts herself in her memoirs as having been traumatized not only by her father—who at times called her "son"—but also by her mentally disturbed mother whom she was compelled to nurse for several years.

Music was not the only means Baum used to escape her repressive family environment. As a teenager, she entered and won a literary contest after having been forbidden to read by her father. At eighteen, she left home to marry Max Prels, a writer. Baum continued to write during their marriage, well enough that Prels sold several of her stories under his name to the German magazine *Velhagen und Klasings Monatshefte*.[84] By 1912, a year after publication of "Rafael Gutmann" in *Ost und West*, Baum divorced Prels and left Vienna to take a position with the Darmstadt city orchestra; she married its conductor, Richard Lert (a non-Jew), in 1916.

Where do Jewish women readers fit into this picture? For his part, the musically gifted ghetto boy Rafael was destined to appeal to bourgeois

Figure 15. Musical notes to Heine's "Das gold'ne Kalb."
Ost und West *(January 1911): 49–50.*

Jewish women. Materially and spiritually impoverished, weak and unmanly, he practically cries out for rescue from the ghetto. Through Western culture, Rafael hopes to break out of his stifling milieu, not unlike Redlich and Glicenstein and other Eastern Jewish artists—and not unlike Baum and the female readers who may have identified with them.

At first glance, it is surprising that Winz and his colleagues would publish any images of Eastern Jews that were even slightly negative. But as we know, *Ost und West* did not always object to negative representations of Jewish ghettos or their inhabitants. Rather, the critique of the traditional Jewish milieu became a way to promote ethnic ideals of the new Jew, a Jew liberated from centuries of mental and physical stagnation. In fact, Baum's ambivalent portrayal of Yiddish-speaking *Ostjuden*[85] reflected competing receptions of the ghetto story (*Ghettogeschichte*). One school expressed longing for the old world; the other regarded it with disdain.[86] At the turn of the century, the critique of the European Diaspora was a flourishing industry among Jewish intellectuals, whether Eastern or Western, socialist or Zionist.[87] According to Scholem, Eastern Jewish discourse about the Jews, particularly in elitist Hebrew-language forums, could be even harsher than German-Jewish stereotyping of Jews.[88] Micha Joseph Berdichevsky (1865–1921), representing the Nietzschean fringe, found no redeeming value in the Diaspora era. Aḥad Ha⁵am, in contrast, argued for tolerance: "If someone declares 'our entire people is degenerate,'—why not, if he loves that entire people with his soul?"[89] Both the ghetto and the *goles* ("Diaspora") were backward and deplorable, but to judge them required an insider's sensibility. Such a view suggested that Jewish self-criticism was necessarily of a different tenor from non-Jewish criticism of the Jews.[90]

Ost und West's ambivalence toward the Diaspora was influenced by Aḥad Ha⁵am and cultural Zionism at least as much as by anticapitalism or antimodernism. But its Eastern Jewish empathy for the ghetto did not stop the presses when Baum's stories came along. In short, *Ost und West* promoted Eastern Jewish nationalism in more than one way, further revealing Winz's public relations savvy. Double-edged messages, in fact, could only work to the magazine's benefit and enable it to reach several audiences. Baum's ghetto stories were no less polysemic, in both their range of discourses and their suggestive, elliptical style. Furthermore, the criticism of the ghetto in Baum's "Rafael Gutmann" did not contradict the pro-Eastern Jewish discourse of *Ost und West* as German-Jewish women had come to know it.[91] Within the broad framework of Diaspora criticism, it was permissible to portray the figure of Rafael as a powerless but talented victim in need of Western philanthropy and *Bildung*.

The editors of *Ost und West* allowed these associations to resonate in their choice of illustrations to accompany "Rafael Gutmann." The interplay of text and image was meant to encourage German-Jewish women (and men) to act philanthropically toward East European Jews. See, for instance, the commemorative medal designed by Hugo Kaufmann and titled "Den Helfern in der Not" (February 1911) (fig. 16). This medal, juxtaposed with Rafael's final attempt at leaving the ghetto, thematizes the uplifting of the enslaved to freedom. One page later, we find a reproduction of Kaufmann's "Freiheit" (fig. 17), a section of the "Unity Monument" (*Einheitsdenkmal*) in Frankfurt am Main. This sculpture of a seminude Herculean male epitomizes Western respectability—a stark contrast to Rafael's weak and dependent nature. To drive the point home, a long article on Kaufmann directly precedes the final installment of Baum's story. In this piece, Kaufmann serves as an icon of a Western Jewish artist who is successful and

Figure 16. Hugo Kaufmann, "Den Helfern in der Not." Ost und West *(February 1911): 133.*

established. The reference to his spacious atelier in the Western suburbs of Berlin returns us full circle to the Western Jewish audience of *Ost und West*.

Savvy promotion, as public relations people know, does not always function as intended. By bringing more German-language fiction about Jews to a largely German-Jewish audience, the editors of *Ost und West* may have been hoping to compensate for the failed literary contest of eight years earlier. In the end, however, their tolerance toward Jewish ghetto fictions was stretched to its limits by Baum's "Rafael Gutmann." When written from an Eastern Jewish perspective, a ghetto story typically excoriated the Diaspora ghetto. After all, this milieu was perceived as the breeding ground of Western parvenus. But when written from a Western Jewish perspective, as in the case of "Rafael Gutmann," the stereotypes were potentially more detrimental to Jews. On the sensory level, for example, Baum associates the smell of onions and chicken fat with "ghetto Jews" (*Ghettojuden*).[92] In addition, synagogue scenes in "Rafael Gutmann" are exotic and depict the worshipers as near-hysterics.[93] And for any reader, the most conspicuous feature of the story is that many Jewish characters do not speak standard German.[94] The stereotyping of *Mauscheln* (Yiddish-accented German) had a long history. Both Western- and Eastern-based writers employed the myth of the "corrupt and corrupting" language of the Jews when looking at the ghetto, but it was not difficult to discern an anti-Eastern bias in "Rafael Gutmann."[95] For Baum's story appeared in the original German; there was no indication that it (like others in *Ost und West*) had been translated from Yiddish or Hebrew.

One did not have to examine the title carefully, however, to see that Baum's analysis of the Jewish Diaspora was likely more influenced by

Figure 17. Hugo Kaufmann, "Freiheit."
Ost und West *(February 1911): 137–38.*

enlightened Western (Jewish) thought than by Eastern Jewish tradition-alism. Taken to its logical extreme, her thinking equated Rafael's Judaism with femininity, madness, and a counterfeit creativity. Such an equation had become a centerpiece of turn-of-the-century science, in particular in the theories of Baum's Viennese contemporary, Otto Weininger (1880–1903). Derided today as a paragon of "Jewish self-hatred," Weininger's views on race and gender mirrored those of his time and place; hence the popular appeal of his revised dissertation, *Geschlecht und Charakter* (1904, *Sex and Character*),[96] which was praised by Freud, Karl Kraus (1874–1936), and others.[97] It is not surprising that Vicki Baum, like many other Central European Jews, came under the spell of this young philosopher. In fact,

Baum was an adolescent and a student in Vienna when the influence of Weininger was at its summit (between 1903 and 1910), and she refers to him in her autobiography.[98]

Weininger's contribution to the debate on racial degeneracy rests upon a strict dichotomy between the categories of "Jew" and "Aryan." This corresponds in turn to a dichotomy between "masculine" and "feminine." By extending the category of the feminine to the Jews (a move that gave Arthur Schopenhauer's misogyny a "scientific" grounding), Weininger attempted to link them with psychopathology. The protagonist of "Rafael Gutmann" can be read as an exemplar of such "Jewish" symptoms. In his impotent attempts to assimilate to "Aryan" culture, Rafael resembles Weininger himself: a baptized Jew, repressed homosexual, and young suicide. In fact, the circumstances of Weininger's self-destruction at age twenty-three may have influenced Baum's novella. Weininger's suicide became a cause célèbre and helped publicize his ideas. That he killed himself in the house where Beethoven died suggests a desire to identify with a Christian, "masculine" genius. Similar patterns can be found in "Rafael Gutmann." Not only is Rafael stereotyped as an inferior, feminized Jew, but his suicide is also linked to Beethoven. This episode thus merits closer examination.

In part one of "Rafael Gutmann," Rafael's only escape from the darkness of the squalid Jewish quarter (*Judengasse*) has been music; he is infatuated with the opera and with the singer Corinna. The second installment of the novella relates Rafael's atrophy in the ghetto environment. Prevailed upon by his father to abandon his musical aspirations, he gives up his starring role in the choir, and his confidence diminishes. Meanwhile, the ghetto continually "works on" Rafael, destroying his "fine, dreamy nature." Externally and internally, he is transformed back into a "typical" ghetto Jew, and this retrograde Jewishness is described in terms suggesting impotence: Rafael is variously depicted as "unaware," "without will," "full of horror," and "helpless."

By the second half of "Rafael Gutmann," a full year has passed without song and without visits to the opera. Deprived of Corinna, and therefore of music, Rafael is rendered a neurotic dreamer and hysteric. As if secretly aware of Rafael's defiant unconscious, his father and his employer keep him under steady watch. Yet one February night while sleeping in the stifling kitchen of his parents' flat, Rafael dreams of melodies and awakens in tears. This is a prelude to his final attempt at breaking out. As the store where he works is closing for the Sabbath, Rafael randomly glimpses a newspaper. There he sees a (dated) advertisement for Beethoven's *Fidelio*, and, shedding his restraint, he decides to attend the opera one last time. This new resolve reiterates a dynamic that defines the novella as a whole: a movement between desire and repression—and, correspondingly, between assimilation and dissimilation.[99] In perfect analogy, the play of desired and repressed dominates Beethoven's *Fidelio*. The opera's plot reflects Rafael's wish to be rescued from ghetto imprisonment. The rescue of Don Fernando Florestan by his wife, Leonora—in the disguise of a male prison guard—points to Rafael's passive hope that the Christian Corinna will rescue him from the scourge of the ghetto. Fidelio, as a politicized feminine body, calls male operatic roles into question; in the context of *Rafael Gutmann*, the opera's cross-dressing motif evokes Weininger's feminizing of the (male) Jew.

In deciding to attend the opera, Rafael's pathology reaches its summit. Proceeding with his plan to attend *Fidelio*, Rafael takes his week's wages and heads into town. But having just descended happily into the colorful, inviting city, his desire is met with resistance when he bumps into Moritz Belft, the son of his employer. The caricature of an Eastern Jew, Belft wonders out loud where Rafael might be going on the Sabbath. Rafael, undaunted by Belft's "tricky questions," emerges into the illuminated, sensual metropolis, and, arriving at the opera, he is taken in by the seductive smells of silk, perfume, and women's hair.[100] His red ticket underlines the dream atmosphere, suddenly punctuated by the appearance of Corinna, "lean[ing] against the wall, slender, pale, and blond" (140–41). Presumably leaning away from Menkis, who is seated, she has extended her hand down to him. This ultimate patronizing pose is reinforced by her gently affected smile. Her entire habitus suggests the condescension of the bourgeois philanthropist for the ghetto Jew.[101] The suspense is heightened when the lights go down before Corinna can return Rafael's glance. To his surprise, the opera is *Tristan* rather than *Fidelio*. As a devoted Wagnerian—like many other European Jews, especially women[102]—he soon grows receptive to *Tristan* and its theme of forbidden, decadent love. With head in hands, he trembles and sobs. At this point, Corinna lays her "free" hand on his head, a gesture elucidated by the accompanying illustration of Hugo Kaufmann's "Einheit" (fig. 18). Kaufmann's sculpture of an Athena-like female not only suggests the fatal unity of Tristan and Isolde; it also reinforces the symbolism of Corinna as assimilation, as the Enlightenment way out of the ghetto. In extending the succor of philanthropy, she functions in this text as a cipher for the middle-class Jewish female reader.

Demoralized after *Tristan*, Rafael reverts back to his effete, excitable Jewishness. In addition, he becomes aware of the rift between himself and his less than satisfactory benefactors. Menkis admonishes him in patronizing fashion: "Come again, Rafael. . . . Only, you can't be so weak—a little backbone, and keep your head up!" (141). Here, Rafael's inner lack of resolve is explicitly linked to his inferior Jewish body, suggesting that his future attempts to assimilate himself are condemned to failure. Listening to Rafael's steps as he takes his leave, Menkis is apprehensive that he will not find the right path (*Weg*) for himself. Corinna—at a greater "racial" distance, as it were—articulates Menkis's pessimism more fully: "Maybe— there is no right path for his kind [*Art*]." Both are convinced that this prisoner of the ghetto is doomed and that he does not have the power

Figure 18. Hugo Kaufmann, "Einheit."
Ost und West *(February 1911): 141–42.*

or will to save himself. Though still not conscious of his own decision to die (he returns briefly to gaze at his parents' window), Rafael accepts it as a fait accompli. He is content to be leaving the corrupt and corrupting ghetto; when he kills himself, he will be killing off one more incarnation of its "Platonic form" (a favorite term of Weininger's). In his last moments, Rafael is not sad. Engulfed in reverie, he feels a "strange, happy intoxication." He acknowledges, as Menkis suspected earlier, that he is "without direction" (*ohne Weg*). (The repeated references to Rafael's having lost his *Weg* may allude to Arthur Schnitzler's comprehensive *Zeitroman, Der Weg ins Freie* (1908), which treats similar themes of Jewishness and aestheticism.) Oblivious to the snow and the biting cold, he reprises "Fatal Yearning" ("Todessehnsucht"), the introduction to *Tristan*, while waiting on the tracks for the approaching train.

How are we to interpret the allusions to Wagner in "Rafael Gutmann"? In Jewish nationalist (and Zionist) literature, the encounter with Wagner and his music is overshadowed by the maestro's antisemitic pamphlet "Das Judenthum in der Musik" (1850).[103] One of *Ost und West*'s serial novellas, Heinrich York-Steiner's "Koriander, der Chasan" (October 1904, November 1904, December 1904), is typical of such a reading of Wagner. In this proto–*Jazz Singer* narrative, the protagonist's Hungarian *shtetl* roots enable him to overcome negative Wagnerian influences and the allure of a Gentile diva (fig. 19) and become a successful (but proudly Jewish) opera star. Yet, in "Rafael Gutmann," the role played by Wagner is different. Because Rafael is inherently unworthy of the great Beethoven's legacy, he shares a kinship with the modern decadent Wagner and, by extension, Weininger. What is more, in Weininger's eyes, even the great antisemite Wagner was polluted because of a reputed accretion of "Jewishness" in his art.[104] In his regression to ghetto Jewishness, Rafael thus shares Wagner's proclivity for death and the Dionysian.[105]

It matters little for our interpretation of "Rafael Gutmann" that Wagner was not a genius by Weininger's standards. More important are Weininger's judgments of Jewish notables such as Spinoza and Heine, who, like women, possess either superficial genius or no genius at all. Weininger's conjectures here are linked with music and language. For him, women's language is lies, as is the Jew's deformed language (*Mauscheln*), and Weininger's insistence on this point illuminates Baum's focus on Yiddish, song, and Wagner in "Rafael Gutmann." In fact, Rafael becomes the classic Jew of Weininger's schema. Much as he, in the first part of the story, shows little fear that the way he speaks or sings German is embarrassing, his career ends so rapidly as to suggest that his golden choirboy days had been a lie. A key passage from *Sex and Character* sheds light on Rafael's flightiness and oversensitivity and radical shifts between assimilation and dissimilation: "This temptation [to lie] has to be stronger in a being such as w[oman], because, unlike that of man, her memory is not continuous; rather she lives only in moments, as it were, discrete, unconnected, discontinuous, swayed by transitory events instead of dominating them."[106] Rafael, too, has degenerated back into a mendacious "ghetto-ness": he thinks like a Jew and like a woman. He lacks the capacity for dominance necessary to be a Nietzschean creator who "wills" his life.

Baum's protagonist Rafael is thus a distillate of "feminine" and "Jewish" characteristics. In his impotent attempts to assimilate to "Aryan" culture, Rafael directly resembles Weininger. Through allusions to Weininger as well as Oscar Wilde and *Jugendstil*, Baum created an emasculated Jewish "queer." For while Rafael is depicted as a fan of a cross-dressing opera (Beethoven's *Fidelio*) and a decadent, self-mortifying one (Wagner's *Tristan*), he is a failure at assimilation, indeed at "passing."[107] On the one hand, he is a sympathetic teenage singer struggling to escape his Eastern Jewish ghetto

Figure 19. Isaak Snowman, "Sardanopolis."
Ost und West *(November 1904): 789–90.*

milieu. On the other hand, he bears the classic symptoms of degeneracy: *Ostjudentum*, unmanliness, hysteria, and pseudo-genius.

In the end, however, "Rafael Gutmann" was too multivalent for any single interpretive framework. *Ost und West's* audience of German-Jewish women (and men) was thus free to identify with and then dissociate itself from the Eastern Jewish boy-artist. In effect, Baum's novella invited Jewish readers to graft negative self-images onto a perceived "Other": a nonthreatening ghetto *Ostjude*. A feminized Western Jewish self might be projected onto the East European Jewish subgroup, exemplified by Rafael. At the same time, the publication of "Rafael Gutmann" revealed how flexible the editors of *Ost und West* could be in their choice of contributions, even when those contributions appeared to attack Eastern Jewry, as in the case of Baum's antighetto fictions. These fictions ironically empowered Western Jewish women (and men) to escape their own inner ghettos by means of Jewish antisemitism.[108] Such a move, however, was at cross-purposes with *Ost und West*'s agenda and became the occasion for redefining editorial policy.[109]

If Baum's use of Weininger's stereotypes was intended as just another critique of Diaspora Jewry in *Ost und West*, it soon backfired. Grounded in negative images of *Ostjuden*, Weininger's Jewish antisemitism immediately elicited a response from the journal's editors and contributors. Even if an effete, effeminate Eastern Jew like Rafael was granted some sympathy by Western Jewish women, he was likely to be rejected by Western Jewish and Eastern Jewish (nationalist) men whose "manliness" he called into question.[110]

A degree of anti-Eastern sentiment was permissible in *Ost und West*, as the publication of Baum's stories shows. Indeed, for a time, the editors had used such sentiments—recast positively—to appeal to Western Jewish women. But while this kind of nonpartisanship was a guiding principle of *Ost und West*, some of the magazine's producers felt that fictions such as "Rafael Gutmann" went too far in their anti-Eastern sentiment. While there is no record of a direct editorial response to "Rafael Gutmann," there is evidence that Baum—or at least her approach—came under attack. Ultimately, her point of view showed how Jewish philanthropy functioned in the class posturing of Western Jewish women. In fact, was not Rafael the castoff skin of Vicki Baum, her negative image of social failure?[111]

Baum's double-edged attitudes toward Eastern Jews required some damage control so that *Ost und West* could protect its reputation as *the* advocate of East European Jewry. In order to counteract the ambiguities of "Rafael Gutmann," the journal subtly addressed the same issues in a number of contributions in 1911. Some responses even appeared in the same issues as the installments of the novella.[112] For example, Segel—Winz's main associate by 1911—offered a mainstream Jewish nationalist response to Baum in "Das Judenelend in Galizien" (February and March 1911) and "Volkswohlstand und Volksaufklärung" (July 1911), both under the pseudonym of "B. Samuel." This series of strongly worded editorials on Galician Jewry depicts Eastern Jewish men not as emasculated boys but as independent and strong. At the same time, they show that the editors of *Ost und West* could not tolerate the definition of Jewishness implicit in Baum's fiction. Even though Segel strove to be neutral in his writings, he now became vehement in attempting to defend Eastern Jewish masculinity.[113] His arguments suggested that an effeminate pathological character such as Rafael was a dubious role model for Jewish males, thus revealing the boundaries of what (East) European Jews considered respectable on the eve of World War I.[114]

Segel, a dedicated exponent of ethnic Judaism and Eastern Jewish nationalism, had already been *Ost und West*'s chief editorialist for several years.[115] In the 1905 opinion piece on philanthropy (discussed above), he had shown a willingness to defend unpopular positions—as he had in the *Altneuland* controversy of 1903—and to criticize the leading Jewish charity organizations. All of this suggested that he would dislike Baum's brand of Jewish philanthropy. In fact, his first response to Baum followed the first installment of "Rafael Gutmann" in *Ost und West*. This two-part editorial, entitled "Das Judenelend in Galizien," is an apologia for Jewish poverty and political inactivity throughout Austro-Hungary. The essay is thus an indirect response to the Weiningerian elements in Baum's novella, for Galicia was the probable place of origin for nearly all Jews in Baum's Viennese ghetto stories, and Segel was an acknowledged expert on Jewish life in this Austrian province. In "Das Judenelend in Galizien," Segel provides a justification for Galician Jewry's apparent lack of organization: it has been repeatedly victimized by non-Jewish politicians. Its weakness, then, is conditioned by history rather than "race." What is more, the few native Jewish politicians there also have acted opportunistically.

Segel's invective was so fierce in "Das Judenelend in Galizien" that an editor's note (*Anmerkung der Redaktion*) was appended to the essay. Such a disclaimer, though rare in *Ost und West*, functioned as a preemptive warning, signaling to the audience that the journal wished not to offend but that it was going to publish the objectionable material anyway. Whether Winz or Segel actually found any of these essays objectionable is a matter for speculation.[116] But it is unlikely that Segel's "Das Judenelend in Galizien" was unacceptable. First, the pseudonym used by Segel, "B. Samuel," was fairly identifiable by 1911 and was easily decoded as "B. Segel." Second, Winz and Segel wanted to counter the negative stereotypes found in Baum's fiction, a move in keeping with the new trend toward antidefamation in *Ost und West*.

In March 1911, Segel criticized Baum's outlook more directly. Having just issued the final installment of "Rafael Gutmann," *Ost und West* allowed Segel to have the last word in a continuation of "Das Judenelend in Galizien." Here he insists that Jewish pride and self-sufficiency can be developed only from within Jewry. The westernizing philanthropy of Baron Hirsch's Jewish Colonial Association offers a cosmetic and hopelessly incomplete solution, in Segel's opinion. Then, in a July 1911 editorial entitled "Volkswohlstand und Volksaufklärung," Segel continued on the same path followed in "Das Judenelend in Galizien." Leaving the political realm, he takes aim at the philosophy of Enlightenment as practiced by Western philanthropists, showing that even Orthodox Galician Jews preferred to attend Christian schools over Baron Hirsch's Reform Jewish schools which disputed their beliefs and practices. As an alternative to Hirsch's enlightened Western Judaism, Segel promotes the Eastern-based *Haskalah* of Aḥad Haᶜam and other cultural Zionists over the philanthropic, political Zionism of Baum's stories.

Other *Ost und West* essays of 1911 took issue with the patronizing uplifting of Eastern Jews sanctioned by Baum. In "Genug der Versäumnisse. Ein Ruf zur Tat" (October 1911), Segel returned to the issue of centralized relief in order to attack the proponents of mass Jewish migrations from one continent to another. His editorial also established the need for an interterritorial congress on behalf of Russian and Rumanian Jewry, both largely forgotten by the international community. By calling for such a congress on immigration, Segel hoped to advance his own arguments in favor of Jewish autonomy. Winz, agreeing with Segel, launched two new monthly features in the same October 1911 issue. The new rubrics, entitled "Illustrationen zur russischen Judenpolitik in den letzten Monaten" and "Revue der Ereignisse," were probably written by Segel and appeared continuously until 1914.

"Der stille Pogrom. Wehruf eines russischen Juden" (November 1911) represents the summit of Segel's polemics against "philanthropic" stereotyping of the *Ostjude*.[117] In this editorial, Segel criticizes indecision and inaction on the part of Western Jewry as tantamount to a "cultural pogrom" (*Kulturpogrom*). In contrast to Baum, he regards Jews in the *West* as feminine and weak, a position thoroughly in keeping with the masculinist, "tough Jew"[118] slant of *Ost und West*. Segel's main example of Western Jewish cowardice was the delayed reaction of English Jewry to the recent pogrom in South Wales. The fact that violent pogroms had ebbed in Russia by this time was perceived as a legacy of the Jewish freedom fighters who valiantly defended themselves in the Pale in 1905 and earlier. *Ost und West* recounted the exploits of these Jewish self-defenders in articles and graphic photos (fig. 20 and fig. 21).[119]

Segel's response to Western-style philanthropy à la Baum reflects the shrewd propaganda at which *Ost und West* so excelled. It was also closely bound up with the issues of independence and masculinity. Segel's tough editorials, moreover, seemed designed to upstage the imminent publication of a similar journal, Fritz Mordechai Kaufmann's *Die Freistatt*, though *Die Freistatt* was hardly competition for *Ost und West*. *Ost und West*'s resolve to publish as it pleased was characteristic of the years between 1912 and 1914— the heyday of the magazine.[120] These years also form a minor turning point in German-Jewish history as a result of the victory of cultural Zionism over political Zionism and—of more direct consequence to *Ost und West*—the demise of the German branch of the Alliance Israélite Universelle.[121] This demise, brought on by the Zionists, compelled the Paris Central Committee to take over the Berlin office from the German branch of the Alliance (*die Deutsche Conferenz-Gesellschaft der A.I.U.*).

Figure 20. "Gruppe hingeschlachteter Mitglieder der jüdischen 'Selbstwehr' in Odessa." Ost und West *(October–November 1905): 609–10.*

Owing to the recent success of the women's movement, 1913 witnessed more contributions than ever by women in *Ost und West*. Winz, perhaps bowing to pressure, published the journal's first (belated) feature on Jewish women's philanthropy, Stephanie Forchheimer's "Jüdische soziale Frauenarbeit in Frankfurt am Main" (January 1913). In fact, the flurry of public activity by the *Jüdischer Frauenbund* and other Jewish women's organizations just prior to 1913 was likely perceived as a threat to the hegemony of *Ost und West* and other male-dominated Jewish institutions. In May and June 1913, *Ost und West* came out with an ingenious parvenue sketch by Segel (under the pseudonym "A. Warszawski") entitled "Die Lehrerin." Here, Segel took the old scare tactics and developed a stereotype of the Western Jewess that still might appeal to German-Jewish female readers.[122] The ensuing novella is a serialized, two-part sketch that contrasts two unnamed teachers. In typical philanthropic fashion, a teacher from an upper-middle-class family has devoted her career to working-class children—a perfect role model for the Jewish female audience. The affection of her pupils (whose *"Rotwälsch"*[123] she has managed to learn) persuades her ultimately to reject the prospect of marriage to a high-ranking diplomat so that she can pursue her metier. But just as the reader is prepared to identify with

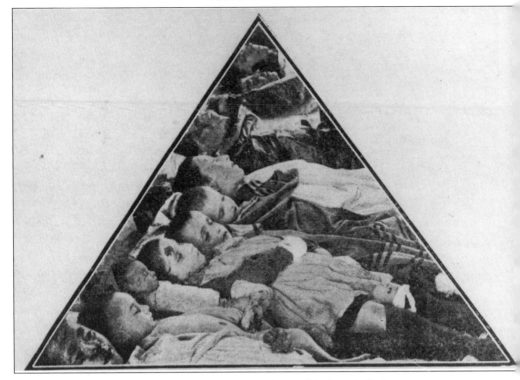

Figure 21. "Von Hooligans und Militär hingeschlachtete jüdische Kinder in Russland." Ost und West *(August–September 1906): 569–70.*

this paragon of middle-class virtue, Segel has her express gratitude that her adoring charges are not "Jewish children," thus revealing her to be an antisemite and a likely non-Jew. The second teacher, in the second installment of "Die Lehrerin"—a Jewish woman—proves to be equally flawed. The product of a poor family, this Jewish educator is revealed to be a social climber who betrays her roots in search of status. (Her siblings have sacrificed their own educations so that she can earn a doctorate. That her brothers also give up professional careers signals her egotism; girls usually had to make sacrifices for the boys' educations in Jewish families.)[124] Since she is a paragon of Western parvenuism, she harbors negative attitudes toward *Ostjuden,* caring more about her publishing career than about her "snot-nosed, Yiddish-screeching" pupils. Ironically, she chooses to marry a boorish, affluent Galician-Jewish businessman at the story's end.

In "Die Lehrerin," the cold parvenu woman becomes the antithesis of bourgeois philanthropy. Segel had succeeded in creating a new stereotype:

the educated careerist Jewess. Like Baum's Rafael, Segel's *Bildungsparvenue* functioned as a foil onto whom middle-class German-Jewish women might project negative feelings about themselves (or others who had chosen a career path). At the same time, the philanthropic teacher fared no better in Segel's estimation owing to her shallow philanthropy and anti-semitism.[125]

This episode of *Ost und West*'s history ended with a surprising return to Western Jewish parvenu characters. In earlier chapter, we saw how the parvenu stereotype helped male intellectuals construct their Jewish identities and build coalitions between Eastern and Western Jewish nationalists. It was hoped that the female parvenu in "Die Lehrerin" might give philanthropic Jewish bourgeoises a common foil for their Jewish identities and enlist their support in the pan-Jewish project. Segel's satire, precisely because of its antifeminism, tacitly acknowledged that women now occupied a central place in German-Jewish public life.

In the period before World War I, the parvenu stereotype was also closely tied to the *stereotype*, as opposed to the *phenomenon*, of Jewish self-hatred. When used in *Ost und West*, this stereotype encouraged readers to project the stain of self-hatred onto other Jews. The main targets of this stereotype were Western Jewish men, and attempts were made to control its spread. When it was specifically directed at women, however, as in "Die Lehrerin," the charge of self-hatred was a reaction to the fear of female careerism and other forms of enlightened Judaism. *Ost und West*'s willingness to disseminate such images suggests misogyny. Segel, at numerous points in the magazine, made sexist remarks and analogies; see, for example, "Der Niedergang des österreichischen Antisemitismus" (October 1910).

At the same time, the journal's editors did not—and could not, given their significant female readership—call for a return to traditional, pre-Enlightenment roles for women. When viewed in the context of the fin de siècle, *Ost und West*'s antifeminism was moderate. Above all, Winz, Segel, and their associates wanted to ensure that the journal's texts were read according to male Eastern Jewish values, what some might call an "androcentric" perspective.[126] Baum herself, in accepting Weininger's equation of the woman and the Jew, was implicitly encouraging an androcentric reading of her works.

The editors of *Ost und West* had always postured themselves as tough and masculine, and the argumentative style of the journal derided opponents as weak and cowardly. But the journal's "masculinity" and that of its German-Jewish and Eastern Jewish male audiences were called into question in 1914 as doubts spread regarding the fitness (*Tauglichkeit*) of Jews in the armies of Europe. The next chapter addresses these conflicts, which are present *in nuce* in the contradictions between Baum's and Segel's fiction. Hatred of one's femininity, of one's Jewish body, of one's Jewish culture—these issues became central to German-Jewish soldiers in World War I, and *Ost und West* sought to capitalize on the fears and hopes of its male readers who were not part of the Jewish intelligentsia.

5

Antisemitism and the German-Jewish Male: *Ost und West*'s Promotion of Ethnic Jewish Identity to German-Jewish Men

By 1914, *Ost und West*'s promotion of Jewish ethnicity had become highly sophisticated. The stereotypes of Jews that Winz and his colleagues developed to appeal to both Jewish intellectuals and middle-class Jewish women showed a thorough understanding of what shaped Jewish identity in Imperial Germany. In their flexible approach to stereotyping, the editors of *Ost und West* played upon the fears and desires associated with the Eastern-traditional and Western-enlightened identities of their audiences. Yet one audience of Jewish readers in Germany seemed to elude *Ost und West* in its first decade or so: middle-class men. The average German-Jewish man was different from his wife, his sisters, and his daughters in terms of socialization and self-image. He was also different from his brothers and sons in the German-Jewish intelligentsia who seemed intent on using their newfound Jewish nationalism to distance themselves from him.

To interest the average German-Jewish *Bildungsbürger* ("educated middle-class man") or *Besitzbürger* ("property-holding middle-class man") in Jewish ethnicity, *Ost und West* would be compelled to refine its approach once again. But why were German-Jewish men so difficult to attract during the first years of the journal? Their disinterest had, in fact, many sources. First, these individuals had the most to lose by associating themselves with Jewish nationalism. As status-conscious as some of their wives, these men identified with the German nation and the *Mittelstand* (middle class),[1] and they found it difficult to act demonstratively Jewish. Second, they worked in the public sphere, whereas Jewish women stayed largely at home and the Jewish literati inhabited the coffeehouses. German-Jewish men were also made painfully aware that they were overrepresented in business, banking, and the professions. Third, the quintessential *Westjude* was uncomfortable, at times even unfriendly, in the presence of *Ostjuden*. Though there always had been highly acculturated male readers of *Ost und West*, it would require something special to interest them in Eastern Jewish identity.

It took a cataclysmic event to transform middle-class Jewish men into a significant audience of *Ost und West*. That event was World War I, an acknowledged watershed both in modern German-Jewish history and in the history of the magazine.[2] For most Jews, the war meant an end to the relative security of the *Kaiserreich* and the beginning of more open antisemitism. For Jewish men, it meant an unrelenting attack on their fitness (*Tauglichkeit*) for military service, culminating in attempts by antisemites to deny the extent of Jewish participation in the war. The most infamous of these measures was the October 1916 order for a census of Jewish soldiers in the Prussian military, the so-called *Judenzählung*. Whereas *Ost und West*'s primary concern before the war was with intellectuals and middle-class Jewish women, its primary concern between 1914 and 1918 was with older middle-class Jewish men. Knowing how loyal most German-Jewish men were to the liberal, anti-Zionist *Centralverein deutscher Staatsbürger jüdischen Glaubens* (Central Association of German Citizens of the Jewish Faith), *Ost und West* likened anti-German sentiment to antisemitism when the war broke out, projecting onto the Entente powers images of cowardice, Germanophobia, and self-hatred that antisemites had repeatedly associated with Jewish men.

German-Jewish *Bürger*, for all their acculturation, had never completely abandoned the Jewish religion. By no means fully secularized, many of these men retained a modicum of observance into the twentieth century. Since most still had some knowledge of Judaism, their religious allegiances were fair game for an enterprising journal such as *Ost und West*. For this reason, stereotypes of nonobservant Jews—"religious" self-haters—figured as prominently in wartime as they had previously in the magazine. These "old" images were ingeniously woven into a prowar stance in the magazine's first series of war-related editorials in the autumn of 1914. Yet, soon thereafter, *Ost und West* suppressed negative images of the Jew as part of the fight against wartime antisemitism. In its longest-running serialized novella ever, *Am Tage des Gerichts* [On the Day of Judgment] by Binjamin Segel (December 1915, January–February 1916, March–April 1916, May–June 1916), *Ost und West* featured a pious Eastern Jew in prewar Poland. Even though he is morally flawed, this Jew's faults are overshadowed by those of his hostile foil, a rapacious East European antisemite. As we shall see, this non-Jewish villain embodies both charges associated with the *Judenzählung*:

that Jews profited from the war and that they were unsoldierly. Several of Segel's novellas and editorials, which literally filled the pages of *Ost und West* during the war, were published in special editions for German-Jewish soldiers at the front. The Eastern Jewish editors of the magazine thus came to the aid of their Western Jewish brethren in their hour of need, as they were under attack from antisemites. In a sense, this reversed the customary West-to-East movement of relief.

Ost und West's ideal of ethnic Jewish identity thus began to look more attractive as Western Jewish identity came to look more illusory. Antidefamation become the magazine's first priority after 1915, as Jew haters attacked all Jews in Germany. The apologetics moved into high gear when Polish Jews were forced to enter the *Reich* as laborers in the last months of the war. Yet the need to combat Western antisemitism also strengthened the case of Jewish nationalism. By reaching out to German-Jewish males in a wartime atmosphere demanding the utmost conformity, *Ost und West* was merely appealing to a new market; it was not changing its message of pan-Jewishness. Because World War I eventually signaled the failure of Jewish acculturation in Germany, Jewish middle-class men were ready to take a second look at *Ost und West* and its message of ethnic Jewish identity.

Prior to 1914, the potential male Jewish audience of *Ost und West* was about 300,000 (nearly 25 percent of those being in Berlin).[3] In comparison with non-Jewish men, these German Jews were fairly homogeneous in occupation (trade and commerce), age (older), class (overwhelmingly middle), and place of residence (urban). Compared to the Jewish male educated class, most Jewish (propertied) men in Germany were more secure, socially and financially.[4] They were similar to their middle-class female counterparts in this respect; at the same time, gender roles divided bourgeois men from bourgeois women. Thus, even though wealthy Jewish women were periodically caricatured in *Simplicissimus* and *Fliegende Blätter*, male German Jews were always the principal targets of ridicule. They were even the butt of criticism in *Ost und West* since they most closely resembled the parvenus satirized in the journal. Self-conscious about their wealth and status, not to speak of their Jewishness, some of these men strove to escape the stereotype of the Jewish social climber.[5]

This stereotype of the German-Jewish parvenu is so powerful that it continues to slant our perspective in the post-Holocaust era, and historians have labored in vain to redress negative images of middle-class Jewish men.[6] (The cliché of the *yekke*—the uptight, jacket-wearing, foolish German Jew—is alive and well in Israel half a century after World War II.) The Jews of Germany are invariably represented as prototypical assimilators: wealthy, self-satisfied, and self-deluding. As opposed to the honored writers and thinkers—the Einsteins, Kafkas, and Benjamins—of German Jewry, the average Jewish *Bürger* seem best remembered for making money, for intermarrying, and for passively accepting German culture.[7] In fact, they are typically faulted for not having foreseen the "inevitable" rise of Nazism.

These misconceptions demand correction. In the last fifteen years, a number of historians have presented evidence of German-Jewish dissimilation.[8] By no means completely Germanized or self-hating, many German-Jewish men were fairly devout. They also married Jewish women in greater proportion than late-twentieth-century American-Jewish males do.[9] Just because many of them were integrated and well-to-do did not mean that they—consciously or unconsciously—excluded all forms of Jewish culture from their lives. They still socialized, by and large, with other Jews, and many wrote of "feeling" Jewish and of sharing in a community of fate (*Schicksalsgemeinschaft*).

One example of how Jewish men "assimilated" to German society is cited repeatedly: their willingness to fight for the *Kaiserreich* in World War I. Jewish support for the war, from pamphlets to poetry, also has led many today to see these Jews as German lackeys.[10] The idea that Jews became even more Germanized through the war experience can be found in one of the most recent overviews of Wilhelminian Jewry:

> The war provided a situation in which Jews, too, could work in highly visible positions for the common cause. Like most Germans, Jews believed that their fatherland was in grave danger and that the fight against "czarism" was a righteous one. . . . The war also seemed to offer them the opportunity to feel that they belonged; they seemed to be part of a nation under siege, working together with other Germans for a common cause. Moreover, their labor might also convince the most obdurate antisemite of their honesty and generosity.[11]

This standard account suggests that for Jews in the *Kaiserreich*, the early months of the war symbolized "one brief shining moment" in German-Jewish history. August 1914 seemed to present a window of opportunity in which Jewish Germans might demonstrate that they did not harbor dual allegiances, that they did not collude with the enemy, that they did not profit from wars, and that they did not shirk military service.

If this window of opportunity ever truly existed, however, it was soon closed shut. The charge that Jewish citizens were not contributing their part to the war effort was heard in the highest echelons of the German state and military. This allegation culminated in the 1916 *Judenzählung* ("Jewish census"). Although this statistical survey confirmed the fact that Jewish males volunteered and died in numbers roughly proportional to their non-Jewish compatriots, it was instigated by anti-Jewish sentiment.[12] For Jewish contemporaries, the *Judenzählung* came to represent a major break in German-Jewish history, marking a renewal of the antisemitism in Germany that led to National Socialism and the Holocaust.[13] Yet, strangely, some historians in the post-Holocaust era discern an overwhelming pro-German euphoria on the part of Wilhelminian Jews at the outset of the war.[14] What these historians omit is that the "spirit of 1914" required Jews to conform to a homogenized ideal of Germany identity and thus to repress any competing affiliations. The conventional emphasis on German-Jewish war zeal hides the conscious and unconscious pressures to which Jews were subjected in Imperial Germany and ignores their attempts to resist German monoculturalism. Moreover, Jewish sensitivity to the Germanophobia of the *Reich*'s enemies, far from being a sign of "Jewish antisemitism," points to an emerging "ethnic" Jewish identity among male Jews who lived in and/or served Imperial Germany.

The cliché about German-Jewish war enthusiasm merits reexamination. Despite the fact that most German Jews loyally identified with Imperial war aims in August 1914, the kaiser's declaration of a "civic truce" (or *Burgfrieden*) was violated almost immediately. As illustrated in diaries, letters, and publications such as *Ost und West*, World War I was not a time for open displays of Jewishness. According to the few surviving testimonies of military life, Jewish fighting men experienced a range of difficulties linked to their Jewishness. These ranged from physical violence to subtle exclusion and mental harassment.[15] With good reason, many Jewish soldiers preferred to keep their Jewishness a secret. Others, however, showed pride in being Jewish.[16]

Many a Jew considered it a religious duty to defend the fatherland and found ways to reconcile his belief with Jewish values.[17] But for the more Orthodox among the German-Jewish bourgeoisie, life at the front was difficult.[18] Against considerable odds, a number managed to carry out the required rituals.[19] Even among nonobservant soldiers, "the gravity of the war situation seemed to promote religious seriousness and religious conscientiousness."[20] Homesickness and alienation were not uncommon, and many a Jew returned home after the war "more religious and 'more Jewish' " than before.[21] Much of the literature directed at the Jewish soldier sought to ease his separation from family and community.

Whereas Jews had socialized predominantly with other Jews before the war, they were now thrown together for an extended time with non-Jews in the field. Some individuals, such as Julius Marx, censured friendliness between Jewish soldiers in public.[22] His attitude ultimately expressed a preference for respectability, that Jewishness be kept under wraps. At the same time, Marx details in his memoir how Jews distinguished themselves in battle. (His coreligionists are, in fact, so remarkable and courageous in his account that one begins to doubt the existence of less-than-perfect Jewish soldiers.)

For Jewish antidefamation leagues (*Abwehrorganisationen*) such as the *Centralverein*, the war represented an opportunity to be proven worthy, to achieve full equality before the law for Jews. Zionists in Germany, by being among the first to volunteer for the war, had more in common with their enemies at the *Centralverein* than they wished to admit. Like the average

German-Jewish man who had little interest in settling in Palestine, most Western Zionists were financially secure and more or less satisfied with life in the *Kaiserreich*.[23]

But in an unexpected paradox of World War I, antisemitism made German Jews more sensitive to their common ethnic heritage. Before the war, Jewish men in the *Kaiserreich* had more acute fears than being branded ignorant of Jewish learning and culture. In the life-and-death drama of battle, the German-Jewish soldier was more aware of his Jewishness than ever before. In addition, he had to live with the anxiety that his superiors or the troops he commanded might accuse him of cowardice or his family of war profiteering.[24] The situation was similar on the homefront, where the pressure of Jew hatred pointed more and more Jews in the direction of Jewish nationalism. The Orthodox community in Germany, impressed by the ethnic-national sentiments of pious Jews from the East, passed its most Zionist resolution ever at a convention in 1918.[25] Wartime antisemitism was thus an effective goad to Jewish nationalism, and *Ost und West* seized upon the opportunity to attack it. Contrary to most historiography, the outbreak of war did not bring Germans and Jews any nearer to each other than they already were.

One stereotype central to any discussion of Jewish identity in Germany is the image of the Jew as weak and unmanly. The notion that Jews might be physically inferior can be traced back to the Enlightenment. As George Mosse (and others) have argued, the origins of "respectability" were closely linked to a sublimated ideal of male sexuality in which the naked body is interpreted as a symbolic, spiritual vessel.[26] In the nineteenth century, respectability became the prevailing ideology of both the German and the German-Jewish middle classes, providing a pretext for excluding Eastern Jews as unmasculine. As a distancing mechanism, then, Western Jews "repudiate[d] the stereotype of the ghetto Jew of the past who through his appearance and behavior seemed to deny that ideal of manliness basic to respectability, and therefore to the process of Jewish assimilation."[27] The male body and force of character played critical roles in *Ost und West*'s appeals to German-Jewish *Bürger*.[28]

By the onset of the twentieth century, virile strength had become the sine qua non of Western-style nationalisms, both Jewish and non-Jewish. Discourse in the Jewish nationalist *Ost und West* could also be rigidly masculinist, a type of verbal combat. Jewish Zionists often felt compelled to prove that they were more martial than Jewish liberals, if only in their rhetoric. In the same period, Jewish nationalist students were demanding *Satisfaktion* in duels and showing prowess in sport.[29] By 1914, Jewish gymnastics (*Turnen*) and and similar activities had become more mainstream. Most of the luminaries of the Democratic Faction and the *jungjüdische Bewegung* now had assumed positions of responsibility in the Jewish community.[30] Like their elders, nearly all Jewish young men

144

went to war or supported Germany's war aims.[31] In a major political shift, they reconciled with the establishment in the official Jewish communities (*Gemeinden*) so that Zionists and liberals worked together to some extent during the war.[32]

In response to the prevailing stereotype of the Jew as a faint-hearted weakling, German Jews of all persuasions created fantasies of themselves as manly. The Jewish body once again served as a receptacle of values for both its defenders and its detractors. Among the former, influenced by Max Nordau's idea of "Jewish muscularity" (*Muskeljudentum*), a cult of Hebrew prowess evolved:

> The cult of the tough Jew as an alternative to Jewish timidity and gentleness rests on ideals of "masculine beauty," health, and normalcy that are conceived and articulated as if their validity were obvious and natural. They have, in other words, internalized unquestioningly the physical and psychological ideals of their respective dominant cultures. In doing so they forget that, far from being self-evident cultural universals, those ideals are predicated on a series of exclusions and erasures.[33]

At the turn of the century, tough Western Jewish nationalists tended to denigrate the Eastern Jewish body. This does not mean that they were antisemites or that they—as Paul Breines argues above—"internalized unquestioningly" the Western ideal of masculinity.[34] Yet *Ost und West*, though it did not denigrate the body of the *Ostjude*, was not prepared to submit the Eastern Jewish scholar as a masculine ideal based on intellect rather than force.[35]

In fact, any search for new models of Jewish masculinity stopped abruptly in August 1914.[36] At this time, the common element in *Ost und West's* defense of Jewish manhood became the denigration of weak men, particularly those who were not Jewish. The magazine did not counter the images of weak Jewish males through stereotypes rooted in traditional Eastern or enlightened Western Judaism. Instead, for the first time after 1914, the journal's stereotypes of masculinity were based on criteria that were more genuinely ethnic or pan-Jewish.

Prior to World War I, *Ost und West* consistently had sought to be neutral in scholarship and nonpartisan in politics in its quest to be *the* leading ethnic Jewish magazine in Europe. This impartiality was in keeping with its self-image as popularized "Science of Judaism," as pan-Jewish *Wissenschaft des Judentums* of Eastern Jewish paternity. Such a scholarly approach to religion was brought to bear on *Ost und West's* first war editorial, "Der Krieg als Lehrmeister" [The War as Teacher] (September–December 1914). Though unsigned, the essay was written by Binjamin Segel and managed to appeal to the residual Judaism of middle-class Jewish men at the same time as it affirmed the German cause. Since objectivity in nineteenth-century Western Europe had come to be associated with virility, it was important to the men of *Ost und West*—now more than ever—that they project a image of being in control. *Ost und West* presented itself as above the fray to defuse potential conflicts between competing ideals of German and Jewish manhood.

For all its pretensions to impartiality, the journal's rejoinders to the war mobilization of August 1914 were almost unanimously pro-German.[37] For example, "Der Krieg als Lehrmeister"—which was almost certainly uncensored[38]—made no mention of Winz's expulsion from the *Kaiserreich* in the first days of conflict. Winz, like other Russian Jews residing in Germany, had never been granted citizenship and was thus subject to deportation. Because Segel was an Austrian national, he was permitted to stay in Berlin, where, in place of Winz, he presumably helped carry out much of the day-to-day work of publishing *Ost und West*.[39] Winz, then, spent much of the war in Copenhagen, and the nature of his activities there is shrouded in mystery; he probably worked for the Zionist office and for the German consulate as the Jewish affairs adviser, and possibly even for German intelligence.[40] Winz was also permitted to return to Germany to publish the first wartime issue of *Ost und West*, a mission having the endorsement of German officials.[41] Wars make strange bedfellows, but neither the Alliance Israélite Universelle nor other anti-German Jews ever forgave Winz for siding officially with the *Kaiserreich*.[42]

Even though Winz aligned himself with Germany, the *Deutschtum* of *Ost und West* diverged in important respects from the nationalism of other German-Jewish periodicals in 1914. The Liberal-Jewish press and the Zionist press called on German-Jewish males—regardless of whether they resided in the Palatinate or in Palestine—to sacrifice their lives for the fatherland. In contrast, *Ost und West* delivered a relatively muted, if still patriotic, response in December 1914. Four months into the war, Winz and his colleagues were aware of growing antisemitism in the German ranks. But the journal called for objectivity rather than oversensitivity in counteracting the charge of dual loyalty. Anti-Jewish sentiment was to be brushed off and not answered with hatred, lest Jews be viewed as malicious or negative (and thus in violation of the Kaiser's *Burgfrieden*). To promote this agenda in "Der Krieg als Lehrmeister," Segel recycled an old promotional strategy by projecting conventional stereotypes of Jews as spiteful and treacherous onto both Jewish and non-Jewish groups. First and foremost among Segel's perceived "others" are the hate-filled, pathological enemies of Germany in the war; they embody the stereotype of the vengeful Jew. The second group he singles out is made up of the disloyal men of German ancestry in the enemy camp. These individuals—all non-Jews—are described as self-hating apostates.[43] Segel then turns the tables by projecting the stereotype of the vindictive renegade not onto Eastern Jews but rather onto a third group: Western Jewish apostates.[44]

One stereotype Segel projects onto the "others" is that of the "corrupt and corrupting" discourse of the Jews.[45] If Sander Gilman's theory is correct, fin-de-siècle Jews such as Segel who used language to shape their identity internalized this stereotype and saw themselves as flawed. In turn, they sought to rid themselves of the taint of Jewishness in their writing by displaying firm command of the German language and of the rational discourse of *Wissenschaft* ("science" or "scholarship").[46] Segel's editorial, while difficult to fit into Gilman's project, does show a preference for objectivity over partisanship and hence a need to demonstrate the fitness not only of the Jewish male body but also of "Jewish discourse." In order to retain control over his Jewish discourse, Segel had to resolve the tension inherent in being both the observer and the observed.[47] Although Segel was a Galician Jewish folklorist and ethnographer, his war editorials revealed his inability "objectively" to master ethnological discourse about the Jew. In striving to be a man of science (a *Wissenschaftler*), he also distanced himself from a related fiction about the Jews, namely that Jewish journalism was imitative, polemical, and devoid of beauty. To contain this Jewish discourse, a Jewish publicist such as Segel had to avoid extremes of emotion. If he were chauvinistically pro-German, he would be branded as opportunistic; if he were too Eastern Jewish, he would be labeled hysterical or too subjective.

In "Vom grundlosen Haß" (Of Unfounded Hatred), the first of three sections of "Der Krieg als Lehrmeister," Segel refutes the myth that Jews are deranged by "Christian hatred." Still, only after six hundred words and a page turn does it emerge who hates whom and whose side *Ost und West* will be taking in the war. The first sentences are deliberately vague: "A tidal wave of blood-red, fire-scorching, wildly roaring *hatred* has stunned the world. It seems to have burst out of infernal depths. It is as deep as the ocean, and rolls oppressively like smelt metal over the civilized [*gesittete*] Earth, destroying all the seeds of refined [*edel*] culture, smothering all stirrings of humane feeling" (625; emphasis added). While the allusions to "culture" and "civilization"[48] betray *Ost und West*'s pro-German stance, Segel's advocacy of cultured respectability here is implicitly a defense against the image of the vindictive, corrupted Shylockian Jew. As if to compensate for this anti-Jewish image, Segel now takes an ethnological approach to hatred, in effect delivering a popularized lecture on the formation of stereotypes: "Hatred is a natural, human affect. It can be refined if it emanates from anger, the anger over a wrong suffered, an undeserved humiliation. . . . Hatred is pathological (*krankhaft*) if it is unfounded (*grundlos*), hatred for the sake of hatred, barren, subversive, and festering" (626). Here Segel develops a theory of affects and presents himself as a psychoanalyst and physician of the spirit. He thus regards himself as competent to distinguish between pathological and nonpathological hatred. Germany's hatred toward its enemies is seen as rational, even healthy; its foes, by contrast, are unscientific and therefore diseased.

Antisemitism as a form of unjustified hatred is so far missing from the editorial, as if it were a taboo topic. Whereas many German Jews

147

by December 1914 already were comparing the situation of the outcast *Reich* to the pariah status of the Jews, Segel makes no explicit analogy between antisemitism and anti-Germanism until another thousand words into the argument. Instead, he begins by deriving the distinction between pathological and nonpathological hatred from the Jewish ethical tradition. So imperative is it to debunk the myth that Jews resent Christians that Segel actually quotes the Hebrew term for "groundless hatred" (*sin'at ḥinnam*) in the original Hebrew script and concludes that "the hatred towards Germany is deeply related to *antisemitism*" (629). Such a strategy, in fact, was calculated to interest German-Jewish men in ethnic Jewish identity. At the same time, it was a response to the growing controversy over the popular "Haßgesang auf England" (Hate-Hymn for England) by Ernst Lissauer (1882–1937), a German Jew. While the antisemite Houston Stewart Chamberlain (1855–1927) maintained that only a Jew could have composed such a song (thereby breaking his promised wartime silence on the so-called *Judenfrage*), Segel, in a later editorial—"Erziehung zum Haß" (Education in Hatred) (January–May 1915)—summarized interviews with sixty German-Jewish personalities, all of whom rejected Lissauer's song of hatred as un-Jewish.[49]

Three pages into "Der Krieg als Lehrmeister," Segel still has not referred directly to the Jews. He has simply appealed to readers to understand the mechanisms of hatred. By equating anti-Germanism and antisemitism in the last passage, Segel puts off the crucial issue of Jewish masculinity yet again. Since addressing this topic would call his own Jewish masculinity into question, he is careful to focus on anti-German stereotypes as much as possible: (1) the representation of Germans as overly industrious and driven to succeed (626, 628); (2) the representation of Germans as uncivilized and without manners (628); and (3) the representation of Germans as "fetid men" (*stinkende Männer*), a cliché promulgated by the Belgians (628). Upon reexamination, however, these stereotypes reveal more than coincidental affinities with anti-Jewish stereotypes. The final representation, in fact, evokes the canard of the *foëtor judaicus*, the reputed stench of the Jew.

This pattern, whereby stereotypes of the Germans turn out to be stereotypes of the Jews, continues into the second part of Segel's editorial, titled "Die Rassentheorie und der Krieg." Here Segel unmasks the pseudoscience of "race," especially as practiced by Chamberlain. The war, for Segel, has brought forth little evidence of "Aryan" solidarity. If anything, conflicts are rampant within the ranks of the so-called master race, and Segel singles out disloyal men of German ancestry, rendering these individuals self-haters while continuing to ignore the idea of Jewish self-hatred. To this end, he harps on Germans who must struggle with competing allegiances. Tsar Nicholas, for example, becomes the worst example of self-renunciation. Married to a German and himself a blood relative of German royalty, he exemplifies pathological hatred that has been transformed into self-hatred. Other self-hating Germans Segel cites include men from the neutral countries as well as British and Russian envoys to the Central Powers.

By delaying any mention of Jewish soldiers until the editorial's third segment, entitled "Die Juden als Krieger," Segel rescues Jewish males from the scourge of apostasy. Even though the defense of Jewish masculinity, from swordsmanship to scholarship, forms the rationale for the entire editorial, Segel's defense of Jewish masculinity is still understated. At first, he argues that peace is the true measure of a people's moral mettle. This disclaimer involves a view of Jewish manhood that stresses mind over muscle, a view held by the herald of *Muskeljudentum*, Nordau.[50] Having repudiated brute force in this way, Segel now can view the war as a unique historical event that tests a people's capacity for bravery, discipline, organization, sacrifice, and physical performance (635). His catalogue of Jewish war heroes, from the Bible and Bar Kochba to the *Befreiungskriege* ("Wars of Liberation") and the Franco-Prussian war, spans an entire page.

It should be noted, however, that these arguments applied to Jews who were fighting on *both* sides of the conflict. If Jews were also in the enemy armies, how could Segel applaud their heroic attacks on Germans and still be a German (or Austro-Hungarian) patriot? The possibility of Jewish disloyalty is addressed in a fashion appropriate to a Jewish man of the quill. After consistently overlooking Jewish self-hatred, Segel finally lets the self-hating Jews out of the closet, admitting most of the way through his seven-page essay that men of German descent are not alone in being renegades. Instead of citing actual Jewish soldier-traitors, however, he picks on a favorite target, Maximilian Harden (1861–1927), publisher and editor of *Die Zukunft*. Harden, a convert to Christianity, once declared that no Aryan would ever deign to obey a Jewish soldier. Segel ridicules him as having "never smelled gunpowder" (639).[51] But the attack on Harden ultimately fails; Segel is, after all, accusing a fellow journalist of Jewish origin of being self-hating. That all of this is too close for comfort is suggested in Segel's curious remark that the legend of Jewish physical inferiority found in novels and humor magazines would soon disappear, and he notes optimistically: "Particularly in the East, the traditional humble behavior [*Haltung*] of lower-class Jews toward the 'gentleman' and representative of armed power will give way to a dignified, fearless, more composed demeanor" (640). For Segel, this Jewish attitude of humility (which resembles the Eastern Jewish male style) will be redeemed by the "blood sacrifices" (*Blutopfer*) of thousands of European Jewish warriors.[52]

Such a pan-Jewish attitude suggests, quite implausibly, that Jews are incapable of betraying other Jews. Segel anticipates this objection in an earlier comment by suggesting that writers, not warriors, betray themselves and their nations. Arguing that the soldiers of 1914 do not hate in a pathological manner, Segel (like the profoundly un-Jewish Ernst Jünger a few years later)[53] describes these men of valor as feeling emotion, even respect, for the courage of the enemy. While exonerating the 600,000 Jewish fighters involved in this greater European struggle, the editorial goes on to indict the sneaky civilian snipers of the *pen*, who are said to be conducting the discursive equivalent of ritual murder. These franc-tireurs are likened to the pogromists who in autumn 1914 were cutting off Jewish "eyes, ears, hands, and legs" (627). Using the same reasoning, Segel, in a signed article following the editorial—"Eine Verirrung (Zangwill als Anwalt Rußlands)" (September–December 1914)—denounces the British-Jewish writer Israel Zangwill, whom he links with the franc-tireurs of the pen. Alleging that Zangwill has never seen a pogrom with his own eyes, Segel also depicts him as a self-hating Western Jew who is unable to read Yiddish and who has no understanding of Jewish history or Jewish thought (646). Worst of all, Zangwill has betrayed his father, the Eastern Jewish proletarian who emigrated from Russia, by siding with the Tsar in World War I. By characterizing his more successful Jewish colleague as a renegade, Segel comes full circle and promotes a stereotype that was familiar to readers of *Ost und West*: that of the Western Jewish parvenu.[54] By the middle of the first wartime issue of the journal, Segel has thus rendered nearly everyone—the Germans, the English, the Russians, and the Western Jews—as self-hating and duplicitous. Excluded are the Russian Jews, such as Winz, and the Galician Jews, such as Segel himself, who produced *Ost und West*.

The inner conflicts experienced by warriors of the pen in 1914 were not limited to Jewish war publicists such as Segel, Harden, or Zangwill. But while Segel's relentless search for the self-hating "other" suggests the psychological pressures to which Jewish writers were subjected during the war, his conscious projection of Germany's antisemitism onto enemy nations remains a form of political propaganda.[55] It is likewise propaganda when he argues that *Ost und West*'s rational, objective approach to the war is indebted to the "German scholarly spirit and German method" (647). For, according to Segel, all research on Jews—whether in English, French, or Polish—ultimately draws on the German *Wissenschaft des Judentums*, which itself derives from German philosophy. In short, Segel's rhetorical acrobatics in the essay on Zangwill are better explained as the self-assuredness of the propagandist than as the self-consciousness of a Jew who despises himself. Segel thus provides a revisionist historiography—a public attempt at mastering recent German history—for an audience presumed to be German, Jewish, and male. He contends that all Eastern Jews know that Germany is the country where antisemitism originated: "Of course, all of these [East European] Jews know that antisemitism in Germany is far from being extinguished and simply appears to be waiting for the right moment to flare up with renewed violence" (647). But then he presents an antithetical argument that plays down the significance of German antisemitism: "In the public and spiritual life of Germany, antisemitism is a merely dismal phenomenon if juxtaposed with the thousand other positive ones" (647). In a final passage, Segel's justifications for German antisemitism anticipate the so-called *Historikerstreit* unleashed in 1986 inasmuch as he diagnoses Russia as Germany's wicked *Doppelgänger* in matters of antisemitism:

> As powerful as antisemitism in Germany has been at times and as fatefully as it has affected the situation of the Jews in other countries, especially in Russia, it still has never achieved predominance here, it has never become the leitmotiv of all governmental activity; in particular, however, it has never degenerated into a well-considered, organized, and effectively maintained system of persecution. As much as the Jews of Germany and, as a result, all other Jews have had to suffer emotionally [*seelisch*] due to antisemitism, all of these sufferings are only a droplet in the sea in comparison to the unspeakable disaster that the Russian *Doppelgänger* of German antisemitism has brought upon our people. (647–48)

Turning the *Judenfrage* into a *Tsarenfrage* was only the first of *Ost und West's* wartime attempts to deal with increasing antisemitism. Not content to publish editorials alone, Winz and Segel soon added fiction to their arsenal of apologies for German-Jewish masculinity.

Segel's earliest appeals to middle-class German-Jewish men in World War I subtly played upon their fears of apostasy and excessive emotionality. These fears were in turn rooted in attachments to traditional and enlightened Jewish identity. Such attachments were the basis for *Ost und West's* ideal of ethnic Jewish identity, and the climate of war promoted Jewish ethnicity, in part because criticism of German-Jewish men was growing. Indeed, as the war progressed, *Ost und West's* pan-Jewish agenda indirectly benefited from antisemitic attacks questioning the patriotism of Jewish men who saw themselves as loyal German citizens. The canard of Jewish male weakness grew more pervasive in the press, and by the time the war had descended into the trenches, antisemitic stereotyping of the Jewish male body had sunk to new lows.

The most significant assault on German-Jewish political and physical integrity was the 1916 census of Jewish soldiers in the Prussian army. *Ost und West's* response to this challenge was typical: it altered the way it promoted ethnic Jewishness. Because the *Judenzählung* seemed designed to expose Jewish cowardice, the magazine responded with case histories of Jewish military prowess.[56] The journal also phased out most negative Jewish characters in its fiction and began with heightened resolve to introduce positive ones. This strategy is evident in one of *Ost und West's* longest novellas, Binjamin Segel's *Am Tage des Gerichts*.

Am Tage des Gerichts was, by all standards, a carefully choreographed success. As though he were anticipating the *Judenzählung*, Segel created a strong Jewish male character, perhaps the most believable Eastern Jewish protagonist in the history of *Ost und West*.[57] And even though the narrative contained a Jewish parvenu, he was ultimately overshadowed by a weak and degenerate Polish antisemite. Furthermore, long passages extolled the traditional and enlightened identity of Polish Jewry and were thus aimed at rejuvenating ethnic Judaism. In addition, the story's Yom Kippur setting and the presence of a "jazz singer" character (the cantor David Chasan) capitalized on the strong associations most Jews—even the *Dreitagejuden*[58] of Germany—had with this most sacred of Jewish holy days. Since *Am Tage des Gerichts* appeared sequentially in *Ost und West,* Segel was able to deliver his strongest apologetics in the final segment of May–June 1916, just a few months before the official announcement of the *Judenzählung.* Published separately as a book, the novella sold around 5,000, one of many publications intended for Jewish soldiers at the front.[59] In addition, Segel's wartime publications—many of which were based on essays in *Ost und West*—went through several printings, in one case reaching 12,000 copies.[60]

Am Tage des Gerichts also followed on the heels of Segel's most successful book, *Die polnische Judenfrage* (completed in December 1915), and his novella is in many ways the fictional realization of arguments in the book, particularly in its proposed synthesis of Western Jewish emancipation and Eastern Jewish tradition.[61] The impetus this time for Segel's ethnic Jewish standpoint was the need to expose the double standard of Max Bodenheimer's distinctly Western Jewish "Committee for the East" (*Komitee für den Osten*).[62] Established after the outbreak of the war to secure "national autonomy" for the Jews of Poland, the *Komitee*'s German-interventionist program, Segel argued, was destined to perpetuate Jewish inequality.[63] Bodenheimer's notions of *Volk* and *völkische Emanzipation* were pure abstractions; only individuals can be genuinely emancipated.[64] Segel thus encouraged the *Komitee,* tongue in cheek, to try out Jewish national autonomy in Germany first, for to maintain separate Jewish cultural and linguistic institutions in Poland would only further isolate the already powerless Jews living there.[65] Lastly, Segel was opposed to treating Eastern Jews as pawns of German war policy and thus demanded an end to propaganda clichés that linked *Ostjudentum* to *Deutschtum.*[66]

Am Tage des Gerichts was a defense of Polish Jewry designed both to influence policy and to bring German-Jewish men into the ethnic Jewish fold. The story thus recapitulates the historical stages of traditional, enlightened, and ethnic Judaism in Poland—all against the backdrop of one man's life. This Jewish Everyman is Simon Berg, the managing director of a factory.[67] The story documents Berg's struggle with his conscience on Yom Kippur, three months after embezzling 9,000 gulden from Stefan Gemba, the local antisemite. When Gemba, an abusive drunkard and usurer, accidentally overpays a debt to Berg's boss, the otherwise pious Jew succumbs to the "evil impulse" (in Hebrew, *yetser hara*) and steals the excess. There is a motive for Berg's lapse: the thirty-six-year-old[68] widower, with two children and a younger sister to provide for, has little to show for his two decades with the firm. His boss, Heinrich Rebenstein, is recently deceased, and the younger

Rebenstein, who is selling off his deceased father's assets, does not offer Berg severance pay; he is only prepared to excuse his debts. Such behavior is unjustified. For, unlike his patron's son, who is arrogant and dishonorable, Berg is a Jewish version of Gustav Freytag's Anton Wohlfahrt,[69] the Horatio Alger of nineteenth-century German literature: he is disciplined, well liked, and respected by all. The new boss's resolve to live the dissolute life in Paris[70] is contrasted with Berg's life of virtue prior to his crime.

What starts out as a critique of Jewish parvenuism is, however, given little room to develop, and the younger Rebenstein harmlessly disappears from the story. Instead, the narrator shows how Berg deals with the Eastern-traditional Jewish implications of his transgression, extensively detailing his reactions to the Yom Kippur liturgy. Like his fellow worshipers at the town synagogue, he is caught up in the drama of the day. Sobbing, wailing, and breast beating express the guilt of the community (or *kehillah*), and individuals recount numerous tales of how sinners have repented in public on previous Days of Atonement. Because the communal admission of sins is such an integral part of Yom Kippur observance, Berg wishes to feel united with his coreligionists, but this circumstance is dependent on his contrition. Whenever he considers his predicament, he is overcome by a feeling of separation from his community. This separation is analogous to the isolation felt by German-Jewish soldiers, the target audience of the story. Because this audience is made up of Western-enlightened Jews, the narrator must define the status of embezzlement in Jewish law: a thief not only stains his own soul, but he also dismantles God's order, spreading injustice in the world. (It does not matter what the offended party knows, or whether he or she is hurt; the more secretly the larceny takes place, the worse the sin.) Worst of all, however, is sinning against a non-Jew, which is regarded as a transgression against God's name (*ḥillul ha-shem*) that sullies His teaching and His chosen people.[71]

But religious arguments are not enough to convince Berg to repent. Part II of *Am Tage des Gerichts* targets the Western-enlightened background of most German-Jewish men. It implicitly censures antisemitism, especially the myth that Jews profited from World War I. For, on top of the misrepresentations of their fitness for military service, Jewish men increasingly had to contend with accusations that they were exploiting the war for personal gain. The story's theme of misappropriated funds was addressed both to German-Jewish civilians and to soldiers, encouraging them to resist the temptation to cheat or disobey non-Jews.[72] Even so, the temptation for Jews to indulge in reverse discrimination was understandable, if not pardonable, and this is reflected in *Am Tage des Gerichts*. Antisemitism reaches its breaking point for Berg in part II, and for the first of three times in the narrative, he has misgivings about repenting. Even though he is consumed here with self-pity and is worried that his standing in the community will be jeopardized should knowledge of his crime leak out, his nihilistic excurses at the end of part II are really an angry response to antisemitism. He fears that innocent Jews will be persecuted if his secret is exposed, that his case will be taken as confirmation that Judaism allows Jews to cheat those outside the fold (65). The existence of antisemitism makes God seems unjust, indeed absent. In his delirium, Berg asserts in Karamazovian fashion that everything is allowed, and he threatens to convert, even on Yom Kippur.

But in rejecting Eastern religious Judaism and flirting with nihilism, Berg has allowed the pendulum to swing too far to the West. In the third part of the novella, he regains his composure and contemplates a more Eastern version of enlightened Jewish identity that signals his movement toward atonement. The mechanical repetition of the liturgy is faulted, but with one interesting exception: a prayer that especially moves Berg and resembles the Lord's Prayer (*das Vaterunser*). In *Am Tage des Gerichts*, as elsewhere in his oeuvre, Segel adds christological features to heighten the effect.[73] The title of the story means "On the Day of Judgment," and at times it presents an almost Christian notion of unconditional forgiveness (121) that enables Berg to overcome his hatred of antisemites.[74] Knowing how easily one can lapse, Berg now pledges to show more consideration for others and to be less prejudicial.

A further, and more significant, critique of Eastern Jewish formalism comes in the fourth and final installment of *Am Tage des Gerichts*. In this key dramatic scene, Berg leaves the synagogue, resolved to confront Gemba. But as he arrives at home to retrieve the money from the chest, he realizes that he has left the keys with his sister. His only option, short of confessing to her, is to open the chest with a crowbar. Yet Berg hesitates to break the lock, painfully aware that to do so would constitute a horrible transgression on Yom Kippur. This hesitation is all the more conspicuous: up to this point, it has been a manly test of will to fulfill the commandments in the face of obstacle. The Rabbinic principle of *marit 'ayin* ("what the eye perceives")—of conveying the appearance of piety—is never mentioned.

The German-Jewish readers of this story were bound to view Berg's hesitation as hair splitting. Segel thus came up with an elaborate justification for making an exception to the commandments, a justification that would appeal to German-Jewish men while still fulfilling *Ost und West*'s pan-Jewish agenda. At first, Berg's literalist obedience to Torah prevails on the basis of religion (the body is the external instrument of Torah) and aesthetics (Torah gives poetry, style, and rhythm to life). But when confronted with the long history of the Jewish people prior to Rabbinic Judaism—essentially an ethnic criterion—he refuses to delay his confession to Gemba any longer: "A hundred proud voices awakened in Simon Berg, a hundred witnesses from the past drew near and stood round his bed. The apparition of piety and learnedness [that had plagued him] became more and more blurred. Soon it had dissolved away into emptiness; its voice had disappeared" (201). This ethnic criterion also persuades Berg to overcome the racism implicit in the argument that a Jew may be impious on account of a Gentile. By acknowledging the ethnic-historical nature of his identity, he tacitly admits the legitimate rights of other peoples. In addition, since the Jews were once strangers in the land of Egypt, they are now, as a "holy people" (*heiliges Volk*), obliged to protect the stranger against thievery and other injustices. In finally deciding to break open the chest on a holy day, Berg breaks with the supremacy of religious and aesthetic concepts of Judaism in favor of a pan-Jewish ethnic identity.

Only after having overcome second thoughts on three separate occasions does Berg subject himself to possible humiliation: before the sun sets, he returns the money to Gemba and asks his forgiveness. Yet he strikes a balance between humility and toughness in his meeting with Gemba, illustrating a new synthesis of universalism with ethnic particularism. The Jewish hero is redeemed as masculine and respectable: "He had regained his composure and looked his adversary straight [*fest*] in the face" (202). At the dramatic high point of the novella, Gemba erupts in a drunken tirade upon hearing Berg's dispassionate confession, "I misappropriated the money" (202), forcing the protagonist to defend himself: "Simon Berg stood there, his hand propped on the edge of the table, and let Gemba's rage pass over him. Gemba, fuming with anger, grabbed his dog whip. Then he lifted his hand to attack Simon Berg. Berg turned pale, seized Gemba forcefully by the wrists, and divested him of the whip with a quick movement. Then, with a shove, he forced his defenseless rival into his chair. Stefan Gemba groaned in pain under his iron-like grip" (202). Insofar as Gemba only respects signs of physical superiority, he virtually compels Berg to respond with force, only to plea for mercy from Berg's "fingers of steel" (202). In successfully subduing Gemba, Berg effectively saves Jewish men as a group from the denunciations of antisemites. At the same time, his righteous example influences Gemba, who (for the time being) stops beating his servant and his dog.

In the conclusion to *Am Tage des Gerichts*, Segel prefigures how his narrative is to be read. His implied audience is not German-Jewish women but rather their brothers, fathers, and husbands. In fact, Berg desists from telling anything to his beloved sister and confidante. Although he could reveal his experience to her as something that had happened to a third person, he demurs, claiming that her "pure and childlike sensibility" (204) would not grasp the full significance of such a story. One can similarly imagine German-Jewish soldiers sparing women descriptions of their own humiliations at the front. To comprehend the story thus requires a masculine consciousness. No weakling, Berg is characteristically referred to as a "strong-willed man of deeds" (68). Because his tale is inappropriate for a female—or effeminate—audience, he expressly resolves to tell it to his son when he has reached manhood and to recall it frequently to himself.

The language of the novella's closing passages urges an ethnic return to the fold (*Umkehr*) and underlines the theme of a universalist but particularist

Judaism. In addition, the conclusion ties together earlier evidence of an East-West ethnic reconciliation in the story, most notably the eclectic clique of *maskilim* in Berg's pluralistic Polish *shtetl*. This clique includes a humble student of philosophy in Berlin, the author Segel's alter ego.[75] This student, out of love for Yom Kippur, returns every year to the *shtetl*, demonstrating the power that the Day of Atonement exercises even over the local "Deutsche" (in Yiddish, *daytshe* or westernized Jews) and, by extension, over Segel's German-Jewish readers. Although the would-be head of the *kehillah*, David Schamler, is obsessed with his hunger every Yom Kippur, the Berlin student argues that it is better to be "master in one's own house" (190)—and thus more virile—for twenty-four hours. But Schamler, while he despises the poor Berlin student, is never denounced as a westernized parvenu; Segel renders him with humor, not acerbity. In keeping with this day of reconciliation, the visiting student also draws a parallel between the learned men of the East and the West. The *Ostjude* Reb Jossele, who wishes that Yom Kippur happened twice a year, shares this attitude with the *Westjude* Professor Steinthal, confirming a "peculiar affinity" (190) between the wretched scribe from Tarnow and the eminent Berlin scholar of *Völkerpsychologie* ("ethnic psychology"). One final instance of East-West symbiosis is the common talmudic discourse of two boys from divergent backgrounds. Engaged in a dispute on theodicy (which Segel links to Berg's predicament), the two have been friends since early childhood and remain so despite the fact that the one attends a secular school and the other a *heder*.

At times, Segel's egalitarian *shtetl* in *Am Tage des Gerichts* is so idealized that it virtually becomes a cult of the *Ostjuden*. Class distinction appears to matter little in this idyllic community: both rich and poor Jews are united by the years spent worshiping and studying Talmud together at the same *shul*. Even a simple person such as the blind *melamed* is esteemed; this poor but wise old man is frequently consulted as an expert in questions of Talmud. Non-Jews in Segel's narrative do not fare nearly as well. True, there is the good Polish noblewoman, just as there are a few upright Poles in Segel's *Die polnische Judenfrage.*[76] But Stefan Gemba is portrayed as a drunken beast in *Am Tage des Gerichts*, as is Onufry, the pilfering, unrepentant *shabbes goy* (non-Jewish Sabbath helper). In fact, Berg shouts at Onufry in a scene meant to evoke humor. In a final dig, the narrator suggests that Onufry subscribes to the Polish peasants' proverb: "To rob the nobleman is no crime; to rob the priest is no sin; to rob the *Jews* is a service" (191). In short, Segel exalts the history of Polish Jewry at the expense of Polish Christians, setting up the divided, colonized culture of the Poles as a foil for a new Jewish ethnicity. As in *Ost und West*'s wartime journalism, negative stereotypes of the Jews re-emerge—in slightly altered form—as negative stereotypes of non-Jewish groups. Only in this way, it appeared, was it possible to imagine an ethnic Judaism that appealed to the broader German-Jewish middle class.

As we have seen, *Am Tage des Gerichts* defended the Jews of Poland by rejecting the religious and enlightened identities of German-Jewish men for a more encompassing idea of Jewish ethnicity. Because antisemitism toward both Eastern and Western Jews intensified in World War I, it was all the more imperative that *Ost und West* promote a viable model of ethnic Jewishness, which meant suspending virtually all negative images of Jews. In response to the *Judenzählung*, then, the journal effectively relegated the Jewish parvenus and other Jewish villains to the closet.

Eliminating pretexts for antisemitism was impossible. Nor was it easy to create models of Jewish ethnic identity with which German-Jewish men (including soldiers) could identify. Understandably, *Ost und West's* fiction held out greater promise for positive marketing than its editorials. In addition, the careful interweaving of the Yom Kippur liturgy with the protagonist's tribulations in *Am Tage des Gerichts* was designed to draw in otherwise unreligious readers. Traditional Jewish practices were carefully clarified in the text for *Ost und West's* Western Jewish audience.[77] In another concession to Jewish males, the story's defense of Jewish masculinity and integrity surpassed that of the journal's prewar literature. The unmanly Jewish parvenu was played down in the wartime issues of the magazine in order to make way for positive images.[78] Like his editorials, Segel's story had few (if any) weak Jews, exploitive Jews, or Jews without some knowledge of Jewish customs.

After 1914, the battle lines were drawn differently in *Ost und West*. Fighting the common enemy was of greater necessity than fighting internal Jewish turf battles. Yet the journal's message, especially in *Am Tage des Gerichts*, was contradictory. On the one hand, Jews were urged to watch their behavior; on the other, they were exhorted publicly to challenge antisemitism. In Segel's fiction, embezzlement was condemned and linked to war profiteering, yet it was also understandable—almost justified—since the victim of the crime was a ruthless antisemite. After 1916, contesting antisemitism increasingly took precedence in *Ost und West* over the nascent Western cult of Eastern Jewry. The promoters of this self-styled cult viewed the Eastern Jews as "a genuine national proletariat, authentic embodiments of a proud tradition."[79] For them, the *Ostjude* became a symbol of community and spirituality in a materialistic world at war. The cult of the *Ostjuden* was also of interest to the average German-Jewish readers of *Ost und West* who were eager to find a way to coopt criticism of their values by Jews and non-Jews.

But Winz and the other contributors were quite suspicious of these newcomers to *Ostjudentum* and Jewish ethnicity. Segel, as we have seen, was less than enthusiastic about the Western-oriented *Komitee für den Osten*. More than ever, *Ost und West* was convinced that East-to-West transmission had to take place cautiously, without blind chauvinism. Thus, Winz and his circle did not blindly idealize the Jews of the East, and after the war, they grew even more critical of discourse on Eastern Jews and Jewish ethnicity. At the same time, even where Eastern Jews were depicted as having significant faults, such as in *Am Tage des Gerichts*, these faults were usually overshadowed by those of non-Jews.

For all their criticism and ad hominem arguments, Segel's war stories and essays stand up to comparison to the coffee-table literature of the "cultists" of Eastern Jewry.[80] In the tradition of *Ost und West*, Segel brought the *Ostjuden* to the *Westjuden* and adapted the promotion of Jewish nationalism to the demands of wartime. At the same time, the journal clearly assessed the needs of its German-Jewish male constituency and showed that their needs, as well as those of the Eastern Jews under Russian siege, could not be met by the *Komitee für den Osten* or related groups. Unfortunately, *Ost und West*'s skepticism toward the new friends of the *Ostjuden* also proved prescient. After November 11, 1918, the activist aficionados of Polish Jewry could not prevent verbal and physical assaults on *Ostjuden* living in Germany. The violence reached its peak in the little-known pogrom of November 1923 in Berlin's Scheunenviertel, just half a year after *Ost und West*'s demise. But having foreseen such events, Winz, Segel, and their associates could not predict the ultimate fate of twentieth-century German—and European—Jewry.

The Meaning of *Ost und West*:
Jews and Germans, Identity and Self-Hatred

This study has been concerned with *Ost und West*'s promotion of Jewish ethnicity and its impact on Jewish identity in the *Kaiserreich*. The conclusion will assess how successful Winz and his colleagues were in promoting the idea of cultural pluralism for European Jewry. Sharing in multiple cultures, and thus identities, was perceived negatively by most German Jews in this period. What *Ost und West* accomplished was to create an alternative space for a minority culture within German culture and European culture at large.[1] The journal may thus furnish a model for contemporary ethnic and nonethnic minorities: from African Americans and Latinos to lesbians, gays, and bisexuals. Seeing one's minority—or minorities—anew inevitably means adapting and reclaiming images of one's group that have been created by hostile outsiders. Taking older stereotypes and giving them new meanings is part of the process by which "new" identities are formed.

After the fall of the monarchy and the outbreak of revolution in November 1918, the political and social situation of Jews in Germany, despite great promise, improved little. Equality before the law in the new German democracy did not protect self-proclaimed "German Citizens of the Jewish Faith" against the proliferation of anti-Jewish myths, ranging from the idea of a Jewish world conspiracy (*Weltverschwörung*) to the stab-in-the-back theory (*Dolchstoßlegende*).[2] Attacks on Jews were not only ideological but also physical, revealing how woefully thin the line between prejudice and bodily assault had become. Left-wing activity as a whole came to be associated with Jews, and the assassinations of a number of Jewish political leaders of all shades—Rosa Luxemburg, Kurt Eisner, Walther Rathenau, Eugen Leviné, Gustav Landauer—were only the most public reminders of anti-Jewish violence in the first five years of the new German republic.

Discrimination against Eastern Jews did not make the headlines, however. The large-scale deportations of Jews from Bavaria in October 1923 and the pogrom that took place in Berlin's Scheunenviertel on November 8 and 9, 1923, were quickly forgotten.[3] Clearly, *Ost und West* no longer could fight the propaganda battles of the *Ostjuden* by itself. New political organizations sprang up to fill the vacuum in leadership (such as the *Jüdische Volkspartei*), but efforts on behalf of the Eastern Jews in Germany came, for the most part, too late. In fact, it must have seemed to Winz and his associates as if history were repeating itself in this latest revival of anti-*Ostjude* sentiments—and deeds. Hatred toward Jews had never disappeared entirely from German society; it was always lurking beneath the surface. At the same time, the experience of wartime antisemitism had given *Ost und West* and other Jewish periodicals time to anticipate the extremes of German political life between 1918 and 1923. The promotion of stereotypes in the journal now yielded to a more pressing need for apologetics to stem the tide of Jew hatred. Antidefamation proved as necessary in a Weimar Republic struggling to assert its authority as in a *Kaiserreich* at war.

Justifying ethnic Jewish identity became, in fact, a more urgent desideratum as 100,000 *Ostjuden* migrated to Germany between 1914 and 1921, almost double the number that had lived in the country prior to World War I.[4] In spite of repeated calls to close the border during the war,[5] the German Military High Command imported Polish Jewish labor for jobs in manufacturing and agriculture. As a result, approximately 30,000 Jews from Poland moved to Imperial Germany after 1916.[6] That these were the only Jews permitted to immigrate during the war—the other 60,000 to 70,000 arrived after November 1918—confirms that many were either attracted by false claims or forced into servitude.[7] In fact, antisemitic excesses and unemployment in Germany compelled 40 percent (40,000) of these immigrants to return home to Poland. The long-standing policy of limiting Jews in Germany to certain occupations also applied (often with greater restrictions) to Jewish immigrants from the East. Under the monarchy, Jews with money or significant business interests were given preference over other would-be immigrants. The few Eastern Jewish proletarians who managed to enter the country were employed in cigarette factories (Berlin), the fur and tanning business (Leipzig), and, to a lesser extent, the textile industry. Jewish immigrants also were singled out for economic prejudice in Weimar Germany. The goal now was to keep out Polish Jews. A job requiring bodily labor became the precondition for all Jewish entry and residency permits.[8] Even so, few Jews actually found work in heavy industry and mining, with the exception of pockets in Upper Silesia and in the Ruhr region. In short, German administrative decisions continued to dictate the situation of the *Ostjuden* in Germany as they had since the eighteenth century.

Because restrictions on Jewish immigration from the East were a staple of German history, it was senseless of antisemites to speak of an Eastern Jewish menace (*Ostjudengefahr*).[9] There were simply no grounds to fear that Jews were overrunning German borders. That, however, did not stop citizens of the Weimar Republic from believing this canard. In fact, they were bombarded with all kinds of Jewish images that were palimpsests of older stereotypes. It became clear to *Ost und West* that the *Ostjuden* had become a metaphor for all Jews; moreover, few antisemites cared to distinguish between Eastern and Western Jews.[10]

Even though Jews and non-Jews increasingly came into contact in the 1920s, their prejudices toward each other apparently changed little. (By the same token, relations between Eastern and Western Jews were not always friendly.)[11] In fact, antisemitism became more visible as non-Jews and Jews came into greater social proximity in the Weimar Republic. Resentment and envy were typical responses in the immediate postwar climate of inflation and unemployment. Yet, because of the stridency and political savvy of antisemitism, we tend to discount signs of a German-Jewish symbiosis all too quickly. To many Jews before World War I, antisemitism seemed less alarming in Germany than in other West European countries—most notably France. Is it true, then, that the *Kaiserreich* was somehow better to the Jews?

Nostalgia is a powerful sentiment, and it is understandable that some Weimar Jews yearned for the halcyon days of stability under the monarchy. But the preponderance of evidence points to a democratic Germany as a better place for Jews, if only on legal grounds. There were also hints that the situation had improved socially. Despite their tendency to attract attention, flare-ups of ethnic friction in post-1918 Germany can be read as a sign that Jews were becoming (somewhat) integrated.[12] After all, that Jews could legally organize to defend their rights suggested progress, and the antidefamation leagues that had existed since 1893 achieved their highest profile in the Weimar Republic. As a result, antidefamation and Jewish nationalism now existed on a continuum, a development reflected in *Ost und West*'s editorial policy: after the war, it published as much political writing as it did fiction and art. Having already influenced other periodicals to define Jewishness as an ethnicity, *Ost und West* now could afford to give more space to countering slander against the Jews.

The cause of *Ost und West*'s ultimate demise was the horrific inflation of 1918–1923 which also obliterated other publishing ventures in Germany (including Buber's *Der Jude* in 1924). Whereas the rate of exchange bene-fited Jewish journals such as *Milgroym/Rimon* (Berlin, 1922–1924) which had sponsors outside Germany, it effectively buried any Jewish journal that was financed with German currency. In July 1923, one dollar was worth 353,412 marks; in September, it was worth 98,860,000; in November, 4,200,000,000,000.

The creators of *Ost und West*, however, did not cease to promote ethnic Judaism after 1923. Segel, for instance, became a part-time propagandist for the *Centralverein*.[13] Winz was more active than ever in Jewish publishing and in Palestine-related business ventures, including film production and distribution.[14] Perhaps Winz's greatest accomplishment was the *Gemeindeblatt der jüdischen Gemeinde zu Berlin*. By sprucing up its image, he built it into the most highly circulated Jewish newspaper in Weimar Germany.[15] Although it was distributed freely to all households registered in the Berlin community, it no longer depended on subsidies from the *Gemeinde* thanks to Winz's successful advertising strategies. What had functioned as little more than a news bulletin before he (and his wife) took over in 1928 rose in circulation from an average of 58,000 to 77,000 in less than three years. Winz, however, was only applying what he had learned in promoting the *Ostjuden* at *Ost und West*: attracting readers meant more illustrations, more fiction, better publicity, professional management—and stereotyping.

We shall now examine the implications of the thesis that *Ost und West* promoted Eastern Jewish culture and Jewish national identity in Germany by means of stereotypes. Winz, Segel, and their colleagues showed a high level of self-awareness in their understanding of the workings of stereotyping, an understanding that enabled *Ost und West* to change with the times and to attract three different Jewish audiences. As a contribution to the history of promotion, the history of minority culture in Germany, and the history of European Jewry, this study has called into question received notions about ethnic identity, particularly the notion that Jews were somehow self-hating or that they eagerly assimilated to German society.

Since it marketed models of Jewish identity, *Ost und West* is ideal for the study of Jewish self-stereotyping. Which kinds of stereotypes were the most popular among Germany's Jews? Most striking in *Ost und West* was the journal's reliance on older images of religious renegades. But eventually, it was the parvenu, a figure whose social position was at least as important as his religious status, who proved flexible enough to appeal to each of *Ost und West*'s audiences. Far from being a new creation, then, stereotyping in the magazine simply inverted aspects of both Western/enlightened and Eastern/traditional Jewish identity.

Most positive stereotypes of Eastern Jewry came from the wartime "cult of the *Ostjuden*." Yet, since Winz and his friends at *Ost und West* saw themselves as the first German-based advocates of the Eastern Jews, they increasingly differed with the "cult." The "cultists" were not only, with few exceptions, Jews from the West, but they were also naive and

162

uncritical in their idolizing of the Jewish East.[16] While Martin Buber, Fritz Mordechai Kaufmann, and others were writing paeans to Eastern Jewry in a neoromantic vein, *Ost und West* was dutifully fighting antisemitism—in the West *and* the East. While the new idealization of the East was expanding, actual Jewish life in Poland was on the decline. Socially and politically, there was little reason to romanticize the lives of Eastern Jews. Polish and other Jewries had been mired in poverty and malaise even under the German occupation.

The Polish contributors to *Ost und West* knew better than to accept any glowing accounts of life in Germany's Eastern neighbor. Segel, for one, shrewdly demythologized the *Ostjude* in 1921 in an article in the *Centralverein* monthly, *Im deutschen Reich*.[17] With characteristic invective, he criticized those who would revere the ignorance, economic helplessness, and lack of worldliness (*Kulturlosigkeit*) of Jews in Poland. Those who were investing the *Ostjuden* with a romantic aura had rendered their unkempt appearance "aesthetic," their superstition "mysticism," and their crudeness "poetic." Hasidic *rebbes* and fashionable revolutionaries were being touted as heroes, instead of great German-Jewish intellectuals such as Mendelssohn or Abraham Geiger (1810–1874). Instead of fantasizing about Eastern Jewish liberation, Segel advocated a form of autonomism: Jews should stay in their present countries and participate in their democratization. Ultimately, Segel's sobriety vis-à-vis his Eastern Jewish compatriots was so pronounced that he placed the word *Ostjuden* in quotation marks.

Ost und West was opposed to contrived mythologies and hagiographies of the *Ostjuden*, believing that the fight against antisemitism had become by 1918 the more urgent agenda. But people tend to prefer positive images, and although the post-1945 historical situation is quite different from that of *Ost und West*, positive stereotypes of the *Ostjuden* and their communities are still popular. (Even in the early twentieth century, the nostalgic antithesis to middle-class European Jewish life was embodied in the *shtetl*—an affectionate synonym for the negatively loaded *ghetto*.) Since the 1960s, Yiddish and East European Jewish culture have undergone a renaissance in America that includes literary anthologies, new editions, picture books, exhibitions, and films. This renaissance also extends to postwar Germany. Typical for the (mainly Western) German manifestation of this renaissance are publications on Eastern Jewish life in Germany in the 1920s in which Berlin—*Ost und West*'s hometown—has become romanticized as the last great holdout of Yiddish and Hebrew culture in pre-Hitler Europe. As in the United States, the memory of the *Ostjude* in Germany is highly sentimentalized, at once exotic and fascinating. But the German commemoration of the Eastern Jews—and the majority of the Jews murdered in the Holocaust were from Eastern Europe—is also an attempt to come to terms with the legacy of National Socialism. After the fall of the German Democratic Republic in 1989–90, Germans are now faced with their own internal divisions

(*Westdeutsche* versus *Ostdeutsche*). These East-West problems are not only reminiscent of *Ost und West* but also raise the question of German self-stereotyping and the possibility of German self-hatred.

In Germany, positive stereotyping of the *Ostjude* has always involved a simple reversal of negative stereotyping of the *Westjude*. For average German Jews, such idealization was the prism through which they could reject negative self-images, images deriving from antisemitism. As a result of their Eastern origins, the editors of *Ost und West* knew how thin the line was between idolizing *Ostjuden* and vilifying them. The favorite stereotype of Western Jewish nationalists, the self-hating Jewish parvenu, was a distillate of calumnies about East European Jews.

Just because stereotypes of self-haters were preeminent in *Ost und West* did not mean that they depicted a reality. On the contrary, they were always distortions, incapable of representing actual individuals. The stereotype of the self-hater, Winz and his associates realized, might be put to new uses. In the specifically Jewish context of *Ost und West*, then, self-hatred became a tool for promoting Eastern Jewry while criticizing Western Jewry.

Precisely because Winz and company used it as a promotional tactic, self-hatred took on a dimension beyond its psychological definition as internalized racism. *Ost und West* shows that "self-hatred" is a label, indeed a slander, that can be affixed to any group or individual at any time. This means that the psychology of self-hatred is historically and culturally conditioned. At the same time, some critics fail to recognize that self-hatred can serve as a fictional device that is governed by the cultural and textual contexts in which it appears. Circulating images of self-hating Jews among a turn-of-the-century audience that was primarily Jewish is thus very different from publishing similar images twenty years later in the Nazi *Der Stürmer.* The ascent of the Jewish self-hater as a stereotype enabled the readers of *Ost und West*— who may or may not have been self-hating at moments—to project the stain of self-hatred onto Western Jewish parvenus and others. In short, *Ost und West* used self-haters as part of its rhetoric of social criticism. As already mentioned, the magazine's images of self-haters were not always images of Jews from one group or another. For example, *Ost und West* stereotyped non-Jewish groups as self-hating after August 1914 as part of a wartime plan to suppress negative images of Jews that might fuel antisemitism.

Yet *Ost und West* was not always consistent in dealing with the idea of self-hatred. While using the concept as a cultural construct, Winz and Segel sometimes appeared to take self-hatred as a reality, perhaps hoping to "cure" readers of its scourge by externalizing it and projecting it onto other individuals or groups. Sander Gilman, despite historicizing the discourse of self-hatred in his *Jewish Self-Hatred*,[18] offers no explicit guidelines for differentiating between cultural representations and historical individuals or between pathological and nonpathological stereotyping. As a result, the stain of self-hatred seems to linger on most of the personalities discussed in his book (even though the "self-splitting" of Jewish writers may be nothing more than a way to set up the distance prerequisite for artistic creation). In Gilman's work, a critical-cognitive approach to self-hatred clashes with a simplistic psychological approach that conceives of Jewish identity before the Holocaust as preordained by antisemitism.[19]

It is one thing to examine professional writers, a group that provides the student of self-hatred with numerous test cases. But other historians of self-hatred encounter less self-hatred in the materials they examine. "Self-hatred may have been endemic to intellectuals; the majority of German Jews managed to exist without recourse to it," writes social historian Henry Wassermann.[20] Wassermann's view flies in the face of the typical Zionist account of Jewish self-hatred that sees Diaspora Jews as trapped between conflicting cultures, a double bind that is typically resolved by repudiating one's Jewishness. For extreme Zionists, then, Jews who challenge the view that all German Jews were (or are) self-haters are themselves either renegades or mentally ill. This amounts to a charge of dual loyalty which overlooks the fact that "German Jews, like other minorities, could adhere to conflicting positive reference groups for generations with minimal psychological damage."[21] As we have seen, Winz and Segel also lived poised between two cultures, indeed two identities, but the experience did not mar their psyches. Marion Kaplan explains: "What has become a paradox for historians appeared reasonable and consistent to the German Jews themselves: they were at one and the same time agents of acculturation and tradition and of integration and apartness."[22]

The same analysis applies to antisemitism in the *Kaiserreich*. Owing to the influence of the Holocaust and thinkers such as Jean-Paul Sartre and Gershom Scholem, we today tend to think of antisemitism as something of an unchanging existential crisis. Nothing could be further from the reality of German-Jewish life at 1900. For most German Jews at this time, antisemitism became a mundane part of life, something one endured. As a result, not all criticism of Wilhelminian Jews was automatically antisemitic "hate speech."[23] At the same time, Wilhelminian Jews were not involved in wide-scale denial, nor were they bent on assimilation or self-hatred. Instead, much like their counterparts in France and Russia, they took new forms of Jew hatred at face value: as a continuation of older anti-Jewish prejudices prevalent since the Middle Ages. For this reason, some German Jews misrecognized the new quality of "racialistic" antisemitism, unable to see the vital ways in which it superseded traditional Jew hatred.

The responses of German Jews also closely resemble those of their Eastern Jewish cousins. Most of these Jews habitually took a degree of Jew hatred in their lives for granted. As mentioned in chapter 1, Chaim Weizmann and other Eastern Jewish students found antisemitism to be more latent in Germany than in Russia. In a similar vein, Binjamin Segel wrote in 1923: "Here in Germany pogroms were talked about; in Russia, they were carried out."[24] According to literary historian David Roskies, the Jews of the Pale "were overprepared for catastrophe, and nothing could really take them by surprise."[25] In fact, Eastern Jewry bequeathed to the West a "liturgy of destruction" that originated at the time of the Crusades and attempted to provide comfort to Jews after modern pogroms.[26] Challenges to Jewish existence, far from being eradicable, became instead a way of life and were incorporated into traditional Judaism.

Ost und West's promotional strategy is testimony to the power of this Jewish liturgy of destruction. The journal's very last editorial, Segel's "Philosophie des Pogroms," shows how second-nature this tradition had become after the pogroms of 1881–82, 1903–6, and 1919–20. Since November 1918, *Ost und West* had been barraged constantly with anti-Jewish "pogrom propaganda," and Hans Blüher's *Secessio Judaica* (1922), the subject of the editorial, was no different. Segel's attitude toward antisemitism, as it emerged in the essay, was surprisingly nonchalant in light of the escalation of violence and agitprop activity at this time. Since the purpose of his editorial was antidefamation, however, he was careful to respond with cool objectivity to Blüher's accusations that liberalism and socialism were Jewish creations. With characteristic insight, Segel also debunked the foundations of Blüher's ideology and its foreboding call for a "world pogrom" (89).[27] By defining German *Geist* as "the factory where the weapons to destroy the Jews are produced" (90), he turned those weapons into stereotypes of German antisemites, who now became the prototypical assimilators. As in Segel's war editorials, a number of these Jew haters were accused of having behaved like traitors and self-haters between 1914 and 1918, and, in the manner of renegades, they were said to be "mimicking" (80) the enemies of the fatherland.

Even as Segel denied in "Philosophie des Pogroms" that it was possible for those Germans to have a dual identity, he suggested that Jews could transcend competing allegiances. While insisting that the Jews never actually wanted to assimilate to German culture (83–84), he pointed out that no *Westjude* was ever exclusively "Jewish." Segel, in fact, delved deep into the past to locate examples of German-Jewish interdependence that contrasted starkly with the rhetoric and reality of post-1918 Germany. He cited evidence of an ancient coexistence, if not yet symbiosis, of Germans and Jews, claiming that Jews had resided in Germany since Roman times (2,000 years). He also claimed, in an article following the editorial, that the medieval *Minnesänger*, Süßkind von Trimberg, was Jewish.[28]

"Never have two peoples, a very large and a very small one, permeated each other more deeply than the Jews and the Germans" (91). In this way, Segel concluded his editorial, which he knew would be *Ost und West*'s last. But lest he be thought of as an idealist, his last sentence challenged the idea of a German-Jewish symbiosis by suggesting that new influences, such as antisemitism, were corrupting the legacy of Lessing (92).[29] In allying *Ost und West* with the great Enlightener and his friend Moses Mendelssohn, Segel affirmed just how central the German Enlightenment was in encouraging tolerance of different peoples. Without the Enlightenment, there also would have been no *Haskalah* or *Wissenschaft des Judentums* and hence no intellectual basis from which to launch a defense of Jewry, a defense that was grounded in a critical understanding of stereotyping.

Exposing the errors of antisemitism was an agenda that went beyond the intellectual call for ethnic Judaism in *Ost und West*, and in this final editorial of March–April 1923, Segel promoted an ethnic Judaism that combined the best of *Haskalah* with the best of Ashkenazic tradition. But what did the Eastern Jewish nationalism of *Ost und West* mean in political terms at a time when the fledgling Weimar democracy came under increasing attack? At best, one could hope for a pluralistic, or "multicultural," polity, and Jewish cultural autonomy on a nonterritorial basis was considered by Segel and his allies the best way to combine rational universalism with ethnic particularism.[30]

Neither territory nor political sovereignty was a prerequisite for Jewish national longings. And, as *Ost und West* shows, neither was needed for a group to promote minority culture in a textual medium. The main accomplishment of the bicultural editors of *Ost und West* was to demonstrate that pluralism was feasible even in Imperial Germany despite a longstanding tradition of German monoculturalism. *Ost und West*'s idea of a common European Jewish culture, like the idea of a common German culture, had its sources in competing versions of European nationalism, one "conservative" (or "ethnic") and one "liberal" (or "civic"). Because conservative nationalisms sought to exclude and dominate even the most integrated of minority groups, the journal rejected them. Instead, *Ost und West*'s liberal nationalism, like the German nationalism of Liberals and Social Democrats in the *Kaiserreich*, made it clear that nationalism was not synonymous with racism or antisemitism.[31] Conservative and liberal nationalisms often coexisted within the same political framework: Zionism had political and cultural wings that corresponded to opposing factions in Bismarck's coalition (the National Liberals and the Freethinkers), and after 1886, Bismarck rejected the *Kulturkampf* against Catholics—representing one third of the German population—in favor of a hesitant pluralism. In addition, there were other targets besides Jews and Catholics. The German "nation" always could vent its frustrations upon the Poles, the Danes, the Alsatians, and other minorities.

One important "minority" often overlooked is the bourgeoisie. Since most German Jews belonged to this socioeconomic group, their political fortunes often rose and fell with it, even though non-Jews had been emancipated before Jews. The price the German bourgeoisie paid to be integrated into the larger German state was unwavering German nationalism. Yet this group embraced not only conservative nationalism, which deviated into antisemitism, but also liberal nationalism. In support of this thesis, a new generation of historians have argued that the integration of the middle classes was more pervasive than previously thought. They insist, moreover, that recent German history has not followed a peculiar linear path since 1848.[32] They thus oppose the so-called *Sonderweg* theory that Germany, prior to Nazism, had a strong antidemocratic tradition in comparison with other Western nations because it never went through a bourgeois political revolution. For it is difficult to argue that Germany did not assume a "normal" line of development as did Britain and France when the latter two also practiced imperialism and other forms of autocracy. The fact that the Prussian *Junker* or large landowners remained politically dominant into the industrial age does not ipso facto render other European nations more democratic; indeed, all of them had institutionalized antisemitism to some extent.

The prevailing conception of German Jewry as passive and assimilating overlaps, in many respects, with the *Sonderweg* view of the German bourgeoisie as having timidly abdicated political responsibility. But if the bourgeoisie could be integrated into the German mainstream, why were their loyal allies, the fewer than 1 percent of Jews living in Germany, still objectionable? What emerged was that antisemitism was different from class hatred (or "classism"), and German (bourgeois) antisemites were fundamentally opposed to admitting Jews into the ranks of "Germanhood" (*Deutschtum*). Since it offered an alternative to this antisemitism, the moderate Jewish nationalism of *Ost und West* appealed to many German Jews. In fact, these Jews were willing to integrate *Jewish* minorities, and foremost among them, the *Ostjuden*, into their own ranks—if not into their private lives, then at least into their public pronouncements. And by 1923, *Ost und West* was not alone in trying to bridge the gap separating European Jews from each other. Effective promotion, like that of Winz and Segel, could help build coalitions between opposing Jewish factions and their notions of Jewish culture. *Ost und West* thus merged the universal with the particularistic and espoused an Eastern Jewish nationalism that was compatible with Western liberal humanism. The realization of the journal's ideas in Weimar Jewish politics shows that a qualified form of Jewish separatism was acceptable to German Jews, if not to Germans in general.

Resentments between different groups of Jews always have existed and will continue to influence attitudes. But instead of assuming that *Westjuden* could never be tolerant of *Ostjuden*, historians should inquire into the conditions that made German Jews favor ethnic Jewishness.[33] By posing such questions, this study may enrich American and other contemporary Jewish communities that are struggling to sustain a distinctive culture in the face of a powerful majority culture.[34] In *Ost und West*, Eastern and Western

Jews were vocal and visible in overcoming the allures of assimilation. Their resistance to monoculturalism might serve as a model for the ethnic behavior of non-Jews.

As Reinhard Rürup, a leading historian of nineteenth-century German Jewry, maintains, it is unreasonable to demand that minority groups subordinate their cultural behavior (language, religion, culture) to every aspect of the majority culture. But if minority groups move too far to dissimilate themselves, they run the risk of being treated as separate or being cut off from participation in the mainstream culture.[35] Winz and Segel, in their writings and life choices, recognized this danger. They thus staked their claim with the *Rechtsstaat*, the state governed by law. A diverse polity, so long as it guaranteed a range of individual rights, seemed less prone to antisemitism than a profusion of small "self-determined" states. Having grown up in the Austro-Hungarian empire, Segel believed in the larger multiethnic state ruled by law, not in some radical form of democracy. He and his colleagues thus pointed out how destructive self-determination could be: it involved a constant need to redraw territorial boundaries, resulting in wars with neighboring states and a constant need to limit its definition of who was a citizen. Restrictions on citizenship, in turn, could lead to the harassment and deportation of residents of other ethnicities.

The historical search for a balance of power between cultures has important implications for the study of ethnic groups and minorities today. The study of *Ost und West* can shed light on the tension between group identity and assimilation and thus on the debate between the idea of the multiethnic state and that of the national homeland. As events since 1989 have revealed, the terms of this debate have changed little in East Central Europe since World War I. The ideas of self-determination and minority rights influence political discourse as much today as they did after 1918, promising that national identities will not soon disappear from a "united Europe." In addition, the call by national groups for "ethnic cleansing" in a disintegrating Yugoslavia (and elsewhere) has resurrected the specter of genocide in our time. An "antisemitism without Jews" also has emerged. Seeking to draw attention away from their national rivalries and feuds, extremists in Western and Eastern Europe yearn for the days when Jews were more convenient scapegoats.[36]

Only if nations with ethnic minorities are prepared to confront the presuppositions they have about the groups living in their midst, as well as the subgroups within their *own* groups, can the unique subcultures of Jews, Kurds, Palestinians, Bosnians, Armenians, and many others continue to survive.[37] Presuppositions about such groups are still pervasive today, even in supposedly pluralistic societies such as the United States, where Jews, Blacks, Arabs, Hispanics, and nonethnic groups such as homosexuals continue to be stigmatized. The example of *Ost und West* suggests a way to overcome this stigmatization: to recognize both the contingency and the necessity of stereotyping. More often than not, stereotypes are forms of bias used to slander and to wound. But since stereotypes—understood in the perspectivist terms of *cognitive* psychology—are the wellsprings of human thinking, they also can serve as a means of bridging cultures and inverting received images. Stereotyping, impossible to do without, still might be elevated to a form of criticism used to promote an end to ethnic prejudice.

NOTES

Unless otherwise noted, all translations are my own.

INTRODUCTION

1. On the terms *acculturation* and *assimilation*, see David Sorkin, "Emancipation and Assimilation—Two Concepts and Their Application to German-Jewish History," *Year Book of the Leo Baeck Institute* 35 (1990): esp. 27–33. Recent researchers prefer *acculturation* because of the negative connotations of *assimilation* (which many Zionists used as a term of opprobrium). For the purposes of this study, acculturation is defined as the adoption of non-Jewish cultural traits. According to sociologist Milton Gordon, assimilation is a continuum. Beginning with what he calls "acculturation," a type of "cultural assimilation," an ethnic group adopts the dress, recreational tastes, economic patterns, language, cultural baggage, and political views of the general society without necessarily losing its sense of group identity. Total assimilation and group disappearance, however, do not take place unless primary contacts—friendships, associations, marriage and family ties—have disappeared. This "structural assimilation" and the final stage of "marital assimilation" render the minority indistinguishable from the culture at large. Milton M. Gordon, *Assimilation in American Life: The Role of Race, Religion and National Origins* (New York: Oxford University Press, 1964). See also the discussion in Trude Maurer, *Die Entwicklung der jüdischen Minderheit in Deutschland (1780–1933). Neuere Forschungen und offene Fragen*, special issue 4 of *Internationales Archiv für Sozialgeschichte der deutschen Literatur* (Tübingen: Niemeyer, 1992).

2. *Identity* or *self-understanding* is properly understood as a system of allegiances one assigns to oneself or to others. On the term "ethnic," see chapter two below.

3. The term *pan-Jewish* is adopted from *pan-Slavism*, a political ideology which has its intellectual roots in Herder and Schelling.

4. Peter Pulzer, *Jews and the German State: A Political History of a Minority, 1848–1933* (Oxford: Blackwell, 1992), 43.

5. In this study, *Western Jewry* and *Eastern Jewry* refer to West-Central and East European Jews. But "Western Jewish" and "Eastern Jewish" refer to *cultures* and cultural tendencies, for what is "Eastern Jewish" and what is "Western Jewish" cannot always be demarcated geographically. On the history of the term *Ostjude* to refer to East European Jews, see Steven E. Aschheim, *Brothers and Strangers: The East European Jew in German and German Jewish Consciousness, 1800–1923* (Madison: University of Wisconsin Press, 1982), 257 n. 1; and Trude Maurer, *Ostjuden in Deutschland, 1918–1933* (Hamburg: Hans Christians, 1986), 12–13. Aschheim and Maurer maintain that the term did not achieve popular currency until 1910. Although the term did become more widespread in connection with the German occupation of Poland in World War I and the related ideas of an *Ostjudenfrage* and an *Ostjudengefahr,* the ideology of the *Ostjude* was thoroughly developed by the mid-nineteenth century. Even if it was not labeled as such, there was a generalized understanding in Germany of what an *Ostjude* was. There, the names *Polacken* and *Schnorrer* designated Jews from Poland, Galicia, and Russia who were regarded as dirty, loud, unmannered, and culturally backward. The awareness of the plight of Rumanian and Russian Jews—publicized by *Ost und West,* among others—dates at least from the last decades of the nineteenth century. In spite of its pejorative connotations, *Ostjude* will be used neutrally throughout this book to make a real and crucial distinction between East European and West European Jewish life and culture. This usage is further justified with respect to the title of the magazine—"Ost und West"—even though the terms were rarely employed in *Ost und West* itself.

6. Until 1906, *Ost und West* was subtitled *Illustrierte Monatsschrift für modernes Judentum,* and after that time *Illustrierte Monatsschrift für das gesamte Judentum.* According to Winz's and independent estimates, the journal had anywhere from 16,000 to 23,000 subscribers in the period between 1906 and 1914. Allowing for families, cafés, reading rooms, and libraries, these figures should be multiplied by three (or more). The result: a broad resonance in the Jewish population in Germany. According to Michael Brenner, "[p]robably most German Jews read a Jewish newspaper" by the Weimar period. Brenner, *The Renaissance of Jewish Culture in Weimar Germany* (New Haven: Yale University Press, 1996), 219.

7. On the notion of a German-Jewish public sphere, see David Sorkin, *The Transformation of German Jewry, 1780–1840* (New York: Oxford University Press, 1987), 5, 104.

8. I would argue that the reception of a text, not its producers or its contents, ultimately makes it "Jewish."

9. Trietsch, who was Winz's "co-editor" in the first year of *Ost und West,* may have learned much about magazines and marketing in the several years he spent in the United States in the 1890s.

10. For an account of the role of projection and transference in historiography, especially with respect to the Holocaust, see Dominick LaCapra, *Representing the*

Holocaust: History, Theory, Trauma (Ithaca: Cornell University Press, 1994), 192–203. For a recent critical survey of the scholarship on German-Jewish identity, see Samuel Moyn, "German Jewry and the Question of Identity: Historiography and Theory," *Year Book of the Leo Baeck Institute* 41 (1996): 291–308.

11. See the discussion of the "revenge of the *Ostjuden*" in Jack Wertheimer, "The German-Jewish Experience: Toward a Useable Past," *American Jewish Archives* 40 (November 1988): 422.

12. Just because *Ost und West* was marketing Eastern Jewish culture to the West does not somehow make its version of Eastern Jewry an utter fabrication. On the formidable, lasting nature of Western stereotypes of "the East," see Edward W. Said, *Orientalism* (1978; New York: Vintage, 1979), 5–6.

13. Sander L. Gilman, *Jewish Self-Hatred: Anti-Semitism and the Hidden Language of the Jews* (Baltimore: Johns Hopkins University Press, 1986), 1–5.

14. Maurer, *Ostjuden in Deutschland*, 741–44.

15. See Shulamit Volkov, *Jüdisches Leben und Antisemitismus im 19. und 20. Jahrhundert* (Munich: Beck, 1990), 178–79. Applying the arguments of Norbert Elias to relations between Eastern and Western Jews, Volkov differentiates between two types of embarrassment. These are *Scham* (evinced by one's own social behavior) and *Peinlichkeit* (evinced by others' behavior); together, they constitute the emotional poles of civility (*Zivilisation*). See Norbert Elias, *Über den Prozeß der Zivilisation: Soziogenetische und psychogenetische Untersuchungen* (Basel: Haus zum Falken, 1939), 2: 397–409, 424–34.

16. See Jack Wertheimer, *Unwelcome Strangers: East European Jews in Imperial Germany* (New York: Oxford University Press, 1987). Neither Wertheimer nor Aschheim denies that Eastern Jews also shunned or condescended to their Western brethren.

17. Wertheimer, *Unwelcome Strangers*, 149. For a somewhat different view, compare Wertheimer's own conclusion to *Unwelcome Strangers*, 176–81. Other than Winz, the financial backers of *Ost und West* were largely Western Jewish, including Heinrich Meyer-Cohn, Otto Warburg, Eduard Lachmann, and others; see Leo Winz Papers, Central Zionist Archives, Jerusalem, A136/41 and others. *Ost und West* and other Eastern Jewish publishers required a degree of help from Western Jews, for German state policies demanded that Russian and other foreign Jews avoid attracting attention. Thus, *Ost und West* was radical for its time in openly displaying Eastern Jewishness; see Wertheimer, *Unwelcome Strangers*, 16–18.

18. Wertheimer may be correct in claiming that Eastern Jews formed few public or political organizations, instead preferring synagogal associations and *Gemeinde* activities. However, he is too categorical when he denies that the foreigners created cultural institutions of their own. See Wertheimer, *Unwelcome Strangers*, 179–80. According to historian Eric Hobsbawm, the redefinition of cultural texts and representations is necessary and ongoing in every modern society; "Introduction: Inventing Traditions," in *The Invention of Tradition*, ed. Eric Hobsbawm and Terence Ranger (1983; reprint, Cambridge: Cambridge University Press, 1984), 1–14. This "reinvention" of traditions—often alleged to be authentic—was no less characteristic of *Ost und West*, which adapted elements of Judaic civilization within already existing textual/institutional frameworks.

19. While Aschheim attempts to examine both "high" and "low" culture, he rarely cites the German-Jewish popular press.

20. *Discourse* is understood here as a system of language and symbols (or symbolic acts) that are not reflective but rather constitutive of human cultures, identities, and experiences. See Michel Foucault, *The Archaeology of Knowledge*, trans. A. M. Sheridan Smith (New York: Pantheon, 1972); Michel Foucault, *The Order of Things: An Archaeology of the Human Sciences* (New York: Pantheon, 1971); Michel Foucault, *The History of Sexuality: An Introduction*, trans. Robert Hurley (New York: Pantheon, 1978); and Clifford Geertz, "Ideology as a Cultural System," in *Ideology and Discontent*, ed. David E. Apter (New York: Free Press, 1964), 47–76. For Foucault, "discourse" is understood as a set of statements which claims to be "true" or "objective." This claim, however, must be approached with skepticism, since a discourse constructs knowledge about an object (e.g., "identity," "the Jew," "objectivity") according to rules specific to itself and in relation to institutions in a specific social context.

Chapter 1

1. The Yiddish name of the *Bund* was Der allgemeyner idisher arbeyterbund in Lita, Poylen un Rusland.

2. This account of East European Jewish migration derives, in part, from Wertheimer, *Unwelcome Strangers*, 11–22.

3. Ibid., 12. Other important issues for policymakers were: "How could officials encourage Jews to transmigrate through the *Reich* from Russia, Austro-Hungary, and Rumania on their way west, yet at the same time bar such travelers from lingering and even settling in the country? By what mechanisms could governments filter out undesirable 'trouble makers' from the population of Eastern Jews who resided in Germany temporarily as legitimate business people, students, and intellectuals? Would the relatively large representation of Russian Jews at German institutions of higher learning harm the quality of those schools, or would it enrich the process of education by adding diversity to the student body? And how could governments determine whether potential Jewish immigrants would prove an asset to Germany by virtue of their skills and knowledge, or a burdensome population of unproductive and unassimilable foreigners? The arrival of East European Jews in the Second *Reich* challenged German leaders to address these difficult questions." Ibid., 21–22.

4. Aschheim, *Brothers and Strangers*, 32–36.

5. Between 1871 and 1914, 5.8 million non-Germans embarked at North Sea ports, 38 percent of them Russians and 51 percent Austrians. Jews made up a significant portion of the latter and the preponderant majority of the former. Wertheimer, *Unwelcome Strangers*, 14.

6. Barring religious discrimination rendered void the Prussian Jewry Law of 1847 requiring alien Jews (as opposed to other aliens) to obtain a special work permit from the Ministry of Interior.

7. Officials from the different German states frequently worked together to coordinate policies for dealing with different alien populations in the *Kaiserreich*.

8. Quoted in Wertheimer, *Unwelcome Strangers*, 21. See also David Brenner, "Making *Jargon* Respectable: Leo Winz, *Ost und West*, and the Reception of Yiddish Theater in Pre-Hitler Germany," *Year Book of the Leo Baeck Institute* 42 (1997): 51–66.

9. Wertheimer, *Unwelcome Strangers*, 21.

10. See Maimon's autobiography, *Salomon Maimons Lebensgeschichte*, ed. Karl Phillipp Moritz (Berlin: Friedrich Vieweg, 1792–93).

11. The *numerus clausus* applied to individual faculties at Russian universities. In addition, admission to secondary schools (*Gymnasien*) was severely curtailed for Jews after 1887, bringing about an exodus westward. Restrictions also were imposed to limit the number of Jewish *Externen*, those Jews permitted to take exams but not classes.

12. See Jack Wertheimer, "The 'Ausländerfrage' at Institutions of Higher Learning: A Controversy over Russian-Jewish Students in Imperial Germany," *Year Book of the Leo Baeck Institute* 25 (1982): 187–215; and Jack Wertheimer, "Between Tsar and Kaiser: The Radicalization of Russian-Jewish University Students in Germany," *Year Book of the Leo Baeck Institute* 28 (1983): 329–50.

13. Wertheimer, "Between Tsar and Kaiser," 192.

14. Robert C. Williams, *Culture in Exile: Russian Émigrés in Germany, 1881–1941* (Ithaca: Cornell University Press, 1972), 20, 25.

15. See Botho Brachmann, *Russische Sozialdemokraten in Berlin, 1895–1914* (Berlin: Akademie-Verlag, 1962), 1–20 and appendices.

16. Between 1900 and 1905, the foreign Jewish population of Berlin nearly doubled, rising from 11,615 to 18,316. Yet in the census of 1910, of 137,000 Jews in Greater Berlin, only 15.8 percent were born outside the *Reich*. Moreover, only 9.5 percent of all Jews in Greater Berlin were *Ostjuden*, that is, from Russia, Galicia, or Rumania. See Gabriel Alexander, "Die Entwicklung der jüdischen Bevölkerung in Berlin zwischen 1871 und 1945," *Tel Aviver Jahrbuch für deutsche Geschichte* 20 (1991): 287–314.

17. See Wertheimer, "Between Tsar and Kaiser," 189.

18. Shalom Adler-Rudel, *Ostjuden in Deutschland 1880–1914*, Schriftenreihe wissenschaftlicher Abhandlungen des Leo Baeck Instituts 1 (Tübingen: Mohr, 1959), 21–22.

19. Moshe Zimmermann, "Jewish Nationalism and Zionism in German-Jewish Students' Organisations," *Year Book of the Leo Baeck Institute* 27 (1982): 129–54; Marsha L. Rozenblit, "The Assertion of Identity—Jewish Student Nationalism at the University of Vienna before the First World War," *Year Book of the Leo Baeck Institute* 27 (1982): 171–87; and other essays from the same volume of the *Year Book of the Leo Baeck Institute*.

20. Wertheimer, "Between Tsar and Kaiser," 190 and table 211.

21. For the significant parallel case of a Black American student in Berlin at the turn of the century, see W. E. B. Du Bois, *The Autobiography of W. E. B. DuBois* (New York: International Publishers, 1968).

22. Chaim Weizmann, *Trial and Error* (New York: Harper, 1949), 33.

23. Wertheimer, "Between Tsar and Kaiser," 190.

24. Weizmann repudiated the Pale in his letters, having had to return there for a year before resuming his studies. Jehuda Reinharz, *Chaim Weizmann: The Making of a Zionist Leader* (New York: Oxford University Press, 1985), 417 n. 17. See also DuBois, *Autobiography*.

25. Ibid., 36–37.

26. "The Pale" designates those provinces in Imperial Russia where Jews had the right of permanent residence. Making up 4 percent of Russian territory, it

contained 94 percent of the Jewish population. Formally declared in 1791 under the reign of Empress Catherine, it encompassed by 1887 the ten provinces of the so-called kingdom of Poland (Warsaw, Kalisz, Kielce, Lomza, Lublin, Piotrków, Plock, Radom, Suwalki, and Siedlce), as well as the northwest provinces of Vilna, Kovno, Grodno, Minsk, Vitebsk, and Mogilev; the southwest provinces of Volhynia, Podolia, Kiev, Chernigov, and Poltava; and the southern provinces of Bessarabia, Kherson, Ekaterinoslav, and Tauris. Within the Pale, Jews were permitted to live only in urban areas, and certain cities and towns were open only to privileged Jews. Numerous other restrictions also applied.

27. The surface resemblance of these debates to Talmudic-style learning in the yeshiva is striking.

28. Predecessors to the *Verein* include the first European Jewish fraternity, *Kadimah* (Vienna, 1882), and the *Akademischer Verein für jüdische Geschichte und Literatur* (founded 1883) and others. Jehuda Reinharz, ed., *Dokumente zur Geschichte des deutschen Zionismus, 1882–1933*, Schriftenreihe wissenschaftlicher Abhandlungen des Leo Baeck Instituts 37 (Tübingen: Mohr, 1981).

29. Other members of the *Verein* during different periods included Eliyahu Davidson, Lazare Kunin, David Maklin, Isidore Eliashev, Joseph Lurie, Israel Motzkin, Selig Soskin, Judah Vilensky, Yehoshua Thon, Mordechai Ehrenpreis, David Farbstein, and Leo Estermann.

30. Reinharz, *Chaim Weizmann*, 418 n. 29. On Winz and *Jung Israel*, see Heinrich Loewe Papers, Central Zionist Archives, Jerusalem, A146.

31. Reinharz, *Dokumente*, 18.

32. See Wertheimer, "Between Tsar and Kaiser," 336.

33. Ibid.

34. Reinharz, *Chaim Weizmann*, 34.

35. See Winz's *Studienbücher* in Leo Winz Papers, A136/1.

36. Rozenblit, "The Assertion of Identity," 163–64. At the end of World War I, Habsburg Jews faced a grave crisis as the supranational monarchy fell apart into hypothetically homogeneous nation-states.

37. Ibid., 164.

38. See Jacob Toury, *Die jüdische Presse im österreichischen Kaiserreich. Ein Beitrag zur Problematik der Akkulturation 1802–1918*, Schriftenreihe wissenschaftlicher Abhandlungen des Leo Baeck Instituts 41 (Tubingen: Mohr, 1983).

39. The members of the *Verein* were known for being nonconformists; see Reinharz, *Chaim Weizmann*, 32. They also preferred ideological debate to the cultural offerings of Berlin, probably because of lack of money, living as they did on the edge of destitution. Having studied or worked hard all day, they enjoyed an evening of discussion at cafés. In short, they perceived themselves as "Russian-Jewish intellectuals," distinguished by class, education, culture, and geographical origin from other Eastern Jews.

40. For a prime example, see Heinrich Loewe, "Wer spricht Jargon?" *Jüdische Rundschau* (January 22, 1904): 33–35.

41. Loewe's other cultural activities actively spread Eastern-style Jewish nationalism. Loewe earned a doctorate in Berlin, but discrimination compelled him to seek work as a librarian and archivist. Eager to build more formal organizations for raising consciousness, Loewe was instrumental in the establishment of *Jung Israel*

in Berlin in 1892. Together with Max Bodenheimer, he founded the *Verein Jüdischer Studenten* in 1895, intended as the first Jewish nationalist students' association in Germany, designed to foster Jewish self-consciousness and pride. Members included Martin Buber and Leo Winz, among many others.

42. The predecessor of the *Jüdische Lesehalle* was the Russian Reading Room, which dated from the 1880s. Wertheimer, "Between Tsar and Kaiser," 332. See also Ulrike Schmidt, "Jüdische Bibliotheken in Frankfurt am Main: Vom Anfang des 19. Jahrhunderts bis 1938," *Archiv für die Geschichte des Buchwesens* 29 (1987): 235–67.

43. Leo Winz and *Ost und West* contributed money to Jewish reading rooms. See Leo Winz Papers, A136/98. A thorough study also would reveal what impact these institutions had on the circulation and distribution of *Ost und West* and other Jewish periodicals.

44. The same criterion may have applied to other Jewish newspapers known to Winz, such as the British weekly *Jewish Chronicle* (London, 1847–) and the weekly *Die jüdische Presse* (Berlin, 1869–1923, edited by Esriel and Meier Hildesheimer).

45. Like *Ost und West*, the *Israelitisches Familienblatt* has rarely been analyzed in depth by historians. See David Brenner, "Reconciliation before Auschwitz: The Weimar Jewish Experience in Popular Fiction from the *Israelitisches Familienblatt*," in *Borders and Crossings: Evolving Jewish Identities in German Minority Culture*, ed. Linda Feldman and Diana Hinze (Westport, Conn.: Greenwood/Praeger, forthcoming).

46. Other Jewish nationalist forerunners of *Ost und West* include Max Jungmann's five issues in 1897–98 of *Die jüdische Moderne* and Ruben Brainin's Vienna-based monthly (and later yearbook) *Mi-mizraḥ u-maʿarev* [From East and West], also subtitled *Hebräische Monatsschrift. Sammelbuch für Literatur und Wissenschaft* (1894–96).

47. Quoted in Yehuda Eloni, *Zionismus in Deutschland. Von den Anfängen bis 1914* (Gerlingen: Bleicher, 1987), 155. On the origins of the *Jüdische Rundschau*, see 155–61.

48. For a full account of the *Verein*'s attempt to develop "Jewish feelings" among Western Jews, see ibid., 66–67.

49. Jean-Paul Sartre offered the problematic formulation of Jewish identity as the invention of antisemites in *Anti-Semite and Jew*, trans. George J. Becker (New York: Schocken Books, 1948).

50. Benedict Anderson, *Imagined Communities: Reflections on the Origin and Spread of Nationalism*, rev. ed. (London: Verso, 1991), 15.

51. For an attempt to differentiate these two related terms, see Franz Oppenheimer, "Stammesbewusstsein und Volksbewusstsein," *Die Welt* (February 18, 1910): 139–43. This essay sparked a major controversy.

52. Defining Jewish nationhood was more the province of Jewish cultural elites than that of other Jews.

53. This concept may be related to the Yiddish notion of *dos pintele yid*, "the little bit of Jew" to be found within every Jew.

54. Marsha Rozenblit, "The Jews of the Dual Monarchy," *Austrian History Yearbook* 23 (1992): 162.

55. Several ethnic-national awakenings took place in mid-nineteenth-century Central and Eastern Europe. Loewe and other Western Zionists even published articles on how the Zionist movement began in the 1840s. See Heinrich Loewe, "Zur

Vorgeschichte des Zionismus," *Israelitische Rundschau [Jüdische Rundschau]* (June 27, 1902): 3–4 and (July 4, 1902): 3–4.

56. For an overview, see Arthur Hertzberg, ed., *The Zionist Idea: A Historical Analysis and Reader* (Garden City, N.Y.: Doubleday, 1959).

57. For a contemporary's view of the difference between Jewish nationalism and Zionism, see Hermann Jalowitz, quoted in Joachim Doron, " 'Der Geist ist es, der sich den Körper schafft': Soziale Probleme in der jüdischen Turnbewegung (1896–1914)," *Tel Aviver Jahrbuch für deutsche Geschichte* 20 (1991): 240–41.

58. See Friedrich Meinecke, *Weltbürgertum und Nationalstaat: Studien zur Genesis des deutschen Nationalstaats* (Munich: R. Oldenbourg, 1908). Meinecke's distinction is deceptive, however. Stemming from Western Europe, it fails to account for the political origins of cultural Zionism and its popular resonance in Eastern Europe. For a discussion of non-European nationalisms, see John Breuilly, *Nationalism and the State* (Manchester: Manchester University Press, 1982), 235.

59. The Territorialist movement, led by the British-Jewish writer Israel Zangwill (1864–1926), had goals similar to those of the political Zionists but was not Palestinocentric in its choice of a site for the Jewish nation-state.

60. Still, Herzl was politically savvy enough to take into account objections from East European Jews, whose numbers far outranked those of Jews in the West.

61. One of the Democratic Faction's inspirations, besides Aḥad Haᶜam, was Micha Joseph Berdichevsky (1865–1921), also known as Bin Gurion. Berdichevsky preferred the Israelite prophecy of the Bible over the "fossilized" law (*halakhah*) of the Diaspora age. The Faction, often to the chagrin of Herzl, opposed political Zionism and its religious allies (rabbis, preachers, clerics) in the Mizrachi faction of the organization. Moreover, they protested against the nondemocratic organization of the party. At the same time, they were criticized for being too elitist and too intellectual themselves, and their existence was short-lived (1900–1905).

62. Many historians assume a rivalry between political and cultural Zionists, yet some evidence shows that the movement's factions coexisted peacefully. According to Michael Berkowitz, they even "jointly popularized and disseminated many of the vital unifying myths, symbols and ideological postulates of Zionism througout the prewar period. In many respects, the argument can be made that the intensive and successful *Propagandaarbeit* of these years was possible because there was fundamental accord in the Zionists' cultural outlook, not a fundamental divergence." Michael Berkowitz, " 'Mind, Muscle, and Men': The Imagination of a Zionist National Culture for the Jews of Central and Western Europe, 1897–1914," Ph.D. dissertation, University of Wisconsin, 1989, 16. See also Michael Berkowitz, *Zionist Culture and West European Jewry before the First World War* (Cambridge: Cambridge University Press, 1993). *Ost und West*'s response to the *Bund* was a sign of a dilemma in its ideological program. In favor of tolerance toward "backward" Eastern Jewish culture, the journal sought at the same time to be "modern," that is, to be scientific and cultured according to Western principles. Through the efforts of the Democratic Faction, the Zionists also tried to attract and coopt the growing constituency of young Jews leaning in a socialist direction, specifically those inclined toward the Bundists or, somewhat later, the Zionist Socialists (*Poᶜalei Tsiyyon*). Founded in Vilna in 1897 as the unification of several preexisting Jewish socialist groups, the *Bund* adopted its ethnocultural program in 1905, going beyond

its previous opposition to anti-Jewish discrimination and advocating Jewish cultural autonomy based on secular Yiddish culture.

63. The terms *kleindeutsch* and *großdeutsch* have a long and involved history.

64. See David Blackbourn, "Catholics, the Centre Party, Anti-Semitism," in *Nationalist and Racialist Movements in Britain and Germany before 1914,* ed. Paul Kennedy and Anthony Nicholls (Oxford: Macmillan, 1981), 108. Other significant minority groups in Germany include the Danes, the Poles, and the populace of Alsace.

65. Reinharz, *Chaim Weizmann,* 42.

66. The Jews' fear that emancipation would be set back was equally strong where acculturation had been at its most successful. In France and England, suppression of all distinctiveness and national exclusivity was legally required of the Jews.

67. Aschheim, *Brothers and Strangers,* 33–35, 262 n. 2. Whereas millions of transmigrants—some Jewish—passed *through* Germany in the nineteenth century, one third of East European Jewry (74.5 percent of the world's Jewish population) was eventually permitted to settle in the United States. See also David Vital, *The Origins of Zionism* (Oxford: Oxford University Press, 1975), 49–64.

68. See Gilman, *Jewish Self-Hatred,* 308.

69. See Shmuel Almog, *Zionism and History: The Rise of a New Jewish Consciousness,* trans. Ina Friedman (New York: St. Martin's Press, 1987), 174–75.

70. Like German nationalism, other European nationalisms had a conservative face. As liberalism waned, these nationalisms lost their liberating force, often deviating into xenophobia and antisemitism. For a discussion of the continuities between Jewish nationalism and *völkisch* racialism, see chapter 4 in George L. Mosse, *Germans and Jews: The Right, the Left, and the Search for a "Third Force" in Pre-Nazi Germany* (New York: Howard Fertig, 1970), 77–115.

71. As late as 1910, certain German Zionists made a distinction between themselves and all East European Jews, Zionists included. See Oppenheimer, "Stammesbewusstsein und Volksbewusstsein," 139–43.

72. Herzl's programmatic *Altneuland,* published in October 1902, cannot be discussed fully in this context. It is sufficient to note that cultural Zionists reacted very critically. For the most part, criticism of the work focused on its Western style and its complete lack of concern for culture. Furthermore, negative clichés abound of Hebrew and Yiddish languages, of narrow-minded Eastern Jewish nationalists, and also of assimilationist Jews. *Altneuland*'s combination of racialist concepts (*Rassenzugehörigkeit, Stammesbewußtsein, Muskeljuden*) and its call for duty-bound work and bourgeois virtues derived almost without exception from West European models. See Aḥad Haᶜam, "Altneuland," *Ost und West* (April 1903): 237–44.

73. See Nordau's trenchant reply: "Achad Haᶜam über Altneuland," *Die Welt* (March 13, 1903): 1–5. *Ost und West*'s editorial, "Die Juden von Gestern" (April 1903): 217–26, was probably penned by Binjamin Segel but did not quite match Nordau's performance in its acerbity. On Herzl's monarchical disposition, see Ernst Pawel, *The Labyrinth of Exile: A Life of Theodor Herzl* (New York: Farrar, Straus and Giroux, 1989). For a résumé of the controversy, see Winz's letter of August 15, 1903, to Adolf Friedemann (who also had supported Aḥad Haᶜam), in *The Uganda Controversy,* ed. Michael Heymann (Jerusalem: Israel University Press, 1970), 1: 68–71.

74. Herzl and Nordau had ambivalent attitudes toward Eastern Jewry. The Zionist satire magazine *Der Schlemiel*, however, was originally published by Winz under the slightly different title *Der Schlemihl*.

75. See Berkowitz, *Zionist Culture*, 28–33. See Weizmann's reaction to Herzl as quoted in Aschheim, *Brothers and Strangers*, 91.

76. *Ost und West*'s undeservedly tarnished reputation in the wake of these events was shared even by friends of Winz such as Sammy Gronemann, who failed to appreciate Segel's editorial on Nordau. See Sammy Gronemann, "Erinnerungen" (1948), an unpublished memoir at Leo Baeck Institute, New York, 138.

77. The *Jüdische Rundschau*, even after Loewe's tenure as its editor, continued to throw barbs at *Ost und West*. These attacks were so frequent as to require frequent disclaimers from the Alliance Israélite Universelle, the erstwhile sponsor of *Ost und West* between 1906 and 1914. Because the Alliance had considerable ideological disagreements with Winz and his associates, it urged Zionist critics to attack *Ost und West* and not the Alliance itself. According to Wertheimer, "Loewe's relationship with Eastern Jews deserves study; the childlike tone of his letters to Leo Motzkin is quite remarkable." Wertheimer, *Unwelcome Strangers*, 340 n. 24.

78. Herzl financed and published *Die Welt* (1897–1914) until his death in 1904. It also should be noted that Herzl himself had an acute intuitive sense of public relations. See Berkowitz, " 'Mind, Muscle, and Men,' " 74. At the Zionist Congress of 1905, Sammy Gronemann called on the delegates to make greater use of visual images and symbols in order to increase the organization's following.

79. Later, however, Buber committed the ultimate act of political heresy by writing a negative obituary of Herzl (alongside positive ones), in which he maintained that Herzl had never understood Eastern Jewry. See Martin Buber, "Herzl und die Historie," *Ost und West* (August–September 1904): 583–94.

80. See Reinharz, *Chaim Weizmann*, 183–85. For Buber's conception of the periodical, see Maurice S. Friedman, *Martin Buber's Life and Work: The Early Years, 1878–1923* (New York: Dutton, 1981), 60.

81. Buber's impact on the image of East European Jewry is habitually exaggerated over that of *Ost und West*. See, for example, M. Brenner, *The Renaissance of Jewish Culture*, 142.

82. Whereas at the beginning of the nineteenth century, German Jews were still regarded as "ghetto Jews" (*Ghettojuden*), the term applied exclusively to Eastern Jews by the end of the century. *Ghetto* became the pejorative rubric for the cultural and geographic milieu of Eastern Jewry. In addition, the concept of the ghetto "referred to the simple fact of Jewish physical concentration regardless of its coercive or voluntary origins, and even more crucially, to the perception of the separatist culture generated by such concentration." Aschheim, *Brothers and Strangers*, 5–6.

83. See Jehuda Reinharz, *Fatherland or Promised Land? The Dilemma of the German Jew, 1893–1914* (Ann Arbor: University of Michigan Press, 1975).

84. See Leo Winz Papers, A136/41.

85. For more on the genre of the *Kulturrundschau*, see Karl Ulrich Syndram, *Kulturpublizistik und nationales Selbstverständnis* (Berlin: Mann, 1989).

86. Ury later would become something of a canonical figure in German-Jewish art; his *Jeremias* hung in the entrance hall of the Jewish Museum in Berlin after 1932.

87. For the role of respectability in the constructing of *Ost und West*'s readership, see chapter 2 below.

88. "Ost und West," *Ost und West* (January 1901): 1–2. Further references are to the relevant year of *Ost und West* with column numbers in parentheses.

89. On the reader's "horizon of expectations" and its role in reception theory, see Hans Robert Jauss, *Literaturgeschichte als Provokation* (1967; reprint, Frankfurt a.M.: Suhrkamp, 1970).

90. The later signet of the Jüdischer Verlag, the publishing house of the Zionist movement founded by Buber, Feiwel, Weizmann, and Lilien, appears in the background. Also designed by Lilien, it depicts a Star of David superimposed on a smaller menorah.

91. See Lilien's lithograph "Zion" in Borries von Münchhausen's *Juda: Gesänge* (Goslar: F. A. Latimann, 1900), as well as his famous "angel" postcard from the Fifth Zionist Congress (1901), reproduced and discussed in Berkowitz, *Zionist Culture*, 128–29.

92. On early Zionist iconography, see Berkowitz, *Zionist Culture*.

93. See Aḥad Haᶜam, *Äussere Freiheit und innere Knechtschaft: Eine zeitgemässe Betrachtung* (Berlin: Achiasaf, 1901[?]).

94. On the *Berliner Illustrirte Zeitung*, see Lynda King, *Best-sellers by Design: Vicki Baum and the House of Ullstein* (Detroit: Wayne State University Press, 1988), 29–31, 52–53. On illustrated magazines in Germany, see Hartwig Gebhardt, "Illustrierte Zeitschriften in Deutschland am Ende des 19. Jahrhunderts," *Börsenblatt für den deutschen Buchhandel*, Frankfurt ed., 150–51, 48 (June 16, 1983): B41–65, under the heading "Buchhandelsgeschichte."

95. Though their approach was not strictly historical, Buber and the Jewish socialist/anarchist Gustav Landauer (1870–1919) aptly distinguished between Eastern and Western Jews in terms of *Gemeinschaft* ("community") and *Gesellschaft* ("society"), respectively. See Ferdinand Tönnies, *Gemeinschaft und Gesellschaft. Grundbegriffe der reinen Soziologie* (Leipzig: R. Reisland, 1887). Whereas *Gemeinschaft* designated a close-knit, cooperative community, *Gesellschaft* represented atomized, Western urban society. See also Noah Isenberg, *Between Redemption and Doom: German Modernism and the Strains of Jewish Identity* (Lincoln: University of Nebraska Press, forthcoming).

96. German bourgeois history as a whole may gain from an understanding of *Ost und West*. By examining German-Jewish journals, we have access to the private lives of the German *Bürgertum*, a group that recently has attracted the interest of social historians who hitherto favored the working class, thus inadvertently excluding the Jews from their purview. This study (especially chapters 2–5 below) explores how the emerging Jewish middle classes were influenced by reading journals.

97. Anderson, *Imagined Communities*, 47–49.

98. Winz's publishing principles were a smaller-scale version of those practiced by the blockbusting but politically liberal Ullsteins, who recommended: (1) eliminating chance and sticking with a successful product as long as possible; (2) appealing to the lower classes (this includes *Ost und West*'s populist appeal to the Eastern Jews); (3) using advertising and promotion; and (4) using other media to promote success of products (such as Winz's other businesses). See King, *Best-sellers by Design*, 60–63. That Winz himself survived for so long is also testimony to his business savvy. It suffices merely to look at the second half of his career, where he served as a public relations representative for Tel Aviv, as the publisher of the largest newspaper in

Germany (the *Gemeindeblatt der jüdischen Gemeinde zu Berlin*), as a copublisher of the first sensationalist Hebrew newspaper in Israel, and so forth.

99. Winz to *Vorstand der Jüdischen Gemeinde Berlin*, July 12, 1927, Leo Winz Papers, A136/49.

100. The ordering of genres in *Ost und West* was fairly consistent. Although people did not always read it from front to back, the hierarchy of genres expressed a constancy at odds with the heterogeneity of the genres and contributions. This was part of the inevitable process of canonization that took place in the journal.

101. See Buber's letter to Herzl of May 26, 1903, in Martin Buber, *Briefwechsel aus sieben Jahrzehnten*, ed. Grete Schaeder (Heidelberg: Lambert Schneider, 1972), 197. See also the argument that Winz and his associates treated Eastern Jews as "liebevoller," in Victor Klemperer, *Curriculum Vitae. Jugend um 1900* (Berlin: Siedler, 1989), 2: 489. On Kaufmann, see the first issues of *Die Freistatt* (1912–14).

102. According to lawyer, writer, and Zionist leader Sammy Gronemann, "Winz war . . . Protektor schlechthin. Immer wieder entdeckte er in die Klemme geratene Personen, denen er ueber die Schwierigkeiten hinweghalf, junge Maler, Schauspieler etc.—bald war es eine russische Taenzerin, bald eine in Scheidung liegende Fürstin oder eine Diplomatinfrau, vor allem aber interessierte er sich fuer Sportsleute aller Art, und schliesslich wurde er in der Sportpresse als der Bekannte 'Protektor des Box-Sportes' zitiert." Gronemann, "Erinnerungen," 139.

103. See Winz's contracts with the Alliance under the heading "Berlin/Winz" at the archives of the Alliance Israélite Universelle in Paris, file Archives-Allemagne, VII.A.14–16, VII et XIV.

104. In late 1905, Winz secured an agreement from the Alliance whereby the organization agreed to finance part of the journal's production in exchange for eight to ten pages in each monthly issue and discounted subscriptions for its 10,000 German members. The pages devoted to the Alliance in each monthly issue appeared under the heading "Mitteilungen aus dem deutschen Bureau der Alliance Israélite Universelle" (October 1906–December 1911) or "Mitteilungen des Central-Comités der Alliance Israélite Universelle in Paris" (January 1911–August 1914)—hereafter referred to as "Mitteilungen." This section was edited independently of *Ost und West* (by M. A. Klausner, an outstanding publicist in his own right and the political editor of the *Berliner Börsen-Courier*), and philosophical differences with *Ost und West* were not unusual. Although the newsy, derivative "Mitteilungen" were probably ignored by most readers, the stereotypes of North African and Middle Eastern Jews purveyed there were more objectionable than those in the main body of the magazine.

105. Personal communication from Professor Aron Rodrigue, January 2, 1993. See also Aron Rodrigue, *French Jews, Turkish Jews: The Alliance Israélite Universelle and the Politics of Jewish Schooling in Turkey, 1860–1925* (Bloomington: Indiana University Press, 1990), 121–45.

106. The Alliance routinely depicted Sephardic and Falasha Jews as "feminine" and "childlike" in their reports appearing in *Ost und West*. In contrast, Winz and his colleagues never published anything as blatantly westernizing as the Alliance's Orientalist travelogues and reports on Jewish ghettos in North Africa and the Levant.

107. A few letters of protest are preserved in the archives, especially from the climactic year of 1912, when the German-based Alliance was divided by conflict.

See, e.g., the letter of Dr. Max Mainzer to Dr. Eduard Baerwald of the Frankfurter Lokalcommite der Alliance, November 11, 1912. Winz, "Berlin/Winz," 7565/3.

108. See Andre Lefevere, *Translating Literature: Practice and Theory in a Comparative Literature Context* (New York: Modern Language Association, 1992). See also D. Brenner, "Making *Jargon* Respectable."

109. The most obvious imitator of *Ost und West* was the Hungarian-Jewish art and cultural journal *Mült és jövó* (Budapest, 1912–1944).

110. Gershom Scholem, *Mi-berlin li-yerushalayim* [From Berlin to Jerusalem], expanded Hebrew ed. (Tel Aviv: Am Oved, 1982), 47.

111. On the Jewish renaissance of Weimar Germany, see M. Brenner, *The Renaissance of Jewish Culture*.

112. See Michael Brenner, "The *Jüdische Volkspartei*—National-Jewish Communal Politics during the Weimar Republic," *Year Book of the Leo Baeck Institute* 35 (1990): 219–44.

113. On American magazines and advertising in the same epoch, see Ellen Gruber Garvey, *The Adman in the Parlor: Magazines and the Gendering of Consumer Culture, 1880s to 1910s* (New York: Oxford University Press, 1996), and Richard M. Ohmann, *Selling Culture: Magazines, Markets, and Class at the Turn of the Century* (New York: Verso, 1996).

114. Demonizing the *Westjude* allowed Winz and his associates to ally themselves with Western models of modernization while pretending to shun contact with the West. In an ambiguous manner, it permitted *Ost und West*'s readers to practice a guilt-free type of (Jewish) Orientalism. Cf. Paul Mendes-Flohr, "Fin-de-Siècle Orientalism, the Ostjuden and the Aesthetics of Jewish Self-Affirmation," *Studies in Contemporary Jewry* (1984): 96–139.

115. For a general overview of stereotyping, see Arthur G. Miller, "Historical and Contemporary Perspectives in Stereotyping," in *In the Eye of the Beholder*, ed. Arthur G. Miller (New York: Praeger, 1982), 1–40. For a case study, see Pierre Bourdieu, *Distinction: A Social Critique of the Judgement of Taste*, trans. Richard Nice (Cambridge, Mass.: Harvard University Press, 1984).

116. See Sander L. Gilman, *Difference and Pathology: Stereotypes of Sexuality, Race, and Madness* (Ithaca: Cornell University Press, 1985), 17–18.

117. From early childhood on, we use stereotypes as a conceptual shorthand in making judgments about the world and ourselves. Thus, stereotypes cannot be summarily dismissed as irrational; they are unavoidable. On the need for a sociohistorical approach to stereotyping, see James Elliott, Jürgen Pelzer, and Carol Poore, eds., *Stereotyp und Vorurteil in der Literatur: Untersuchungen zu Autoren des 20. Jahrhunderts* (Göttingen: Vandenhoeck and Ruprecht, 1978), 29–31. For an early cognitive approach, see Walter Lippmann, *Public Opinion* (New York: Macmillan, 1922). Lippmann was very influential in disseminating the term *stereotype*. Stereotypes for him are characteristic of "mass democracy" and of wide-ranging media effects. Also similar to *Ost und West*'s flexible approach to stereotyping is Lippmann's view that the degree and range of stereotyping are determined by the affects and tendencies of each individual. For a sociological approach to stereotyping, see Gordon W. Allport, *The Nature of Prejudice*, 2nd ed. (Garden City, N.Y.: Doubleday, 1958).

118. Ritchie Robertson, "National Stereotypes in Prague German Fiction," *Colloquia Germanica* 22 (1989): 118.

119. Although the rhetoric of stereotypes permeates most textual genres in *Ost*

und West, fiction will receive special attention here owing to its insight into identity and culture.

120. Gilman, *Difference and Pathology,* 23–24.

121. Although there was a long tradition of stereotypes that *Westjuden* held about *Ostjuden*—and vice versa—a complete history of these cultural types and stereotypes would take us too far afield. It suffices here to note that these stereotypes, no matter how compelling their historical similarities, do vary.

122. See John Efron, who argues that "[t]o accept the proposition that historically the Jews were involved in a colonial relationship with Christian Europe is to also recognize that the labors of Jewish physical anthropologists [and historians] were an attempt at reversing the European gaze." John M. Efron, *Defenders of the Race: Jewish Doctors and Race Science in Fin-de-Siècle Europe* (New Haven: Yale University Press, 1994), 3.

123. Only by knowing the nature of the specific subaudience, the reader's position in society, can we ultimately know whether stereotypes are irresponsible, inappropriate, or inaccurate in the contexts in which they appear.

124. Considering that it targeted Jews living in Germany, *Ost und West* achieved an astounding level of saturation. Compare circulation figures of recent print media in America in *The 1988 Media Guide,* ed. Jude Wanniski (Morristown, N.J.: Polyconomics, 1988).

125. See Gershon Shaked, *Die Macht der Identität. Essays über jüdische Schriftsteller* (Königstein/Ts.: Veröffentlichung des Leo Baeck Instituts, 1986), 192.

126. Because systematic study of periodicals is largely neglected in the field of German-Jewish history, one must draw on previous research in periodical studies, particularly coming out of Germany and England. Much of this scholarship characterizes periodicals as collections of texts unique in their mix of constancy and heterogeneity. In a sense, the medium was *Ost und West's* message. To survive, a journal, then as now, had to be flexible. Yet readers also wanted periodicals to show some stability in successive issues. According to Lyn Pykett, the periodical "may offer its readers scope to construct their own version of the text by selective reading, but against that flexibility has to be put the tendency in the form to close off alternative readings by creating a dominant position from which to read, a position which is maintained with more or less consistency across the single number and between numbers." Lyn Pykett, "Reading the Periodical Press: Text and Context," *Victorian Periodicals Review* 52 (Fall 1989): 107. See also Kurt Koszyk, *Deutsche Presse im 19. Jahrhundert* (Berlin: Colloquium, 1966), vol. 2; and Wilmont Haacke, "Der Zeitschriftentypus Revue," *Archiv für Geschichte des Buchwesens* 11 (1970): 1035–56. See both the *Victorian Periodicals Review* and *Archiv für Geschichte des Buchwesens* for more current views in the field.

127. See Janet Swaffar, Katherine Arens, and Heidi Byrnes, *Reading for Meaning: An Integrated Approach to Language Learning* (Englewood Cliffs, N.J.: Prentice-Hall, 1991), 43.

128. Gershom Scholem, quoted in Mark H. Gelber, "Das Judendeutsch in der deutschen Literatur. Einige Beispiele von den frühesten Lexika bis zu Gustav Freytag und Thomas Mann," in *Juden in der deutschen Literatur. Ein deutsch-israelisches Symposion,* ed. Stéphane Moses and Albrecht Schöne (Frankfurt a.M.: Suhrkamp, 1986), 176.

129. On the terms *acculturation* and *assimilation,* see introduction, note 1, above.

CHAPTER 2

1. While few records remain from before 1901, documents in Winz's *Nachlaß* from after that period show a high awareness of market research. See especially Winz's detailed outline (*Exposé*) for a nationwide *Gemeindeblatt*, an illustrated weekly with a different local section for each Jewish community; see also his proposal for an English-language edition of *Ost und West*. Both in Leo Winz Papers, A136/39.

2. Some of the following considerations also apply to Jews living in the Habsburg empire.

3. For recent examples, see Monika Richarz, ed., *Jüdisches Leben in Deutschland. Selbstzeugnisse zur Sozialgeschichte*, 3 vols. (Stuttgart: Deutsche Verlags–Anstalt, 1976–82); Marsha L. Rozenblit, *The Jews of Vienna, 1867–1914: Assimilation and Identity* (Albany: State University of New York Press, 1983); and Marion A. Kaplan, *The Making of the Jewish Middle Class: Women, Family, and Identity in Imperial Germany* (New York: Oxford University Press, 1991).

4. The word *national* resonated differently in early twentieth-century ears, connoting "ethnic" more than "nationwide." The German noun prefixes *Stammes-* and *National-*, in their historical setting, are roughly equivalent to the present-day English term *ethnic*. It is related to *Abstammung* ("descent") and *Stammesgemeinschaft* ("community of common ancestry"). According to Michael Brenner, "[t]he popularity of its [*national*'s] use can be partly explained by its vagueness. Assimilationists interpreted it in the sense of a German *Stamm* analogous to Bavarians or Saxons, but for Zionists it became a synonym for a Jewish *Volk.*" M. Brenner, *The Renaissance of Jewish Culture*, 228 n. 12.

5. See chapter 3 below.

6. Ezra Mendelsohn, *The Jews of East Central Europe between the World Wars* (Bloomington: Indiana University Press, 1983), 6–7.

7. On the "semi-neutral society," see Jacob Katz, *Out of the Ghetto: The Social Background of Jewish Emancipation, 1770–1870* (New York: Schocken, 1978), 42–57.

8. Not all components of European Jewish identity can be subsumed under these three categories. In this study, however, broad cultural trends will take precedence in the attempt to reconstruct Jewish identities along East-West lines.

9. See Jeffrey A. Grossman, "The Space of Yiddish in the German and German-Jewish Discourse," Ph.D. dissertation, University of Texas, 1992, 28–63.

10. The Reform movement has had no "doctrinal essence" even though certain teachings—the historical nature of Judaism, progressive revelation, and universalized messianism—achieved dominance for long periods. See Michael A. Meyer, *Response to Modernity: A History of the Reform Movement in Judaism* (New York: Oxford University Press, 1988), ix.

11. This rejection of East European Judaism is a fine example of the power of negative definition in identity formation. See ibid., xi.

12. On the significance of Jewish religion, see Winz's rationale for sending his son, Viktor, to study and live at the neo-Orthodox *Gymnasium* in Halberstadt. Leo Winz Papers, A136/179.

13. Many Jews regarded the avoidance of baptism as evidence of character. See Fabius Schach, *Über die Zukunft Israels. Eine kritische Betrachtung* (Berlin: M. Poppelauer, 1904), 12–13.

14. At least one contributor to *Ost und West*, Binjamin Segel, published concurrently in *Der Israelit*, a neo-Orthodox newspaper.

15. Although they did not urge a return to the ghetto, some Jewish nationalists made the autonomous communal organization, the *kehillah* (or, in Yiddish, *kehile*) into a paradigm. The *kehillah* had served as the political basis for Ashkenazic Jewish communities until the granting of limited individual rights under Western-style emancipation and had been treated as a corporate body under European feudalism. It negotiated as a collective in order to secure the rights and status of the Jews in each specific territory and thus differed significantly from Western *Gemeinden* and their umbrella organizations in the early twentieth century.

16. Michael Stanislawski, *For Whom Do I Toil? Judah Leib Gordon and the Crisis of Russian Jewry* (New York: Oxford University Press, 1988), 5.

17. On Orthodox Zionists and the Mizrachi faction, see Ehud Luz, *Parallels Meet: Religion and Nationalism in the Early Zionist Movement, 1882–1904* (Philadelphia: Jewish Publication Society, 1988).

18. Robert D. King, "Migration and Lingustic Change as Illustrated by Yiddish," in *Trends in Linguistics: Reconstructing Languages and Cultures*, ed. Werner Winter and Edgar Polomé (Berlin: Mouton de Gruyter, 1992), 419–39.

19. Western Jews even differentiated between themselves and the Easterners as *Ashkenaz* and *Polacken*. See Moses A. Shulvass, *From East to West: The Westward Migration of Jews from Eastern Europe during the Seventeenth and Eigtheenth Centuries* (Detroit: Wayne State University Press, 1971); and "Die Beschreibung fun Ashkenaz un Polack" (ca. 1675), reproduced in Max Weinreich, "Zvey yidishe shpotlider af yidn," *Filologishe shriften* (Vilna: YIVO, 1929), 3: 537–54.

20. On the pejorative Yiddish term *daytsher* ("German-style" or "Europeanized" Jews), see Aschheim, *Brothers and Strangers*, 21. While S. Y. Agnon may have strived to destroy this stereotype, he was by no means typical. Nor do I concur with Michael Brenner's assessment that "[i]t took an East European Jew to accomplish what German-Jewish writers failed to achieve: a portrayal of the varieties of Jewish life in Germany, without bias." M. Brenner, *The Renaissance of Jewish Culture*, 208–9.

21. On the history of Eastern *Betteljuden* in Germany, see Shulvass, *From East to West*, 44–45, 67–70, 97–104, 108–10.

22. Aschheim, *Brothers and Strangers*, 4.

23. Wertheimer, *Unwelcome Strangers*, 147.

24. Mendelsohn, *The Jews of East Central Europe*, 7.

25. Ibid.

26. It is not surprising, then, that *Ost und West*, as the first magazine to promote the *Ostjuden*, was published in Berlin and was directed primarily at German-Jewish readers. On the special history (or *Sonderweg*) of Germany with respect to Jewish emancipation and acculturation, see Sorkin, *The Transformation of German Jewry*.

27. Joshua Fishman maintains that within the Jewish fold, secularism can be defined negatively or positively. More frequently defined negatively, secularism is the position that traditional orthopraxis is antiquated or counterproductive and that "religion is a 'private matter' of no collective or institutional significance for Jewish survival and creativity." Positively viewed, secularism implies Jewish affiliation on the basis of language and literature (non-Hebrew and non-Yiddish as well), party

politics, arts, the mass media, etc. Joshua A. Fishman, *Ideology, Society and Language: The Odyssey of Nathan Birnbaum* (Ann Arbor: Karoma, 1987), 270.

28. This transformation was often thematized in both Jewish and non-Jewish publications. See "Die Transformation der russischen Juden," *Ost und West* (September 1901): 673–74, which depicts the physical and cosmetic transformation of Russian-Jewish immigrants to Germany over four generations. See also Th. Th. Heine's caricature, "Die Verwandlung," *Simplicissimus*, June 2, 1903.

29. On Mendelssohn, see Alexander Altmann, *Moses Mendelssohn: A Biographical Study* (University, Ala.: University of Alabama Press, 1973); and David J. Sorkin, *Moses Mendelssohn and the Religious Enlightenment* (Berkeley: University of California Press, 1996).

30. See the incident with the Swiss theologian Johann Caspar Lavater (the so-called *Lavaterfrage*), who confronted Mendelssohn in 1769 regarding his unwillingness to convert to Christianity. On Mendelssohn's essential conservatism, see Meyer, *Response to Modernity*, 13–16.

31. On policy toward the Romani people (the "gypsies") in the German lands, see Heinrich Moritz Gottlieb Grellmann, *Die Zigeuner: Ein historischer Versuch über die Lebensart und Verfassung Sitten und Schicksahle dieses Volks in Europa, nebst ihrem Ursprunge* (Dessau and Leipzig: Buchhandlung der Gelehrten, 1783).

32. For more on Dohm, see Uwe J. Eissing, "Christian Wilhelm von Dohm, die bürgerliche Verbesserung der Juden und die Vision einer 'judenfreien' Welt," *Bulletin des Leo Baeck Instituts* 88 (1991): 27–58.

33. Many converted Jews did not eliminate their ties to Germany's distinctive Jewish subculture. Rejection by the official Jewish *Gemeinde* also mattered less once Judaism came to be regarded as just another denomination in a German state made up of many confessions. Former Jews were not prohibited from associating with their former coreligionists.

34. See Lessing's *Die Juden: Ein Lustspiel in einem Aufzuge* (1749) for an example of a positively drawn, presumably Sephardic Jew from Hamburg. For the first published edition of 1754, see Gotthold Ephraim Lessing, *Schrifften* (Berlin: C. F. Voss, 1753–1755), vol. 4.

35. In the emancipation debates in revolutionary France, the Ashkenazic Jews of Alsace-Lorraine were not considered for the same rights as their Sephardic coreligionists. For a full treatment, see Paula E. Hyman, *The Emancipation of the Jews of Alsace: Acculturation and Tradition in the Nineteenth Century* (New Haven: Yale University Press, 1991).

36. See George L. Mosse, "Jewish Emancipation: Between Bildung and Respectability," in *The Jewish Response to German Culture: From the Enlightenment to the Second World War*, ed. Jehuda Reinharz and Walter Schatzberg (Hanover, N.H.: University Press of New England, 1985); and George L. Mosse, *Nationalism and Sexuality: Middle-Class Morality and Sexual Norms in Modern Europe* (1985; Madison: University of Wisconsin Press, 1986), 1–22.

37. Mosse, "Jewish Emancipation," 4.

38. At the same time, *Ost und West* sought to distance itself from the Jewish *Familienblätter* ("family journals").

39. Male and female roles were regarded as separate and distinct, a common pattern in nineteenth-century national iconography in Germany and England. This iconography, in turn, became the model for "respectable" Jewish nationalism.

40. See Fritz Ringer, "*Bildung:* The Social and Ideological Context of the German Historical Tradition," *History of European Ideas* 10 (1989): 193–202. For a dissenting view, see Rozenblit, who argues that "most historians have greatly exaggerated the role of *Bildung* in the lives of most German-speaking Central European Jews in the nineteenth century." Rozenblit, "The Jews of the Dual Monarchy," 165. Whereas Jacob Katz has placed the origins of Jewish modernization in the small circles of Enlightenment intellectuals who created a secular, semi-neutral society open to Jews, Rozenblit and others find that an economically generated neutral space was more important in Jewish-Gentile interaction than intellectual circles could ever be. Social historians have demonstrated repeatedly the important link between industrialization and Jewish modernization in Germany. See Rozenblit, "The Jews of the Dual Monarchy," 170–71; and William O. McCagg, Jr., *A History of Habsburg Jews, 1670–1918* (Bloomington: Indiana University Press, 1989).

41. W. H. Bruford, *The German Tradition of Self-Cultivation: "Bildung" from Humboldt to Thomas Mann* (London: Cambridge University Press, 1975), ix.

42. See Ringer, "*Bildung,*" 196.

43. George L. Mosse, *German Jews beyond Judaism* (Bloomington: Indiana University Press, 1985), 72–82.

44. Bruford, *The German Tradition of Self-Cultivation,* 22–26, 206–25.

45. On Yiddish and respectability, see Grossman, "The Space of Yiddish," 77–78. See also Mosse, "Jewish Emancipation," 6. Mosse has argued quite persuasively that respectability, both as ideology and as practice, was closely linked to a sublimated ideal of male sexuality. In nationalist thought of the epoch, calls were made to integrate eros into male communities (in German, the phenomenon of the *Männerbünde*).

46. Ibid., 30, 78.

47. See Berkowitz, *Zionist Culture,* 107–8. See also chapter 5 below.

48. See "Earl of Reading," *Ost und West* (January–February 1921): 29–32.

49. On the pitfalls of the term *Mittelstand* as a designation for the middle classes in Germany, see Thomas Childers, "The Social Language of Politics in Germany: The Sociology of Political Discourse in the Weimar Republic," *American Historical Review* 95.2 (1990): 331–58.

50. See Jacob Toury, *Soziale und politische Geschichte der Juden in Deutschland, 1848–1914: Zwischen Revolution, Reaktion und Emanzipation* (Düsseldorf: Droste 1977), 114. The Jews made up approximately 1 percent of the population at any given time in the *Kaiserreich.*

51. See Mosse, *Nationalism and Sexuality,* 181.

52. In the nineteenth century, both Jewish secularism and Jewish nationalism offered themselves as replacements for messianism and other forms of religious expression. Zionist professions of faith were powerful devices because they were so nebulous. Similar to the Yom Kippur liturgy, Zionist practice involved collective "admission of sins, vows, and mutual responsiblity. . . . In some ways, Herzl . . . obscured the boundary between Jewish nationalism as a secular ideology and Judaism's traditional religious faith." Berkowitz, "Mind, Muscle, and Men,'" 76.

53. Eastern Jews shared many norms of "bourgeois ideology" and *Bildung.* See Paul Mendes-Flohr, review of *German Jews beyond Judaism* by George L. Mosse,

Studies in Contemporary Jewry 5 (1989): 379. In the documents left to us, Eastern Jews fashion themselves as middle class in their aspirations to education and social mobility.

54. Kaplan, *The Making of the Jewish Middle Class*, 232–33.

55. To be sure, the ideal of respectability proved dangerous to the process of emancipation which it had once encouraged. But, as Mosse writes, "[r]espectability itself was part of the narrowing vision of German society. Liberalism could remain alive even while respectability attempted to tighten the reins, for political and economic freedoms were not supposed to entail freedom of manners and morals; rather the cohesion respectability provided was necessary to supply liberal freedoms with a stable base. Liberalism seemed to provide a secure anchor for Jewish assimilation, despite the remaining obstacles to full citizenship." Mosse, "Jewish Emancipation," 13. The success of respectability in nineteenth-century Jewish circles also may have been related to demography: the Jewish population was comparatively older than the German population.

56. Kaplan claims that "Jewish families were more liberal politically—that is, less xenophobic, more tolerant of pluralism, more supportive of one of the liberal parties." Kaplan, *The Making of the Jewish Middle Class*, ix.

57. On Jewish voting, see Pulzer, *Jews and the German State*, 323. On socialism and Zionism, see Berkowitz, " 'Mind, Muscle, and Men,' " 112. Socialism became increasingly attractive to Jewish intellectuals and protest voters as a party that opposed antisemitism. Liberals did not fret over Prussia's militarism; instead, Prussia was seen as progressive in education, communications, and its respect for technology. Contrary to myth, constitutionalism did succeed partially in the *Kaiserreich*, as well as legal and constitutional safeguards. See David Blackbourn, "The German Bourgeoisie: An Introduction," in *The German Bourgeoisie: Essays on the Social History of the German Middle Class from the Late Eighteenth to the Early Twentieth Century*, ed. David Blackbourn and Richard J. Evans (London: Routledge, 1991), 20–21. *Ost und West* flirted more with socialism than the party Zionists, who saw it as conflicting with their ideal of a liberalism that curtailed arbitrary government. At the same time, the journal seemed at times elitist and antidemocratic—despite the fact that considerable social and extralegal barriers to full legal emancipation remained at least until the Weimar period. In fact, the average Jewish voter, as a member of the German middle class, perceived socialism as immoderate and potentially destabilizing. See Pulzer, *Jews and the German State*, 139.

58. Kaplan, *The Making of the Jewish Middle Class*, 12.

59. Blackbourn, "The German Bourgeoisie," 12. Along with social organizations, German Jewry shared the propertied middle class's suspicion of the boheme and avant-garde.

60. Jacob Katz, "German Culture and the Jews," in *The Jewish Response to German Culture: From the Enlightenment to the Second World War*, ed. Jehuda Reinharz and Walter Schatzberg (Hanover, N.H.: University Press of New England, 1985), 85.

61. As of the mid-nineteenth century, the German bourgeoisie showed muted antagonism toward the aristocracy and toward the "uncivilized" and "dependent" peasantry. Blackbourn, "The German Bourgeoisie," 14.

62. See Richarz, ed., *Jüdisches Leben in Deutschland*, 12–22.

63. Kaplan, *The Making of the Jewish Middle Class*, 232.

64. Sorkin, *The Transformation of German Jewry*, 6–7.

65. In contrast to the German-Jewish middle class, the Jewish traders of Galicia and the Pale often lived on the edge of destitution. And in the Weimar republic, non-Jewish Germans "caught up" with the Jews, achieving similar economic success. See Donald Niewyk, *The Jews of the Weimar Republic* (Baton Rouge: Louisiana State University Press, 1980), 11–21.

66. The gospel of work, for example, hastened the integration of Jewish men into the German middle classes. A number of contributors to *Ost und West* called for an immediate restructuring of Jewish occupations to stem the tide of German-Jewish upward mobility. In 1901 alone, see the two essays by Ernst Tuch, "Die wirtschaftliche Aufgabe der deutschen Judenheit" (January 1901): 55–58 and "Jüdische Bauern auf deutschem Boden" (July 1901): 499–512.

67. Aḥad Haʿam created his own elite, Masonic-like Jewish order called *B'nei Moshe.*

68. Eli Lederhendler, "Modernity with Emancipation or Assimilation? The Case of Russian Jewry," in *Assimilation and Community: The Jews in Nineteenth-Century Europe*, ed. Jonathan Frankel and Steven J. Zipperstein (Cambridge: Cambridge University Press, 1992), 324–43.

69. See Raphael Mahler, *Hasidism and the Jewish Enlightenment: Their Confrontation in Galicia and Poland in the First Half of the Nineteenth Century* (Philadelphia: Jewish Publication Society, 1985).

70. These successors to the early *maskilim* came from less prosperous families, and they took to heart the promise of Jewish national redemption. Part of the largest population boom in East European Jewish history, this group disseminated ethnic as well as secular Jewish identity. An entire generation aspired to be Hebrew or Yiddish writers, worshiping literature as an *Ersatztalmud*. See Dan Miron, *A Traveler Disguised: A Study in the Rise of Modern Yiddish Fiction in the Nineteenth Century* (New York: Schocken, 1973).

71. On "re-ethnification," see Fishman, *Ideology, Society and Language*, 64–65 n. 7, and the discussion in chapter 3 below.

72. Nathan Birnbaum, *Die jüdische Moderne*, ed. Henryk M. Broder (Augsburg: Ölbaum Verlag, 1989), 104. The book was originally published in Czernowitz in 1910 by "Dr. Birnbaum and Dr. Kohut."

73. Hence the rendering of Eastern-style cultural Zionism into German as *Kulturzionismus*. Whereas *Zivilisation* is roughly equivalent to "respectability," *Kultur* also may refer to "civilization," as in the frequent *Ost und West* phrase *"Kultur und Bildung."*

74. George L. Mosse, *The Culture of Western Europe: The Nineteenth and Twentieth Centuries* (New York: Rand McNally, 1961), 1–2. On the use of *Kultur* by German thinkers in the nineteenth century, see George L. Mosse, *The Crisis of German Ideology: Intellectual Origins of the Third Reich* (New York: Grosset and Dunlap, 1964). On Birnbaum and *Kultur*, see Berkowitz, *Zionist Culture*, 53–54.

75. Birnbaum, "Etwas über Ost- und Westjuden" (1904), in *Die jüdische Moderne*, 152–53.

76. Ibid., 153–54.

77. Ibid., 155.

78. Birnbaum and *Ost und West* developed an Eastern version of the *Wissenschaft des Judentums*, which called for scientific inquiry into Judaism and demanded that Jewry assume a role commensurate with its contributions to civilization.

79. On Aḥad Haᶜam, see Steven Zipperstein, *Elusive Prophet: Aḥad Haᶜam and the Origins of Zionism* (Berkeley: University of California Press, 1993).

80. Alan Mintz, "A Sanctuary in the Wilderness: The Beginnings of the Hebrew Movement in America in the Pages of *Hatoren*," *Prooftexts* 10 (September 1990): 411.

81. See Joseph Goldstein, "The Zionist Movement in Russia, 1897–1904," Ph.D. dissertation, Hebrew University of Jerusalem, 1982. Discussions of Jewish identity among Russian Jews mirrored debates of the time about whether to adopt Western traditions or move along "native" Russian lines.

82. Compare the somewhat more "Western" *Kulturzionismus* of Micha Joseph Berdichevsky. Influenced by Nietzsche, he sought to liberate Eastern Jewry from its "ghetto" lethargy. See Aschheim, *Brothers and Strangers*, 123–24.

83. Franz Kafka, "[Rede über die jiddische Sprache]," *Hochzeitsvorbereitungen auf dem Lande: und andere Prosa aus dem Nachlaß* (Frankfurt a.M.: Fischer Taschenbuch, 1983), 306; in *Gesammelte Werke*, ed. Max Brod. See Kafka's letter to Bauer of October 27, 1912, in *Briefe an Felice und andere Korrespondenz aus der Verlobungszeit*, ed. Erich Heller and Jürgen Born (Frankfurt a.M.: Fischer, 1967), 59.

84. The foremost historian of German-Jewish marginality is Peter Gay. See his *Weimar Culture: The Outsider as Insider* (New York: Harper and Row, 1968) and *Freud, Jews, and Other Germans: Masters and Victims in Modernist Culture* (New York: Oxford University Press, 1978).

85. Specifically, *Ost und West* used juxtaposition in the magazine itself, placing articles and images side by side in order to suggest the compatibility of Eastern and Western Jewish culture and to guide their reception.

86. See Anderson, *Imagined Communities*, 47–49. Like much of the nationalist media, *Ost und West* also made "populist" concessions to lower-class groupings within the "nation"—specifically the Eastern Jews.

87. See Haacke, "Der Zeitschriftentypus Revue," 1035–56; and Wolfgang Martens, *Die Botschaft der Tugend: Die Aufklärung im Spiegel der deutschen Moralischen Wochenschriften* (Stuttgart: Metzler, 1968).

88. Karl Ulrich Syndram, *Kulturpublizistik und nationales Selbstverständnis* (Berlin: Mann, 1989), 35–39.

89. On the *Gebildeten*, see the contributions in *Das wilhelminische Bildungsbürgertum*, ed. Klaus Vondung (Göttingen: Vandenhoeck and Ruprecht, 1976). The *Bildungsbürgertum* was made up of civil officials (schoolteachers, clergymen, academics) and members of the free professions, whereas the *Besitzbürgertum*, or propertied bourgeoisie, included merchants, businessman, and independent master craftsmen. See Blackbourn, "The German Bourgeoisie," 3.

90. According to Syndram, the rhetoric of the *Kulturrundschau* consistently emphasized culture over politics. This resulted as much from German *Innerlichkeit* and distaste for interest politics as from censorship. See Syndram, *Kulturpublizistik*, 152–56. In contrast, *Ost und West* was rather political considering its tenuous status as an *Ostjuden*-sponsored magazine. A more significant parallel between German and Jewish *Rundschauzeitschriften* was that their producers shared a similar educational

background and similar attitudes on intermarriage, integration, the family, and leisure—in spite of the fact that they parted ways on ethnicity and religion.

91. Syndram, *Kulturpublizistik*, 154.

CHAPTER 3

1. Recognizing that all stereotypes are bipolar in nature, *Ost und West*, as indicated in chapter 1 above, adopted the characteristics usually associated with "ghetto" Jews—dishonesty, perversion, illness, etc.—for its stereotypes of Western "bad" Jews.

2. Hannah Arendt may have introduced the term "Jewish parvenu" into scholarly discourse. See Hannah Arendt, "The Jew as Pariah," in *The Jew as Pariah: Jewish Identity and Politics in the Modern Age*, ed. Ron H. Feldman (New York: Grove, 1978), 67–90.

3. See Shulvass, *From East to West*, 53–54.

4. In current usage, a *Protz* is a "show-off" or a "boaster." *Jüdische Geldprotz* became common coinage in the late nineteenth century. See Henry Wassermann, "The *Fliegende Blätter* as a Source for the Social History of German Jewry," *Year Book of the Leo Baeck Institute* 28 (1983): 126.

5. It is difficult to estimate the size of the intellectual audience of *Ost und West*. In 1902, Winz reported that the journal had a readership of 5,000 in its first year. See *Sperlings Zeitschriften-Adressbuch. Hand- und Jahrbuch der deutschen Presse* 41 (1902): 16. Such a high figure—if correct—suggests that German-Jewish intellectuals were not the sole readers of *Ost und West* at its inception. See the following chapters for profiles of other readers of the magazine.

6. *Ost und West*'s contribution to the so-called Jewish Renaissance went hand in hand with the vogue of literary naturalism, artistic *Jugendstil*, and secular Jewish culture. On the young Jewish avant-garde, see Mark H. Gelber, "The *jungjüdische Bewegung:* An Unexplored Chapter in German-Jewish Literary and Cultural History," *Year Book of the Leo Baeck Institute* 31 (1986): 105–19.

7. On Jewish students in the *Kaiserreich*, see Norbert Kampe, "Jews and Antisemites at Universities in Imperial Germany (I): Jewish Students: Social History and Conflict," *Year Book of the Leo Baeck Institute* 30 (1985): 357–94. Kampe generally argues that academic antisemitism was a response to a perceived social conflict between the Jewish *Bildungsbürgertum* and the non-Jewish *Bildungsbürgertum*. See also Fritz K. Ringer, *The Decline of the German Mandarins: The German Academic Community, 1890–1933* (Cambridge, Mass.: Harvard University Press, 1969); and Konrad Jarausch, *Students, Society and Politics in Imperial Germany: The Rise of Academic Illiberalism* (Princeton: Princeton University Press, 1982).

8. Anti-Jewish sentiment was a part of university life since the early nineteenth century prior to the Wars of Liberation (*Befreiungskriege*). See Alfred D. Low, *Jews in the Eyes of the Germans: From the Enlightenment to Imperial Germany* (Philadelphia: Institute for the Study of Human Issues, 1979).

9. See Wertheimer, "The Ausländerfrage," 191–92.

10. Even though most Eastern Jewish students in Germany hailed from the Pale of Settlement, many had little intention of returning permanently to Tsarist Russia. Jewish students in Austro-Hungary, in contrast, could attended universities in Vienna, Prague, Lemberg, and other places. The majority of Jewish Russians

studied medicine, a profession that permitted them more mobility once they had passed the hurdle of *numerus clausus*. Still, admission to medical and engineering colleges did not preclude all forms of discrimination.

11. Wertheimer, *Unwelcome Strangers*, 92–93.

12. Having persisted throughout the Wilhelminian period, academic Jew baiting was thought to have reached the apex of its popularity in 1912, only to reach new heights after the so-called fortress peace (*Burgfrieden*) of World War I, when expulsions of Eastern Jewish immigrants took place on a level not previously witnessed.

13. Negative views of the Jewish occupational structure have a long history and continued despite the antisemitism of World War I, as Socialist Zionists hoped that the rise of a laboring Jewish proletariat in Germany would transform traditional prejudices and demonstrate that not all Jews were unproductive capitalists. Aschheim, *Brothers and Strangers*, 191.

14. See Toury, *Soziale und politische Geschichte*, 60.

15. The rise in conversions also reflects the prosperity of the final decades of the Wilhelminian empire. See Arthur Ruppin, *Die Juden der Gegenwart: Eine sozialwissenschaftliche Studie* (1911; Berlin: Jüdischer Verlag, 1920), 190. Moreover, 36 percent of all men leaving the *Gemeinde*—converts or dissidents—between 1873 and 1906 were members of the academic professions.

16. Richarz, ed., *Jüdisches Leben in Deutschland* 2:15, 49–50. *Trotzjuden* formally renounced their membership in the Jewish community by choosing not to pay communal taxes (*Gemeindesteuer*). At the same time, Jews formed the overwhelming number of this class of Germans who were officially classified as *konfessionslos*. Even the antisemite court preacher Adolf Stoecker preferred *Trotzjuden* over converts and modernized, enlightened Jews. See Benjamin Segel, *Die Entdeckungsreise des Herrn Dr. Theodor Lessing zu den Ostjuden* (Lemberg: Hatikwah, 1910), 49.

17. Samter, N., *Judentaufen im neunzehnten Jahrhundert. Mit besonderer Berücksichtigung Preußens* (Berlin: M. Poppelauer, 1906), 145–48.

18. For an early thematicization of the generation gap in *Ost und West*, see the discussion below of Ernst Guggenheim's "Der Rabbi." Demographically, the younger Jews of Germany were less numerous and more East European in origin than their elders.

19. Because the gains of 1869 and 1871 rapidly deteriorated into an era of antisemitism, the German-Jewish intellectual readers of *Ost und West* had a very different experience from their seniors. See Toury, *Soziale und politische Geschichte*, 360–61.

20. Aschheim, *Brothers and Strangers*, 191.

21. Fishman, *Ideology, Society and Language*, 64–65. Fishman extends the term *ba'alei teshuvah* to "genuine returners" (to be distinguished from "metaphorical returners") in other movements which attempted to attain modernization without embracing so-called westernization. He finds such transethnified elites, for example, in nineteenth- and twentieth-century Greek, Arabic, Slavic, and other contexts, arguing that they represent "a vastly overlooked subclass within the study of ethnicity movements" (85).

22. See the parodies on Buber, titled "Nach berühmten Mustern" and "Des Magiers Tod," in *Der Schlemiel* (September 1, 1904): 76–78.

23. Jonathan Frankel, *Prophecy and Politics: Socialism, Nationalism, and the Russian Jews, 1862–1917* (Cambridge: Cambridge University Press, 1981), 172–73.

24. Fishman, *Ideology, Society and Language*, 64–65.

25. Ibid.

26. See Winz, letter to Adolf Friedemann.

27. See Ulrich Linse, "Die Jugendkulturbewegung," in *Das wilhelminische Bildungsbürgertum. Zur Sozialgeschichte seiner Ideen*, ed. Klaus Vondung (Göttingen: Vandenhoeck und Ruprecht, 1976), 120.

28. According to writer Alfred Kurella: "Man konnte in der Anfangszeit der [Jugendb]ewegung, in den Glanzjahren des 'Wandervogel' einen Kampf in der Jugend des Mittelstandes selbst beobachten. Mit grenzenloser Verachtung sonderten sich die 'Wandervögel,' als die Vertreter der eigentlich 'gebildeten,' traditionsreichen Familien innerhalb des Mittelstandes ab von der großen Mehrzahl der Altersgenossen, die, teils aus ähnlichen Kreisen, teils aus denen des 'neuen Reichtums' stammend, sich früh in den Künsten des modernen bürgerlichen Lebens übten und auf eine erfolgreiche Anteilnahme an der . . . Ausbeutertätigkeit ihrer Väter vorbereiteten." Quoted in ibid., 23.

29. See Richarz, ed., *Jüdisches Leben in Deutschland*, 2: 34.

30. As maintained above, this crisis in middle-class identity was resolved by means of stereotyping. In the case of the Jewish parvenu stereotype, the combined fear of the parvenu and fear of the Eastern Jewish immigrant drew on existing antisemitic images.

31. *Ost und West* might accept Western-style modernization while at the same time pretending to shun contact with the West. At the same time as it demonized the most assimilated *Westjuden*, it also might participate in a dishonor-free form of Orientalism directed at the Jewish East. Like the "new ethnicity" that pervades the United States today, ethnic Judaism helped Jewish elites in the West maintain their economic and political influence over their perceived ethnic constituencies. See Richard H. Thompson, *Theories of Ethnicity: A Critical Reappraisal* (New York: Greenwood Press, 1989).

32. There exists no comprehensive and comparative history of parvenuism.

33. On the thesis of the "invisible" Jewish community, see Sorkin, *The Transformation of German Jewry*.

34. Todd M. Endelman, "The Social and Political Context of Conversion in Germany and England, 1870–1914," in *Jewish Apostasy in the Modern World*, ed. Todd M. Endelman (New York: Holmes and Meier, 1987), 98. See also Felix A. Theilhaber, *Der Untergang der deutschen Juden: Eine volkswirtschaftliche Studie*, 2nd ed. (Berlin: Jüdischer Verlag, 1921), 117. It is possible that as many as 100,000 converts and their children and grandchildren lived alongside 620,000 German Jews on the eve of World War I. See Gershom Scholem, "On the Social Psychology of the Jews in Germany, 1900–1922," in *Jews and Germans from 1860 to 1933: The Problematic Symbiosis*, ed. David Bronsen (Heidelberg: Winter, 1979).

35. See the discussion below of Lothar Brieger-Wasservogel's "Das alte Testament," *Ost und West* (November 1901): 849–54. This story exemplifies the narrative tradition of anti-apostate, anti-parvenu fictions.

36. A typical early example of the Jewish parvenu stereotype is found in Karl A. B. Sessa's drama *Unser Verkehr: Eine Posse in einem Aufzuge* (1815; Leipzig: Dycksche Buchhandlung, 1816), a thoroughgoing satire of a ghetto Jew desperate

to become *salonfähig*. For a discussion of the popularity of the Jewish parvenu in non-Jewish media, see the analysis of the *Fliegende Blätter* in Wassermann, "The *Fliegende Blätter*," 126–27.

37. On the court Jew (*Hofjude*) as a possible precursor of the Western Jewish parvenu stereotype, see Selma Stern, *The Court Jew: A Contribution to the History of the Period of Absolutism in Central Europe*, trans. Ralph Weiman (Philadelphia: Jewish Publication Society, 1950).

38. Early essays on the Western Jewish parvenu in *Ost und West* include Alfred H. Fried, "Das soziale Motiv der Tracht und die Judenfrage," *Ost und West* (April 1903): 259–64; and Fabius Schach, "Zur Psychologie des Renegatentums," *Ost und West* (July 1903): 451–62.

39. Few Western Jews were actually fanatical in their parvenuism, and of those who were, a number remained observant and sustained ties to other Jews; for examples, see Werner E. Mosse, *The German-Jewish Economic Elite, 1820–1935* (New York: Oxford University Press, 1991), 13–23. Fully aware of the actual parvenus in a specific sense, Winz and his associates reasoned that if actual parvenus identified with Jewish religiosity and enlightened Judaism, its target audience of all German Jews would as well.

40. The following chapters analyze the nonintellectual audiences of *Ost und West*.

41. At a meeting with Berlin's liberal Jewish representatives who were inveighing against Eastern Jewish infiltration, Zionist leader Alfred Klee went around the room and demonstrated that without exception, those present were themselves from Posen, Breslau, or elsewhere in Poland, or at the very least had forebears from that part of the world; see Gronemann, "Erinnerungen," 137.

42. Treitschke's exact quotation is: "Über unsere Ostgrenze . . . dringt Jahr für Jahr aus der unerschöpflichen polnischen Wiege eine Schaar strebsamer hosenverkaufender Jünglinge herein, deren Kinder und Kindeskinder dereinst Deutschlands Börsen und Zeitungen beherrschen sollen; die Einwanderung wächst zusehends und immer ernster wird die Frage, wie wir dies fremde Volksthum mit dem unseren verschmelzen können." See Heinrich von Treitschke, "Unsere Aussichten," *Preußische Jahrbücher* 44–45 (November 1879), quoted in *Der Berliner Antisemitismusstreit*, ed. Walter Boehlich (Frankfurt a.M.: Insel, 1988), 112.

43. While success stories about Russian and Galician Jews who had built up business empires within one generation were not unheard of, it was statistically more likely in the *Kaiserreich* that Jewish family dynasties had humble Western or Central European origins. See Mosse, *The German-Jewish Economic Elite*, 11–12.

44. Hebrew-language debates on the *Haskalah* (Jewish Enlightenment) regularly criticized Western Jewish social climbers.

45. See Itta Shedletzky, "Some Observations on the Popular Zeitroman in the Jewish Weeklies in Germany from 1870–1900," *Canadian Review of Comparative Literature* 9 (September 1982): 349–56; Itta Shedletzky, "Bellestristik und Literaturdiskussion in den jüdischen Zeitschriften in Deutschland, 1837–1918," Ph.D. dissertation, Hebrew University, Jerusalem, 1985. See also Hans Otto Horch, *Auf der Suche nach der jüdischen Erzählliteratur: Die Literaturkritik der "Allgemeinen Zeitung des Judentums" (1837–1922)*, Literaturhistorische Untersuchungen 1 (Bern: Peter Lang, 1985).

46. On Berlin specifically, see Katherine Roper, *German Encounters with Modernity: Novels of Imperial Berlin* (Atlantic Highlands, N.J.: Humanities Press International, 1991), 146–63.

47. For an introduction to German Realism including a discussion of stereotyping, see Robert C. Holub, *Reflections of Realism: Paradox, Norm, and Ideology in Nineteenth-century German Prose* (Detroit: Wayne State University Press, 1991).

48. Brieger-Wasservogel was a native of Freytag's hometown, Breslau, and, like Freytag, he went on to produce improbable and idiosyncratic works of pulp literature about Jews. Later, as a Zionist art critic, Brieger-Wasservogel utilized the stereotypes of *Rassenjudentum* in order to censure Jewish parvenuism and other Diaspora institutions for not providing "tough" Jewish role models.

49. To most *Westjuden*, idealized depictions of East European Jewry compensated for the loss of an unproblematic Jewish identity. In fact, much of the Eastern Jewish fiction carried in *Ost und West* likely was received by Westerners as an image of a simpler, premodern Judaism.

50. For negative—if at times ambivalent—portrayals of Eastern Jews, see Karl E. Franzos, *Aus Halb-Asien* (1876) and idem, *Die Juden von Barnow* (1878). See also Mark H. Gelber, "Ethnic Pluralism and Germanization in the Works of Karl Emil Franzos (1848–1904)," *German Quarterly* 56 (1983): 376–85; and Grossman, "The Space of Yiddish," 184–99.

51. The Naturalist subgenre of the satirical sketch proves an excellent vehicle for the propagating of these stereotypes. As a "modern" magazine keeping pace with literary fashion, *Ost und West* was attracted by the Berlin Naturalism in its own backyard. The dominant prose genre of the *Moderne*, the *Skizze*, can be defined as follows: "Was das Märchen für die Romantik gewesen war, wurde die 'Studie' für den Naturalismus, denn wie die romantische Weltanschauung in jener Form zur vollen Entfaltung gekommen war, realisierte sich in dieser Form der von den Naturalisten erstrebte Lebensausschnitt ohne Anfang und Ende als Schilderung eines rein qualitativ gesehenen, nie als 'komplett' anzugebenden Milieus. Man schuf keine eigengesetzliche Welt mehr. Man 'studierte' und beschrieb wissenschaftlich bloß die gegebene, von der man—weil sie rein quantitativ verstanden wurde— lediglich eine 'Skizze' bieten konnte." Roy Cowen, "Naturalismus," in *Geschichte der deutschen Literatur*, ed. Ehrhard Bahr (Tübingen: Francke, 1988), 3: 135.

52. Brieger-Wasservogel, more commonly known as Brieger, was born in Zurchau, the son of an optometrist who was also a composer. Brieger spent most of his life as a book dealer in Berlin-Charlottenburg. His novel *Rene Richter: die Entwicklung eines modernen Juden. Berliner Roman in 3 Büchern* (Berlin: Schröder, 1906) is his best-known work on German Jewry. Further references are to the relevant issue and year of *Ost und West* with column numbers in parentheses.

53. The term *Altes Testament* underlines Goldstein's distance from Jewish traditions. The traditional terms would be *tanakh*, *torah* (*toyre*), or *ḥumash*. The double meaning of *Testament* as "witness" and "will" was the subject of many jokes by German Jews and Eastern Jews.

54. In "Das alte Testament," one military officer asks the other what such an interethnic couple is doing together. The other quips: "Wahrscheinlich will er [i.e., Goldstein] ihre alten Kleider kaufen" (849).

55. *Ost und West* offered prizes valued at 150 and 100 marks, respectively, for literary and artistic works.

56. This banishment was a modern version of the *ḥerem*, excommunication from the Jewish religious community.

57. *Ost und West*'s literary contest, while an excellent marketing idea, was beset by problems. First disseminated in "Unsere Preisschreiben," *Ost und West* (February 1902): 129–30, the results were not announced until the September issue. The art contest, to be juried by E. M. Lilien, Hermann Struck, and Lesser Ury, never even came to fruition. The judges of the literary contest, Theodor Lessing, Fabius Schach, and Berthold Feiwel, were all known for their use of literary stereotyping. Lessing himself was known for excoriating Eastern Jews and went on to write the first explicitly titled work on Jewish self-hatred, *Jüdischer Selbsthaß* (Berlin: Jüdischer Verlag/Zionistischer Bücher-Bund, 1930). For his part, Schach indulged in reverse stereotyping in an article praising Yiddish, "Der deutsch-jüdische Jargon," *Ost und West* (March 1901): 179–90. Feiwel, a major voice in the call for a Jewish *Zeitroman*, maintained in his anthology *Jüdischer Almanach* (Berlin: Jüdischer Verlag, 1902), that Jews possessed a "rassentümlicher Einschlag," a racially based element.

58. See Horch, *Auf der Suche nach der jüdischen Erzählliteratur*, 240.

59. Herzl's "Mauschel" was reprinted in the special Herzl issue of *Ost und West* (August–September 1904): 545–50.

60. By all accounts, roughly 5 percent of the Berlin population at the turn of the century was Jewish. In addition, it is no accident that the opponents of *Haskalah* referred to the Jewish Enlighteners as *Berliner*. See Jakob Katz, "Vom Ghetto zum Zionismus: Gegenseitige Beeinflussung von Ost und West," *Bulletin des Leo Baeck Instituts* 64 (1983): 9.

61. See especially Gronemann's distinction between Berlin E. and Berlin W. in "Erinnerungen," 136–37. For maps of Jewish settlement in Berlin, see Pulzer, *Jews and the German State*, xiv.

62. Siegbert Salter (pseudonym for Simon Salomon) was born in 1873 in Speicher near Trier. Son of a businessman, he studied in Bonn, Heidelberg, and Berlin and later lived in Paris, London, and Milan, writing for popular magazines such as *Die Koralle, Die Zeit im Bilde*, and *Das Leben im Bilde* and editing *Europa auf Reise*. The first fiction of Salter's printed in *Ost und West* was "Kleine Ursachen" (October 1904): 709–14, featuring a parvenu Jew. The eleven-year-old Jewish hero of the novella, Mäxchen, inherits the hypocrisy of the older generation, growing into a self-hating assimilationist as an adult. The sketch is not, however, set among Berlin's *Tiergartenjudentum*.

63. Thomas Mann, *Wälsungenblut* (Berlin: Phantasus-Verlag, 1921). On *Wälsungenblut*, see Jacques Darmaun, "Thomas Mann und die Juden—eine Kontroverse? Thomas Manns Bild des Judentums bis zur Weimarer Republik," *Kontroversen, alte und neue, Akten des VII. Internationalen Germanistenkongresses*, Göttingen, 1985, vol. 5 of *Auseinandersetzungen um jiddische Sprache und Literatur; Jüdische Komponenten in der deutschen Literatur—die Assimilationskontroverse*, ed. Albrecht Schöne, Walter Rolle, and Hans-Peter Bayerdörfer (Tübingen: Niemeyer, 1986), 208–14. See also Gelber, "Das Judendeutsch," 172–73; and Ruth Angress-Klüger, "Jewish Characters in Thomas Mann's Fiction," in *Horizonte: Festschrift für Herbert Lehnert zum 65. Geburtstag*, ed. Hannelore Mundt, Egon Schwarz, and William J. Lillyman (Tübingen: Niemeyer, 1990), 161–72.

64. Mann wrote *Wälsungenblut* in 1905 but withdrew it from publication in the *Neue Rundschau* on the suggestion of Oskar Bie (a Jew and the journal's editor).

While it was finally published (in a limited edition) in 1921, it is not unlikely that it, like Mann's other unpublished works, already had been talked about beyond the Munich literary scene. Regardless of whether Mann's novella preceded Salter's, the trope of the *Tiergartenparvenu* was timely and thus available for any writer to use.

65. "White Negro" may have originated with Houston Stewart Chamberlain. See Gilman, *Jewish Self-Hatred*, 172–75. See also Clementine Krämer, "Getauft," *Ost und West* (January 1913): 77–80. In this short sketch, the analogy is made that blacks cannot become white by means of a ceremony. *Der Schlemiel* at times stereotyped blacks in order to elevate Jews. See, for instance, the March 1904 issue, or any issue with the "Brief aus Afrika." The identification with the African is a recurring theme of Jewish writing in this epoch; often the black person takes the semiotic place of the Eastern Jew. See Sander L. Gilman, ed., *On Blackness without Blacks: Essays on the Image of the Black in Germany* (Boston: G. K. Hall, 1982); and Reinhold Grimm and Jost Hermand, eds., *Blacks and German Culture: Essays* (Madison: University of Wisconsin Press, 1986).

66. For a complete discussion of Jewish self-hatred in relation to *Ost und West*, see the conclusion to this study.

67. Aschheim, *Brothers and Strangers*, 191–92.

68. See Jürgen Born, *Kafkas Bibliothek: Ein beschreibendes Verzeichnis* (Frankfurt a.M.: S. Fischer, 1990), 116; Kafka, letter to Felice Bauer, 59. Herrmann Kafka was not a Galician or Russian Jew but a Moravian Jew and thus relatively westernized. For this reason, Franz Kafka was justified in considering him a West European Jew since birth.

69. After 1880, each pogrom was worse than the previous one, and they also occurred with greater frequency. *Ost und West* published several graphic photos of Jews slain in self-defense. According to David Roskies, "in all the pogroms of 1881–1883, fewer Jews were killed than in Kishinev during Passover of 1903. The forty-nine casualties of Kishinev, in turn, paled before the 800 dead in the pogroms of 1905–1906. . . . To compound the irony, each wave of violence was preceded by a period of hope: the pogroms of the 1880s followed the liberalization under Alexander II. Kishenev was supposed to usher in a century of promise." David Roskies, *Against the Apocalypse: Responses to Catastrophe in Modern Jewish Culture* (Cambridge, Mass.: Harvard University Press, 1984), 82–83.

70. When refugees from the pogroms arrived in Berlin, even wealthy Jews such as the Tietz family housed and cared for them. See the Georg Tietz memoir, quoted in Annegret Ehmann et al., *Juden in Berlin, 1671–1945: Ein Lesebuch* (Berlin: Nicolai, 1988), 159.

71. Notwithstanding the overwhelming number of failures within five years of startup, most new periodicals in the *Kaiserreich* were founded roughly between 1896 and 1914. Foundings of newspaper and book enterprises were also more frequent in this epoch.

72. For more on the relationship of *Ost und West* to the Alliance, see chapter 1 above and chapter 4 below.

73. *Ostjuden* in Germany, however, also had Russian, Hebrew, and Yiddish periodicals at their disposal and did not have to rely solely on an organ such as *Ost und West*.

Chapter 4

1. In prefacing two letters from Solomon Munk (a German founder of the Alliance) to his friend Bernhard Weiss, M. A. Klausner uses direct address ("schöne Leserin")—evidence of an appeal to women readers. The theme strikes at the heart of *Ost und West*'s and of women's concerns: Munk claims to have persuaded a former girlfriend not to convert. See Bernhard Weiss, "Zwei Freunde (Ungedrückte Briefe von Salomon Munk aus den Jahren 1827–1860)," *Ost und West* (June 1908): 373–86.

2. Without a doubt, male identity was an issue for the Russian and Galician men who produced *Ost und West* (see the discussion of Jewish masculinity in chapter 5 below). Moreover, the Jewish Renaissance and Jewish nationalism were mostly male-driven affairs, at least in the public sphere. The pre-1906 parvenu narratives in *Ost und West* were thus meant to reflect the intellectual predilections of the journal's core audience, and for these Western-educated men, culture was a more pressing concern than gender.

3. In pre–World War I Germany, Eastern Jewish women were outnumbered by their male compatriots. Kaplan, *The Making of the Jewish Middle Class*, 5.

4. Some of the female readers of *Ost und West* may have been Orthodox Jews, for the tendency toward women's equality in civic life, Jewish life, and education even affected Orthodox women. Many read Nahida Ruth-Lazarus's *Das jüdische Weib* (Leipzig: G. Laudien, 1892), which glorified great Jewish women of the past, and Ellen Key's *Das Jahrhundert des Kindes*, trans. Marie Franzos (Berlin: Fischer, 1903), which had an "overwhelming impact on Orthodox women and girls." Mordechai Breuer, *Modernity within Tradition: The Social History of Orthodox Jewry in Imperial Germany*, trans. Elizabeth Petuchowski (New York: Columbia University Press, 1992), 279.

5. See Endelman, "The Social and Political Context of Conversion," 98; see also Marion A. Kaplan, "Tradition and Transition—The Acculturation, Assimilation, and Integration of Jews in Imperial Germany—A Gender Analysis," *Year Book of the Leo Baeck Institute* 27 (1982): 18.

6. On the virtual equivalence of *Eastern* and *ghetto* after 1850, see Aschheim, *Brothers and Strangers*, 7.

7. See Daniel Boyarin, *Unheroic Conduct: The Rise of Heterosexuality and the Invention of the Jewish Man* (Berkeley: University of California Press, 1997), 157–62.

8. *Ost und West* understood that the German-Jewish subculture was reformulating German culture, not merely copying its manners and mores. For a similar reading of imitation and assimilation, see Homi K. Bhabha, *The Location of Culture* (London: Routledge, 1994), 85–92. Contrast Paula E. Hyman, *Gender and Assimilation in Modern Jewish History: The Roles and Representations of Women* (Seattle: University of Washington Press, 19XX), 27–28.

9. See the review of Felix Perles, *Bousset's "Religion des Judentums im neutestamentlichen Zeitalter" kritisch untersucht* (Berlin: Wolf Peiser, 1903), by A. D. Bender (a pseudonym for Binjamin Segel?), "Eine Apologie des Judentums," *Ost und West* (July 1903): 427–32. Here Bender lists fifteen prowoman quotes from Talmud. On the idealization of Jewish women, see Binjamin Segel, "Die Frau im jüdischen Sprichwort," *Ost und West* (May 1903): 167–76. Segel claims to have found no sayings that Jewish women were "unfaithful" or "promiscuous."

10. On the Jewish salon women at the turn of the century, see Deborah Hertz, *Jewish High Society in Old Regime Berlin* (New Haven: Yale University Press, 1988). The salons of Berlin Jews at the close of the eighteenth century were only the prologue to what became a social revolution in Western Europe: the division of labor into private and public spheres and the subsequent rise of domestic middle-class culture. On the ambivalent modern and traditional nature of German-Jewish women, see Kaplan, *The Making of the Jewish Middle Class.*

11. See Kafka, letter to Felice Bauer, 59.

12. On the *Volksheim* and Jewish adult education generally, see M. Brenner, *The Renaissance of Jewish Culture*, 69–99.

13. The role played by non-Jewish bourgeoises in German culture and society has been similarly underestimated.

14. The reference here is to the vast *t'khine* (women's devotional) literature. On the importance of women readers of Yiddish, see Shmuel Niger, "Di yidishe lezerin," *Der Pinkes: yorbukh far der geshikhte fun der yudisher literatur un shprakh* 1 (1912): 85–138. *Der Pinkes* was published in Warsaw by B. Klatzkin.

15. According to Marion Kaplan, "the language of class formation was gendered" for Jewish women in the *Kaiserreich*. Kaplan draws on Davidoff and Hall, who argue that "consciousness of class always takes a gendered form." See Lenora Davidoff and Catherine Hall, *Family Fortunes: Men and Women of the English Middle Class, 1780–1850* (London: Hutchinson, 1987), 450, quoted in Kaplan, *The Making of the Jewish Middle Class*, 231.

16. See Andrew Heinze, *Adapting to Abundance: Jewish Immigrants, Mass Consumption, and the Search for American Identity* (New York: Columbia University Press, 1989), 4–8. The rise of an urban-oriented Jewish culture was much more rapid in America than in Germany. Historians have fostered the myth of the monumental, culture-producing Jews of Germany by emphasizing production-oriented history at the expense of a consumption orientation. This study of *Ost und West* should be understood as a preliminary investigation of the consumption history of this group. Like their counterparts in the United States, Eastern Jews who migrated to Western Europe in the nineteenth century may have used the ownership of luxury items to express a change in their identities. The possession of luxury items, such as those advertised repeatedly in *Ost und West*, also signaled a degree of integration into German society.

17. Kaplan, *The Making of the Jewish Middle Class*, 120–21.

18. Ibid., 133.

19. See "Urteile der Presse über die 'Jüdischen Volksliederabende,'" *Ost und West* (December 1912): 1169–1200. For a negative review, see Fritz Mordechai Kaufmann, *Vier Essais über ostjüdische Dichtung und Kultur* (Berlin: Welt Verlag, 1919), 61. See also the positive review by Kaufmann's mentor, Nathan Birnbaum (under the name "Matthias Acher"), "Auf dem Volksliederabend von 'Ost und West,'" *Ost und West* (January 1912): 17–24. Prior to World War I, Winz distributed a multitude of records of Jewish music. M. Brenner, *The Renaissance of Jewish Culture*, 160.

20. See Maurer, *Ostjuden in Deutschland*, 723.

21. "Ost und West," 2. See also Leo Winz Papers, A136/42.

22. In the same programmatic editorial of 1901, *Ost und West* appealed to the "modern"—that is, enlightened or Westernized—Jew (compare the journal's

subtitle until March 1906: "Illustrierte Monatsschrift für modernes Judentum"). The vague but fashionable term *modern* would have appealed equally to female and male readers. On gender, magazines, and advertising, see Garvey, *The Adman in the Parlor.*

23. Compare the Haasenstein and Vogler *Zeitungskatalog* (Berlin: Haasenstein and Vogler, 1910).

24. According to Winz, " 'Ost and West' z. b. musste trotz verhältnismässig hoher Abonnenmentsgebühren ca. vierzigtausend Mark jährlich zu den Abonnenten buchmaessig zulegen und konnte nur durch Inserate diesen Verlust nebst einem erheblichen Gewinn wieder einbringen." See Leo Winz, letter to the Vorstand der Jüdischen Gemeinde zu Berlin, July 12, 1927, Leo Winz Papers, A136/49. Acquiring advertisers was hard work, involving approximately thirty visits to customers and one hundred letters of solicitation per month. In addition, only 5 percent of the firms advertising in *Ost und West* were owned by Jews; the figure was equally low for the *Gemeindeblatt der jüdischen Gemeinde zu Berlin.*

25. Rural non-Jewish women believed that German-Jewish middle-class women were on the cutting edge of fashion. See Kaplan, *The Making of the Jewish Middle Class,* 31.

26. See Leo Winz, letter to the Vorstand der Jüdischen Gemeinde zu Berlin, z. H. Dr. Ismar Freund, September 30, 1927, Leo Winz Papers, A136/44.

27. Ernst Keil's *Die Gartenlaube* (founded in 1853) inaugurated the tradition of the *Familienblatt* ("family journal") and was the most popular German-language periodical of the epoch. See Kirsten Belgum, *Popularizing the Nation: Audience, Representation, and the Production of Identity in* Die Gartenlaube, *1853–1900* (Lincoln: University of Nebraska Press, forthcoming). See also D. Brenner, "Reconciliation before Auschwitz."

28. On average wages, see Walther G. Hoffmann, *Das Wachstum der deutschen Wirtschaft seit der Mitte des 19. Jahrhunderts* (Berlin: Springer-Verlag, 1965), 461, 469, 489. *Ost und West* was affordable not only to the haute bourgeoisie but also to lower-middle-class Jews in Germany, indeed even to Eastern Jews there. A worker's household budget published in 1900 provides an idea of the value placed on reading: 2 percent of the yearly income was spent on books, and 4 percent went for newspapers and magazines. Moreover, a week's wages for a German worker at the turn of the century averaged at least ten marks, though the average workday in 1880 was twelve hours long (compared with eight hours as first legislated in 1919). It is difficult to assess how much money workers had at their disposal in order to pay six months of a subscription in advance, as was customary for periodicals at the time. At the same time, even lower-class Germans appear to have had extra leisure time to spend with books, magazines, and newspapers. See Reinhart Meyer, *Novelle und Journal,* vol. 1, *Titel und Normen: Untersuchungen zur Terminologie der Journalprosa, zu ihren Tendenzen, Verhältnissen und Bedingungen* (Stuttgart: F. Steiner, 1987), 21.

29. One example is Else Croner [-Kretschmer], *Die moderne Jüdin* (Berlin: Axel Juncker, 1913).

30. To an extent, *Ost und West* sought to keep stride with new feminine ideals, such as the "New Woman Type." In addition, the so-called *Jugendstil* directly influenced the magazine's layout and self-presentation. Instead of raising Jewish bourgeoises to be "Salome-like" marriage properties, one commentator in *Ost und West* suggested applying the English model of "vitality," being fresh, wealthy,

tennis-playing, and not so sensual. See Georg Hermann, "Eugen Spiro," *Ost und West* (April 1905): 231–40. On the Salome analogy and other stereotypes of German-Jewish women, see Croner, *Die moderne Jüdin*, 78.

31. Kaplan, *The Making of the Jewish Middle Class*, 31.

32. Ibid., 57–58. See Theodor Zlocisti, "Jüdische Volkslesehallen," *Ost und West* (April 1903): 277–82. Even Zlocisti's complaints that Jewish women were not reading Jewish books and journals seem to be directed at Jewish women. Zlocisti criticizes the "daily press, chlorotic magazines [*Zeitschriften*], syrupy novels," but he suggests that Jewish journalism will one day supersede the reading of books (282). He also cites the tradition of women reading Yiddish texts (especially translations of the Bible and of liturgical texts).

33. Correspondingly, only 18 percent of German-Jewish women worked outside the home in 1907, compared to 31 percent of their non-Jewish counterparts. See Kaplan, *The Making of the Jewish Middle Class*, 158.

34. Fearing that modern, independent young girls would become less feminine, Orthodox German Jews were not prepared to open the way for women to study at universities, but they admitted they had the aptitude for it. Breuer, *Modernity within Tradition*, 280.

35. Kaplan, *The Making of the Jewish Middle Class*, 192–211.

36. *Zeitschrift für Demographie und Statistik der Juden* (May 1909): 77, quoted in ibid., 199.

37. Ibid.

38. In an age of competing claims of what constituted Jewishness, welfare and philanthropy became primary expressions of Jewish identity, especially Jewish female identity. In the nineteenth century, mutual aid societies became widely developed among German Jews. Between 1870 and 1899, no fewer than 297 new Jewish welfare associations (*Wohlfahrtsvereine*) were established in the *Kaiserreich*. See ibid., 202–4. Not coincidentally, the years between 1896 and 1914 represent the most prosperous period in an otherwise economically depressed Imperial Germany.

39. Half of the women's organizations existing in 1908—be they social, charitable, political, or professional—were founded after 1900. Kaplan, *The Making of the Jewish Middle Class*, 202. On the *Jüdischer Frauenbund*, see Marion A. Kaplan, *The Jewish Feminist Movement in Germany* (Westport, Conn.: Greenwood Press, 1979), 59–103.

40. Examples include Lina Morgenstern, Jeanette Schwerin, Henriette Goldschmidt, and Alice Salomon (1872–1948). See Kaplan, *The Jewish Feminist Movement*, 82. In addition, the widespread participation of Jews in social welfare proves that these Jewish women maintained an identity separate from that of other German middle-class women, even at the dawn of the twentieth century. Kaplan, *The Making of the Jewish Middle Class*, 21.

41. German-Jewish women, who had always participated in both Jewish and non-Jewish guilds for women, were now potential members of male-dominated organizations. Kaplan, *The Making of the Jewish Middle Class*, 68–69.

42. Ibid.

43. *Paternalism* is defined as a system under which an authority (male or female) undertakes to supply the needs and regulate the conduct of social inferiors such as *Ostjuden*.

44. Baron Hirsch's Jewish Colonial Association was a philanthropic, liberal organization established in 1891 which worked closely with the Alliance Israélite Universelle.

45. The 1913 restatement of the Alliance's goals by its secretary, Jacques Bigart, may have been a response to Western Jewish women's concern about the so-called white slave trade. In addition to building schools, Bigart sees it as a fundamental responsibility of the Alliance to "raise up" Oriental Jewish women through education and the inculcation of bourgeois virtue. See Jacques Bigart, "Die Tätigkeit der A.I.U. in der Türkei (Vortrag des Herrn J. Bigart, gehalten am 24. Mai 1913 in der jüdischen Volksuniversität zu Paris)," *Ost und West* (October 1913): 819–34. This address appeared under the rubric "Mitteilungen des Central-Comités der Alliance Israélite Universelle in Paris." It should also be noted that Segel's "Philosophie der Zerstreuung" appeared in *Ost und West* before the Alliance agreed in 1906 to finance part of the journal's production.

46. The giving of money served as an entry ticket into Jewish culture, and Zionists strove to render this gesture "visible and dignified." See Berkowitz, " 'Mind, Muscle, and Men,' " 294.

47. *Ost und West*'s strategy of charitable paternalism was sincerely designed to attract the female Western Jewish reader to the preservation of Eastern Jewish culture. The journal's "maternalistic" project thus should be seen as part of its conscious promotion of Eastern Jewish nationalism. Not only a leading publicity organ for relief efforts in Eastern Europe and elsewhere, *Ost und West* also served as a patron to Eastern Jewish artists and writers.

48. Kaplan, *The Making of the Jewish Middle Class*, 198.

49. See Wertheimer, *Unwelcome Strangers*, 149. The possibilities (and limitations) of East-West Jewish relations are partly symbolized by Winz's marriage to Else Jacoby. The betrothal took place in Czechoslovakia, for Jacoby might have lost her German citizenship and even risked deportation by marrying a noncitizen such as Winz. Still, it was more common for German-Jewish women (who were, especially after World War I, numerically greater than German-Jewish men) to marry Eastern Jewish men than for German-Jewish men to marry Jewish women from the East.

50. For a slightly different view, see Kaplan, *The Making of the Jewish Middle Class*, 192. Kaplan prefers the term *acculturation* to describe the goal of female Jewish philanthropists with respect to immigrant Eastern Jews.

51. See Wertheimer, *Unwelcome Strangers*.

52. See Kaplan, *The Making of the Jewish Middle Class*, 198.

53. Leon Kellner, "Eine jüdische Toynbee-Halle in Wien," *Ost und West* (April 1901): 291–98.

54. Bertha Pappenheim, "Das Interesse der Juden an V. Internationalen Kongress zur Bekämpfung des Mädchenhandels," *Ost und West* (August 1913): 601–6. On Pappenheim, see especially Kaplan, *The Jewish Feminist Movement.*

55. Pimps involved in the white slave trade also promised Eastern Jewish women positions as household servants; this was a ruse to lure them into prostitution. Also, a large percentage of former maids became prostitutes. Kaplan, *The Jewish Feminist Movement*, 103–7.

56. In actuality, German-Jewish women might have viewed a marriage to a

composer as marrying "down." Personal communication from Professor Marion Kaplan, October 3, 1993. See also *Ost und West*'s first literary-historical piece, Ludwig Geiger's "Der Estherstoff in der neuen Litteratur" (January 1901): 27–34. The biblical Queen Esther was a key figure in this debate on apostasy. Although married to the non-Jew Ahasuerus, she still acts on behalf of her people.

57. The veritable obsession in *Ost und West* with the high rate of mixed marriage and conversion in Vienna can be read as an attempt to displace criticism away from similar conditions in Berlin and the *Kaiserreich*. On the "baptism epidemic" in Vienna, see Maximilian Paul-Schiff, "Die Judentaufen in Wien," *Ost und West* (March 1904): 193–98. See also —m—g— [Benjamin Segel], "Die Taufseuche in Wien," *Ost und West* (June 1905): 361–72 and (December 1905): 749–62. For the treatment of baptism in Berlin, see N. Samter, "Berliner Judentaufen," *Ost und West* (November 1902): 783–86 and (December 1902): 811–20.

58. For an early example of the *belle juive* image, see the character of Laurabella in Moritz Hartmann, "Bei Kunstreitern," *Ost und West* (March 1901): 211–22.

59. Because they appeared at Passover season, this and other March and April issues of *Ost und West* took on a certain importance; the same was true of issues appearing at the time of Rosh Hashanah and Yom Kippur.

60. Rothstein is an early instance of the "jazz singer" motif.

61. The antisemites harp on the imagined belief that Rothstein has money (269).

62. See Kunstverlag Phönix, *Illustrierter Katalog* (Berlin: Kunstverlag Phönix, 1903).

63. In this passage, Schach makes it appear that the fight against Jewish parvenuism was originally a Western Jewish idea.

64. The original German quote is as follows: "Ich sitze des nachts in meinem Kämmerlein beim Kerzenschein und lese verstohlen deutsche Bücher, mit einem heiligen Schauer, wie ein zarte Jungfrau, die die Liebesbeteuerungen ihres Auserwählten liest."

65. The original German quote is as follows: "Und über mich kommt es wie ein himmlisches Rauschen, wie wenn eine neue, lichte, freie Seele in mich einzöge. Und jedes deutsche Gedicht ist mir eine Offenbarung, jeder neue Gedanke ein Quell reinen Wissens, und mich packt eine wilde, verzehrende Sehnsucht, hinaus aus der dumpfen Atmosphäre, aus der Welt der starren Formeln und toten Buchstaben! hinaus in die Welt der Schönheit und Freiheit! Die erste knospenhafte Liebe kann nie zarter, heiliger aufkeimen als diese Bildungsinbrunst."

66. Schach became more westernized himself. Starting in World War I, he became a publicist for the liberal, antidefamation *Centralverein*, an act regarded by some as a defection from the Zionist movement.

67. See the journal's programmatic statement, "Ost und West."

68. See the discussion of the literary contest above in chapter 3.

69. It is unlikely that the many visual images of Eastern Jewish men and boys in *Ost und West* were intended to keep Western Jewish women's desires in check, to keep them from marrying—or lusting after—Gentile men. On the pale, gentle, "effeminate" Talmud scholar (*yeshive bokher*) as a marriage—and potential *erotic*—object for Jewish women in the nineteenth century, see Boyarin, *Unheroic Conduct*, 68–73, 157.

70. An alternative spelling is *Glitzenstein*.

71. Interestingly, the Prinzregent of Bavaria who let Glicenstein paint his portrait was not bothered by the artist's deficient German.

72. On the stereotype of "the Jew's language," see Gilman, *Jewish Self-Hatred*, 22–28.

73. Much of the published research on the life and work of Baum, arguably the first female literary celebrity of twentieth-century Germany, omits any discussion of her Jewish background. Indeed, Baum herself was eager to disown her Jewishness, as her posthumously published autobiography (*Es war alles ganz anders* [Cologne: Kiepenheuer und Witsch, 1987; originally published 1962)] makes abundantly clear. At one point in the memoir, which was posthumously edited by her daughter-in-law (Ruth Lert), Baum claims that her father's ancestors may have been (non-Jewish?) Swabians (*Es war*, 137). Specifically, the memoir reveals ambivalent attitudes toward Jews. Such attitudes were not atypical for a person raised in fin-de-siècle Vienna, yet Baum's father—the parent of Jewish descent—is primarily described in negative terms, as "shabby," "ugly," "humped over," "uncouth," and a "schlemiel," not to speak of associations with homosexuality, spying, and megalomania (*Es war* 90–99, 105–9). The widespread anxiety of mixed-race Jews in this epoch concerning their creativity, virtue, and intelligence may illuminate Baum's love-hate relationship with her Jewish parent, as chronicled in a chapter of the autobiography titled "My Father, My Enemy." See Sander Gilman, *Smart Jews: The Construction of the Image of Jewish Superior Intelligence* (Lincoln: University of Nebraska Press, 1996), 142–43.

74. Like Winz, Baum also had an understanding of mass market appeal, and it is no accident that she became a pop icon at the end of the "Golden Twenties." On the latter, see King, *Best-sellers by Design*.

75. The "star system" and "the picture personality" such as Mary Pickford have been dated by film historians to late 1909, at the time when "quality films" produced by Vitagraph and Biograph were experiencing a boom and were being heavily exported to Europe. The event-driven focus of Baum's technique in "Rafael Gutmann" brought narrative flow and film elements to the conventional ghetto novella (*Ghettogeschichte*).

76. Often, Jewish women artists are characterized in the terms reserved for male colleagues: "restrained melancholy" and full of "deep inner feeling" (*Innerlichkeit*). But usually they are marginalized. Heinz Schnabel asks, "why do great German women talents act masculine?" and he notes that Käthe Kollwitz (1864–1945) "does work impossible for a female." See Heinz Schnabel, "Sophie Blum-Lazarus," *Ost und West* (June 1908): 357–60. The best example for the eroticization of Jewish women, especially Eastern Jewish women, is the art of Leo Bakst, featured in the September 1912 and March 1913 issues. More traditional Jewish women would have objected to images of naked women in the magazine.

77. A quote from the commentary: "An interesting needlework. . . . A piece, like this curtain here, should serve as a model to our women."

78. Managing a *mikve* suggests that the protagonist is Eastern Jewish in background though not necessarily an immigrant from Eastern Europe.

79. These photos (notably absent from the magazine's table of contents) were reprinted from E. N. Adler's *Vom Ghetto zu Ghetto*, reviewed under "Literarische Rundschau," *Ost und West* (January 1910): 41–44; Adler's book is also critical of the Alliance. See also the series of photos of the New York Lower East Side ghetto, titled "Aus dem New Yorker Judenviertel," *Ost und West* (July 1909): 461–66. The advent

of photography may have made it more difficult to imagine the ghetto in Baum's terms. See, for instance, Stephanie Forchheimer, "Ein Gang durch das Judenviertel in Amsterdam," *Ost und West* (November 1913): 889–96.

80. The article is signed "N. O." Its author was possibly Karl M[artha] Baer, the author of the memoir of a Jewish boy raised as a girl. See N. O. Body, *Aus eines Mannes Mädchenjahren* (1909; Berlin: Edition Hentrich, 1993). On Baer, see David Brenner, " 'Re-Dressing' the German-Jewish: A Jewish Hermaphrodite and Cross-dresser in Wilhelmine Germany," in *Borders, Exiles, and Diasporas*, ed. Elazar Barkan and Marie-Denise Shelton (Stanford: Stanford University Press, forthcoming).

81. On the reclaimed stereotype "queer," see Boyarin, *Unheroic Conduct*, 13–15.

82. Yet the *Judengasse* where Rafael lives resembles the Jewish quarter of Vienna.

83. Rafael's namesake in Herman Heijermans's (1864–1924) socialist work *Ghetto*, an 1899 drama of the Amsterdam *Judenviertel*, does not give in to his father. Also, the character of Menkis is related to that of the blind father in Heijermans's *Ghetto*.

84. Winz and Segel (who spent much of his time in Vienna) can be credited with having "discovered" Baum or at least with having had contact with her husband, Max Prels.

85. The analysis in note 78 above is also valid for Rafael and his family.

86. Hans Otto Horch maintains that there is a basic ambivalence inherent in ghetto fictions. See Horch, *Auf der Suche nach der jüdischen Erzählliteratur*, 165–68. It might be added that this is conditioned by competing receptions of the *Ghettogeschichte*.

87. A recent example of criticism of the Diaspora is the Israeli disdain for most expressions of Diaspora culture, including Yiddish culture, which dominated until the 1970s.

88. See Scholem quoted in Gelber, "Das Judendeutsch," 174.

89. Quoted in Mathias Acher (Nathan Birnbaum), "Ghetto," *Ost und West* (March 1903): 537. The original German quote is: "Wenn jemand verkündet 'unser ganzes Volk ist entartet'—warum nicht, wenn er dieses ganze Volk mit seiner Seele liebt?"

90. Baum's fiction was influenced not only by the already familiar colonializing narratives sponsored by the Alliance and by *Ost und West* but also by the tradition of the *Dorf- und Ghettogeschichte* set in Europe. There is no canonical Jewish "ghetto story," and most attempts to define the genre have been haphazard and oversimplified. Most of all, the diversity of Jewish populations in Europe and their modes of expression renders illusory any attempt to characterize the ghetto story adequately. Nearly every size of settlement is depicted (village, town, city), and nearly every region where Jews settled brought forth its own ghetto poets (Germany, Bohemia, Poland, Galicia, Ukraine, Russia, etc.). From Posen to Moscow and from Prague to Odessa, the Jewish ghetto was part of the landscape—not to speak of areas beyond Eastern Europe. The *Ghettogeschichte* shows correspondences with the vogue of regionality in German and other literatures, beginning with Realism of 1848 and extending to Naturalism and the *Heimatkunstbewegung* (e.g., Liliencron, Viebig, Thoma, Hauptmann). The last obstacle to a binding definition is the fact that the literary genres employed (sketch, novella, novel) and the type of authorial intent

(idealization, lament, satire) vary greatly. See especially Horch, *Auf der Suche nach der jüdischen Erzählliteratur,* 165–66. One of the best examples of the multivalence possible in the interpretation of the ghetto fiction is the reception of Stefan Zweig's 1902 novella "Im Schnee," which appeared in the *Jüdischer Almanach.* Mark H. Gelber writes: "Es ist möglich, daß Buber und Feiwel die Geschichte 'Im Schnee' anders auslegten als Zweig. Sie sahen darin vielleicht einen Versuch zur Wiederaufrichtung des jüdischen Selbstbewußtseins, eine Warnung und einen verzweifelten Aufruf zur 'Verjüngung' des jüdischen Lebens, eine Richtung, die in ihr kulturell-zionistisches Schema paßte. . . . Buber's Ansicht, daß die jüdische Ghettoexistenz in Osteuropa einer der wahren inneren Feinde des jüdischen Volkes sei, entsprach Franzos' eigener Ablehnung des Ghettos. Für beide war die Judenfrage eine Kulturfrage, obwohl ihre Vorschläge zur Lösung des Problems äußerst verschieden waren." Mark H. Gelber, "K. E. Franzos, Achad Haᶜam und S. Zweig," *Bulletin des Leo Baeck Instituts* 27 (1982): 43.

91. Instead of judging *Ost und West* by a rigid standard of consistency, we can see it as a set of coexisting compatibilities. This explanation accounts for the fact that the journal attracted opposing audiences.

92. Compare Wagner's olfactory stereotypes, discussed in Marc A. Weiner, *Richard Wagner and the Anti-Semitic Imagination* (Lincoln: University of Nebraska Press, 1995).

93. Exotic descriptions of Jews praying have a long history in European culture. Goethe describes a rabbi in the Frankfurt ghetto as praying with "fanatic zeal . . . repulsive enthusiasm, wild gesticulations . . . confused murmurings . . . piercing outcries . . . effeminate movements . . . the queerness of an ancient nonsense." See Aschheim, *Brothers and Strangers,* 7.

94. For Baum, language is intimately connected with cultural difference. The holy language of the Jews, like their vernacular Yiddish, is marked by corrupting influence and is described as "a strange sing-song . . . distorted by an excessive number of screeching sounds (*Quetschlauten*)." This causes Rafael to slowly "unlearn" the "language of the city" ("Rafael Gutmann," 135). The caricature of Jewish speech in German culture, especially of Yiddish, goes back to Karl B. A. Sessa's *Unser Verkehr,* but it is not present in all ghetto stories. Unlike *Mauscheln,* which parodies a native Yiddish speaker's attempts to speak "proper" German, the typologizing of the "improper" Jewish characters in "Rafael Gutmann" is a fairly neutral reproduction of how one dialect of Yiddish may have sounded in the Viennese milieu where Baum grew up. (In fact, Baum's attitudes toward Yiddish are somewhat more nuanced in her autobiography: "Jiddisch—eine größere Schande war nicht möglich für die verfeinerten und ihrer Umgebung sorgsam angepaßten österreichischen und deutschen Juden" [*Es war,* 86]). Nevertheless, Yiddish retains the markings of degeneracy in the story, participating in the centuries-old discourse of the language of the Jew. In the 1922 version of the story, which appeared in a rather different contest (the *[Leipziger] Illustrirte Zeitung*), the Yiddish was completely Germanized (Baum, "Raffael").

95. Sander Gilman uses this phrase repeatedly in his works.

96. Otto Weininger, *Geschlecht und Charakter. Eine prinzipielle Untersuchung* (Vienna: Braumüller, 1904). See especially part 2, chapter 13 on "Das Judentum," 403–41.

97. *Ost und West's* reviewer was ambivalent regarding Weininger, agreeing on his view of women but defending Judaism as a great religion. See Bernhard Münz, "Das Judentum in der Beleuchtung eines jungen Philosophen," *Ost und West* (December 1903): 823–26.

98. See Baum, *Es war,* 196.

99. Rafael seems different to his employer, who, as if acting in unison with the dictates of Freudian symbolism, requires Rafael to put another cold, salted carp on ice before leaving.

100. The reader is implicitly asked to compare the pleasant odors of the Gentile city with the stereotypical Eastern Jewish smell of garlic and onions. Similar olfactory prejudices are discussed at length by Weiner in *Richard Wagner,* 24–25. According to Weiner, Tristan "came to be viewed by Wagner's contemporary audiences as an explicitly erotic work, shocking to bourgeois sensibilities of the time. . . . If such a response seems all too literal to listeners today, it may serve to underscore the distance between Wagner's world and our own; in Wagner's time, his music—like his texts and stage directions—was both intended and perceived to convey physiological states." Isolde's orgasmic apotheosis and union with her lover at the conclusion to the drama are accompanied by unparalleled aromas, for *Tristan und Isolde* is "the most synesthetic of Wagner's synesthetic works, and the highly charged Oedipal nature of its suggestive psychological content is enhanced by the aesthetic merging of elements in the text. In *Tristan und Isolde* the borders are sexual, social, and olfactory; a sexual union is implied in the union of sense perceptions, and the union is, in terms of the sociey depicted in the drama, a *forbidden* one" (201–2).

101. The femme fatale Corinna is not the first non-Jewish women to disappoint a Jewish male in *Ost und West.* See also the character of Elsa in Hartmann's "Bei Kunstreitern" and the diva character in Heinrich York-Steiner, "Koriander, der Chasan" (October 1904): 687–92, (November 1904): 783–90, and (December 1904): 859–72.

102. Jewish women, in particular, attended opera and theater in numbers far exceeding their proportion within the German population. If the multiple references to it in her memoirs are any indication, *Tristan und Isolde* was Vicki Baum's favorite opera in Wagner's repertoire. Baum, *Es war,* 62, 137, 191.

103. Wagner's "Das Judenthum in der Musik" (*Neue Zeitschrift für Musik,* September 3 and 6, 1850) appeared anonymously in its early editions. Weininger was doubtless familiar with it—and the fact that its author was Wagner.

104. Weininger, *Geschlecht und Charakter,* 404 (*Sex and Character,* 305).

105. Compare Thomas Mann's early stories, where Wagner functions as a destructive decadent, a threat to bourgeois stability. For a somewhat different interpretation of Wagner, Jewishness, and masculinity, see Boyarin, *Unheroic Conduct,* 73–79.

106. Weininger, *Geschlecht und Charakter,* 187–88.

107. On stereotypes of opera, degeneracy, and Jews, see Sander L. Gilman, *Disease and Representation: Images of Illness from Madness to AIDS* (Ithaca: Cornell University Press, 1988), 55–81.

108. Jewish antisemitism and self-hatred will be discussed at length in chapter 5 below.

109. It would be valuable to compare the reception of "Rafael Gutmann" when it appeared elsewhere; for instance, in the *Illustrirte Zeitung* (Leipzig; October 12, 1922; October 19, 1922; November 2, 1922) under the title "Raffael Gutmann."

110. For a reading similar to mine of the perception of Weininger as a threat to Jewish "masculinity," see Boyarin, *Unheroic Conduct*, 257. For related overviews on Weininger, see John Hoberman, "Otto Weininger and the Critique of Jewish Masculinity," in *Jews and Gender: Responses to Otto Weininger*, ed. Nancy A. Harrowitz and Barbara Hyams (Philadelphia: Temple University Press, 1995), 141–53; and Susan C. Anderson, "Otto Weininger's Masculine Utopia," *German Studies Review* 19.3 (October 1996): 433–54.

111. By projecting fear of her own inadequacy onto Rafael, Baum also may have been distancing herself from the charge that Jews were egotistical careerists. Compare the discussion below of "Die Lehrerin."

112. As discussed already, Hugo Kaufmann's sculpture "Freiheit" was carefully juxtaposed with "Rafael Gutmann" to promote a more acceptable image of masculinity.

113. On Segel's neutrality and objectivity as a writer, see chapter 5 below.

114. The existence here of moderate Jewish nationalist discourse that denigrates effeminate East European Jews also feeds into later Zionist critiques of Diaspora life in the post-Holocaust era.

115. To advance his doctrine of Jewish empowerment through self-help, Segel adduced historical examples and enlisted horror stories of pogroms in his writings. Although he almost always used a pseudonym (having been persona non grata in Zionist circles since the *Altneuland* affair), his commentaries were easily recognizable by means of their well-crafted and often audacious rhetoric.

116. Editorial disclaimers in *Ost und West* may have served merely as a marketing ploy in order to create suspense.

117. "Der stille Pogrom. Wehruf eines russischen Juden" also puts to rest suspicions that *Ost und West* had somehow allied itself with the Jewish establishment between 1906 and 1914.

118. Although Paul Breines does not include *Ost und West* in his study, his discussion of Jewish attitudes toward masculinity since the nineteenth century applies to the journal. See Paul Breines, *Tough Jews: Political Fantasies and the Moral Dilemma of American Jewry* (New York: Basic Books, 1990).

119. See also B. Wolff (Benjamin Segel), "Die Juden als Wehrvolk," *Ost und West* (October 1913): 869–76.

120. In 1912 *Ost und West* had more pages than ever. In general, page numbers underwent a rise and fall, from 968 in 1901, to around 850 until 1907, then slight decline in high 700s until 1910 (814) then a jump to 1144 and to 1200 in 1912, then dropping to 1000 in 1913 and 696 in 1914 and declining through 1923.

121. Contemporaneous to the victory of the new generation of Zionists was the so-called *Kunstwartdebatte* unleashed by Moritz Goldstein. See Moritz Goldstein, "Deutsch-Jüdischer Parnaß," *Der Kunstwart* (March 1912): 281–94. A scandal erupted over this essay, in which Goldstein maintained that Jews dominated the culture industry in Germany. Goldstein went on to argue that Jews should choose between German and Hebrew culture. For a complete discussion, see Horch, *Auf*

der Suche nach der jüdischen Erzählliteratur, 227–36; see also Eloni, *Zionismus in Deutschland,* 266–69.

122. To produce a fiction that might overcome "Rafael Gutmann," Segel also knew he would have to come up with a character negative enough to overshadow Rafael's weakness of resolve. At the same time, the presumed setting of "Die Lehrerin" in Poland was meant to deflect attention away from more relevant arenas such as Vienna or Berlin.

123. *Rotwelsch* is the common designation for the Germanic thieves' jargon. It is related to Yiddish and a clue that the Christian teacher is a stand-in for a Western Jewish bourgeoise. The technique of indirect free speech (*erlebte Rede*) and the fact that the characters are unnamed both heighten reader involvement in "Die Lehrerin."

124. On Jewish women and careers, see Kaplan, *The Making of the Jewish Middle Class,* 168–91. The Jewish teacher in "Die Lehrerin" not only edits a literary magazine for the young but also yearns to have her own private academy to preside over.

125. For all her advantages, the good Gentile does not look superior in Segel's depiction; her approach to education and welfare is "maternalistic." The critique is therefore of *both* women.

126. *Ost und West* ultimately contradicted the norms of androcentric Jewish literary history, according to which only Jewish males produce Jewish culture. On androcentric reading, see Patricinio P. Schweikart, "Reading Ourselves: Toward a Feminist Theory of Reading," in *Speaking of Gender,* ed. Elaine Showalter (New York: Routledge, 1989), 17–44.

CHAPTER 5

1. On the problematic use of the term *Mittelstand* in German historiography, see Childers, "The Social Language of Politics in Germany."

2. See the collected essays in Werner E. Mosse and Arnold Paucker, eds., *Deutsches Judentum im Krieg und Revolution, 1916–1923,* Schriftenreihe wissenschaftlicher Abhandlungen des Leo Baeck Instituts 33 (Tübingen: Mohr, 1971).

3. With the exception of the histories of German-Jewish women already cited (e.g., Kaplan, *The Making of the Jewish Middle Class*), few historians have attempted to differentiate German-Jewish men from their female counterparts in a systematic manner, particularly for the period of the *Kaiserreich* and in the realm of audience studies.

4. On the disappointing quality of university life for (Eastern) Jewish students in Germany, see Lazarus Friedmann, *Die Emanzipation der Ostjuden und ihr Einfluß auf die Westjuden: Ein Wort zur rechten Zeit* (Frankfurt a.M.: J. Kauffmann, 1917), 13.

5. See Hans Dieter Hellige, "Generationskonflikt, Selbsthaß und die Entstehung anti-kapitalistischer Positionen im Judentum. Der Einfluß des Antisemitismus auf das Sozialverhalten jüdischer Kaufmanns- und Unternehmersöhne im Deutschen Kaiserreich und in der K. u. K. Monarchie," *Geschichte und Gesellschaft* 5 (1979): 476–518.

6. See Wertheimer, "The German-Jewish Experience," 423.

7. For an introduction to these post-Holocaust stereotypes, see ibid., 421–24.

8. See the works of Volkov, Aschheim, Kaplan, and others, cited above.

9. See Wertheimer, "The German-Jewish Experience," 241.

10. It is nearly a commonplace among American and Israeli Jews today to see the Jews of Germany as having been pathologically "pro-German." See Tom Segev, *The Seventh Million: The Israelis and the Holocaust*, trans. Haim Watzman (New York: Hill and Wang, 1993), 15–67.

11. Kaplan, *The Making of the Jewish Middle Class*, 220. For similar arguments, see *Deutsche jüdische Soldaten, 1914–1945*, Militärgeschichtliches Forschungsamt, ed., 3rd ed. (Bonn: Mittler, 1987), 59–60. For a more in-depth treatment, see Egmont Zechlin, *Die deutsche Politik und die Juden im Ersten Weltkrieg* (Göttingen: Vandenhoeck and Ruprecht, 1969). István Deák's arguments also point to heightend Jewish chauvinism for the Axis powers: "World War I marked the apogee of Jewish participation in the life of Central Europeans. In the delirious enthusiasm of August 1914, Jews were among the greatest enthusiasts. They endorsed the war, in part because the enemy was the antisemitic Russian empire, in part because the outcome of the conflict promised to bring their final and complete acceptance. Jewish writers and journalists did signal service as war propagandists, and thousands of Jewish reserve officers willingly assumed command of their troops. Never again would Jews be allowed to play such a dignified role in the history of German-Austrians, Magyars, and Slavs. Yet it appears that for the first time in the history of the monarchy, the valor of individual Jewish soldiers did not help to dampen antisemitism. As the situation worsened, the right-wing press increasingly attacked the Jews, despite censorship, for their alleged cowardice, war profiteering, and treason." István Deák, "Jewish Soldiers in Austro-Hungarian Society," *34th Annual Leo Baeck Memorial Lecture* (New York: Leo Baeck Institute, 1990), 21–22.

12. See especially Jakob Segall, *Die deutschen Juden als Soldaten im Kriege, 1914–1918* (Berlin: Philo Verlag, 1922), 38; and Franz Oppenheimer, *Die Judenstatistik des preußischen Kriegsministeriums* (Munich: Verlag für Kulturpolitik, 1922). For a summary of the above arguments, see Rolf Vogel, *Ein Stück von uns: Deutsche Juden in deutschen Armeen 1813–1976: Eine Dokumentation* (Mainz: Hase and Koehler, 1977), 8–9. Of 100,000 German-Jewish soldiers in World War I, approximately 12,000 were reported as dead or missing, approximately 30,000 (30 percent) decorated, more than 20,000 promoted (20 percent). Of those promoted, 2,000 (2 percent) became officers. In the same proportion as non-Jews, 20 percent of Jewish men fought in the conflict. The percentage of Jewish casualties was also roughly equivalent. In similar proportion to their German compatriots, 80 percent of Jewish soldiers served at the front and only 20 percent behind the lines.

13. Eva Reichmann, "Der Bewußtseinswandel der deutschen Juden," in *Deutsches Judentum im Krieg und Revolution, 1916–1923*, ed. Werner E. Mosse and Arnold Paucker, Schriftenreihe wissenschaftlicher Abhandlungen des Leo Baeck Instituts 33 (Tübingen: Mohr, 1971), 516.

14. For but one example of such revisionist historiography, see Gershom Scholem, "On the Social Psychology of the Jews in Germany."

15. See Julius Marx, *Kriegstagebuch eines Juden* (1939; reprint, Frankfurt a.M.: Ner-Tamid, 1964).

16. See ibid., 181.

17. Breuer, *Modernity within Tradition*, 385. Some Orthodox Jewish spokesmen asserted that their support for the war originated in Jewish values. See, for instance,

Joseph Wohlgemuth, *Der Weltkrieg im Lichte des Judentums* (Berlin: Jeschurun, 1915). This book was based on wartime articles appearing in his journal *Jeschurun* between 1914 and 1915.

18. It is not far-fetched to compare the experience of German-Jewish soldiers with that of Russian-Jewish soldiers, nearly all of whom, prior to World War I, were forced to convert.

19. The number of traditionally observant young men who volunteered for the military was probably larger than the ratio of Orthodox Jews to the total number of German Jews; see Breuer, *Modernity within Tradition*, 385. Nonetheless, rabbis serving as chaplains were limited in their sphere of influence, and Orthodox ones were all but excluded from service; see ibid., 388–89.

20. Ibid., 389–90. While Jewish Germans stationed in Eastern Europe occasionally visited synagogues in Vilna and Kovno, they were hardly inspired to worship there. See Klemperer, *Curriculum Vitae*, 2: 686–87. To some, the symbolic power of religious Judaism remained palpable, however. See Sammy Gronemann, *Hawdolah und Zapfenstreich: Erinnerungen an die ostjüdische Etappe 1916–1918* (Berlin: Jüdischer Verlag, 1924).

21. Breuer, *Modernity within Tradition*, 390.

22. Marx urged one coreligionist to behave more "militarily." Marx, *Kriegstagebuch eines Juden*, 36.

23. See Berkowitz, *Zionist Culture*.

24. For an example of the linkage of the two stereotypes, see Klemperer, *Curriculum Vitae*, 2: 316.

25. Breuer, *Modernity within Tradition*, 391, 393.

26. See George L. Mosse, *The Image of Man: The Creation of Modern Masculinity* (New York: Oxford University Press, 1996).

27. For the nineteenth century, G. Mosse cites the case of a well-known liberal rabbi: "During the 1830s, Gotthold Salomon inveighed against the danger presented by vacillating men who were described as effeminate and debauched. Like his Protestant colleagues, he blamed such unsteadiness upon the fulfillment of desire, just as gratification of sensuality must needs produce criminals. But there is a tone of urgency here, an effort to stress the image of masculinity so central to the concept of respectability as over against the prevailing stereotype of the Jew." Mosse, "Jewish Emancipation," 6.

28. In *Ost und West*, Jews were called on to show *Willensstärke* and *Festigkeit*. See "Earl of Reading."

29. On Jews and dueling, see Ute Frevert, "Bourgeois Honour: Middle-Class Duellists," in Blackbourn and Evans, eds., *The German Bourgeoisie*, 255–92; see also Ute Frevert, *Ehrenmanner: Das Duell in der bürgerlichen Gesellschaft* (Munich: C. H. Beck, 1991). For a different viewpoint, see Kevin McAleer, *Dueling: The Cult of Honor in Fin-de-Siècle Germany* (Princeton: Princeton University Press, 1994). In contrast to the *Kaiserreich*, non-Jews in Austro-Hungary usually were required to accept Jewish challenges. See Deák, "Jewish Soldiers," 21.

30. Doron, " 'Der Geist ist es,' " 240–41.

31. Martin Buber and Stefan Zweig affirmed the war effort early on, as did the most eminent figures of the postwar "cult of the *Ostjuden*" who came of age after 1900 and included Julius Berger (1883–1948), Arnold Zweig (1887–1968), Siegfried Lehmann (1892–1958), and Fritz Mordechai Kaufman (1888–1921).

32. Aschheim, *Brothers and Strangers*, 157–68. Like the upwardly mobile "rebels" of the Democratic Faction, the men behind *Ost und West* also had become more like the Jewish establishment. After nearly two decades of Jewish journalism in Germany, Winz knew most of the German Jews in high positions. See correspondence in Leo Winz Papers.

33. Breines, *Tough Jews*, 167.

34. In his analysis of "Rambowicz" pulp fiction since 1967, Breines highlights stereotyping of Arabs, effeminate men, homosexuals, women, pacifism, and gentleness. One point, however, must be added to Breines's interpretation: far from (only) internalizing the "tough Jew" ideal, some German-Jewish men consciously promoted it in their (positive) stereotyping of the heroes of ancient Israel.

35. See Tamar Somogni, *Die Schejnen und die Prosten: Untersuchungen zum Schönheitsideal der Ostjuden in Bezug auf Körper und Kleidung unter besonderer Berücksichtigung des Chassidismus* (Berlin: Reimer, 1982).

36. At the same time, it is questionable whether there was truly a tradition of a "tough" Eastern Jew before the Holocaust. Even though the ideal of manliness inherent in the ideal of respectability served to brand Eastern Jews as "uncivilized," *Ostjuden* themselves (the heirs of rabbinic Judaism) appeared undaunted by the charge. From Lithuania to Poland to Bessarabia, Eastern Jews did not share non-Jewish, much less Western, body ideals. While Jewish thinkers in the West distanced themselves more and more from physical stereotypes of Eastern Jews, the thin, pale Jewish scholar was considered to be the epitome of male beauty in East European milieus. Whereas Western Jewry by the end of the nineteenth century idealized martial culture, physical prowess, superior health, and strong nerves, many Eastern Jews still subscribed to ideals of male gentleness, physical restraint, and nonviolence. Specifically, traditional Eastern Jews may have distinguished between the *sheyner* (the "beautiful" male) and the *proster* (the "simple" male). The *sheyner* embodied "intellect, a sense of moderation, cherishing of spiritual values, and the cultivation of rational, goal-directed activities," whereas the "un-Jewish" *proster* (or *bal-guf*) was the epitome of "emphasis on the body, excess, blind instinct, sexual instinct and ruthless force." Mark Zborowski and Elizabeth Herzog, *Life Is with People: The Culture of the Shtetl* (1952; New York: Schocken, 1962), 142. At the same time, with the onset of new pogroms in Kishenev, Odessa, and elsewhere, Eastern Jewish socialist and labor militants showed that they were prepared to defend themselves against hooligans and soldiers. *Ost und West* is thus replete with photographs of bloodstained "freedom fighters" between 1903 and 1906. Western Jews, however, saw World War I as an opportunity to demonstrate their manliness and thus win honor in male society (the *Männerbund*). See also Boyarin, *Unheroic Conduct*.

37. Compare G. Mosse's somewhat different interpretation of *Ost und West* during World War I. George L. Mosse, "The Jews and the German War Experience," *Leo Baeck Memorial Lecture 21* (New York: Leo Baeck Institute, 1977), 14, 15.

38. Preemptive censorship was unusual in wartime Germany, at least until the court decision of July 1916 and new command directives that followed it. Kurt Koszyk, *Deutsche Pressepolitik im Ersten Weltkrieg* (Düsseldorf: Droste, 1968), 14–15.

39. Lemberg (Austro-Hungary) is given as the place of publication for several of Segel's war writings, but Segel was likely living in Berlin. (He may have said he was in Lemberg in order to lend his arguments greater credibility.)

40. See Isaiah Friedman, *Germany, Turkey, and Zionism, 1897–1918* (Oxford: Clarendon Press, 1977), 251, 344 n. 38.

41. See Sammy Gronemann's eulogy for Winz in "Leo Winz, s. A.," *Mitteilungsblatt des Irgun Oley Merkuz*, March 28, 1952. In his autobiography, Gronemann refers to the continuous publication of *Ost und West* during World War I as a typical "Kunststück" of Winz. Gronemann, "Erinnerungen," 137.

42. The Alliance was especially dismayed; see "Berlin/Winz," VII.A.14–16, VII and XIV. According to some reports, Winz was never fully rehabilitated from the accusations of being a spy for the German government during the World War I, Michael Heymann, personal communication, August 30, 1992.

43. It may be argued that the stereotype of "Jewish self-hatred" was alive and flourishing by the outbreak of World War I.

44. See Gilman, *Jewish Self-Hatred*, 243–85, where the projection of anti-Jewish images onto *Ostjuden* is the hallmark of Jewish self-hatred.

45. Ibid.

46. *Ost und West* affected a more "Germanic" orthography in 1914, as is evident in Segel's essay. For the first time in thirteen years, *Ost und West* uses the "ss-tset" (*ß*). (Interestingly, the word *Haß* is the immediate topic of the essay.)

47. In striving to be like German "scientific " and "scholarly" discourse, *Ost und West's* war editorials are designed to make visible the objectivity of the Jewish observer. Otherwise, the observer might be accused of opportunistic lying, war profiteering, or shifting loyalties—in short, of embodying stereotypes of the Jews.

48. *Gesittet* is a Germanism for "civilized" (or *zivilisiert*).

49. Binjamin Segel, *Der Weltkrieg und das Schicksal der Juden* (Berlin: Georg Stilke, 1915), 143. See also "Erziehung zum Haß," *Ost und West* (January–May 1915): 13–22, which was almost certainly written by Segel.

50. For a view of Jewish manhood related to Nordau's, see Segel's essay, "Morija und Golgotha," *Ost und West* (January–May 1915): 45–60. This essay was also expanded and published separately as a pamphlet for soldiers (*Feldbuch*). See Binjamin Segel, *Morija und Golgotha* (Berlin: M. Poppelauer, 1915). Just after the Easter season, Segel debunks the myth that Jews are filled with hatred; he also praises staying alive over sacrificing oneself. At the same time, Segel also equates obeying God and obeying one's fatherland, even when this requires one to kill others.

51. Harden later became an opponent of World War I, although he was perhaps best known for his homophobic campaign of 1906–09 against Prince Philipp zu Eulenburg and Count Kuno von Moltke and other members of the kaiser's general staff and clique.

52. This comment also may be read as a veiled call for an anti-Tsarist revolt. It also alludes to the fact that the war raged in the areas of the most dense Eastern Jewish populations: Congress Poland, Galicia, and much of the Pale of Settlement.

53. See Ernst Jünger, *Der Kampf als inneres Erlebnis* (Berlin: E. S. Mittler, 1922).

54. It should be recalled that Zangwill was the founder of the International Territorialist Organization, which broke away from mainstream Zionism in 1906.

55. For one example of self-hating "other," see Segel's series of 1917–18 in *Ost und West* entitled "Rümänien und seine Juden" (published under the name "Dr. S. Schiffer") and later published separately as Binjamin Segel, *Rumänien und seine Juden. Zeitgemässe Studien* (Berlin: Nibelungen, 1918).

56. See B. Saphra (Binjamin Segel), "Jüdische Kämpfe um Freiheit um Recht. Ein Rückblick auf die letzten 125 Jahre jüdischer Geschichte," *Ost und West* (January 1916): 29–66; (February–March 1916): 123–38; (June–July 1916): 243–54. This series of articles, juxtaposed in the same issues with Segel's *Am Tage des Gerichts*, maintained that Jewish men were fit for military service.

57. One reason Segel's Berg was such a compelling character is that he was depicted using stream-of-consciousness (more specifically, indirect free speech or *erlebte Rede*). This device was also pervasive in the Hebrew and Yiddish literature of this epoch.

58. "Dreitagejuden," or "three-day Jews," was an ironic reference to those Jews who observed only the most important days in the Jewish religious calendar: the first and second days of the New Year (Rosh Hashanah) and the Day of Atonement (Yom Kippur).

59. One publisher who specialized in pamphlets for Jewish soldiers in the field was Louis Lamm. See Lamm's *Jüdische Feldbücherei*, Verlag Louis Lamm, no. 28, Berlin. One such pamphlet reviewed in *Ost und West* was Marcus Brann, *Ein kürzer Gang durch die jüdische Geschichte* (1895; Berlin, 1916) under the rubric "Kriegsliteratur," *Ost und West* (January–February 1916): 71–72.

60. Most of Segel's wartime pamphlets had printings of at least 5,000.

61. Binjamin Segel, *Die polnische Judenfrage* (Berlin: Georg Stilke, 1916).

62. On the *Komitee des Ostens*, see Aschheim, *Brothers and Strangers*, 157–68.

63. Misconstruing the reports of the *Komitee*, the German High Command endangered the lives of Russian Jews in late 1914 by distributing leaflets urging the "German-dialect-speaking" Jews across the border to foment revolution. While careful not to endanger the status of Jews living along the Russian front, who now faced renewed pogroms, *Ost und West* did not feel that its Eastern Jewish orientation came into conflict during the war with its efforts on behalf of a German victory in World War I.

64. Segel, *Die polnische Judenfrage*, 83. Aschheim argues that Segel may have underestimated the historical and sociological problems of applying a Western model of individual emancipation to East European circumstances. Aschheim, *Brothers and Strangers*, 158.

65. Aschheim, *Brothers and Strangers*, 161–62.

66. Ibid., 158.

67. Many Jewish soldiers in World War I served in desk jobs, not unlike Berg's. In fact, Jews were preferred in these positions primarily owing to their higher rate of literacy and education.

68. That Berg is thirty-six years old suggests that Segel is portraying him as a *lamedvovnik*, one of the thirty-six righteous men living in the world in every generation according to a Jewish legend originating in the Babylonian Talmud. The most important trait of the *lamedvovnik*, besides his humble nature and vocation, is that he is unaware that he is a *lamedvovnik* and truly a holy man.

69. Anton Wohlfahrt is the model protagonist of Gustav Freytag's *Soll und Haben* (1855).

70. Segel once again shows anti-Belgian sentiment in one passage, where he (accidentally?) maintains that the parvenu is going to live in Brussels, not Paris (486).

71. Because sinning against a non-Jew is a direct sin against God, Berg must atone for his transgression before the close of Yom Kippur.

72. For a similarly oblique defense of Jewish obedience, see Segel's "Morija und Golgotha," 45–60.

73. See Binjamin Segel, "Die Einweihung des Tempels," *Ost und West* (March 1908): 167–76. This anti-assimilationist novella contains several christological symbols. A group of rustic *shtetl* Jews attend the unveiling of a new *"Tempel"* (Liberal Jewish synagogue) and recoil in horror at the stiff, noiseless worship (*Gottesdienst*) there and the rabbis garbed like priests. Jesus's confrontations at the Temple in Jerusalem are alluded to. Finally, the Eastern Jewish *rov* leading his students is more a Christ figure than a *meshiah*.

74. In this passage of *Am Tage des Gerichts*, the narrator nearly implies that *all* sins can be forgiven by God, yet under Jewish law, those committed against individuals must be atoned for by person-to-person reconciliation.

75. Segel studied ethnology and *Geisteswissenschaften* (humanities) as a student in Berlin at the turn of the century.

76. See Segel, *Die polnische Judenfrage*, 4–5; see also Binjamin Segel, "Elisa Orzeszko," *Ost und West* (July 1912): 443–50.

77. Specific terms also were glossed in the back of the book edition of *Am Tage des Gerichts*.

78. Stereotypes of the Eastern Jewish nouveau riche made a comeback in wartime, especially in the non-Jewish media. See Aschheim, *Brothers and Strangers*, 172–73.

79. Ibid., 191.

80. The best example of such illustrated pro-*Ostjude* books is Hermann Struck and Arnold Zweig, *Das ostjüdische Antlitz* (Berlin: Welt-Verlag, 1919).

CONCLUSION

1. For an interesting discussion on minority literature and culture, see the interpretation of this study's epigraph from Kafka by Gilles Deleuze and Félix Guattari, *Toward a Minor Literature*, trans. Dana Polan, Theory of History and Literature 30 (Minneapolis: University of Minnesota Press, 1986).

2. See Binjamin Segel, *Welt-Krieg, Welt-Revolution, Welt-Verschwörung, Welt-Oberregierung* (Berlin: Philo Verlag, 1926), recently translated as *A Lie and a Libel: The History of the Protocols of the Elders of Zion*, trans. and ed. Richard S. Levy (Lincoln: University of Nebraska Press, 1995). It is an abbreviated version of Segel's *Die Protokolle der Weisen von Zion, kritisch beleuchtet. Eine Erledigung* (Berlin: Philo Verlag, 1924).

3. On Jewish life in the Scheunenviertel, see Eike Geisel, ed., *Im Scheunenviertel. Bilder, Texte und Dokumente* (Berlin: Severin und Siedler, 1981). See also D. Brenner, "Reconciliation before Auschwitz."

4. See Maurer, *Ostjuden in Deutschland*, 63–73.

5. See Zechlin, *Die deutsche Politik*, 260–77.

6. The majority of these *Ostjuden* were from Congress Poland. Whereas approximately half of foreign Jews in prewar Germany came from the Habsburg empire and approximately a quarter from Russia, nearly half of all foreign Jews in Germany after World War I were Polish in origin. See Wertheimer, *Unwelcome Strangers*, 195–97; and Maurer, *Ostjuden in Deutschland*, 78–80.

7. Maurer, *Ostjuden in Deutschland*, 36–44.

8. Ibid., 527.

9. Unlike the United States, Germany never had a tradition of absorbing large numbers of immigrants. Even newcomers to the Habsburg empire may not have become integrated as rapidly as those to the United States. For a summary, see Klaus J. Bade, *Deutsche im Ausland, Fremde in Deutschland. Migration in Geschichte und Gegenwart* (Munich: C. H. Beck, 1992).

10. Aschheim, *Brothers and Strangers*, 245.

11. One proven method, however, for creating pan-Jewishness was close and repeated contacts with *Ostjuden*, in particular in Poland and Lithuania, where the wartime cult of the *Ostjuden* got under way.

12. Susan Olzak, *The Dynamics of Ethnic Competition and Conflict* (Stanford: Stanford University Press, 1991).

13. Eva Reichmann, who served as *Referentin* in the Berlin central office of the *Centralverein*, casts doubt on the widespread notion that Segel was an official member of (or consultant to) the *Centralverein*. Maurer, *Ostjuden in Deutschland*, 914 n. 245.

14. For an introduction to Winz's involvement in the film industry, see Leo Winz Papers, A136/181.

15. See ibid., A136/42 and A136/46.

16. Perhaps Winz and his cohorts saw themselves as better promoters and better schooled in the methods of stereotyping than the cultists of *Ostjudentum*.

17. Verax [Binjamin Segel], "Jüdische Rundschau," *Im deutschen Reich* 27 (January 1921): 18–26. For evidence that Segel was "Verax," see Reichmann, "Der Bewußtseinswandel der deutschen Juden," 562.

18. See especially the chapter titled "The Development of the Concept of Self-Hatred," in Gilman, *Jewish Self-Hatred*, 286–308.

19. For another cogent critique of Gilman's work, see Leslie A. Adelson, "Der, die oder das Holocaust? A Response to Sander L. Gilman's Paper, " *German Quarterly* 62.2 (1989): 205.

20. Wassermann, "The *Fliegende Blätter*," 138.

21. Ibid.

22. Kaplan, *The Making of the Jewish Middle Class*, 11.

23. For a recent analysis of "hate speech," stereotyping, and discourse that parallels my own, see Judith Butler, "Sovereign Performatives in the Contemporary Scene of Utterance," *Critical Inquiry* 23 (Winter 1997): 372–77.

24. Binjamin Segel, "Philosophie des Pogroms," *Ost und West* (March–April 1923): 89.

25. Roskies, *Against the Apocalypse*, 83. See also Alan L. Mintz, *Hurban: Responses to Catastrophe in Hebrew Literature* (New York: Columbia University Press, 1984).

26. For an example in *Ost und West*, see Segel, "Morija und Golgotha."

27. See Hans Blüher, *Secessio Judaica. Philosophische Grundlegung der historischen Situation des Judentums und der antisemitischen Bewegung* (Berlin: W. Ritter, 1922). On Blüher's synthesis of homoeroticism and German nationalism, see G. Mosse, *Nationalism and Sexuality*, 87–88.

28. Thekla Skorra (Binjamin Segel), "Süßkind von Trimberg: Ein jüdischer Minnesänger," *Ost und West* (March–April 1923): 95–100. The latest research

suggests that Süßkind was a Christian *Minnesänger* using a Jewish persona in his poetry. See Edith Wenzel, "Friedrich Torberg: 'Süßkind von Trimberg'. Jüdische Identitätssuche in Deutschland," in *Mittelalter-Rezeption II*, ed. J. Kühnel, H.-D. Mück, Ursula Müller, U. Müller, Göppinger Arbeiten zur Germanistik (Göppingen, 1982), 367–81.

29. See the Zionist *Jüdische Rundschau's* similar reaction to the Scheunenviertel pogrom: "Die Früchte der Emanzipation sind ins Wanken geraten." "Die Schicksalsstunde des deutschen Judentums," *Jüdische Rundschau* (November 9, 1923): 559.

30. See the useful documents on Jewish "extra-territorial" or "cultural" autonomism and on the theory and practice of "minority rights" collected in *The Jew in the Modern World: A Documentary History*, ed. Paul Mendes-Flohr and Jehuda Reinharz, 2nd ed. (New York: Oxford University Press, 1995), 417–48.

31. See G. Mosse, *Nationalism and Sexuality*, 190–91.

32. Geoff Eley and David Blackbourn, *The Peculiarities of German History: Bourgeois Society and Politics in Nineteenth-Century Germany* (Oxford: Oxford University Press, 1984).

33. For a paradigmatic statement of the "older" approach, see Gershom Scholem, who argued in 1962 that "[t]he allegedly indestructible community of the German essence with the Jewish essence consisted, so long as these two essences really lived with each other, only of a chorus of Jewish voices, and was, on the level of historical reality, never anything else than a fiction, a fiction of which you will permit me to say that too high a price was paid for it." Gershom Scholem, "Against the Myth of the German-Jewish Dialogue," *On Jews and Judaism in Crisis: Selected Essays* (New York: Schocken, 1976), 63. My study, as an analysis of Jewish self-stereotyping in Germany, agrees in a very limited sense with Scholem when he states: "To whom, then, did the Jews speak in that much-talked-about German-Jewish dialogue? They spoke to themselves . . ." Ibid.

34. See Wertheimer, "The German-Jewish Experience," 423–24.

35. Reinhard Rürup, *Emanzipation und Antisemitismus. Studien zur "Judenfrage" der bürgerlichen Gesellschaft*. Kritische Studien zur Geschichtswissenschaft 15 (Göttingen: Vandenhoeck and Ruprecht, 1975), 478.

36. Poland's Jews had always lived amidst Poles, Ukrainians, Russians, Lithuanians, Latvians, and others.

37. As in the case of Israelis and Palestinians, the presuppositions between majority and minority groups can (begin to) be overcome only through dialogue, contact, and an awareness of each group's history and stereotypes.

Primary, Secondary, and Archival Sources Cited

Acher, Mathias [Nathan Birnbaum]. "Auf dem Volksliederabend von 'Ost und West.'" *Ost und West* (January 1912): 17–24.

———. "Ghetto." *Ost und West* (March 1903): 533–40.

Adelson, Leslie A. "Der, die oder das Holocaust? A Response to Sander L. Gilman's Paper." *German Quarterly* 62.2 (1989): 205–9.

Adler-Rudel, Shalom. *Ostjuden in Deutschland, 1880–1914*. Schriftenreihe wissenschaftlicher Abhandlungen des Leo Baeck Instituts 1. Tübingen: Mohr, 1959.

Aḥad Haᶜam. "Altneuland." *Ost und West* (April 1903): 237–44.

———. *Äussere Freiheit und innere Knechtschaft: Eine zeitgemässe Betrachtung*. Berlin: Achiasaf, 1901(?).

Alexander, Gabriel. "Die Entwicklung der jüdischen Bevölkerung in Berlin zwischen 1871 und 1945." *Tel Aviver Jahrbuch für deutsche Geschichte* 20 (1991): 287–314.

Allport, Gordon W. *The Nature of Prejudice*, 2nd ed. Garden City, N.Y.: Doubleday, 1958.

Almog, Shmuel. *Zionism and History: The Rise of a New Jewish Consciousness*. Trans. Ina Friedman. New York: St. Martin's Press, 1987.

Altmann, Alexander. *Moses Mendelssohn: A Biographical Study*. University: University of Alabama Press, 1973.

Anderson, Benedict. *Imagined Communities: Reflections on the Origin and Spread of Nationalism*, rev. ed. London: Verso, 1991.

Anderson, Susan C. "Otto Weininger's Masculine Utopia." *German Studies Review* 19.3 (October 1996): 433–54.

Angress-Klüger, Ruth. "Jewish Characters in Thomas Mann's Fiction." In *Horizonte: Festschrift für Herbert Lehnert zum 65. Geburtstag*, 161–72. Ed. Hannelore Mundt, Egon Schwarz, and William J. Lillyman. Tübingen: Niemeyer, 1990.

Arendt, Hannah. "The Jew as Pariah." In *The Jew as Pariah: Jewish Identity and Politics in the Modern Age*, 67–90. Ed. Ron H. Feldman. New York: Grove, 1978.

Aschheim, Steven E. *Brothers and Strangers: The East European Jew in German and German Jewish Consciousness, 1800–1923*. Madison: University of Wisconsin Press, 1982.

"Aus dem New Yorker Judenviertel." *Ost und West* (July 1909): 461 66.

"Aus den letzten blutigen Judenkrawallen in Russland (Die gefallenen Helden von Shitomir)." *Ost und West* (July–August 1905): 457–58.

B. . . . .d [Simon Bernfeld?]. "Die Transformation der russischen Juden." *Ost und West* (September 1901): 673–74.

Bade, Klaus J. *Deutsche im Ausland, Fremde in Deutschland: Migration in Geschichte und Gegenwart*. Munich: C. H. Beck, 1992.

Baum, Vicki. *Es war alles ganz anders*. Cologne: Kiepenheuer and Witsch, 1987.

———. "Im alten Haus." *Ost und West* (January 1910): 15–32.

———. "Rafael Gutmann." *Ost und West* (January 1911): 37–50, (February 1911): 131–44.

———. "Raffael Gutmann." [Leipziger] *Illustrirte Zeitung*, Oct. 12 and 19, Nov. 2, 1922.

"Beethoven's erste Liebe." *Ost und West* (January 1901): 69–70.

Behrend, Alice. "Das Ghetto in Venedig." *Ost und West* (June 1904): 397–400.

Bender, A. D. [Binjamin Segel?]. "Eine Apologie des Judentums." *Ost und West* (July 1903): 427–32.

Benesra, A. [Binjamin Segel]. "Philosophie der Zerstreuung." *Ost und West* (January 1905): 7–16.

Berkowitz, Michael. " 'Mind, Muscle, and Men': The Imagination of a Zionist National Culture for the Jews of Central and Western Europe, 1897–1914." Ph.D. dissertation, University of Wisconsin, Madison, 1989.

———. *Zionist Culture and West European Jewry before the First World War*. Cambridge: Cambridge University Press, 1993.

"Die Beschreibung fun Ashkenaz un Polack" (ca. 1675). Reprinted in Max Weinreich, "Zvey yidishe shpotlider af yidn." *Filologishe shriften*. Vilna: YIVO, 1929. 3: 537–54.

Bhabha, Homi K. *The Location of Culture*. London: Routledge, 1994.

Bigart, Jacques. "Die Tätigkeit der A.I.U. in der Türkei (Vortrag des Herrn J. Bigart, gehalten am 24. Mai 1913 in der jüdischen Volksuniversität zu Paris)." *Ost und West* (October 1913): 819–34.

Birnbaum, Nathan. "Etwas über Ost- und Westjudentum." In *Die jüdische Moderne*, 152–55. Ed. Henryk M. Broder. Augsburg: Ölbaum Verlag, 1989.

———. *Die jüdische Moderne*. Ed. Henryk M. Broder. Augsburg: Ölbaum Verlag, 1989.

Blackbourn, David. "The German Bourgeoisie: An Introduction." In *The German Bourgeoisie: Essays on the Social History of the German Middle Class from the Late Eighteenth to the Early Twentieth Century*, 1–46. Ed. David Blackbourn and Richard J. Evans. London: Routledge, 1991.

———. "Roman Catholics, the Centre Party, Anti-Semitism." In *Nationalist and Racialist Movements in Britain and Germany before 1914*, 106–29. Ed. Paul Kennedy and Anthony Nicholls. Oxford: Macmillan, 1981.

Blackbourn, David, and Richard J. Evans, eds. *The German Bourgeoisie: Essays on the Social History of the German Middle Class from the Late Eighteenth to the Early Twentieth Century*. London: Routledge, 1991.

Blüher, Hans. *Secessio Judaica: Philosophische Grundlegung der historischen Situation des Judentums und der antisemitischen Bewegung*. Berlin: W. Ritter, 1922.

Born, Jürgen. *Kafkas Bibliothek: Ein beschreibendes Verzeichnis*. Frankfurt a.M.: S. Fischer, 1990.

Bourdieu, Pierre. *Distinction: A Social Critique of the Judgement of Taste*. Trans. Richard Nice. Cambridge, Mass.: Harvard University Press, 1984.

Boyarin, Daniel. *Unheroic Conduct: The Rise of Heterosexuality and the Invention of the Jewish Man*. Berkeley: University of California Press, 1997.

Brachmann, Botho. *Russische Sozialdemokraten in Berlin, 1895–1914*. Berlin: Akademie-Verlag, 1962.

Brann, Marcus. *Ein kürzer Gang durch die jüdische Geschichte*. Breslau: Wilh. Jacobsohn, 1895.

Breines, Paul. *Tough Jews: Political Fantasies and the Moral Dilemma of American Jewry*. New York: Basic Books, 1990.

Brenner, David A. "Making *Jargon* Respectable: Leo Winz, *Ost und West*, and the Reception of Yiddish Theater in Pre-Hitler Germany." *Year Book of the Leo Baeck Institute* 42 (1997): 51–66.

———. "Reconciliation before Auschwitz: The Weimar Jewish Experience in Popular Fiction from the *Israelitisches Familienblatt*." In *Borders and Crossings: Evolving Jewish Identities in German Majority Culture*. Ed. Diana Hinze and Linda Feldman. Westport, Conn.: Greenwood/Praeger, forthcoming.

———. " 'Re-dressing' the German-Jewish: A Jewish Hermaphrodite and Crossdresser in Wilhelmine Germany." In *Borders, Exiles, and Diasporas*. Ed. Elazar Barkan and Marie-Denise Shelton. Stanford: Stanford University Press, forthcoming.

Brenner, Michael. "The *Jüdische Volkspartei*—National-Jewish Communal Politics during the Weimar Republic." *Year Book of the Leo Baeck Institute* 35 (1990): 219–44.

———. *The Renaissance of Jewish Culture in Weimar Germany*. New Haven: Yale University Press, 1996.

Breuer, Mordechai. *Modernity within Tradition: The Social History of Orthodox Jewry in Imperial Germany*. Trans. Elizabeth Petuchowski. New York: Columbia University Press, 1992.

Breuilly, John. *Nationalism and the State*. Manchester: Manchester University Press, 1982.

Brieger-Wasservogel, Lothar. "Das alte Testament." *Ost und West* (November 1901): 849–54.

———. *Rene Richter: Die Entwicklung eines modernen Juden. Berliner Roman in 3 Büchern*. Berlin: Schröder, 1906.

Bruford, W. H. *The German Tradition of Self-Cultivation: "Bildung" from Humboldt to Thomas Mann*. London: Cambridge University Press, 1975.

Buber, Martin. "Herzl und die Historie." *Ost und West* (August–September 1904): 583–94.

———. Letter to Theodor Herzl. May 26, 1903. In *Briefwechsel aus sieben Jahrzehnten*, 197. Ed. Grete Schaeder. Heidelberg: Lambert Schneider, 1972.

Butler, Judith. "Sovereign Performatives in the Contemporary Scene of Utterance." *Critical Inquiry* 23 (Winter 1997): 350–77.

Childers, Thomas. "The Social Language of Politics in Germany: The Sociology of Political Discourse in the Weimar Republic." *American Historical Review* 95, no. 2 (1990): 331–58.

Cowen, Roy. "Naturalismus." In *Geschichte der deutschen Literatur*, 3:135. Ed. Ehrhard Bahr. Tübingen: Francke, 1988.

Croner [-Kretschmer], Else. *Die moderne Jüdin*. Berlin: Axel Juncker, 1913.

Darmaun, Jacques. "Thomas Mann und die Juden—eine Kontroverse? Thomas Manns Bild des Judentums bis zur Weimarer Republik." *Kontroversen, alte und neue, Akten des VII. Internationalen Germanistenkongresses*. Göttingen, 1985. Vol. 5. *Auseinandersetzungen um jiddische Sprache und Literatur; Jüdische Komponenten in der deutschen Literatur—die Assimilationskontroverse*, 208–14. Ed. Albrecht Schöne, Walter Rolle, and Hans-Peter Bayerdörfer. Tübingen: Niemeyer, 1986.

Davidoff, Lenora, and Catherine Hall. *Family Fortunes: Men and Women of the English Middle Class, 1780–1850*. London: Hutchinson, 1987.

Deák, István. "Jewish Soldiers in Austro-Hungarian Society." *34th Annual Leo Baeck Memorial Lecture*. New York: Leo Baeck Institute, 1990.

Deleuze, Gilles, and Félix Guattari. *Toward a Minor Literature*. Trans. Dana Polan. Theory of History and Literature 30. Minneapolis: University of Minnesota Press, 1986.

Dohm, Christian Wilhelm von. *Ueber die bürgerliche Verbesserung der Juden*. Berlin: F. Nicolai, 1781.

Doron, Joachim. " 'Der Geist ist es, der sich den Körper schafft': Soziale Probleme in der jüdischen Turnbewegung (1896–1914)." *Tel Aviver Jahrbuch für deutsche Geschichte* 20 (1991): 240–41.

DuBois, W. E. B. *The Autobiography of W. E. B. DuBois*. New York: International Publishers, 1968.

"Earl of Reading." *Ost und West* (January–February 1921): 29–32.

Efron, John M. *Defenders of the Race: Jewish Doctors and Race Science in Fin-de-Siècle Europe*. New Haven: Yale University Press, 1994.

Ehmann, Annegret, et al. *Juden in Berlin, 1671–1945. Ein Lesebuch*. Berlin: Nicolai 1988.

Eissing, Uwe J. "Christian Wilhelm von Dohm, die bürgerliche Verbesserung der Juden und die Vision einer 'judenfreien' Welt." *Bulletin des Leo Baeck Instituts* 88 (1991): 27–58.

Eley, Geoff, and David Blackbourn. *The Peculiarities of German History: Bourgeois Society and Politics in Nineteenth-Century Germany*. Oxford: Oxford University Press, 1984.

Elias, Norbert. *Über den Prozeß der Zivilisation: Soziogenetische und psychogenetische Untersuchungen*. Basel: Haus zum Falken, 1939. Vol. 2.

Elliott, James, Jürgen Pelzer, and Carol Poore, eds. *Stereotyp und Vorurteil in der*

Literatur: Untersuchungen zu Autoren des 20. Jahrhunderts. Göttingen: Vandenhoeck and Ruprecht, 1978.

Eloni, Yehuda. *Zionismus in Deutschland. Von den Anfängen bis 1914.* Gerlingen:
Bleicher, 1987.

Endelman, Todd M. "The Social and Political Context of Conversion in Germany
and England, 1870–1914." In *Jewish Apostasy in the Modern World.* Ed. Todd M.
Endelman. New York: Holmes and Meier, 1987.

"Erziehung zum Haß." *Ost und West* (January–May 1915): 13–22.

Feiwel, Berthold, ed. *Jüdischer Almanach.* Berlin: Jüdischer Verlag, 1902.

Fishman, Joshua A. *Ideology, Society and Language: The Odyssey Of Nathan Birnbaum.*
Ann Arbor: Karoma, 1987.

Forchheimer, Stephanie. "Ein Gang durch das Judenviertel in Amsterdam." *Ost und
West* (November 1913): 889–896.

———. "Jüdische soziale Frauenarbeit in Frankfurt am Main." *Ost und West* (January
1913): 67–72.

Foucault, Michel. *The Archaeology of Knowledge.* Trans. A. M. Sheridan Smith. New
York: Pantheon, 1972.

———. *The History of Sexuality: An Introduction.* Trans. Robert Hurley. New York:
Pantheon, 1978.

———. *The Order of Things: An Archaeology of the Human Sciences.* New York:
Pantheon, 1971.

Frankel, Jonathan. *Prophecy and Politics: Socialism, Nationalism, and the Russian Jews,
1862–1917.* Cambridge: Cambridge University Press, 1981.

Franzos, Karl Emil. *Aus Halb-Asien: Culturbilder aus Galizien, der Bukowina, Sudruss-
land und Rumänien.* Leipzig: Duncker und Humblot, 1876.

Franzos, Karl Emil. *Die Juden von Barnow: Geschichten.* Stuttgart and Leipzig:
E. Hallberger, 1878.

Frevert, Ute. "Bourgeois Honour: Middle-Class Duellists." In *The German Bour-
geoisie: Essays on the Social History of the German Middle Class from the Late
Eighteenth to the Early Twentieth Century,* 255–92. Ed. David Blackbourn and
Richard J. Evans. London: Routledge, 1991.

———. *Ehrenmänner: Das Duell in der bürgerlichen Gesellschaft.* Munich: C. H. Beck,
1991.

Freytag, Gustav. *Soll und Haben: Roman in sechs Büchern.* Berlin: S. Hirzel, 1855.

Fried, Alfred H. "Das soziale Motiv der Tracht und die Judenfrage." *Ost und West*
(April 1903): 259–64.

Friedman, Isaiah. *Germany, Turkey, and Zionism, 1897–1918.* Oxford: Clarendon
Press, 1977.

Friedmann, Lazarus. *Die Emanzipation der Ostjuden und ihr Einfluß auf die Westjuden:
Ein Wort zur rechten Zeit.* Frankfurt a.M.: J. Kauffmann, 1917.

Friedman, Maurice S. *Martin Buber's Life and Work: The Early Years, 1878–1923.*
New York: Dutton, 1981.

"Die Früchte der Emanzipation sind ins Wanken geraten." *Jüdische Rundschau*
(November 9, 1923): 559.

Garvey, Ellen Gruber. *The Adman in the Parlor: Magazines and the Gendering of
Consumer Culture, 1880s to 1910s.* New York: Oxford University Press, 1996.

Gay, Peter. *Freud, Jews, and Other Germans: Masters and Victims in Modernist Culture.* New York: Oxford University Press, 1978.

———. *Weimar Culture: The Outsider as Insider.* New York: Harper and Row, 1968.

Gebhardt, Hartwig. "Illustrierte Zeitschriften in Deutschland am Ende des 19. Jahrhunderts." *Börsenblatt für den Deutschen Buchhandel* 150–51, no. 48 (June 16, 1983): B41–B65.

Geertz, Clifford. "Ideology as a Cultural System." In *Ideology and Discontent,* 47–76. Ed. David E. Apter. New York: Free Press, 1964.

Geiger, Ludwig. "Der Estherstoff in der neuen Litteratur." *Ost und West* (January 1901): 27–34.

Geisel, Eike, ed. *Im Scheunenviertel. Bilder, Texte und Dokumente.* Berlin: Severin und Siedler, 1981.

Gelber, Mark H. "Ethnic Pluralism and Germanization in the Works of Karl Emil Franzos (1848–1904)." *German Quarterly* 56 (1983): 376–85.

———. "Das Judendeutsch in der deutschen Literatur. Einige Beispiele von den frühesten Lexika bis zu Gustav Freytag und Thomas Mann." In *Juden in der deutschen Literatur: Ein deutsch-israelisches Symposion,* 162–78. Ed. Stéphane Moses and Albrecht Schöne. Frankfurt a.M.: Suhrkamp, 1986.

———. "The *jungjüdische Bewegung:* An Unexplored Chapter in German-Jewish Literary and Cultural History." *Year Book of the Leo Baeck Institute* 31 (1986): 105–19.

———. "K. E. Franzos, Achad Haᶜam und S. Zweig." *Bulletin des Leo Baeck Instituts* 27 (1982): 19–43.

Gilman, Sander L. *Difference and Pathology: Stereotypes of Sexuality, Race, and Madness.* Ithaca: Cornell University Press, 1985.

———. *Disease and Representation: Images of Illness from Madness to AIDS.* Ithaca: Cornell University Press, 1988.

———. *Jewish Self-Hatred: Anti-Semitism and the Hidden Language of the Jews.* Baltimore: Johns Hopkins University Press, 1986.

———. *Smart Jews: The Construction of the Image of Jewish Superior Intelligence.* Lincoln: University of Nebraska Press, 1996.

———, ed. *On Blackness without Blacks: Essays on the Image of the Black in Germany.* Boston: G. K. Hall, 1982.

Goldstein, Joseph. "The Zionist Movement in Russia, 1897–1904." Ph.D. dissertation, Hebrew University of Jerusalem, 1982.

Goldstein, Moritz. "Deutsch-Jüdischer Parnaß." *Der Kunstwart* (March 1912): 281–94.

Gordon, Milton M. *Assimilation in American Life: The Role of Race, Religion and National Origins.* New York: Oxford University Press, 1964.

Grellman, Heinrich Moritz Gottlieb. *Die Zigeuner: Ein historischer Versuch über die Lebensart und Verfassung Sitten und Schicksahle dieses Volks in Europa, nebst ihrem Ursprunge.* Dessau and Leipzig: Buchhandlung der Gelehrten, 1783.

Grimm, Reinhold, and Jost Hermand, eds. *Blacks and German Culture: Essays.* Madison: University of Wisconsin Press, 1986.

Gronemann, Sammy. "Erinnerungen." Unpublished memoir, 1948. Leo Baeck Institute, New York.

[Gronemann, Sammy.] "Leo Winz, s. A." *Mitteilungsblatt des Irgun Oley Merkuz* (March 28, 1952).

———. *Hawdolah und Zapfenstreich: Erinnerungen an die ostjüdische Etappe 1916–1918.* Berlin: Jüdischer Verlag, 1924.

Grossman, Jeffrey A. "The Space of Yiddish in the German and German-Jewish Discourse." Ph.D. dissertation, University of Texas, 1992.

"Gruppe hingeschlachteter Mitglieder der jüdischen 'Selbstwehr' in Odessa." *Ost und West* (October–November 1905): 609–10.

Guggenheim, Ernst. "Der Rabbi." *Ost und West* (November 1902): 767–78.

Haacke, Wilmont. "Der Zeitschriftentypus Revue." *Archiv für Geschichte des Buchwesens* 11 (1970): 1035–56.

Haasenstein and Vogler. *Zeitungskatalog.* Berlin: Haasenstein and Vogler, 1910.

Hartmann, Moritz. "Bei Kunstreitern." *Ost und West* (March 1901): 211–22.

Heine, Th. Th. "Die Verwandlung." *Simplicissimus,* June 2, 1903.

Heinze, Andrew. *Adapting to Abundance: Jewish Immigrants, Mass Consumption, and the Search for American Identity.* New York: Columbia University Press, 1989.

Hellige, Hans Dieter. "Generationskonflikt, Selbsthaß und die Entstehung antikapitalistischer Positionen im Judentum. Der Einfluß des Antisemitismus auf das Sozialverhalten jüdischer Kaufmanns- und Unternehmersöhne im Deutschen Kaiserreich und in der K. u. K. Monarchie." *Geschichte und Gesellschaft* 5 (1979): 476–518.

Hermann, Georg. "Eugen Spiro." *Ost und West* (April 1905): 231–40.

Hertz, Deborah. *Jewish High Society in Old Regime Berlin.* New Haven: Yale University Press, 1988.

Hertzberg, Arthur, ed. *The Zionist Idea: A Historical Analysis and Reader.* Garden City, N.Y.: Doubleday, 1959.

Herzl, Theodor. *Altneuland.* Leipzig: H. Seemann, 1902.

———. "Mauschel." *Ost und West* (August–September 1904): 545–50.

Hoberman, John. "Otto Weininger and the Critique of Jewish Masculinity." In *Jews and Gender: Responses to Otto Weininger,* 141–53. Ed. Nancy A. Harrowitz and Barbara Hyams. Philadelphia: Temple University Press, 1995.

Hobsbawm, Eric. "Introduction: Inventing Traditions." In *The Invention of Tradition,* 1–14. Ed. Eric Hobsbawm and Terence Ranger. 1993. Reprint, Cambridge: Cambridge University Press, 1984.

Hoffmann, Walther G. *Das Wachstum der deutschen Wirtschaft seit der Mitte des 19. Jahrhunderts.* Berlin: Springer-Verlag, 1965.

Holub, Robert C. *Reflections of Realism: Paradox, Norm, and Ideology in Nineteenth-century German Prose.* Detroit: Wayne State University Press, 1991.

Horch, Hans Otto. *Auf der Suche nach der jüdischen Erzählliteratur: Die Literaturkritik der "Allgemeinen Zeitung des Judentums" (1837–1922).* Literaturhistorische Untersuchungen 1. Bern: Peter Lang, 1985.

Hyman, Paula E. *The Emancipation of the Jews of Alsace: Acculturation and Tradition in the Nineteenth Century.* New Haven: Yale University Press, 1991.

———. *Gender and Assimilation in Modern Jewish History: The Roles and Representation of Women.* Seattle: University of Washington Press, 1995.

Isenberg, Noah. *Between Redemption and Doom: German Modernism and the Strains of Jewish Identity.* Lincoln: University of Nebraska Press, forthcoming.

Jarausch, Konrad. *Students, Society and Politics in Imperial Germany: The Rise of Academic Illiberalism.* Princeton: Princeton University Press, 1982.

Jauss, Hans Robert. *Literaturgeschichte als Provokation.* 1967. Reprint, Frankfurt a.M.: Suhrkamp, 1970.

"Die Juden von Gestern." *Ost und West* (April 1903): 217–26.

Jünger, Ernst. *Der Kampf als inneres Erlebnis.* Berlin: E. S. Mittler, 1922.

Kafka, Franz. *Gesammelte Werke.* Ed. Max Brod. Frankfurt a.M.: Fischer Taschenbuch, 1983. 7 vols.

———. Letter to Felice Bauer. October 27, 1912. In *Briefe an Felice und andere Korrespondenz aus der Verlobungszeit,* 57–62. Ed. Erich Heller and Jürgen Born. Frankfurt a.M.: Fischer, 1967.

Kampe, Norbert. "Jews and Antisemites at Universities in Imperial Germany (I): Jewish Students: Social History and Conflict." *Year Book of the Leo Baeck Institute* 30 (1985): 357–94.

Kaplan, Marion A. *The Jewish Feminist Movement in Germany.* Westport, Conn.: Greenwood Press, 1979.

———. *The Making of the Jewish Middle Class: Women, Family, and Identity in Imperial Germany.* New York: Oxford University Press, 1991.

———. "Tradition and Transition—The Acculturation, Assimilation, and Integration of Jews in Imperial Germany—A Gender Analysis." *Year Book of the Leo Baeck Institute* 27 (1982): 3–35.

Katz, Jacob. "German Culture and the Jews." In *The Jewish Response to German Culture: From the Enlightenment to the Second World War,* 85. Ed. Jehuda Reinharz and Walter Shatzberg. Hanover, N.H.: University Press of New England, 1985.

———. *Out of the Ghetto: The Social Background of Jewish Emancipation, 1770–1870.* New York: Schocken, 1978.

———. "Vom Ghetto zum Zionismus: Gegenseitige Beeinflussung von Ost und West." *Bulletin des Leo Baeck Instituts* 64 (1983): 1–10.

Kaufmann, Fritz Mordechai. *Vier Essais über ostjüdische Dichtung und Kultur.* Berlin: Welt Verlag, 1919.

Kellner, Leon. "Eine jüdische Toynbee-Halle in Wien." *Ost und West* (April 1901): 291–98.

Key, Ellen. *Das Jahrhundert des Kindes.* Trans. Marie Franzos. Berlin: Fischer, 1903.

King, Lynda. *Best-sellers by Design: Vicki Baum and the House of Ullstein.* Detroit: Wayne State University Press, 1988.

King, Robert D. "Migration and Lingustic Change as Illustrated by Yiddish." In *Trends in Linguistics: Reconstructing Languages and Cultures,* 419–39. Ed. Werner Winter and Edgar Polomé. Berlin: Mouton de Gruyter, 1992.

Klemperer, Victor. *Curriculum Vitae. Jugend um 1900.* Berlin: Siedler, 1989. Vol. 2.

Kohut, Adolf. "Lina Morgenstern." *Ost und West* (January 1906): 37–42.

Koszyk, Kurt. *Deutsche Presse im 19. Jahrhundert.* Berlin: Colloquium, 1966. Vol. 2.

———. *Deutsche Pressepolitik im Ersten Weltkrieg.* Düsseldorf: Droste, 1968.

Krämer, Clementine [Binjamin Segel?]. "Getauft." *Ost und West* (January 1913): 77–80.

Krauss, Samuel. "Orientalische Spagnolen." *Ost und West* (October–November 1906): 687–700.

"Kriegsliteratur." *Ost und West* (January–February 1916): 71–72.

Kunstverlag Phönix. *Illustrierter Katalog*. Berlin: Kunstverlag Phönix, 1903.

LaCapra, Dominick. *Representing the Holocaust: History, Theory, Trauma*. Ithaca: Cornell University Press, 1994.

Lazarus, Nahida Ruth. *Das jüdische Weib*. Leipzig: G. Laudien, 1892.

Lederhendler, Eli. "Modernity with Emancipation or Assimilation? The Case of Russian Jewry." In *Assimilation and Community: The Jews in Nineteenth-Century Europe*, 324–43. Ed. Jonathan Frankel and Steven J. Zipperstein. Cambridge: Cambridge University Press, 1992.

Lefevere, Andre. *Translating Literature: Practice and Theory in a Comparative Literature Context*. New York: Modern Language Association, 1992.

Lessing, Gotthold Ephraim. *Schrifften*. Volume 4. Berlin: C. F. Voss, 1753–1755.

Lessing, Theodor. *Jüdischer Selbsthaß*. Berlin: Jüdischer Verlag/Zionistischer Bücher-Bund, 1930.

Linse, Ulrich. "Die Jugendkulturbewegung." In *Das wilhelminische Bildungsbürgertum: Zur Sozialgeschichte seiner Ideen*, 119–37. Ed. Klaus Vondung. Göttingen: Vandenhoeck and Ruprecht, 1976.

Lippmann, Walter. *Public Opinion*. New York: Macmillan, 1922.

Loewe, Heinrich. Papers. Central Zionist Archives, Jerusalem. A146.

———. "Wer spricht Jargon?" *Jüdische Rundschau* (January 22, 1904): 33–35.

———. "Zur Vorgeschichte des Zionismus." *Israelitische Rundschau [Jüdische Rundschau]* (June 27, 1902): 3–4, (July 4, 1902): 3–4.

Low, Alfred D. *Jews in the Eyes of the Germans: From the Enlightenment to Imperial Germany*. Philadelphia: Institute for the Study of Human Issues, 1979.

Luz, Ehud. *Parallels Meet: Religion and Nationalism in the Early Zionist Movement, 1882–1904*. Philadelphia: Jewish Publication Society, 1988.

"Des Magiers Tod." *Der Schlemiel* (September 1, 1904): 76–78.

Mahler, Raphael. *Hasidism and the Jewish Enlightenment: Their Confrontation in Galicia and Poland in the First Half of the Nineteenth Century*. Philadelphia: Jewish Publication Society, 1985.

Maimon, Salomon. *Salomon Maimons Lebensgeschichte*. Ed. Karl Phillipp Moritz. Berlin: Friedrich Vieweg, 1792–93.

Mann, Thomas. *Wälsungenblut*. Berlin: Phantasus-Verlag, 1921.

Martens, Wolfgang. *Die Botschaft der Tugend: Die Aufklärung im Spiegel der deutschen Moralischen Wochenschriften*. Stuttgart: Metzler, 1968.

Marx, Julius. *Kriegstagebuch eines Juden*. 1939. Reprint, Frankfurt a.M.: Ner-Tamid, 1964.

Maurer, Trude. *Die Entwicklung der jüdischen Minderheit in Deutschland (1780–1933). Neuere Forschungen und offene Fragen. Internationales Archiv für Sozialgeschichte der deutschen Literatur*, Sonderheft 4. Tübingen: Niemeyer, 1992.

———. *Ostjuden in Deutschland 1918–1933*. Hamburger Beiträge zur Geschichte der deutschen Juden 12. Hamburg: Hans Christians, 1986.

McAleer, Kevin. *Dueling: The Cult of Honor in Fin-de-Siècle Germany*. Princeton: Princeton University Press, 1994.

McCagg, William O., Jr. *A History of Habsburg Jews, 1670–1918*. Bloomington: Indiana University Press, 1989.

Meinecke, Friedrich. *Weltbürgen und Nationalstaat: Studien zu Genesis des deutschen Nationalstaats*. Munich: R. Oldenbourg, 1908.

Mendelsohn, Ezra. *The Jews of East Central Europe between the World Wars.* Bloomington: Indiana University Press, 1983.

Mendes-Flohr, Paul. "Fin-de-Siècle Orientalism, the Ostjuden and the Aesthetics of Jewish Self-Affirmation." *Studies in Contemporary Jewry* 1 (1984): 96–139.

———. Review of *German Jews beyond Judaism,* by George L. Mosse. *Studies in Contemporary Jewry* 5 (1989): 376–79.

Mendes-Flohr, Paul, and Jehuda Reinharz, eds. *The Jew in the Modern World: A Documentary History.* 2nd edition. New York: Oxford University Press, 1995.

Metz, Josefa. "Sünde: Aus dem Leben eines kleinen Mädchens." *Ost und West* (May 1904): 341–48.

Meyer, Michael A. *Response to Modernity: A History of the Reform Movement in Judaism.* New York: Oxford University Press, 1988.

Meyer, Reinhart. *Novelle und Journal.* Vol. 1. *Titel und Normen: Untersuchungen zur Terminologie der Journalprosa, zu ihren Tendenzen, Verhältnissen und Bedingungen.* Stuttgart: F. Steiner, 1987.

Militärgeschichtliches Forschungsamt. *Deutsche jüdische Soldaten, 1914–1945,* 3rd ed. Bonn: Mittler, 1987.

Miller, Arthur G. "Historical and Contemporary Perspectives in Stereotyping." In *In the Eye of the Beholder,* 1–40. Ed. Arthur G. Miller. New York: Praeger, 1982.

Mintz, Alan. *Hurban: Responses to Catastrophe in Hebrew Literature.* New York: Columbia University Press, 1984.

———. "A Sanctuary in the Wilderness: The Beginnings of the Hebrew Movement in America in the Pages of *Hatoren.*" *Prooftexts* 10 (September 1990): 389–413.

Miron, Dan. *A Traveler Disguised: A Study in the Rise of Modern Yiddish Fiction in the Nineteenth Century.* New York: Schocken, 1973.

Morgenstern, Lina. "Heinrich Redlich. Erinnerungen." *Ost und West* (January 1906): 41–50.

Mosse, George L. *The Crisis of German Ideology: Intellectual Origins of the Third Reich.* New York: Grosset and Dunlap, 1964.

———. *The Culture of Western Europe: The Nineteenth and Twentieth Centuries.* New York: Rand McNally, 1961.

———. *German Jews beyond Judaism.* Bloomington: Indiana University Press, 1985.

———. *Germans and Jews: The Right, the Left, and the Search for a "Third Force" in Pre-Nazi Germany.* New York: Howard Fertig, 1970.

———. *The Image of Man: The Creation of Modern Masculinity.* New York: Oxford University Press, 1996.

———. "Jewish Emancipation: Between Bildung and Respectability." In *The Jewish Response to German Culture: From the Enlightenment to the Second World War,* 1–13. Ed. Jehuda Reinharz and Walter Schatzberg. Hanover, N.H.: University Press of New England, 1985.

———. "The Jews and the German War Experience." *Leo Baeck Memorial Lecture 21.* New York: Leo Baeck Institute, 1977.

———. *Nationalism and Sexuality: Middle-Class Morality and Sexual Norms in Modern Europe.* 1985. Reprint, Madison: University of Wisconsin Press, 1986.

Mosse, Werner E. *The German-Jewish Economic Elite, 1820–1935.* New York: Oxford University Press, 1991.

Mosse, Werner E., and Arnold Paucker, eds. *Deutsches Judentum im Krieg und Revolution, 1916–1923*. Schriftenreihe wissenschaftlicher Abhandlungen des Leo Baeck Instituts 33. Tübingen: Mohr, 1971.

Moyn, Samuel. "German Jewry and the Question of Identity: Historiography and Theory." *Year Book of the Leo Baeck Institute* 41 (1996): 291–308.

Münchhausen, Borries von. *Juda: Gesänge*. Goslar: F. A. Lattmann, 1900.

Münz, Bernhard. "Das Judentum in der Beleuchtung eines jungen Philosophen." *Ost und West* (December 1903): 823–26.

N. O. "Lina Morgenstern." *Ost und West* (January 1910): 33–34.

N. O. Body [Karl Martha Baer]. *Aus eines Mannes Mädchenjahren*. 1909. Berlin: Edition Hentrich, 1993.

"Nach berühmten Mustern" and "Des Magiers Tod." *Der Schlemiel* (September 1, 1904): 76–78.

Niewyk, Donald. *The Jews of the Weimar Republic*. Baton Rouge: Louisiana State University Press, 1980.

Niger, Shmuel. "Di yidishe lezerin." *Der Pinkes: yorbukh far der geshikhte fun der yudisher literatur un shprakh* 1 (1912): 85–138.

Nordau, Max. "Achad Ha'am über Altneuland." *Die Welt* (March 13, 1903): 1–5.

Nuhum, Chacham Baschi Maim. "Die Alliance-Expedition zur Erforschung des Falascha-Stammes." *Ost und West* (June 1908): 395–402.

Ohmann, Richard M. *Selling Culture: Magazines, Markets, and Class at the Turn of the Century*. New York: Verso, 1996.

Olzak, Susan. *The Dynamics of Ethnic Competition and Conflict*. Stanford: Stanford University Press, 1991.

Oppenheimer, Franz. *Die Judenstatistik des preußischen Kriegsministeriums*. Munich: Verlag für Kulturpolitik, 1922.

———. "Stammesbewusstsein und Volksbewusstsein." *Die Welt* (February 18, 1910): 139–43.

"Ost und West." *Ost und West* (January 1901): 1–2.

Pappenheim, Bertha. "Das Interesse der Juden an V. Internationalen Kongress zur Bekämpfung des Mädchenhandels." *Ost und West* (August 1913): 601–6.

Paul-Schiff, Maximilian. "Die Judentaufen in Wien." *Ost und West* (March 1904): 193–98.

Pawel, Ernst. *The Labyrinth of Exile: A Life of Theodor Herzl*. New York: Farrar, Straus and Giroux, 1989.

Peretz, Itzhak Leyb. "Vier Testamente." *Ost und West* (September 1901): 697–702.

Perles, Felix. *Boussets "Religion des Judentums im neutestamentlichen Zeitalter" kritisch untersucht*. Berlin: Wolf Peiser, 1903.

Perles, Rosalie. "Henryk Glicenstein." *Ost und West* (March 1903): 177–94.

Pulzer, Peter. *Jews and the German State: A Political History of a Minority, 1848–1933*. Oxford: Blackwell, 1992.

Pykett, Lyn. "Reading the Periodical Press: Text and Context." *Victorian Periodicals Review* 52 (Fall 1989): 101–9.

Reichmann, Eva. "Der Bewußtseinswandel der deutschen Juden." In *Deutsches Judentum im Krieg und Revolution, 1916–1923*, 516–62. Ed. Werner E. Mosse and Arnold Paucker. Schriftenreihe wissenschaftlicher Abhandlungen des Leo Baeck Instituts 33. Tübingen: Mohr, 1971.

Reinharz, Jehuda. *Chaim Weizmann: The Making of a Zionist Leader.* New York: Oxford University Press, 1985.

———. *Fatherland or Promised Land? The Dilemma of the German Jew, 1893–1914.* Ann Arbor: University of Michigan Press, 1975.

———, ed. *Dokumente zur Geschichte des deutschen Zionismus, 1882–1933.* Schriftenreihe wissenschaftlicher Abhandlungen des Leo Baeck Instituts 37. Tübingen: Mohr, 1981.

Reinharz, Jehuda, and Walter Schatzberg, eds. *The Jewish Response to German Culture: From the Enlightenment to the Second World War.* Hanover, N.H.: University Press of New England, 1985.

Review of *Vom Ghetto zu Ghetto*, by E. N. Adler. "Literarische Rundschau." *Ost und West* (January 1910): 41–44.

Richarz, Monika, ed. *Jüdisches Leben in Deutschland. Selbstzeugnisse zur Sozialgeschichte.* Stuttgart: Deutsche Verlags-Anstalt, 1979. 3 vols.

Ringer, Fritz. "*Bildung*: The Social and Ideological Context of the German Historical Tradition." *History of European Ideas* 10 (1989): 193–202.

———. *The Decline of the German Mandarins: The German Academic Community, 1890–1933.* Cambridge, Mass.: Harvard University Press, 1969.

Robertson, Ritchie. "National Stereotypes in Prague German Fiction." *Colloquia Germanica* 22 (1989): 116–36.

Rodrigue, Aron. *French Jews, Turkish Jews: The Alliance Israélite Universelle and the Politics of Jewish Schooling in Turkey, 1860–1925.* Bloomington: Indiana University Press, 1990.

Roper, Katherine. *German Encounters with Modernity: Novels of Imperial Berlin.* Atlantic Highlands, N.J.: Humanities Press International, 1991.

Roskies, David. *Against the Apocalypse: Responses to Catastrophe in Modern Jewish Culture.* Cambridge, Mass.: Harvard University Press, 1984.

Rozenblit, Marsha L. "The Assertion of Identity—Jewish Student Nationalism at the University of Vienna before the First World War." *Year Book of the Leo Baeck Institute* 27 (1982): 171–87.

———. "The Jews of the Dual Monarchy." *Austrian History Yearbook* 23 (1992): 162ff.

———. *The Jews of Vienna, 1867–1914: Assimilation and Identity.* Albany: State University of New York Press, 1983.

Ruppin, Arthur. *Die Juden der Gegenwart. Eine sozialwissenschaftliche Studie.* 1911. Berlin: Jüdischer Verlag, 1920.

Rürup, Reinhard. *Emanzipation und Antisemitismus. Studien zur "Judenfrage" der bürgerlichen Gesellschaft.* Kritische Studien zur Geschichtswissenschaft 15. Göttingen: Vandenhoeck and Ruprecht, 1975.

Said, Edward W. *Orientalism.* New York: Vintage, 1979.

Salter, Siegbert. "Das Glück des Hauses Löbenthal. Skizze aus Berlin W." *Ost und West* (December 1905): 797–800.

———. "Kleine Ursachen . . ." *Ost und West* (October 1904): 709–14.

———. "Szene aus Berlin W. Die Tempelfahrt." *Ost und West* (September 1905): 593–96.

Samter, N. "Berliner Judentaufen." *Ost und West* (November 1902): 783–86; (December 1902): 811–20.

———. *Judentaufen im neunzehnten Jahrhundert. Mit besonderer Berücksichtigung Preußens.* Berlin: M. Poppelauer, 1906.

Samuel, B. [Binjamin Segel]. "Das Judenelend in Galizien." *Ost und West* (February 1911): 101–8; (March 1911): 197–206.

———. "Volkswohlstand und Volksaufklärung." *Ost und West* (July 1911): 593–600.

Saphra, B. [Binjamin Segel]. "Jüdische Kämpfe um Freiheit um Recht. Ein Rückblick auf die letzten 125 Jahre jüdischer Geschichte." *Ost und West* (January 1916): 29–66; (February–March 1916): 123–38; (June–July 1916): 243–54.

Sartre, Jean-Paul. *Anti-Semite and Jew.* Trans. George J. Becker. New York: Schocken, 1948.

Schach, Fabius. "Der deutsch-jüdische Jargon." *Ost und West* (March 1901): 179–90.

———. *Über die Zukunft Israels: Eine kritische Betrachtung.* Berlin: M. Poppelauer, 1904.

———. "Zur Psychologie des Renegatentums." *Ost und West* (July 1903): 451–62.

"Die Schicksalsstunde des deutschen Judentums." *Jüdische Rundschau* (November 9, 1923): 559–60.

Schmidt, Ulrike. "Jüdische Bibliotheken in Frankfurt am Main: Vom Anfang des 19. Jahrhunderts bis 1938." *Archiv für die Geschichte des Buchwesens* 29 (1987): 235–67.

Schnabel, Heinz. "Sophie Blum-Lazarus." *Ost und West* (June 1908): 357–60.

Scholem, Gershom. *On Jews and Judaism in Crisis: Selected Essays.* New York: Schocken, 1976.

———. *Mi-berlin li-yerushalayim* [From Berlin to Jerusalem]. Tel Aviv: Am Oved, 1982.

———. "On the Social Psychology of the Jews in Germany, 1900–1922." In *Jews and Germans from 1860 to 1933: The Problematic Symbiosis.* Ed. David Bronsen. Heidelberg: Winter, 1979.

Schweikart, Patricinio P. "Reading Ourselves: Toward a Feminist Theory of Reading." In *Speaking of Gender,* 17–44. Ed. Elaine Showalter. New York: Routledge, 1989.

Segall, Jakob. *Die deutschen Juden als Soldaten im Kriege, 1914–1918.* Berlin: Philo Verlag, 1922.

[Segel, Binjamin.] "Genug der Versäumnisse. Ein Ruf zur Tat." *Ost und West* (October 1911): 833–42.

———. "Der Krieg als Lehrmeister." *Ost und West* (September–December 1914): 625–40.

———. "Der stille Pogrom. Wehruf eines russischen Juden." *Ost und West* (November 1911): 945–50.

Segel, Binjamin. *Am Tage des Gerichts. Ost und West* (December 1915): 481–92; (January–February 1916): 53–72; (March–April 1916): 115–22; (May–June 1916): 189–206.

———. "Die Einweihung des Tempels." *Ost und West* (March 1908): 167–76.

———. "Elisa Orzeszko." *Ost und West* (July 1912): 443–50.

———. *Die Entdeckungsreise des Herrn Dr. Theodor Lessing zu den Ostjuden.* Lemberg: Hatikwah, 1910.

———. "Die Frau im jüdischen Sprichwort." *Ost und West* (May 1903): 167–76.

———. *A Lie and a Libel: The History of the Protocols of the Elders of Zion.* Trans. and ed. Richard S. Levy. Lincoln: University of Nebraska Press, 1995.

———. *Morija und Golgotha.* Berlin: M. Poppelauer, 1915.

———. "Morija und Golgotha." *Ost und West* (January–May 1915): 45–60.

———. "Der Niedergang des österreichischen Antisemitismus." *Ost und West* (October 1910): 671–76.

———. "Philosophie des Pogroms." *Ost und West* (March–April 1923): 59–92.

———. *Die polnische Judenfrage.* Berlin: Georg Stilke, 1916.

———. *Die Protokolle der Weisen von Zion, kritisch beleuchtet: Eine Erledigung.* Berlin: Philo Verlag, 1924.

———. *Rumänien und seine Juden: Zeitgemässe Studien.* Berlin: Nibelungen, 1918.

———. *Der Weltkrieg und das Schicksal der Juden.* Berlin: Georg Stilke, 1915.

———. *Welt-Krieg, Welt-Revolution, Welt-Verschwörung, Welt-Oberregierung.* Berlin: Philo Verlag, 1926.

Segev, Tom. *The Seventh Million: The Israelis and the Holocaust,* trans. Haim Watzman. New York: Hill and Wang, 1993.

Sessa, Karl B. A. *Unser Verkehr: Eine Posse in einem Aufzuge.* Leipzig: Dycksche Buchhandlung, 1916.

Shaked, Gershon. *Die Macht der Identität. Essays über jüdische Schriftsteller.* Königstein/Ts.: Veröffentlichung des Leo Baeck Instituts, 1986.

Shedletzky, Itta. "Belletristik und Literaturdiskussion in den jüdischen Zeitschriften in Deutschland, 1837–1918." Ph.D. dissertation, Hebrew University, Jerusalem, 1985.

———. "Some Observations on the Popular Zeitroman in the Jewish Weeklies in Germany from 1870–1900." *Canadian Review of Comparative Literature* 9 (September 1982): 349–56.

Shulvass, Moses A. *From East to West: The Westward Migration of Jews from Eastern Europe during the Seventeenth and Eigtheenth Centuries.* Detroit: Wayne State University Press, 1971.

Skorra, Thekla [Binjamin Segel]. "Süßkind von Trimberg: Ein jüdischer Minnesänger." *Ost und West* (March–April 1923): 95–100.

Somogni, Tamar. *Die Schejnen und die Prosten: Untersuchungen zum Schönheitsideal der Ostjuden in Bezug auf Körper und Kleidung unter besonderer Berücksichtigung des Chassidismus.* Berlin: Reimer, 1982.

Sorkin, David. "Emancipation and Assimilation—Two Concepts and Their Application to German-Jewish History." *Year Book of the Leo Baeck Institute* 35 (1990): 17–33.

———. *Moses Mendelssohn and the Religious Enlightenment.* Berkeley: University of California Press, 1996.

———. *The Transformation of German Jewry, 1780–1840.* New York: Oxford University Press, 1987.

Sperlings Zeitschriften-Adressbuch. Hand- und Jahrbuch der deutschen Presse 41 (1902): 16.

Stanislawski, Michael. *For Whom Do I Toil? Judah Leib Gordon and the Crisis of Russian Jewry.* New York: Oxford University Press, 1988.

Stern, Selma. *The Court Jew: A Contribution to the History of the Period of Absolutism in Central Europe.* Trans. Ralph Weiman. Philadelphia: Jewish Publication Society, 1950.

Struck, Hermann, and Arnold Zweig. *Das ostjüdische Antlitz*. Berlin: Welt-Verlag, 1919.

Swaffar, Janet, Katherine Arens, and Heidi Byrnes. *Reading for Meaning: An Integrated Approach to Language Learning*. Englewood Cliffs, N.J.: Prentice-Hall, 1991.

Syndram, Karl Ulrich. *Kulturpublizistik und nationales Selbstverständnis*. Berlin: Mann, 1989.

Theilhaber, Felix A. *Der Untergang der deutschen Juden: Eine volkswirtschaftliche Studie*, 2nd ed. Berlin: Jüdischer Verlag, 1921.

Thompson, Richard H. *Theories of Ethnicity: A Critical Reappraisal*. New York: Greenwood Press, 1989.

Tobias, A. "Neues von den Falaschas." *Ost und West* (April 1907): 231–38.

Tönnies, Ferdinand. *Gemeinschaft und Gesellschaft. Grundbegriffe der reinen Soziologie*. Leipzig: R. Reisland, 1887.

Toury, Jacob. *Die jüdische Presse im österreichischen Kaiserreich: Ein Beitrag zur Problematik der Akkulturation, 1802–1918*. Schriftenreihe wissenschaftlicher Abhandlungen des Leo Baeck Instituts 41. Tubingen: Mohr, 1983.

———. *Soziale und politische Geschichte der Juden in Deutschland, 1848–1914: Zwischen Revolution, Reaktion und Emanzipation*. Düsseldorf: Droste 1977.

Treitschke, Heinrich von. "Unsere Aussichten." *Preußische Jahrbücher* 44–45 (November 1879). Reprinted in *Der Berliner Antisemitismusstreit*, 112–16. Ed. Walter Boehlich. Frankfurt a.M.: Insel, 1988.

Tuch, Ernst. "Jüdische Bauern auf deutschem Boden." *Ost und West* (July 1901): 499–512.

———. "Die wirtschaftliche Aufgabe der deutschen Judenheit." *Ost und West* (January 1901): 55–58.

"Urteile der Presse über die 'Jüdischen Volksliederabende.' " *Ost und West* (December 1912): 1169–1200.

Verax [Binjamin Segel]. "Jüdische Rundschau." *Im deutschen Reich* 27 (January 1921): 18–26.

Vital, David. *The Origins of Zionism*. Oxford: Oxford University Press, 1975.

Vogel, Rolf. *Ein Stück von uns: Deutsche Juden in deutschen Armeen, 1813–1976. Eine Dokumentation*. Mainz: Hase and Koehler, 1977.

Volkov, Shulamit. *Jüdisches Leben und Antisemitismus im 19. und 20. Jahrhundert*. Munich: Beck, 1990.

Wagner, Richard. [Freigedank, K.] "Das Judenthum in der Musik." *Neue Zeitschrift für Musik*, September 3 and 6, 1850.

Wanninski, Jude, ed. *The 1988 Media Guide*. Morristown, N.J.: Polyconomics, 1988.

Warszawski, A. [Binjamin Segel]. "Die Lehrerin." *Ost und West* (May 1913): 389–94; (June 1913): 445–58.

Wassermann, Henry. "The *Fliegende Blätter* as a Source for the Social History of German Jewry." *Year Book of the Leo Baeck Institute* 28 (1983): 93–138.

Weiner, Marc A. *Richard Wagner and the Anti-Semitic Imagination*. Lincoln: University of Nebraska Press, 1995.

Weininger, Otto. *Geschlecht und Charakter: Eine prinzipielle Untersuchung*. Vienna: Braumüller, 1904.

Weiss, Bernhard. "Zwei Freunde (Ungedrückte Briefe von Salomon Munk aus den Jahren 1827–1860)." Ed. M. A. Klausner. *Ost und West* (June 1908): 373–86.

Weizmann, Chaim. *Trial and Error*. New York: Harper, 1949.

Wenzel, Edith. "Friedrich Torberg: 'Süßkind von Trimberg.' Jüdische Identitäts-suche in Deutschland." In *Mittelalter-Rezeption II*, 367–81. Ed. J. Kühnel, H.-D. Mück, Ursula Müller, and U. Müller. Göppinger Arbeiten zur Germanistik. Göppingen, 1982.

Wertheimer, Jack. "The 'Ausländerfrage' at Institutions of Higher Learning: A Controversy over Russian-Jewish Students in Imperial Germany." *Year Book of the Leo Baeck Institute* 25 (1982): 187–215.

———. "Between Tsar and Kaiser: The Radicalization of Russian-Jewish University Students in Germany." *Year Book of the Leo Baeck Institute* 28 (1983): 329–50.

———. "The German-Jewish Experience: Toward a Useable Past." *American Jewish Archives* 40 (November 1988): 417–23.

———. *Unwelcome Strangers: East European Jews in Imperial Germany*. New York: Oxford University Press, 1987.

"Das westjüdische Kulturproblem." *Ost und West* (February 1904): 73–88.

Williams, Robert C. *Culture in Exile: Russian Émigrés in Germany, 1881–1941*. Ithaca: Cornell University Press, 1972.

Winz, Leo. "Berlin/Winz." File "Archives-Allemagne." Alliance Israelite Universelle Archives, Paris.

———. Letter to Adolf Friedemann. August 15, 1903. In *The Uganda Controversy*, 1:68–71. Ed. Michael Heymann. Jerusalem: Israel University Press, 1970.

———. Papers. Files A136. Central Zionist Archives, Jerusalem.

Wohlgemuth, Joseph. *Der Weltkrieg im Lichte des Judentums*. Berlin: Jeschurun, 1915.

Wolff, B. [Binjamin Segel]. "Die Juden als Wehrvolk." *Ost und West* (October 1913): 869–76.

York-Steiner, Heinrich. "Koriander, der Chasan." *Ost und West* (October 1904): 687–92; (November 1904): 783–90; (December 1904): 859–72.

Ysaye [Binjamin Segel?]. "Die Jüdin. Eine Wiener Skizze." *Ost und West* (April 1904): 269–71.

Zborowski, Mark, and Elizabeth Herzog. *Life Is with People: The Culture of the Shtetl*. 1952. New York: Schocken, 1962.

Zechlin, Egmont. *Die deutsche Politik und die Juden im Ersten Weltkrieg*. Göttingen: Vandenhoeck and Ruprecht, 1969.

Zimmermann, Moshe. "Jewish Nationalism and Zionism in German-Jewish Students' Organisations." *Year Book of the Leo Baeck Institute* 27 (1982): 129–54.

Zipperstein, Steven. *Elusive Prophet: Aḥad Haʿam and the Origins of Zionism*. Berkeley: University of California Press, 1993.

Zlocisti, Theodor. "Jüdische Volkslesehallen." *Ost und West* (April 1903): 277–82.

—m—g— [Binjamin Segel]. "Die Taufseuche in Wien." *Ost und West* (June 1905): 361–72; (December 1905): 749–62.

INDEX

Abwehrorganisation (Abwehrvereine). *See* Antidefamation; Centralverein

Academia, 26–27. *See also* Antisemitism, universities and; East European Jews, as students

Acculturation versus dissimilation, 15, 34, 36, 52, 53, 55, 60, 62, 71, 72, 99, 101, 142, 165, 171n. 1, 199n. 8, 203n. 49, 203n. 50

Adelson, Leslie A., 217n. 19

Advertising, 16, 44–45, 46 (fig. 4), 48, 102, 162, 201n. 24

Agnon, Shmu'el Yosef, 186n. 20

Agudat Yisrael (Agudes Yisroel), 69

Aḥad Haᶜam, 35, 36, 38, 45, 68, 72, 82, 124, 134, 190n. 67

Aleichem, Sholem, 45, 68

Allgemeine Zeitung des Judentums, 31, 40, 74

Alliance Israélite Universelle, 45, 47, 134, 146, 180n. 77, 182n. 104, 182n. 106, 203n. 45

Altneuland controversy, 38–39, 72, 95, 179n. 72, 180n. 76

Anderson, Benedict, 33

Antidefamation (and apologetic anti-antisemitism), 37, 152, 157, 160, 161, 162, 164, 166; in the framework of Abwehrorganisationen, 84, 143; *See also* Centralverein

Antisemitism, 21, 22–23, 24, 33, 34, 50, 67, 70, 78, 79, 80, 81, 84, 88, 90, 111, 136, 140, 151, 154, 165, 166, 167, 169; antijudaism versus, 165; Antisemitic Petition of 1881–82 and, 66, 80; compared with anti-Germanism, 148; comparative European, 27, 36, 151, 166, 167, 169, 179n. 66; during the Weimar period, 159–61; during World War I, 142, 160; ethnic conflict and, 161; in modern German history, 160; in the professions, 67, 79–80; Jewish apologetics for, 34, 142, 147, 150;

Jewish "discourse" and, 146; Jewish psychology and, 143; political parties and, 37, 66; racialistic, 34, 65, 79, 165; universities and, 25–26, 79, 192nn. 7, 8, 10, 193n. 12; war profiteering stereotype and, 153, 157, 211n. 11. *See also* Self-hatred

Apostates. *See* Conversion to Christianity

Arendt, Hannah, 192n. 1

Art, 16, 27, 45; decorative, 118, 119 (fig. 12); Eastern Jewish, 96; patrons and collectors of, 45, 115–16, 202n. 47; photography and, 42. *See also* Marketing and audience; *and individual artists*

Artists, 116, 124; women, 118. *See also individual entries*

Asch, Sholem, 45

Aschheim, Steven, 18, 19, 20, 173n. 19

Ashkenazic Jewry, 17, 34, 59

Assimilationism, 30, 75, 81; as stereotype, 70–71 *See also* Parvenu stereotype; Self-hatred

Audience. *See* Marketing and audience

Auerbach, Berthold, 86

Austro-Hungary (Habsburg Empire): Jews in, 22, 23, 29, 40, 80, 133, 169, 176n. 36; compared with Jews in Germany, 29, 36

Autonomism, Jewish cultural, 29, 35, 152, 163, 169; Diaspora nationalism, 35, 69; kehillah as model for, 186n. 15

Ba'aalei teshuvah (returners), 30, 80, 81–83, 95, 193n. 21. *See also* Acculturation versus dissimilation

Bakst, Leo, 205n. 76

Bar Kochba, 149

Baron Hirsch (and The Jewish Colonial Association), 133, 203n. 44

Baron Hirsch schools, 133

Bauer, Felice, 73, 101. *See also* Kafka, Franz

Baum, Vicki, 117, 120–34, 137, 205n. 73, 208n. 102; "Im alten Haus," 118, 120; "Rafael Gutmann," 118, 120–34, 207n. 94

Beethoven, Ludwig von, 108, 127, 130; *Fidelio*, 127–28, 130

"Beethoven's erste Liebe," 108

Befreiungskriege, 149

Benjamin, Walter, 141

Berdichevsky, Micha Yosef (Bin Gurion), 124, 178n. 61, 191n. 82

Berkowitz, Michael, 178n. 62

Berlin: Jews in, 15, 26, 28, 30, 60, 85, 88, 96, 100, 102, 115, 125, 162; East European Jewry in, 25, 160, 175n. 16; Jewish settlement in, 92, 175n. 16, 197n. 60; Salondamen in, 100–101, 200n. 10; Tiergarten neighborhood, 92–93. See also *Ost und West*; Pogroms, Scheunenviertel

Berlin Jüdische Lesehalle (und Bibliothek), 30, 31, 32 (fig. 1), 177n. 42

Berliner Illustrirte Zeitung, 44

Bernfeld, Simon, 16

Betteljuden, 21, 22, 24, 59, 67

Bhabha, Homi, 199n. 8

Bible, 51, 60, 89; terms for, 196n. 53

Bigart, Jacques, 203n. 45

Bildung, 25, 59, 64, 101, 124, 188n. 40; as desired by East European Jews, 27, 110–11, 188n. 53. *See also* Respectability

Birnbaum, Nathan, 40, 45, 69–72, 79, 82, 191n. 78; "Das westjüdische Kulturproblem," 69–70; "Etwas über Ost- und Westjudentum," 71

Bismarck, Otto von, 167

Blacks and Africa, 198n. 65; East European Jews and, 198n. 65; in the fiction of *Ost und West*, 93, 94

Bodenheimer, Max, 177n. 41

Brainin, Ruben, 177n. 46

Breines, Paul, 145, 209n. 118, 213n. 34

Brenner, Michael, 186n. 20

Breslau, 114, 115

Brieger-Wasservogel, Lothar, 87, 89, 91, 196n. 48, 196n. 52; "Das alte Testament," 89–90

Buber, Martin, 16, 17, 29, 36, 39, 40, 45,

82, 163, 177n. 41, 180n. 79, 181n. 95, 193n. 22, 212n. 31

Bund, Di, 21, 35, 82, 178n. 62

Butler, Judith, 217n. 23

Catholics, 37, 167

Centralverein deutscher Staatsbürger Jüdischen Glaubens, 31, 143, 162, 204n. 66

Chamberlain, Houston Stewart, 148, 198n. 65

Class, German-Jewish middle, 63, 65–66, 74, 144, 167–68, 189n. 61, 190n. 65, 192n. 7, 200n. 15; Besitz- versus Bildungsbürgertum, 83, 138, 191n. 89; conflict within German-Jewish middle, 83, 84, 95, 103 (116 women); crisis of Bildungsprole- tariat, 79–80; historiography of middle, 181n. 96; middle-brow cul- ture and, 44; terminology, 200n. 15, 210n. 1; the public sphere and de- velopment of, 200n. 10. See also Fe- male readers; Generation gap; Male readers; Marketing and audience

Conservatism, political, 65, 66, 89. See also Nationalism

Conversion to Christianity ("apostasy") or Baptism, 57, 60, 62, 80–81, 84, 85, 89, 93, 99, 108, 109, 110, 111, 154, 187n. 33, 194n. 34, 204n. 57, 212n. 18; as stereotype, 89, 146, 149; compared to Trotzjuden, 81, 193n. 16; susceptibility of univer- sity students to, 81, 193n. 15. See also Genres, anticonversion and anti-intermarriage fiction

Democratic Faction (Demokratische Fraktion) of Zionist Organization, 36, 37, 79, 82, 144, 178n. 61

Department stores, 46 (fig. 4), 102. See also Tietz family

Deutsche Rundschau, 73

Dissimilation. See Acculturation versus dissimilation

Dohm, Christian Wilhelm von, 62, 63, 70

Dolorosa, 118

Domestic workers, 107

Dreyfus trials, 21, 36

Dubnow, Simon, 35. See also Auto- nomism

East European Jews, 15–16, 21–32, 40, 47, 77, 86, 168; as students, 25, 80, 192n. 10, 210n. 4; as source of embarrassment for Western Jews, 19, 173n. 15; "cult" of the Ostjuden, 18, 47–48, 72, 81, 157–58, 162–63, 212n. 31, 217n. 16; during the Weimar period, 160; demograph- ics, 179n. 67; forced labor in Ger- many and, 140, 160; Galician ver- sus Russian, 29; gender, 99, 199n. 3; German language and, 40; mar- riage with Western Jews, 203n. 49; negative portrayal of, 196n. 50; stereotype of the "ghetto Jew," 64, 122–27, 67, 70, 100, 180n. 82, 199n. 6; shtetl romanticism and, 77, 156, 163; post-Holocaust renais- sance of, 163, 173n. 11; promotion of by means of positive and neg- ative stereotyping, 49, 77–78, 99–100, 108, 162, 163; public-sphere symbiosis with Western Jewry and, 156, 195n. 41. See also Berlin; Bil- dung; Eastern/traditional model of Judaism; Ethnic Judaism/Jewish- ness; Female readers; German Jewry; Immigration of East Euro- pean Jews to Germany; Intellectual readers; Marketing and audience; Male readers; Masculinity; Ostju- den; Philanthropy; Ost und West; Pogroms; Respectability; Western Jewry

Eastern/traditional model of Judaism, 44, 55–59, 75, 76, 88–90, 100–101, 108–9, 153–54, 162

Edinburgh Review, 74

Education and schools. See Female read- ers; Maskilim

Efron, John, 184n. 122
Ehrenpreis, Markus, 29
Einstein, Albert, 141
Elias, Norbert, 173n. 15
Emancipation (of Jews), 24, 36, 37, 59, 62, 63, 167, 189n. 55
England, Jews in, 60, 80, 85. *See also* Antisemitism; Immigration of East European Jews to Germany
Enlightenment: European, 15, 17, 25, 34, 36, 41, 56, 57, 144; German (Aufklärung), 62, 167
Enlightenment, Jewish. *See* Haskalah
Ethnic Judaism/Jewishness and Pan-Jewishness (or Jewish nationalism, Jewish Renaissance), 15, 16, 20, 30, 31, 32, 33, 39, 42, 44, 48, 51–52, 53–54, 56, 67–76, 79–81, 82, 101–2, 103–4, 110–12, 123, 137, 144, 145, 151, 152, 154–57, 160, 167, 168, 192n. 6, 194n. 31, 217n. 11; Eastern compared with Western, 33, 36, 37, 69, 73; gender and, 199n. 2; Orthodoxy and, 72, 144; state versus cultural Jewish nationalism, 35, 40; stereotyping and, 52, 54; terminology, 172n. 3, 185n. 4; universalism versus particularism, 41, 155; visibility and conspicuousness of, 16, 35, 42, 44, 85, 86, 140, 143, 169; Zivilisation versus Kultur, 70–71. *See also* Female readers; Male readers; Pluralism, cultural; Marketing and audience; Stereotyping
Ethnic magazines: *Ost und West* as prototype, 53, 159.
Ethnicity: as source of competition and conflict, 161; contemporary American, 159, 167; in Kaiserreich, 167. *See also* Antisemitism; Ethnic Judaism/Jewishness; Pluralism, cultural
Ethnography, 147, 216n. 75

Feiwel, Berthold, 36, 197n. 57
Female readers (of *Ost und West*), 44, 98–138; Alliance Israélite Universelle and, 105; artistic depiction of, 104, 106; as consumers (of culture), 100–103, 202n. 32 (reading habits); class and, 103, 116, 132, 201n. 25; domesticity and family and, 99, 100, 102, 103, 111; education and, 101, 103, 136; historiography and, 102, 210n. 3; Jewish Women's League (*Jüdischer Frauenbund*) and, 104, 107, 118, 135; professional structure of, 99, 202n. 33; promotion of the uplifted (artist) Ostjude as object of idealization and philanthropy and, 99, 107, 110–37, 202n. 47; religious observance and, 100, 104, 199n. 4, 200n. 14, 202n. 34; social work and welfare, 104–6, 116–23, 202n. 38; the middle-brow and, 103; urban modernity and, 102, 200n. 16; women's organizations and, 202n. 39. *See also* Male readers; Marketing and audience; Parvenu stereotype, and parvenue stereotype; Philanthropy
Femininity. *See* Masculinity
Film, 16, 162, 205n. 75
Fishman, Joshua, 82, 186
Fliegende Blätter, 91, 141
Folklore, 29, 44, 45, 116; *See also* Ethnography; Music
Forchheimer, Stephanie, 135
Foucault, Michel, 174n. 20
France: Jews in, 60, 62, 80, 165, 187n. 35. *See also* Antisemitism; Immigration of East European Jews to Germany
Frankfurt am Main, 135, 207n. 93
Franzos, Karl Emil, 86, 88, 196n. 50
Freistatt, Die, 47, 96, 134
Freud, Sigmund, 22, 126
Freytag, Gustav, 87; *Soll und Haben*, 87, 114, 153, 215n. 69

Gartenlaube, Die, 103, 201n. 27
Geiger, Abraham, 163
Geiger, Ludwig, 31
Gelber, Mark H., 207n. 90
Gemeinschaft (community) versus Gesellschaft (society), 181n. 95

Gemeindeblatt der Jüdischen Gemeinde zu Berlin, 16, 103, 162, 201n. 24

Gender. *See* Masculinity

Generation gap, 81, 82, 83, 95, 193n. 18

Genres, 49; anticonversion and anti-intermarriage fiction, 86, 108, 109, 110–11, 130; *Dorfgeschichte* ("village story"), 86, 206n. 90; *Ghetto-geschichte* ("ghetto story"), 86, 120, 123, 124, 125, 127, 206n. 90; historical fiction, 87; in *Ost und West*, 44, 182n. 100; in the *Rundschauzeit-schriften*, 74; Eastern versus Western Jewish, 45; Realist novel, 87, 206n. 90; regionalism and *Heimat-kunst*, 206n. 90; (Naturalist) satirical sketch, 196n. 51; specific functioning of, 151; (satirical) *Zeitprosa* ("contemporary prose fiction"), 78, 87, 88, 90, 92, 100, 129, 135–37, 197n. 57. *See also* Antidefamation; Journals, magazines, and newspapers; Naturalism; *Ost und West*; *Ost und West*, literary contest in

Gentz, Ismael, 112; "Im Tempel zu Tripolis," 112, 113 (fig. 9)

German Jewry, 142, 166; as "subculture," 66, 70, 74, 199n. 8; class profile, 65; nostalgia for the Kaiserreich, 161; political profile, 65; stereotypes of, 141, 165, 167, 173n. 16, 211n. 10; symbiosis and, 18, 89, 166, 218n. 33

Germany, contemporary: East/West distinctions, 9, 163, 172n. 5

Gilman, Sander, 19, 146–47, 164–65, 217n. 19

Glicenstein, Enrico [Henryk], 40, 115–16, 117 (fig. 11), 123, 205n. 71

Goethe, Johann Wolfgang von, 103, 109, 207n. 93

Goldstein, Moritz, 209n. 121

Gordon, Milton, 171n. 1

Gronemann, Sammy, 180n. 78, 214n. 41

Guggenheim, Ernst, 90; "Der Rabbi," 90

Ha-Shiloah (Aḥad Haᶜam, ed.), 38, 44, 74

Ha-Tsefirah (Sokolov, ed.), 31

Habsburg Empire. *See* Austro-Hungary

Harden, Maximilian, 149, 214n. 51

Hasidism, 17, 82, 163

Haskalah, 56, 59, 60, 67, 84, 167

Hebraism and Hebraists, 27, 51, 60, 67; Hebrew language and culture, 31, 40

Heijermans, Herman, 206n. 83; *Ghetto*, 206n. 83

Heine, Heinrich, 120, 123 (fig. 16), 130

Helphand, Alexander (Parvus), 29

Herder, Johann Gottfried, 172n. 3

Herz, Henriette, 100

Herzl, Theodor, 33, 36, 38, 39, 91, 95, 180n. 74, 180n. 78; *Altneuland*, 38; "Mauschel," 91; Winz and, 38. *See also Altneuland* controversy; Zionism and Zionist organization

Hess, Moses, 36

Hirsch, Samson Raphael, 59

Hirshenberg, Samuel, 40, 118

Holocaust (Shoah or *khurbn*): and historiography, 18, 27, 95, 141, 142, 158, 163, 164, 165, 169, 209n. 114; and transference, 18, 141

Homosexuality, 64, 120, 130, 205n. 73. *See* Masculinity

Horch, Hans Otto, 206n. 86

Höxter, John, 93

Humanities and humanists, 26–27, 29, 80, 216n. 75; versus medicine and law as courses of study for East European Jews in Germany, 27

Humboldt, Wilhelm von, 62, 64

Identity, 172n. 2, 184n. 119; alternative identities, 130–31, 159; identity politics, 20. *See* Marketing and audience; Pluralism, cultural; Stereotyping

Immigration of East European Jews to Germany, 19, 21, 22, 23, 25, 37, 58, 62, 161, 217n. 9; administrative control and harassment, 24, 25, 161, 174n. 3; after World War I,

216n. 6; compared with Polish seasonal workers, 23, 24–25; deportation and expulsion, 24, 66, 80, 146, 160, 193n. 12; differences among immigrants, 20, 25, 160; during World War I, 160; emigration of recent immigrants, 160; foreign investment and, 23; illegal, 23, 27; motivations for, 25; naturalization, 24, 80, 168; professional restrictions, 23, 80, 160, 174n. 6; transmigration (to ships), 23, 25, 174n. 5. *See also* East European Jews; Philanthropy

Integration into German society. *See* Acculturation versus dissimilation

Intellectual readers, 77–97, 140. *See also* Democratic Faction (Demokratische Fraktion) of Zionist Organization; Male readers; Parvenu stereotype

Intellectuals, 16, 79, 165. *See also* Intellectual readers

Intermarriage, 56, 60, 80, 130, 142, 204n. 57. *See also* Genres, anticonversion and anti-intermarriage fiction

Israel. *See* Palestine

Israelit, Der, 31, 186n. 14

Israelitsches Familienblatt, 31

Israëls, Jozef, 41

Jaffé, Robert, 16

Jahn, Friedrich Ludwig "Turnvater," 64

Jeschurun, 212n. 17

Jewish Chronicle, 177n. 44

Jewish nationalism. *See* Ethnic Judaism/ Jewishness

Jewish Renaissance. *See* Ethnic Judaism/ Jewishness

Journalism, 18; as a "Jewish" profession, 80, 147

Journals, magazines, and newspapers, 13, 31, 42, 44, 51, 73, 80, 184n. 126, 185n. 1; as a means of imagining the nation, 44, 73; Hebrew-language press, 51–52, 124, 195n. 44; the Rundschauzeitschrift or Kultur-rundschau ("national-cultural review"), 40, 73–74, 191n. 90; technology of, 42. *See also* Marketing and audience; *names of specific publications*

Jude, Der (Buber, ed.), 39, 47, 96, 161

Judenzählung (census of Jews in military), 140, 142, 151, 152, 157, 211n. 12

Jüdische Rundschau, Die (multiple eds.), 31, 32, 39, 40, 180n. 77, 218n. 29

Jüdische Volkspartei, 48, 160

Jüdischer Verlag: signet and *Ost und West,* 181n. 90

Jugendstil, 130, 192n. 6. *See also* Lilien, Ephraim Mose

Jung Israel, 28

Jünger, Ernst, 149

Jungmann, Max, 177n. 46

Kadimah, 28, 176n. 28

Kafka, Franz, 13, 22, 72–73, 95, 101, 141, 198n. 68; "Brief an den Vater," 95; journals and, 13; minoritarian literature and, 13, 216n. 1

Kaplan, Marion, 165, 202n. 50

Karpeles, Gustav, 31

Katz, Jacob, 66, 188n. 40

Kaufmann, Fritz Mordechai, 47, 82, 134, 163

Kaufmann, Hugo, 124; "Einheit" (from "Einheitsdenkmal"), 129 (fig. 18); "Freiheit" (from "Einheitsdenkmal"), 126 (fig. 17), 209n. 112; "Den Helfern in der Not," 125 (fig. 16)

Kellner, Leon, 107

Key, Ellen, 199n. 4; *Das Jahrhundert des Kindes,* 199n. 4

Klausner, M. A., 199n. 1

Klee, Alfred, 195n. 41

Kohut, Adolf, 115, 120; "Lina Morgenstern," 115

Komitee für den Osten, 152, 157, 158

Kompert, Leopold, 86

Königsberg, 115

Kraus, Karl, 126

Krochmal, Nathan, 68

Kunstwart, debate, 209n. 121

Labisch, Richard, 42
Lamm, Louis, 215n. 59
Landauer, Gustav, 181n. 95
Langer, Georg (Jírí), 72, 82
Lazarus, Nahida Ruth, 199n. 4; *Das Jüdische Weib*, 199n. 4
Lehmann, Siegfried, 101
Leipzig, 160
Lemberg, 29, 23n. 39
Lessing, Gotthold Ephraim, 60, 167, 187n. 34
Lessing, Theodor, 197n. 57; *Jüdischer Selbsthaß* 197n. 57
Levin, Shmarya, 28
Liberal Judaism, 31, 57, 86, 120, 185n. 10, 212n. 27
Liberalism, political: German, 37, 65, 167, 189n. 55, 189n. 56
Libraries (and Reading rooms), 30, 31, 102–3, 177n. 43
Liebermann, Max, 41, 112; "Weib mit Ziegen," 112, 114 (fig. 10)
Lilien, Ephraim Mose, 16, 17, 39, 40, 41, 42, 118, 181n. 91, 197n. 57
Lippmann, Walter, 183n. 117
Lissauer, Ernst, 148
Literature, 45, 48, 111; as course of study, 26; Eastern Jewish, 45, 74. *See names of specific texts; names of specific writers*
Liturgy (Jewish), 153, 154; "liturgy of destruction," 166. *See also* Yom Kippur
Loewe, Heinrich, 30, 31–32, 39, 79, 176n. 41, 177n. 55
Lublinski, Samuel, 16

Maimon, Salomon, 25
Male readers, 138, 139–58; as German nationalist, 139, 149, 150; age of, 141; Centralverein and, 140, 143; class and, 139; level of observance of, 142, 143; Zionism and, 144, 145; stereotype of the yekke, 141. *See also* Female readers; Intellectual readers; Parvenu stereotype

Mann, Thomas, 64, 208n. 105; *Bekenntnisse eines Unpolitischen*, 70
Marketing and audience, 16, 17, 20, 32, 39, 40, 44, 45, 49, 51, 52–53, 54, 63, 70, 75, 79, 96, 125, 139, 156, 157, 162, 180n. 78; the middle-brow and, 44, 63, 96, 103; women and, 99, 100, 101
Marr, Wilhelm, 37
Masculinity, 56, 112, 126, 127, 128, 132, 137, 148, 157, 213n. 36; as discursively "objective" or "neutral," 132, 145–50, 214n. 47; Charakter (integrity) and, 81; in the military (*Tauglichkeit*), 137–38, 140–41, 142, 144, 145, 149, 153, 211n. 11, 215nn. 56, 67; in occupations and professions, 56, 79, 80, 160–61; image of the "tough Jew," 143, 144, 145, 155, (149), 196n. 48, 213n. 34; nationalism and, 126 (fig. 17), 144; dueling and, 144; debating and, 28–29, 144; and East European Jewish males, 120, 123, 124, 126–28, 130–32, 134, 143, 145, 149, 154–55, 204n. 69, 209n. 114, 213n. 36; respectability and, 188n. 45, 207n. 93, 212n. 27; Zionism and, 64–65. *See also* Judenzählung; Male readers; World War I
Maskilim, 26, 28, 68, 72, 111, 190n. 70; class and, 68; education in yeshivas, 68, 71, 110; reinvention of traditions, 68. *See also* Ethnic Judaism/Jewishness; Haskalah
Maurer, Trude, 19
Meinecke, Friedrich, 35, 70, 178n. 58
Mendele Moykher-Sforim, 68
Mendelssohn, Moses, 56, 60, 62, 63, 67, 111, 163, 167, 187n. 30
Metz, Josefa, 109; "Sünde: Aus dem Leben eines kleinen Mädchens," 109
Migration. *See* Immigration of East European Jews to Germany
Milgroym, 161

Military: Jews in German, 80, 142. *See also* Masculinity

Mi-mizrah u-ma'aarev (Brainin, ed.), 177n. 46

Minority identity. *See* Ethnic Judaism/Jewishness; Pluralism, cultural

Modernization, 188n. 40. *See also* Western/enlightened model of Judaism

Morgenstern, Lina, 112, 114, 115, 116, 117, 120, 122 (fig. 14), 202n. 40

Mosse, George, 63, 188n. 45, 189n. 55, 212n. 27, 213n. 37

Mosse publishing house, 80

Motzkin, Leo, 28, 36, 82

Mült és jövő, 183n. 109

Mundlak, Rachel, 118

Music, 16, 122, 127–31; collectors, 45; concert and opera attendance of Jewish women, 102, 128, 208n. 102; folk songs, 45, 120, 123 (fig. 16); *Ost und West*'s *Liederabende*, 102, 200n. 19; proto–*Jazz Singer* motif, 130, 152, 204n. 60; recorded, 200n. 19

"Muskeljudentum." *See* Masculinity; Nordau, Max

Nachmärz period, 81

Nadel, Arno, 16, 45

National Socialism (Nazism), 18, 142

Nationalism, 35, 40, 74, 168; comparative European, 35, 179n. 70; conservative versus liberal, 37, 167; state versus cultural, 35, 40. *See also* Ethnic Judaism/Jewishness

Naturalism, 87, 88, 89, 192n. 6, 196n. 51, 206n. 90

Neue Jüdische Monatshefte, 47, 96

Newspapers. *See* Journals, magazines, and newspapers

Nietzsche, Friedrich Wilhelm, 130

Nonbelievers. *See* Conversion to Christianity

Nordau, Max, 38, 39, 64, 145, 149, 180n. 74

Nossig, Alfred, 39

Opera. *See* Music

Orient, Der, 31–32

Oriental Jews, 47, 112, 120, 121 (fig. 13), 182n. 104, 182n. 106

Orthodox Jewry and religious observance (also Neo-Orthodoxy), 33, 55, 56, 57, 60, 86, 212n. 20; in art, 42; in the fiction of *Ost und West*, 120, 125, 126, 127, 153, 156; military and, 143; Mizrachi Zionism and, 58, 144; negative stereotypes of, 125, 133, 207n. 93; *Ost und West* and, 186n. 14; Winz and, 185n. 12; World War I and, 211n. 17, 212n. 19

Ost und West: advertising in, 44–45, 102, 201n. 24; Alliance Israélite Universelle and, 45–47; and androcentricism, 137, 210n. 126; and antifeminism and misogyny, 108, 115, 120, 137; Austro-Hungary and, 30; circulation and popularity of, 16, 50, 96, 172n. 6 184n. 124, 192n. 5; cover art, 41–42, 43 (fig. 2), 112; East European Jewish authors/artists in, 40–41; editorial disclaimers in, 133; "family journals" (Familienblätter) and, 31, 96, 103, 187n. 38; financial profile of, 95–96, 173n. 17; history of, 25, 31, 140, 134; literary contest in, 90, 91, 111, 125, 197n. 56; masthead iconography of, 42, 43 (fig. 3); multivalence (polysemy) and, 42, 48, 51, 75, 91, 117–18, 124–25, 131, 207nn. 90, 91; Orientalism and, 17, 106, 183n. 114, 184n. 122, 194n. 30; privileging of nonpartisanship in, 31, 32, 33, 40, 91, 96; seasonal trends, 204n. 59; subscriptions to, 103, 115, 201n. 28; subtitle(s) of, 47, 54, 69, 172n. 6, 201n. 22; title of, 172n. 5; *See also* Genres; Judenzählung; Music, *Ost und West*'s *Liederabende*; Philanthropy. *See also specific authors and their works*

Ostjuden: as term along with *Westjuden*, 15, 60, 163, 172n. 5. *See also* East European Jews

Ostjüdische Antlitz, Das (A. Zweig, Struck), 216n. 80

Palestine, 33. *See also* Zionism and Zionist organization
Pan-Jewishness. *See* Ethnic Judaism/ Jewishness
Pappenheim, Bertha, 107
Parvenu stereotype, 52, 78, 79, 83, 84–97, 99, 110, 137, 141, 150, 153, 157, 162, 164, 192n. 2, 194n. 30, 195n. 39, 195n. 43, 197n. 62, 204n. 63; and parvenue stereotype, 100, 135–38
Peretz, Isaac Leib, 16, 45, 74, 87
Periodicals. *See* Journals, magazines, and newspapers
Perles, Felix, 45
Perles, Rosalie, 115, 116, 117
Philanthropy, 45, 52–53, 99, 101, 104–6, 117, 133, 140, 202n. 38; as paternalism, 74, 117, 202n. 43; as positive force (or empathy) toward East European Jews, 19, 22, 106, 173n. 16, 198n. 70. *See also* East European Jews; Female readers; Immigration of East European Jews to Germany
Phillipson, Ludwig, 31
Phönix Verlag, 108
Pilichowski, Leopold, 40, 118
Pimonenko, Nicolai, 108; "Baptized Jewess in Her [Home] Village," 108
Pinsker, Leon, 36
Pinski, David, 45
Pluralism, cultural (multiculturalism), 15, 18, 28, 29, 36, 37, 50, 73, 143, 156, 159, 166, 167, 168–69, 189n. 56; accusations of separatism and, 66, 167–68; East-West Jewish symbiosis or biculturalism, 28, 40, 67, 73, 82, 84; Kulturkampf and, 37, 167; myths of cultural homogeneity, 38; within the Jewish community, 145. *See also* Ethnic Judaism/ Jewishness
Pogroms, 21, 135 (fig. 20), 134, 136 (fig. 21), 150, 158, 166, 209n. 115, 213n. 36; in Germany, 158, 160; Kishinev pogrom, 39, 95, 198n. 69, 213n. 36; Scheunenviertel, 158, 160, 218n. 29
Poland, Jewish life in, 163. *See also* East European Jews
Poles, 167; depiction in fiction of, 156
Prague, 73
Press, Jewish. *See* Journals, magazines, and newspapers
Professional structure of Jews, 34, 67, 79–80, 140, 190n. 66. *See also* Antisemitism; Female readers; Immigration of East European Jews to Germany; Male readers
Prostitution and the white slave trade, 107, 203n. 45
Prussia: higher education in, 26
Public sphere (Jewish), 15, 18, 20, 30, 31, 51; versus private sphere, 140, 200n. 10. *See also* Ethnic Judaism/ Jewishness; Female readers; Male readers
Publishing houses. *See names of specific publishers*

Raabe, Wilhelm, 87
Rathenau, Walther, 160
Readers (Readership): of *Ost und West* 44, 50, 79, 138, 139; process of reading, 110. *See also* Female readers; Intellectual readers; Male readers; Marketing and audience
Reading societies (*Lesegesellschaften*), 30
Reception theory, 16, 41, 50. *See also* Marketing and audience
Redlich, Heinrich, 112, 114, 115, 116, 123
Reform Judaism. *See* Liberal Judaism
Respectability, 41, 62, 63–66, 81, 83, 124, 126 (fig. 17), 188n. 45, 189n. 55; and military service, 143
Revue des deux mondes, 74
Riesser, Gabriel, 74, 111
Rimon, 161
Roskies, David, 166, 198n. 69
Rozenblit, Marsha, 34, 188n. 40
Rumania, 22, 60. *See also* East European Jews

Rürup, Reinhard, 169

Russia: Germany and, 23, 40; Jews in, 22, 165; numerus clausus at universities, 26, 175n. 11; opposition to Tsarist regime, 27, 28, 35, 214n. 52; Pale of Settlement defined, 175n. 26. See also East European Jews; Immigration of East European Jews to Germany; Pogroms

Russischer jüdischer wissenschaftlicher Verein, 28, 30, 32, 79, 176n. 28, 176n. 29, 176n. 39

Sacher-Masoch, Leopold, 87

Salomon, Alice, 202n. 40

Salter, Siegbert, 92, 93, 109, 197n. 62; "Szene aus Berlin W. Die Tempelfahrt," 92–93, 109; "Das Glück des Hauses Löbenthal Skizze aus Berlin W.," 92–94

Sartre, Jean-Paul, 165, 177n. 49

Schach, Fabius, 107, 110, 111, 112, 116, 197n. 57, 204n. 63, 204n. 55; "Zur Psychologie des Renegatentums," 110–12

Schatz, Boris, 40

Scheunenviertel pogrom. See Pogroms

Schiller, Friedrich, 103

Schlegel, Dorothea, 100

Schlemiel, Der, 16, 180n. 74, 198n. 65

Schnitzler, Arthur, 129; Der Weg ins Freie, 129

Scholem, Gershom (Gerhard), 47, 72, 124, 165, 218n. 33

Schopenhauer, Arthur, 127

Secularization. See Western/enlightened model of Judaism

Segel, Binjamin, 16, 29, 38, 45, 72, 105, 108, 116, 132–37, 145, 146, 147, 148, 149, 150, 151, 152, 156, 158, 162, 163, 165, 165–67, 168, 186n. 14, 199n. 9, 209n. 115, 213n. 39, 214n. 50, 215n. 56, 216n. 75; Am Tage des Gerichts, 140, 151–58, 215n. 68, 216n. 77; "Die Einweihung des Tempels," 216. n73; "Erziehung zum Haß," 148; "Genug der Versäumnisse. Ein Ruf zur Tat,"

134; "Das Judenelend in Galizien," 132, 133; "Der Krieg als Lehrmeister," 145–51; "Die Lehrerin," 135–37, 210n. 123; "Philosophie der Zerstreuung," 105; "Philosophie des Pogroms," 166–67; Die polnische Judenfrage, 152; "Der stille Pogrom. Wehruf eines russischen Juden," 134

Self-determination, 169

Self-hatred, 19, 23, 34, 95, 124, 126, 138, 162, 164, 197n. 57; as hatred, 138, 140; as stereotype, 18, 95, 107, 137, 140, 146–50, 164, 214n. 55. See also Parvenu stereotype

Sephardic Jews, 62, 182n. 106, 187n. 34, 187n. 35

Sessa, Karl A. B., 194n. 36, 207n. 94

Simmel, Georg, 29

Simplicissimus, 91, 108, 141

Snowman, Isaak, 131; "Sardanopolis," 131 (fig. 19)

Social Democrats, 167

Social work and welfare. See Female readers

Socialism (Jewish), 27, 28, 29, 82, 178n. 62, 189n. 57, 193n. 13; Po'alei Tsiyyon, 30

Sokolow, Nahum, 31

Soldiers. See Masculinity

Sonderweg thesis, 167

Spinoza, Baruch, 130

Steinschneider, Moritz, 30

Steinthal, Chaim, 29, 156

Stereotyping, 38, 49, 51, 52, 77–78, 79, 96, 99–100, 108, 125, 159, 162, 163, 167, 169–70; the belle juive, 108, 204n. 58; as technique or rhetorically self-aware process, 19, 20, 30, 48–50, 52–53, 77, 147, 150, 162, 184n. 123; changing trends of in Ost und West, 52, 140, 157, 184n. 121; discourse and, 174n. 20; formation of, 17, 19, 48–49, 147, 183n. 117, 192n. 1; "hate speech" and, 165, 217n. 23; in institutional context, 19, 20, 50; negative versus positive,

17, 48, 74, 75, 99–100, 108, 164; of antisemite as foil, 140, 155; of Jews as left-wing or radical, 26, 160; revisions, reversals, and reinventions of, 17, 18 47, 48, 52, 82, 86, 87, 94, 95, 111, 135, 136–37, 146, 148, 156, 159; traditional stereotype of Westerners (*daytshe*), 59, 66, 86, 173n. 11, 173n. 16, 186n. 20. *See also* East European Jews; Parvenu stereotype; Self-hatred

Stock Market Crash of 1873 (*Börsenkrach*), 67, 79

Stoecker, Adolf, 37, 193n. 16

Strack, Hermann, 29

Struck, Hermann, 41, 197n. 57, 216n. 80

Student fraternities (*Burschenschaften*): compared to East European Jewish student organizations, 28. *See also* Russischer jüdischer wissenschaftlicher Verein

Süßkind of Trimberg, 166, 218n. 28

Switzerland, 26

Syndram, Karl Ulrich, 73, 74

Talmud, 51, 57, 100, 112, 176n. 27, 199n. 9

Tietz family, 198n. 70

Toynbee Halls, 107

Translations, 45, 74; quality of, 47

Treitschke, Heinrich von, 86, 87

Trietsch, Davis, 17

Trotsky, Leon, 29

Trotzjuden. *See* Conversion to Christianity

Ullstein publishing company, 44, 80, 118, 181n. 98

Unification of 1871, German: Jews and, 24, 37, 66

United States, Jews in the, 179n. 67, 217n. 9

Ury, Lesser, 40, 41, 197n. 57

Ussishkin, Menachem, 36

Völkerpsychologie ("ethnic psychology"), 156

Varnhagen, Rahel, 100

Vienna, 28, 29, 71, 107, 118; epidemic of baptisms in (*Taufseuche*), 108, 204n. 57; in "Rafael Gutmann," 206n. 82

Vilna, 212n. 20

Voskhod, 31, 44

Wagner, Richard, 103, 107, 120, 130, 207n. 92; "Das Judenthum in der Musik," 130; *Die Meistersinger von Nürnberg*, 120; *Tristan und Isolde*, 120, 128, 129, 130, 208nn. 100, 102

Wälsungenblut (Mann), 92, 94, 197n64

Wassermann, Henry, 165

Weimar period: Jews in Germany during the, 159–62, 190n. 65

Weiner, Marc, 208n. 100

Weininger, Otto, 126–27, 128, 130, 132; *Geschlecht und Charakter*, 130; review of in *Ost und West*, 208n. 87

Weizmann, Chaim, 27, 28, 36, 39, 82, 165, 175

Welt, Die, 31, 39, 180n. 78

Wertheimer, Jack, 19, 20, 173n. 18

Western/enlightened model of Judaism (secularization), 34, 44, 55, 56, 59–67, 75, 76, 88, 90–92, 144–45, 154, 162

Western Jewry (*Westjuden*): as stereotype, 17, 141; as writers, 87; *See also* Baʿaalei teshuvah; East European Jews; German Jewry; Parvenu stereotype; Philanthropy; Western/enlightened model of Judaism

Westernization. *See* Western/enlightened model of Judaism

Wilde, Oscar, 130

Winz, Leo, 16, 25, 26, 28, 29, 32 (fig. 1), 39, 45, 48, 57, 68, 82, 84, 95–96, 110, 133, 146, 150, 158, 162, 165, 169, 177n. 41, 177n. 42, 181n. 98, 182n. 101, 182n. 102, 185n. 1, 200n. 20, 213n. 32, 214n. 41; boxing promotion and, 16; Herzl and, 38; wife Elsa Jacoby and, 102–3, 203n. 49

Wissenschaft des Judentums, 145, 147, 150, 167, 191n. 78

Women, Jewish. *See* Female readers *and specific entries*

World War I, 140, 142, 146; calls for *Burgfrieden* and, 146; demands for German-Jewish conformity, 141, 142, 143; *Ost und West* and, 140. *See also* Masculinity, in the military (*Tauglichkeit*)

Yekke stereotype, 141

Yiddish language, Yiddishists, and Yiddishism, 27, 28, 56, 60, 68, 69, 73, 101, 107, 115, 116, 120, 197n. 57, 202n. 32, 206n. 87, 207n. 94, 210n. 123; Mauscheln stereotype, 125, 130, 135, 136, 207n. 94

Yom Kippur, 92, 109, 152, 153, 154, 156, 188n. 52, 204n. 59, 215n. 58, 216n. 71

York-Steiner, Heinrich, 130; "Koriander, der Chasan," 130

Young Jewish Movement (Jungjüdische Bewegung), 79, 144

Youth movement, 79, 81, 83; Wandervägel, 83

Zangwill, Israel, 150, 178n. 59, 214n. 54

Zepler, Bogumil, 123 (fig. 15).

Zionism and Zionist organization (Zionist movement), 17, 29, 33, 35, 36, 37, 69, 81, 87, 105, 177n. 55, 209n. 114; Alliance Israélite Universelle and, 47; as displaced religion, 188n. 52; Congresses, 31, 36; cultural Zionism, 39; discourse of racialism, 38, 179n. 70; during World War I, 145, 146; Gegenwartsarbeit, 37; Gemeinde elections and, 37, 81; historiography and, 165; Jewish Liberalism and, 145; political versus cultural (Kulturzionismus), 35, 38, 190n. 73; practical Zionism, 37; Territorialism (the ITO) and, 35, 178n. 59, 214n. 54; Uganda controvery, 38. *See also Altneuland* controversy; Democratic Faction (Demokratische Fraktion) of Zionist Organization; Ethnic Judaism/Jewishness; Herzl

Zlocisti, Theodor, 16, 45, 202n. 32

Zweig, Arnold, 216n. 80

Zweig, Stefan, 207n. 90, 212n. 31